Words of Praise for *Gotcha!*

"*Gotcha!* disconnects the snooze bar and calls out to humanity, begging us to *"Wake up!"* Like an overdose of adrenalin mainlined to your heart, this book will pull your brain out of self and other induced comas.

In this book, Taylor presents why it's time for the 99 percent to get up, get together, reunite, and speak up, responding wisely, acting without reacting. It is a cosmic dare to reclaim our conscience and free ourselves from the tyranny of fear and greed that has led to narcissistic neediness.

Today we have the knowledge necessary for humanity to evolve. The question is, do we have the courage to fuse conscience and competence and come together to ignite a resolution, rather than ignite a revolution? Compassion, liberty, and justice are values that are worth living for."

~ Lynnclaire Dennis, Scientist, Author & Artist

"WOW! Once again Eldon Taylor delivers a penetrating look into our minds and behavior. Providing detailed insight into the nature of influence and shining a revealing light into its sources, Eldon's research and findings offer the reader an opportunity to break free from their conditioned limitations and ignite a life-changing awareness. This is a must-read for the empowered mind!"

~Dr. Steve Maraboli, Author, Behavioral Science Academic

"Eldon Taylor is so spot-on. *Gotcha!* tells it like it is, and it isn't what we want to happen!"

~ George Noory, Host of Coast to Coast AM

"If you are one of those people who believe that ignorance is bliss, then this book is not for you. So who is it for? It is for enlightened souls who are on a mission to change the world for the better. If you are one of those, then you must read this book! Once again, Eldon Taylor has demonstrated with mastery and ample evidence that our world is not what it seems and that the intention to harm and manipulate the people of America is alive and well. As a holistic physician, I am always counseling my patients to become aware of what goes in, on, and around their minds and bodies. Eldon's book uncovers to what lengths corporations and government will go to in order to keep people numb, dumb, and unhealthy. If you're willing to go through the gamut of so-called negative emotions — shock, indignation, anger, and hopelessness - and come out the other side, you'll be empowered by the knowledge found in this book like I was. Every day we are being "called" to awaken from our unconscious slumber by transformational teachers worldwide in order to save our planet and our children. Eldon Taylor is one of those who I consider a Superhero! Thank you, Eldon, for your courage and willingness to bring others to the Light."

> ~ **Karen Kan, M.D., Holistic Physician,**
> **Bestselling Author of** *Guide to Healing Chronic Pain*

"The overwhelming lesson of this critically important book might be called 'Subliminal Seduction,' which has gradually overwhelmed free will and critical thinking. "The time has come, the walrus said, to speak of many things!" Eldon Taylor has spoken of these most important things better than anyone in the past fifty-plus years! It is time to read, think, and heed."

> ~ **Norm Shealy, M.D., author of** *Living Bliss*

"*Gotcha!* is an eye-opening book on the subject of free will. Is it free? Can we truly will anything? Backed by historical information and cutting-edge science, *Gotcha!* explores the many forces impeding humankind from realizing free will. I enjoyed the book, as the concept/re-ality/unreality of "Free Will" has interested me ever since I came across the work of Mokichi Okada (Jorei) and of Dr. Libet. However, *Gotcha!* was scary as it presents much information that was new to me. Most of this information is not simply of the conspiracy theory ilk, but honest-to-goodness things that give a man Goosebumps! After reading what Dr. Taylor presents in this great book, you will seriously consider moving to Bhutan! I highly recommend this work."

> ~ **John L. Turner, M.D., author of** *Medicine, Miracles and Manifestations*

"I'm just in awe of what Eldon is attempting here and how coura-geous and rational he is about it all."

> ~ **Suzanne Brady, Editor**

"Eldon Taylor's book, *Gotcha!* is a brilliant, eye-opening journey into the subject of mind control and a historical journey into the methods used to set the course of our country and world by controlling those who live in it. It is a study of how we have been unknowingly subjected to differing techniques of control to direct our every thought and the basic drives already hardwired within each of us. Eldon is known worldwide as an expert on the subject of mind control, but he reaches deeper than ever before to show you the proof of how you are being influenced to do the things you do every day. Each and every statement written about is backed up by documented proof and research. Reading *Gotcha!* made me very angry that I have allowed myself to be controlled and directed throughout my life, while all the time mistakenly living as if I were in charge of my thoughts. However, it also left me an informed student, who is now cognizant of what is being done to the masses, and gifted me with the tools of awareness and knowledge in order to realize my potential without falling prey to the controls employed by the few attempting to set my life course. Thank you, Eldon, for the wake-up call."

~ **Richard D. Rowland (retired Sergeant from the Kentucky State Police), author of *Unspoken Messages***

"In 1948 George Orwell wrote the classic book that caught the attention of the academic world and most of the reading public. Eldon has shared with us his profound insights and has Taylor-made a contemporary essay that illustrates the many subtle and not-so-subtle ways we are allowing our individuality and free thinking to be eroded. We are being called to assume responsibility for our freedom of thought. You are warned that once you pick this book up and start reading, you will have trouble putting it down. Even after you have finished reading it, you will flip back to your favorite selections. But we are being called to put down the book and take individual inventory of our own lives so that we can, in our own ways, restore at least a small part of our lost freedom to think. Become more of a sheep rancher and less of a thoughtless hired hand. If Eldon's latest book has even one percent of the impact *1984* had, we will all be the better for it. Thanks Eldon."

~ **Bob Nunley, Ph.D., Professor Emeritus, University of Kansas**

"Gotcha! is another brilliant *Snap Out of It!* book by Eldon Taylor. This should be required reading for every school-aged child. What a gift to really understand how to leverage the power of your mind! What we need today are critical thinkers, not more stinker thinkers! This book gives the real tools required to blast past the fear of failure and rejection and edit the negative movies of the mind propagated by society. Eldon's books and audio programs fill my shelves and are my go-to guides when I'm struggling to *Snap the Hell Out of It!"*

~ DeDe Murcer Moffett, aka "The Snap Out of It! Woman"
Speaker, Author, Entertainer

"Gotcha! is Eldon Taylor's masterpiece. He makes substantial, historical information, based on decades of research and professional experience, read like a crime novel—only we're all in this one together. It is a suspenseful and shocking read. *Gotcha!* allows us to discover just how deceived and manipulated we are in our society and provokes us to question who we truly are underneath the facades we have been conditioned into developing since birth. With his extensive knowledge and entertaining way of delivering his message, Dr. Taylor shakes us out of complacency and forces us to reconsider our identity and to seek to change our belief system before it's too late."

~ Elaine Clayton, author of *Making Marks*

Gotcha!

Also by Eldon Taylor

Please visit: **www.eldontaylor.com**

Gotcha!

The Subordination of Free Will

Eldon Taylor

Published by: R.K. Books
PO Box 1139
Medical Lake, WA
99022
1-800-964-3551

Edited by: Suzanne Brady and Ravinder Taylor
Book Cover: Gaelyn Larrick

ISBN: 978-1-62000-236-0

Publisher's Cataloging-in-Publication (Provided by Quality Books, Inc.)

    Taylor, Eldon, author.
      Gotcha! : the subordination of free will / Eldon
    Taylor.
      pages cm
      Includes bibliographical references.
      LCCN 2015945040
      ISBN 978-1-62000-236-0
      ISBN 978-1-62000-237-7

      1. Manipulative behavior. 2. Elite (Social sciences)
    3. Free will and determinism. 4. Thought and thinking.
    I. Title. II. Title: Subordination of free will

    BF632.5.T39 2015   153.8'52
                   QBI15-600143

To all who seek a free mind.

Contents

The mind is its own place, and in itself
Can make a heaven of Hell, a hell of Heaven

~ John Milton

FOREWORD

For those of you who are regular readers of Eldon's work, this book may come as a bit of a surprise. I have edited a number of his books so I am very familiar with his work, but even so, I was taken aback when he first told me what he wanted to write about. As he progressed through his research and writing, I was often hesitant about the information he shared with me. It was not that the information was not fascinating because oftentimes it was incredibly so, but it was more a question of how this fit in with the rest of his work—his books, radio show, blog, etc. Why would an author who has spent 30 years researching ways to harness the power of the mind to improve the quality of a person's life, write a book that appears at first glance to be about questionable actions by the government, conspiracy theories, psychological operations (PSYOPS), the failings of our education system, the dark side of our entertainment, etc.—in fact, all those things that sit in the background of our society and which most of us pay very little attention to? And even when the story that is being reported is one that we do, in fact, remember (and there are a number of those, too), what is the necessity for reminding us?

Gotcha! is a very expansive book, covering a depth and breadth that can almost seem overwhelming. But it is in this very detail that *Gotcha!* gains its real power, for it is the patterns that emerge that are of most importance. As I read the book, I was amazed not only by the number of stories being reported on, but how many of them had filled me with anger at the time. In fact, there are several stories that had enraged the entire nation—but where did that outrage go? There are very few examples where the story was eventually resolved. Why is it so easy for us all to be lulled back to sleep and with such ease? It is in the depth of its information and the detailed citations backing everything up that *Gotcha!* answers this most important question—and a whole lot more!

Most are familiar with the Greek aphorism, "Know thyself," and this really forms the primary purpose behind *Gotcha!* I believe this book to be vital reading for everyone, regardless of their background and interests—whether they are a theist or an atheist; blue-collar or white-collar; young, old, or somewhere in between; and any other category you can think of. Regardless of how you see yourself, in all likelihood you believe that the viewpoints you hold today are yours because you chose them. Unfortunately, *Gotcha!* shows you how totally wrong you are.

However, all is not lost as knowledge is power! I know that this book has changed me. Today I question a lot more and then I double-check my own conclusions. Television, both news and entertainment, has drastically lost its power to sway my beliefs. I try not to accept the sound bites that are broadcast and shared by everyone in some delusional idea that if the majority agrees then it must be correct. And most importantly, I keep an eye open for the hidden agendas. Now, this may sound a little depressing but it is actually very empowering. It is impossible to 'know thyself' when the power elite knows exactly how to puppet you. But when you have some understanding of how it all works, you can take the power back.

So here is the bottom line: *Gotcha!* is all about helping you to find yourself by peeling back all that you are not. It is about rediscovering your own individuality, which is a universal goal for the religious, the spiritual, and the atheist alike. You can never claim your ideas and beliefs as being solidly your own until you have examined the evidence presented in these pages. It also offers some hope—perhaps there will be some 'hundredth monkey' effect and enough people will read this book to actually effect a national change. Who knows? But without hope, what else do we have?

Now I do want to offer some cautions. *Gotcha!* is all about the forest, not just the individual trees. It is in the way that the patterns keep on repeating themselves that really highlight the important issues. I can promise you that, regardless of your background, there are aspects of the book that will have you wanting to throw it down in disgust. For too long the country has been run on a 'divide and conquer' mentality, where most people pick a side and fight tenaciously to support it without taking the time to listen to the other side. The power elite know exactly how to do this, and it is time we stopped giving them the power to do so. As you read *Gotcha!* always keep in your mind it is about the overall repeating patterns, the size of the entire forest and not the individual trees that matter. Think about the agenda and follow the money. It is also possible that some details may have slipped by our fact checkers, but quite frankly, it does not matter, for once again, it is the overall pattern that is important. And I can assure you, if you read the entire book through, the patterns will become apparent.

Now, some may say that my comments are biased, especially as the author happens to be my husband, but I really don't think so. What I can categorically tell you is that I did not like the idea of the book when he first told me what he wanted to write about, and today I think it is a much-needed and valuable book for our society. Read the book and decide for yourself.

Ravinder Taylor

PREFACE

*Are we like late Rome, infatuated with past glories, ruled
by a complacent, greedy elite, and hopelessly powerless
to respond to changing conditions?*
~ Camille Paglia

The subtitle to this book, *The Subordination of Free Will,* may
sound a bit over the top to you, at least initially, but by the
time you reach the end of this work, I'm certain you will see exactly why this subtitle is so apropos. The rabbit hole, as many
refer to it today, goes deeper than most could ever imagine—and
not only is it unimaginably deep, but like the roots of a persistent
noxious weed, it expands in every possible direction.

Because of this, I have chosen to present this material to you
almost as a research paper. I began this project about four years
ago, collecting relevant facts and building veritable piles several
feet high, filling a table with papers and books to be reviewed
and included in this work. The day came that it was clear that
the only reasonable way to manage all of this information and to
share it in the most credible way was to minimize my comments
and present the data directly from the sources.

Every one of us has encountered at one time or another a
piece of news that disturbed us, news that informed us of unfairness, privacy invasions, deceptions, cover-ups, and more, but
most of us discount this news as an isolated incident that, fortunately, does not impact our own personal lives; unfortunately,
that assumption is not only naïve, it is downright foolhardy!

A Plutocracy

Not long ago I asked a young lady what she thought of the two different stories that were coming out regarding the shooting by police of a suspected terrorist. Usaamah Abdullah Rahim was reported shot by authorities because he was wielding a large knife. Rahim's relatives on the other hand, initially argued that he was shot in the back, insisting that the shooting was unjustified.[1] The answer this young woman provided is tutorial to say the least. Indeed, when one thinks about it in the light of certain statements made by the likes of men such as Edward Bernays and Walt Lippman, their assertions that ordinary citizens are just not smart enough to make decisions seems all too true.[2] Here was her answer: "I don't know. I don't watch the news because I know they manipulate it, and I would have to check out what they said before I knew what to believe. I don't have time for all of that!"

Think about that statement. Yes, we might have to invest some time in doing something other than consuming or planning our next consumption, but then if we don't—well, we must recognize that we don't deserve a democracy or freedom itself for that matter. We can all just hang on to our illusions of democracy and fail to face the fact that we really live in a plutocracy (government by the wealthy).

The Patterns

What I have tried to do with this work is assemble a pattern of activity that impacts all of us. When you look upon isolated incidents, even when we know of others but they are separated by time, we tend not to view the larger fabric that is the pattern. By concatenating the information from all areas of our lives, I hope to show that not only is there a pattern but a dangerous one—at least for those of us who value our freedoms!

Nothing in this book is really unknown. Every item is but a sliver of larger board. Slivers amount to nothing until they're added to one another, and finally, your hit over the head with a 2x4. It is the pattern in *Gotcha* that matters, for every sliver does indeed add to one another until there is no denying the weight of the wooden club held over our heads.

The information in this tome is not all the information. At the time of this writing, I could easily add another 100 pages or more and each day we learn of something new that potentially threatens the lives we have come to cherish in the free world.

In organizing the information, I have tried to do so in a manner that tells a story, one that I hope you find both eye-opening and interesting, and one that offers you the facts and allows you to reach your own conclusions. I am not always a silent narrator, and I recognize that. Some concerns require comment, in my view, and I have been direct with matters that violate human dignity.

I have taken every caution to fact check the information within. That said, something may have slipped by me, but then that would only mean there is a minor flaw in the fabric—not a hole in the pattern.

The Way of Rome

John Stossel once stated on his Sunday program that America has already gone the way of Rome, and it is almost too late to reverse the process. Have we gone beyond the tipping point already? Is the spill too large to reverse? Have we already lost so much of our natural identity as individuals that we no longer have the ability to root out the old programming? Are we already so far down in the rabbit hole that we no longer desire even to recognize that there is a hole? These are but some of the questions you will have to answer.

As for me, I have a strong belief in the human potential. I am convinced that once you are informed, there is a chance that enough of you will become involved in meaningful ways that will turn the tide of propaganda and replace it once again with a strong sense of self-reliance in the Emersonian vein. It was, after all, Ralph Waldo Emerson who said, "Nothing is at last sacred but the integrity of your own mind."[3] It is believed that the informed are forearmed. I hope you find this worthy of your time!

INTRODUCTION

"In youth, it was a way I had,
To do my best to please.
And change, with every passing lad
To suit his theories.

But now I know the things I know
And do the things I do,
And if you do not like me so,
To hell, my love, with you."
~ Dorothy Parker

For the past thirty years, my work has been focused on developing tools and techniques for personal empowerment and in the search for the higher meaning to life. As such, many of my regular readers may be surprised at the material in this book. While I have often discussed ways in which we have been manipulated into making choices that are not our own, never before have I created such an encyclopedia of techniques that are being used against us on a 24/7 basis.

In the arenas where I normally teach, the common attitude is one of positive thinking—the idea that, "what you think is what you are, so therefore you should just focus on the positive and all will be well in your world." I most certainly do agree that there is a time and place for this, but in any substantive search for the spiritual, it is vital that we first discover who we are, the quintessential essence of our being that is part of the gift of life. There is a common saying that goes, "All I have is a gift from the giver. What I do with the gift is my way of giving thanks." However, what I will be revealing to you in this book is the multitude of ways you have been told what to think, how to think, and even how to justify why you think what you do. The vast majority of your thinking processes are really just an expression of how you have been programmed to dance to the tune of a specific drummer—the power elite! How then can you "give back to the giver" by maximizing your own talents and abilities when your real self has long been buried?

I will be the first to say that there is little inspiring or uplifting in this work—in fact; much of it is abhorrent, disgusting, and downright depressing. So what place does this information have in the "search for the spiritual" or the journey to self-empowerment?

Recently I watched the movie *The Giver*. In this movie, the population was medicated to dampen all emotions with the aim of removing those aspects of the human personality that would make the wrong choices, create the divisions that lead to fighting, and to keep the public feeling "satisfied" with their lives. The rules for socially acceptable behavior were strictly defined, and no one questioned the motives behind those who were in power. On the surface it looked like a utopian society. However, by taking away the individuals' ability to question and think for themselves, it was possible to get people to commit atrocious acts while keeping them oblivious to what they were really doing. In essence, their very individuality had been taken from them. This theme has been repeated in a number of movies, including *The Matrix* series where the protagonist is offered the choice between the red pill or the blue pill—the blue pill will enable him to continue in the life of comfortable illusion whereas the red pill will wake him up to the real world, however gritty and unpleasant that may be, but one in which he is truly free to make his own choices.

I would like to suggest that this is the path that we are currently on. Time and time again, the public is outraged by something the government has done, but very quickly the hue and cry dies down and the masses simply accept the new "norm." Those we have entrusted with our safety have repeatedly committed heinous acts, and yet nothing is done about it. The world is choosing to become more and more blind, preferring to enjoy the creature comforts we have rather than rock the boat and take a risk. And even those who claim to be searching for spirituality and enlightenment are lost in the same morass—they just use different words and expressions!

It is my firm belief that knowledge is power. It is only when you clearly see the techniques in play that you are able to protect yourself from them, make your own choices, and begin the journey that is your birthright—the journey to personal empowerment and self-actualization.

My Journey Begins

While I have been writing, researching, and teaching about personal empowerment for about thirty years, the seeds of that work actually began long before, when I set out to search for the underlying principles behind why people do what they do. It has been an investigation that has necessarily included many disciplines. It has also been a journey that for me, when I reflect on it all, has been an innate and fascinating one.

When I was very young, maybe eight or nine, a neighbor lady visited my mother. I heard her tell what I somehow knew was a story rich in imagination and poor in truth. Like an unbridled young colt, not knowing any better, I pranced in and asked, "Why are you making all this stuff up?"

Well, as you might imagine, that wasn't the smartest thing I've done in my life. As it turned out, I was correct, and my mother discovered that soon enough. Still, through that experience, I learned that you are not supposed to tell someone they are lying, even though you are right.

Lie Detection and Criminalistics

In time, my career path led me to lie detection, and I found myself immersed in a daily routine in which I might inform individuals of their lies several times during the day. So for years I practiced criminalistics, specializing in the detection of deception, investigations, counterintelligence, and forensic hypnosis.

Finally, it seemed that what I had been designed for fit what I did—form and function all in sync, except that it still remained difficult to understand why people do what they sometimes do. But alas, that's what I got for thinking that I knew what life holds in store for me.

One of the problems in lie detection is the inconclusives—the person who is so stressed by the test itself that lies are difficult to differentiate, or the person who uses countermeasures to show stress on "innocent" questions. It was through my efforts to eliminate inconclusive tests in my lie detection business that I wound up following a path that would eventually change my focus and career. I heard about a study that was reportedly carried out by the Los Angeles Police Department. In that study, a preparation for a possible terrorist abduction during the 1984 Olympics, the department had allegedly dehydrated cadets studying in the academy by using a subliminal audio program masked by the sounds of a furnace or air conditioner, so-called pink noise. I reasoned that if a subliminal audio program could dehydrate cadets, certainly one could be created that would exaggerate physiological responses during deception and minimize them during truthfulness.

I have shared this story in depth in my books *Choices and Illusions* and *Mind Programming*, so I will spare my regular readers the repeat. Bottom line, I found myself developing a method to do exactly this, although it was not truly an audio subliminal. Eventually the scientific studies, carried out by independent researchers at such leading institutions as Stanford, convinced me that this technology (now known as InnerTalk), indeed primes self-talk, causing a fundamental shift in expectations and thereby leading to some truly remarkable changes in those using the it. Not only did it work in my lie detection practice but also within the prison system with inmates, with children dealing with ADHD, with patients dying of cancer, with students dealing with examination anxiety, with individuals coping with clinical depression, and on and on. Well, the long and the short of that was evidence to me, once again, of the influence our thoughts, beliefs, expectations, and the like have on our lives.

Now all during this time I was studying psychology—first pastoral psychology and then clinical psychology. However, although this knowledge added much to my investigation of why people sometimes behave as they do (as their own worst enemy), it still failed to adequately explain all of it. Then one day I had an epiphany—people are not thinking about their behavior at all! They are on automatic much more than we normally might think. They reason in sound bites provided to them by those who would have them think in a given manner. Their enculturation is much deeper and richer—or impoverished, depending on your perspective—than ever before in human history, and this is due to the influence of the media and technology.

Catch-22

We all know what a catch-22 is—damned if you do, and damned if you don't. Let me tell you what a *gotcha* is. A gotcha comes when you do what you think is best because they have taught you the way to think. In other words, as I have pointed out elsewhere and in some detail in my book *Mind Programming,* you have been educated to conform. Not only have you been trained so thoroughly in how to think, but you have also been given the alternatives by which you could object to thinking a certain way.

My guess is that by the time you finish this book, you will have recognized many clever ways by which you have been exploited in the past. My hope is that by becoming aware of the insidious nature of the mind manipulation that goes on today, you will be empowered to make decisions and choices that are yours and not the results of the thoughts of others. You will then be able to easily answer this question: What was your last truly original thought?

Technology has advanced the many means by which we can all find ourselves manipulated. The propaganda of today resembles that of old in purpose, but the methods are so advanced that privacy, even in our minds, is virtually a thing of the past.

Puzzles

David Hume is famous for pointing out that built into human nature is the need to find causes. For Hume, nature made us in such a way that we judge just as we sense and feel. If we are to understand human nature, then we must acknowledge that our reason may be faulty and we cannot rely on our senses to prove reason, any more than we can rely on reason to prove what our senses tell us. Since that is the human condition, however, it is reasonable to use both the senses and reason in going about our lives.

There are lots of conspiracy theories out there. Some have recently turned out to be true, whereas others remain the product of overactive imaginations. That said, I am well aware that this work will present a pattern that some may be inclined, without research, to dismiss out of hand. I have therefore taken great care to document the information, even though the result may read like a research paper from time to time. It is my intention to present you with the unadulterated facts, giving you, as Sergeant Friday insisted on the TV flick, *Dragnet,* "The truth and only the truth!"

One of the early puzzles I remember working was a simple connect-the-dots drawing. After diligently connecting the dots in numerical order, I was amazed to see that a pony appeared on the page. As a result of reading this book, you will have many dots to connect. As the picture appears, it will still be up to you to decide what, if anything, to do with this new view of the world.

The simple fact is, while the spiritual search is the most important aspect of my life and my teachings, I have learned that this journey must begin by separating out our true self from the artificial self that has been created by the society we live in. It is only when we have fully uncovered our true essence that we can begin the journey of self-growth and self-actualization. I truly hope you gain from this adventure!

Hypothesis: Smiling Masks

*"You wear a mask for so long,
you forget who you were beneath it."*

~ Alan Moore

The journey of life is really about living into our authentic selves. The first big gotcha is to hide that fact from us, to enculturate us in ways that foster the interests of society as a whole or of an elite few, while organizing the rest of us to conform and thereby consume. And that's exactly what most of us do—consume more information (and more goodies!) and in doing so separate ourselves from our real selves.

The Fifth Force

I once enjoyed a wonderful lecture from Professor Carl LaPrecht. In the lecture he spoke of the four human drives, what he referred to as the "four Fs": Fight, Flight, Feeding, and F*king. The students he was addressing were members of law enforcement, so the *f*king* in place of *fornicating* got a big laugh. I have never forgotten the "four Fs" in this context, because at the time I was working on a paper having to do with why there was so much interest in getting more—more money, more power, more time, more, more, more!

I consider the "more" to be a modern human adaptation, or fifth force, forming yet another human drive. Perhaps we have,

1

as a species, always had a "more" drive, but if so, I am quite confident that never in humanity's history has it exerted such a powerful influence as that we witness today.

I remember a conversation with a friend years ago about our economy and cash flow. We happened to be at a home show, where we had a team of salespeople at a booth offering security devices. There were many displays within the tent, and when you looked around, you could see an air pump in the corner literally keeping the tent up. My friend directed my attention to the pump and informed me that cash flow was like the pump. Lose the cash, and the tent will come down.

Consumption has become the air in the tent for our economy. Most of this consumption must now come from the private sector, and that means you. Advertisers are charged with motivating you to buy. Marketing experts develop more and more products and services, and banks create credit power so you can just "charge it." Individual debt increases, national debt increases, more money is printed, and we are told that more consumption is needed to pay back the interest on the debt and perhaps the debt itself.

Dare to Know

It is this circularity, to which more and more individuals give their lives, which diminishes who we are as human beings. Immanuel Kant, the great Prussian philosopher who has been credited with making philosophy professional, considered the human condition to be similar to the way in which Copernicus thought about the solar system. Copernicus observed the solar system and concluded that Ptolemy's idea of an earth-centric solar system made no sense, but with the sun at the center, the observations did make sense. Kant did something like this with human beings. He placed consciousness—the mind of man, mankind itself—in the center of his inquiry, and the individual rights of mankind have been central rather than peripheral ever since. No longer was mankind seen as tangential to meaning; rather, mankind was seen as central to the meaning of everything!

One of Kant's central messages and challenges, that is as

relevant today as ever, is "Dare to know." Modernity has placed an emphasis on our individual rights and freedoms, and this can arguably be traced to the works of Kant. As consumption animals, eager to ring yet another bell and gain another token or prize, anxious that we may miss out on the next big deal or the last one, so anxious that we will indebt ourselves for years to have something we quickly forget we ever needed—as consumption animals, gathering things that when we look around we see no reason to keep, we lose our freedom because we surrender our true identity.

In place of true needs, we often have a whole host of "needs" that define our free time as well as motivate the hours we put into our work. It's all too often about what we get if we just give more of ourselves to these moneymaking needs.

It's no wonder that modern societies are experiencing such a dramatic rise in need for psychological care. When people turn off from themselves, and fail to take time to reflect or become fully mindful, they accept counterfeit roles that are not very different from the roles of those lost in subconscious repository, as portrayed in the movie by the same name. In *The Matrix*, everyone lived in an artificial reality, so immersed in their roles that the vast majority had no idea who they really were!

Who Am I?

I have argued before that we have lost so much of ourselves that today we are driven by this fifth force: MORE! We want more of this and more of that, more, more, more—and all the while we find less and less satisfaction and much less of ourselves in the process. Is this intentional or just a matter of how our culture has evolved? That question is irrelevant to the subject at hand because the first gotcha is to separate you from you. As R.D. Laing says in his book *The Politics of Experience:*

> We are not able even to think adequately about the behavior that is at the annihilating edge. But what we think is less than what we know; what we know is less than what we love: what we love is so much less than what there is. And to that precise extent we are so much less than what we are.[1]

3

At first, a serious question, "Who am I?" one day became trite. Today, the question seems to have become irrelevant. Indeed, it has often been replaced with, "Who can I become?" As we will see in chapters to come, this self-esteem fixation may be the root of a much deeper problem yet.

Thus my hypothesis: "You are not who you think you are!" No, you are both much less and much more. You are actually an experience acting out a mind program, and what's more, as you'll see when we discuss the nature of being human, most of our actions and thinking are unconscious. Indeed, to refine this concept just a little, imagine that over 90% of your choices were being carried out in the unconscious—how would you feel? The fact is, modern technology shows us that this imaginative exercise is indeed a representation of the facts. What then is free will?

Theft of Free Will

Researchers using fMRI watch the brain in real time and with unerring accuracy can determine what we will decide many seconds before we know what we have decided. Indeed, there is a very disturbing video produced by the BBC where Professor Marcus Du Sautoy (Oxford University) demonstrates this fact. You can see the video for yourself here: vimeo.com/106089707. Or simply search for 'Neuroscience and Free Will, Marcus Du Sautoy.'

It is the content of our subconscious that makes most of our decisions, and the fact is, we are unaware of that content. In part, that content is the result of all the input our subconscious has received. In a very real sense, it is as computer programmers put it, GIGO—garbage in, garbage out. Think of all the programming, the advertisements, the political rhetoric, the religious insistence, the cultural imperatives, and so forth that form your beliefs. When you're through with this exercise, then try to find an original thought.

Our minds, the subconscious repository of all we have learned, experienced, and fear, together with our defense strategies, mechanisms, and basic drive-related needs—all of this in one mix, one broth, one cauldron consciously unknown to us—

is actually making our choices. And as you'll see, much of this programming has been the result of deliberate propaganda designed to own our thoughts and motivate our behavior. We have been conditioned to think in certain ways from the very beginning of life and, in that sense, I submit that our free will has been stolen.

Additionally, as part of our framework, you should know that recently we learned through the use of fMRI that "parts of the prefrontal and anterior cingulate cortices, which play key roles in vigilance and skepticism when judging the truth and importance of what people say, were deactivated" in the presence of an authority. Although the first study of this nature I noticed was about the authority figure we know as clergy, other studies show this effect to include anyone we think of as an authority.[2] So when I say conditioned, I do mean conditioned.

Engineering Consent

The purpose of much of today's communication is about winning the hearts and minds of the public, something well labeled as the engineering of consent. What are the ways in which this goal is achieved?

Propaganda fills the news. Intelligent people are continually challenged to sort the nonsense from the facts. Adding to this confusion are armies of folks whose sole task is to confuse the facts by adding lies to the information we consume. Many websites today deal with exposing popular myths and outright lies. Still, even the so-called fact checkers often need to be checked. We will explore in this book why lies, misinformation, and disinformation work so well and how they can engineer consent.

Propaganda comes in a very large variety pack. Some of it is so subtle as to be almost invisible. Take, for instance, the use of art by the CIA during the Cold War. The CIA supported Soviet artists because the artistic movement could be used to encourage cultural and intellectual freedom as well as individual creativity. This would undermine the Communist ideology.[3]

The practice of using free expression as an "engineering-of-consent" tool is not limited to the Cold War or to foreign countries.

The decision to include culture and art in the US Cold War arsenal was taken as soon as the CIA was founded in 1947. Dismayed at the appeal communism still had for many intellectuals and artists in the West, the new agency set up a division, the Propaganda Assets Inventory, which at its peak could influence more than 800 newspapers, magazines and public information organisations. They joked that it was like a Wurlitzer jukebox: when the CIA pushed a button it could hear whatever tune it wanted playing across the world.

The next key step came in 1950, when the International Organisations Division (IOD) was set up under Tom Braden. It was this office which subsidised the animated version of George Orwell's *Animal Farm,* which sponsored American jazz artists, opera recitals, and the Boston Symphony Orchestra's international touring programme. Its agents were placed in the film industry, in publishing houses, even as travel writers for the celebrated Fodor guides. And, we now know, it promoted America's anarchic avant-garde movement, Abstract Expressionism.[4]

So you see, propaganda comes in every shape and color imaginable. If the potential to influence exists, then the topic is fair game.

What you choose to believe is often like the language you speak, in that you acquire it by way of parents, peers, and culture. This enculturation process is generally well known, as we all tend to have our ethnocentric biases. This sort of engineered agreement, or consent, can be thought of as organic or natural.

Then there is the more pernicious form of propaganda that strives to convince you of something—not for your good, however, but to satisfy the needs of some hidden agenda. Being aware of this propaganda is helpful but not sufficient in and of itself.

Overcoming Predispositions

We are all predisposed to want to believe certain things. Once we accept an idea, we are then psychologically compelled to defend it. As you will see, human psychology is such that even when we actually know nothing about a subject, including the most complicated of subjects, we will nevertheless tenaciously cling to our ideas. Learning how to set aside such mental reactions is achieved by first recognizing them and then by personally owning them.

There are many facets of consent engineering, and our purpose here is to expose how consent engineers work hard to own our hearts and minds. Is everything absolutely true that is included in the work? The answer is possibly not—"everything" is a big word! That said, I have tried to include only factual information and to draw your attention to issues that need careful consideration. If you read this book with that in mind, you are much less likely to be offended than if you allow your own preconceived beliefs and engineered consent to control your reactions.

Tin Foil Hats

Now, I have one last thought for you before we start really examining the evidence. An ancient Chinese proverb goes like this: "There is many a good man to be found under a shabby hat." For the purposes of this book, let's restate the proverb this way: "There is many a good argument to be found under the so-called tin foil hat."

Now why would I say that? Simply because what I am about to tell you, the place of beginning, is likely to produce from some people the familiar attack that is labeled with one word but loaded with laughter, jeers, ridicule, and the like. That one word is *conspiracy.* The strategy is this: When in doubt, make an ad hoc attack and bully the advocator, knowing that the public at large will generally be seduced by the logic that one good belly laugh is worth a thousand rational arguments.

Thus, when I begin by suggesting that elements in history have come together in ways that make it possible for modern manipulators to take advantage of your thinking in order to gain control of it, those whose vested interests require them to guard against public dissemination of this type will rush forward with something like, "Here goes—another tin foil hat job."

GOTCHA!

If you allow information to be dismissed on nothing more than this sort of personal attack, then you are living evidence for my case. If, on the other hand, you have at least an open mind, one that is willing to hear out an issue and think independently, then to that degree their programming has failed. Lucky you!

CHAPTER TWO

Basic Protections

Who can hope to be safe? Who sufficiently cautious?
Guard himself as he may, every moment's an ambush.

~Horace

Misconception: *You probably believe as Alan Moore stated, "People shouldn't be afraid of their government. Governments should be afraid of their people."*
Fact: *As Edward R. Murrow stated, "A nation of sheep will beget a government of wolves."*

We all would like to believe that our food, water, and drugs are safe for consumption. We are educated to believe that our government attends to these matters, on a federal as well as state and local level. We have huge government bureaucracies for just those purposes. An allocation of our tax dollars goes to ensure that our water, food, and drugs are the safest in the world. Can we rely on that?

In this chapter we will discuss these issues and you can form your own opinion. Are vaccines safe? Is our food protected? How do GMOs affect agriculture and our lives? What connects pesticides and herbicides to disease? We will tackle these and many other questions in just a moment, but first I wish to draw your attention to the government.

Trust in the government is the essence of an organized civil society. History has repeatedly revealed a story of power corrupting and absolute power absolutely corrupting. Over time, governments tend to become more and more decadent and less and less transparent. This can be true of all in whom we invest power. Take, for example, our health care professionals—our doctors.

When we visit our doctors, can we trust that their interest is in our best interest and not in the number of dollars they may or may not be able to bill based on our insurance policy? When the physician hands us a prescription, can we confidently ingest the magical pill, trusting that our doctor knows best?

Prescribing Placebos

What would you think if you learned that 97% of the doctors in the United Kingdom, a state with socialized medicine, have given their patients placebos?

> Researchers at the Universities of Oxford and Southampton in the UK discovered that 97% of doctors have used 'impure' placebo treatments, while 12% have used 'pure' placebos. 'Impure' placebos are treatments that are unproven, such as antibiotics for suspected viral infections, or more commonly non-essential physical examinations and blood tests performed to reassure patients. 'Pure' placebos are treatments such as sugar pills or saline injections which contain no active ingredients.[1]

This practice is not unique to the UK. Researchers point out that there is a rather widespread idea among doctors that this practice is ethical.

> This widespread use and acceptance of placebos is consistent with similar studies worldwide, yet they are still against General Medical Council ethical codes. "Current ethical rulings on placebos ought to be revisited in light of the strong evidence suggesting that doctors broadly support their use," says Dr. Howick.[2]

When we look at the United States, we discover that at least half of the doctors admit to prescribing placebos regularly.

. . . Many of these doctors are not honest with their patients about what they are doing, the survey found. That contradicts advice from the American Medical Association, which recommends doctors use treatments with the full knowledge of their patients. "It's a disturbing finding," said Franklin G. Miller, director of the research ethics program at the U.S. National Institutes Health and one of the study's authors. "There is an element of deception here which is contrary to the principle of informed consent."[3]

Placebos Work

There is no doubt that placebos work, but did you know that they can work even without deception? In other words, if your doctor informed you that he/she was prescribing a placebo, could the placebo still work? The answer is somewhere between possibly and probably, according to new research carried out at Harvard Medical School's Osher Research Center and Beth Israel Deaconess Medical Center. Researcher Ted Kaptchuk described the method by which the patients were given the placebo this way:

> "Not only did we make it absolutely clear that these pills had no active ingredient and were made from inert substances, but we actually had 'placebo' printed on the bottle. We told the patients that they didn't have to even believe in the placebo effect. Just take the pills."[4]

Many of the patients received benefits as though they were taking real drugs.

> "I didn't think it would work," says senior author Anthony Lembo, HMS associate professor of medicine at BIDMC and an expert on IBS. "I felt awkward asking patients to literally take a placebo. But to my surprise, it seemed to work for many of them."[5]

Drugs

How about this one for a gotcha? You order your prescription and discover that your capsules contain powdered human flesh. Not possible, you say. Well, South Korean customs officials an-

11

nounced that they had discovered just that in a May 2012 article appearing in *Telegraph* and a number of other publications.[6]

> The capsules were made in northeastern China from babies whose bodies were chopped into small pieces and dried on stoves before being turned into powder, the Korea Customs Service said.
>
> Customs officials refused to say where the dead babies came from or who made the capsules, citing possible diplomatic friction with Beijing.
>
> Chinese officials ordered an investigation into the production of drugs made from dead fetuses or newborns last year.
>
> The customs office has discovered 35 smuggling attempts since August of about 17,450 capsules disguised as stamina boosters, and some people believe them to be a panacea for disease, the Customs Service said in a statement.
>
> The capsules of human flesh, however, contained bacteria and other harmful ingredients.[7]

The next time you think about ordering a miracle drug from abroad, or even online, think again.

Aborted Fetal Cells

When I first learned that there was a rather widespread use of aborted fetal cell use in the flavoring research of major food producers, such as Pepsi, I was shocked. (Pepsi has since announced that they no longer join in this practice.) We did almost an entire *Provocative Enlightenment* radio show on this practice, naming companies and examining the practice and the purpose. The question asked most often during and after show can be stated this way, "Who on earth thinks of things like this?"

When companies the size of Kraft, Nestlé, and Pepsi join in testing flavoring this way, one has to ask, who on earth dreamed up the idea in the first place?

> For several years anti-abortion advocates have been warning that a new technology for enhancing flavors such as sweetness and saltiness uses aborted fetal cells in the process.

The biotech company using this novel process, Senomyx, has signed contracts with Pepsi, Ajinomoto Co. (the maker of aspartame and meat glue), Nestlé and other food and beverage companies[8] over the past several years.[9]

The primary goal for many of these processed food companies is to make foods and beverages tasty while reducing sugar and salt content.

While Senomyx refuses to disclose the details of the process, its patent applications indicate that part of the secret indeed involves the use of human kidney cells, known as HEK293, originating from an aborted baby.

It's worth noting that no kidney cells, or part thereof, are actually IN the finished product.[10] Rather they're part of the process used to discern new flavors, which will be discussed below.[11]

There are no labeling requirements for companies that use the flavor-enhancing products. The FDA does not regulate flavor enhancers. What those enhancers actually are is a deeper mystery than the so-called secret recipe for making Coca-Cola.

So what exactly is this magic ingredient that will be appearing in a new version of Pepsi, and how is it made? Unfortunately, those questions are hard to answer. Senomyx . . . refers to them only as 'enhancers' or 'ingredients' . . . The products work by triggering receptors on the tongue and tricking your taste buds into sensing sweetness—or saltiness or coolness, in the case of the company's other programs . . .

So are Senomyx's covert ingredients safe? That, too, is anyone's guess . . . many of its enhancers have 'been granted' GRAS (Generally Recognized As Safe) status, but all that means is that the company did its own assessment and then concluded everything was fine. We don't know whether Senomyx did any testing since the company isn't required to submit anything to the FDA.[12]

There's no reason to think that Senomyx's products will cause harm, but until or unless Pepsi decides to share details about how exactly it's achieving a 60% reduction in sugar while keeping the taste the same, customers will be drinking their 'scientifically advantaged' sodas completely in the dark.[13]

Certified by the Authorities

We hear every year about some food problem. Typically the matter is local and involves only a few people. However, from time to time, many people die in several states because of some sort of contamination. Usually the problem is the result of carelessness, but sometimes it happens despite certification by authorities of farm and farming standards. Take this Listeria case, for instance.

> Two Colorado farmers whose cantaloupes were tied to a 2011 Listeria outbreak that killed 33 people pleaded guilty on Tuesday to misdemeanor charges . . . The charges carry penalties of up to six years in prison and $1.5 million in fines . . .
>
> The brothers have sued the safety auditor who gave their farm a "superior" rating just before the outbreak—the deadliest case of foodborne illness in the nation in a quarter century.
>
> Federal investigators said the melons at Jensen Farms in southeast Colorado likely were contaminated in its packing house because of dirty water on the floor and old, hard-to-clean equipment.
>
> The Jensens filed their lawsuit against PrimusLabs, a Santa Maria, California, food safety auditor that checked Jensen Farms in July of 2011.
>
> The Jensens argued that they asked the auditor about a new processing system, which removed a step of rinsing the melons with chlorinated water. The lawsuit states the PrimusLabs auditor "did not warn Jensen that the new system created a hazard or a risk of contamination."[14]

Protective Agencies

Little by little our food supply has been taken over by regulation. There are areas in the country where citizens can no longer grow vegetable gardens in their own yards for fear that something might become contaminated and others may become ill. I don't ever remember a story about Mom and Dad's garden making a whole host of people sick, to say nothing of killing them, but I have heard of many regulated farms where precisely this occurred, and several of them have been in the past half a dozen years. Now that's not saying it's not possible for Mom to grow something in her garden that makes someone sick, but this will not spread to many states. It just seems to me to be a real over-reach to shut down Mom's garden.

In 2012 the United States was witness to the most sweeping legislation yet. It provides the president with control over all food, farms, fertilizer, farm equipment, livestock, veterinary resources, plant health resources, and food production in America. I am speaking of the executive order titled "National Defense Resources Preparedness." The order can be found online here: **www.whitehouse.gov/the-press-office/2012/03/16/executive-order-national-defense-resources-preparedness**

Nutritional Information

We have become dependent on the authority of the government to ensure our food is safe and as advertised—so much so that we rarely truly read any of the labels. Most of us are satisfied that the label requirements are enforced, so why bother reading labels unless we're looking for something in particular, such as how much sodium a product contains? What we don't usually consider is that labels do not necessarily tell the truth or, at the very least, that they intentionally distort the truth. Take my wife's favorite example, or worst example depending on the light cast on the subject: "Blueberries ought to be blueberries!" she exclaims.

It turns out that it's a pretty common labeling tactic to picture blueberries on muffin and pancake mixes, in cereals and bread, as well as in other products. And guess what—most do not contain blueberries at all!

> Pictures of blueberries are prominently displayed on the front of many food packages . . . on boxes of muffins, cereals, and breads. But turn the packages around, and suddenly the blueberries disappear. They're gone, replaced

in the ingredients list with sugars, oils, and artificial colors derived from petrochemicals.

A bag of blueberry bagels sold at Target stores is made with blueberry bits. And while actual blueberries are found further down the ingredients list, the blueberry bits themselves don't even contain bits of blueberries. They're made entirely from sugar, corn cereal, modified food starch, partially hydrogenated vegetable oil, artificial flavor, cellulose gum, salt and artificial colors like Blue #2, Red #40, Green #3, and Blue #1.

What's missing from that list? Well, blueberries.

Where did the blueberries go?

They certainly didn't end up in Total Blueberry Pomegranate Cereal. This cereal, made by General Mills, contains neither blueberries nor pomegranates. They're nowhere to be found. But the cereal is made with Red #40, Blue #2, and other artificial colors. And it's even sweetened with sucralose, a chemical sweetener. And that's in addition to the sugar, corn syrup, and brown sugar syrup that are already on the label.

A lot of products that imply they're made with blueberries contain no blueberries at all. And many that do contain a tiny amount of blueberries cut their recipes with artificial blueberry ingredients to make it look like their products contain more blueberries than they really do.

Kellogg's Blueberry Pop Tarts shows a picture of plump blueberries right on the front of the box. But inside the box, there's a lot more high fructose corn syrup than actual blueberries. And the corn syrup is given a blueberry color with the addition of—guess what—Red #40, Blue #1, and Blue #2 chemicals.

Kellogg's Frosted Mini Wheats also come in a Blueberry Muffin variety, with fresh blueberries prominently featured on the front of the package. But inside, there are no actual blueberries to be found. Instead, you get "blueberry flavored crunchlets"—yes, crunchlets—made from sugars, soybean oil, Red #40, and Blue #2.

And, if you can believe it, the side panel of this box features the "Frosted Mini Wheats Bite Size" logo, followed by the words "blueberry muffin" with pictures of blueberries, finally followed by "The Whole Truth." Except it really isn't the whole truth at all. It's more like a half-truth.

These marketing deceptions even continue on Kellogg's website, where one page claims, "New Special K Blueberry Fruit Crisps are filled with blueberries and drizzled with vanilla icing." Except they aren't, really. What they're really filled with is apple powder, partially hydrogenated soybean oil, fructose, sugar, artificial colors Red #40 and Blue #1, all enhanced with a dash of blueberry puree concentrate.

Even seemingly "healthy" blueberry products can be deceptive. Betty Crocker's Fiber One Blueberry muffin mix enhances its small amount of actual blueberries with petro-chemical colors, too: Red #40, Blue #1, and Blue #2.

At least Betty Crocker's Blueberry Muffin Mix admits it contains no real blueberries. Well, if you read the fine print, that is. Its ingredients reveal "Artificial blueberry flavor bits" which are made from dextrose, corn flour, partially hydro-genated soybean oil, sugar, citric acid, artificial flavor, and of course the obligatory Blue #1 and Red #40.[15]

So why do they do it, and how do they get away with it? The answer to the first part is obvious: It sells product, and that makes money. As for the second—well, that's just another gotcha, isn't it?

Food Fraud

Deceptive labeling practices are not limited to blueberries by any means. Food Fraud is a nonprofit group that watches and publishes labeling fraud. A recent ABC story informs us of this.

> But a new scientific examination by the non-profit Food Fraud detectives, the U.S. Pharmacopeial Convention (USP), discovered rising numbers of fake ingredients in products from olive oil to spices to fruit juice.
>
> "Food products are not always what they purport to be," Markus Lipp, senior director for Food Standards for the independent lab in Maryland, told ABC News.
>
> In a new database to be released Wednesday, and obtained exclusively by ABC News today, USP warns consumers, the FDA, and manufacturers that the amount of food fraud they found is up by 60 percent this year.

USP, a scientific nonprofit that, according to their website, "sets standards for the identity, strength, quality, and purity of medicines, food ingredients, and dietary supplements manufactured, distributed, and consumed worldwide" first released the Food Fraud Database in April 2012.[16]

That database, by the way, can be found here: **foodfraud.org**

Intentional Mislabeling

Food labels are sometimes also mislabeled, and that can have catastrophic results. Imagine fish mislabeled in such a manner as to raise concerns about fish allergies. Well, imagine no more.

> Nearly 40% of seafood sold in New York City is mislabeled, according to a conservation group's new report on a fishy practice that spells trouble for people with food allergies.
>
> "Recent testing has revealed that dishonest labeling and fraudulent seafood substitution for certain species is rampant and widespread," researchers from the ocean conservation group Oceana wrote in their report, which they said was based on DNA testing of 142 seafood samples collected from unidentified New York City grocery stores, restaurants, and sushi bars.
>
> Oceana previously reported fish mislabeling rates as high as 48% in Boston and 55% in Los Angeles.
>
> Oceana said the findings are particularly troubling given that seafood ranks among the top eight food allergens. And since fish allergies are often species-specific, experts say the bait-and-switch opens the door to dangerous exposures.
>
> "If [a person] is not allergic to the fish they think they are getting, and that fish is substituted with one to which they are allergic, they obviously could have a serious allergic reaction," said Dr. David Fleischer, an associate professor of pediatric allergy and immunology at National Jewish Health in Denver, Colorado. "Patients need to be able to trust the people they purchase fish from."[17]

Now this you should also find reassuring. A recent marketing study revealed that those most inclined to study product labels are the likeliest to be duped, and by now you know that they [marketers, the government, and the like] study everything having to do with how and why you do what you do, and how they can accomplish their aim, and that's simply to get you to do what they want you to do—buy, buy, buy![18]

Word Games

Okay, be smart, know what to look for, but even then, you can't catch it all. Still, this is valuable information:

To make the healthiest choices, scrutinize the nutrition facts and ingredient panels, recommends the July issue of *Bicycling* magazine, published by Rodale. Here's how:

'Made with real fruit'

A claim with no regulations around it. Snacks such as Kellogg's Nutri-Grain Cereal Bar sound like a solid pre-ride bite, but the made-with-real-fruit filling contains pure concentrate (more like sugar than actual fruit) of various types of fruit. The lower a fruit is listed in the ingredients, the less the product contains. To increase fruit intake, rely on whole fruits instead.

'Lightly sweetened'

Unlike "sugar-free" and "no added sugars," this claim isn't regulated by the FDA. And it's easy to be fooled: Wheaties Fuel, a cereal that's marketed specifically to athletes, contains more sugar per ¾ cup serving than the same amount of Froot Loops. Check the nutrition facts panel. The American Heart Association recommends that women keep added sugars below 24 grams per day and men aim for less than 36 grams.

'Gluten-free'

To make this claim, a product must be made without wheat, barley, or rye. But there have been reports of cross-contamination with gluten-containing grains during growing or manufacturing. Look for a seal from the Gluten-Free Certification Organization, the Celiac Sprue Association, or the National Foundation for Celiac Awareness, which test products to make sure they have no gluten.[19]

Heart-Healthy

So what about all those healthy foods? You know, those labeled as heart-healthy and so forth? Well, sorry to hand you another gotcha, but that's all about big business as well.

Food giants like Dannon, Kellogg, and General Mills don't claim these products actually prevent or cure diseases. Such declarations would run afoul of federal regulations. Nor do they sell them as medical foods, which are intended to be consumed under a doctor's supervision.

Rather, food companies market functional foods with health-promoting or wellness-maintaining properties. Such claims are perfectly legal, provided that they are backed up by some credible science.

All those heart-healthy red hearts on your box of Quaker Oats cereal or that can of Planters peanuts? That happy-colon yellow arrow on the tub of Activia yogurt? It's all part of the marketing of functional food.

Over the past decade, despite all those sales pitches for "natural," "organic," and "whole" foods, functional food has turned into a big business for Big Food. And more Americans are buying into the functional story. Sales of these foods and beverages totaled $37.3 billion in the United States in 2009, up from $28.2 billion in 2005, according to estimates from the Nutrition Business Journal, a market research firm.[20]

All Natural

What about natural foods? At least if they're natural, then I'm safe—right? Wrong—but that may change.

The only thing natural about the "natural" label is that such branding, naturally, often confuses consumers. But such misleading terms as "natural" and "healthy" could soon become history, or at the very least, score a makeover. Large food companies have hijacked such terms with dubious results—and never mind the fact "natural" is a loaded term. Is a food product only "natural" if it still has dirt on it after being yanked out of the ground? Is it still natural if ingredients, from whole-wheat flour to goji berries to flax seeds, are pulverized, brominated, pasteurized, and homogenized?

This labeling mayhem could change if The Food Labeling Modernization Act of 2013 becomes law. Congressman Frank Pallone, Jr. (D-NJ) and Congresswoman Rosa DeLauro (D-CT) introduced the new legislation at a press conference on Capitol Hill yesterday. If passed, the law would revise the Food, Drug and Cosmetic Act of 1938 and force companies to become more transparent about their ingredients.[21]

The House Bill is available here: **consumermediallc.files. wordpress.com/2013/09/food-labeling-bill-final.pdf**

I suggest you read it, and if it's still an issue, do what you can to support it—that is, if your food labels really matter.

Poison in Chicken Meat

When as a country we see sarin gas used on the citizens of Syria, the drumbeat to punish the perpetrators is raised sometimes to the drone of war, and many are ready to spend billions to carry out the spanking. When a nuclear disaster such as Fukushima occurs, some of us become concerned, others quickly forget, and most just assume that our government will keep us safe. I hope it's true this time that our government will keep us safe, but that has not always been the case. Big-dollar interests, laziness, and sometimes pure stupidity have combined with best intentions, only to fail at doing exactly this! Take, for instance, the fact that the FDA just came clean about the arsenic in chicken meat sold in America. The FDA has kept this little-known fact in the closet, so to speak, for years.

> The FDA said Wednesday that a new study developed by the agency shows that an ingredient in chicken feed that contains arsenic, called Roxarsone, may make its way into parts of the bird that are eaten. Previous studies have indicated that the arsenic was eliminated with chicken waste.[22]

Natural News reported, "For the last sixty years, American consumers who eat conventional chicken have been swallowing arsenic, a known cancer-causing chemical."[23]

21

The article continued:

> Until this new study, both the poultry industry and the
> FDA denied that arsenic fed to chickens ended up in their
> meat. The fairytale excuse story we've all been fed for sixty
> years is that "the arsenic is excreted in the chicken feces."
> There's no scientific basis for making such a claim . . . it's
> just what the poultry industry wanted everybody to believe.[24]

And, in case you are wondering, it was "back in the 1940s,
[when chicken] producers started using arsenicals to promote
growth, treat disease, and improve meat pigmentation. The practice eventually became standard; according to industry estimates,
by 2010, 88% of all chickens raised for human consumption in
the U.S. were given the arsenic-based drug, Roxarsone."[25]

This explanation still does not adequately answer the reason
why this kind of thing is ever done. I can think of two possible
reasons: Either the people in charge (FDA, the government, experts) are too stupid for the kind of responsibility they have assumed, or they lie for personal benefit!

Chicken Nuggets or Nuggets of ???

While we're on labeling, what if that quick, tasty treat of
chicken nuggets wasn't really chicken after all? What if you
learned that those nuggets contained very little meat and mostly
"other stuff?" What if, as with my two boys, chicken nuggets was
their favorite food for a while, served in school, and treasured for
its convenience as a reasonably healthy fast food, and then you
discovered that it was not much better than pet food?

> Chicken nuggets: Call 'em tasty, call 'em crunchy, call
> 'em quick and convenient. But maybe you shouldn't call
> them "chicken."
>
> So says Dr. Richard deShazo, a professor of pediatrics
> and medicine at the University of Mississippi Medical Cen-
> ter. In a research note published in The American Journal
> of Medicine, deShazo and his colleagues report on a small
> test they conducted to find out just what's inside that finger
> food particularly beloved by children. Their conclusion?

22

"Our sampling shows that some commercially available chicken nuggets are actually fat nuggets," he tells The Salt. "Their name is a misnomer," he and his colleagues write. The nuggets they looked at were only 50% meat—at best. The rest? Fat, blood vessels, nerve, connective tissue, and ground bone—the latter, by the way, is stuff that usually ends up in dog food.[26]

Fukushima Revisited

As pointed out earlier in this chapter regarding a potential gotcha, the Fukushima-Daiichi nuclear plant disaster potentially threatens the world. It turns out that Tokyo Electric Power Company (TEPCO) initially reported radiation levels much lower than the actual levels. In a scathing report of their diligence, or lack thereof, *Natural News* reported in September 2013 that TEPCO had intentionally "used radiation detectors that 'max out' at relatively low levels (i.e. they don't go higher than 100 mSv)."[27]

In actual fact, the radiation leak is eighteen times higher than TEPCO reported, coming in at 1800 mSv. "Ito Tetsuo Professor of Kinki University (radiation biology) said, regarding the level of hourly 1800 mSv, 'There is only a thing called death if you stay exposed to this for four hours. One hundred percent of persons will die within thirty days.'"[28]

TEPCO's history regarding this nuclear disaster is one of repeated lies. Originally only a few gallons of radiated water were leaking from the plant. This lie dissolved away when later they admitted that "300 tons of radioactive water was seeping out of the destroyed nuclear power plant daily into the ocean (and everywhere else), a leak which subsequently was raised from a stage 1 to stage 3 in radioactive severity, and that it had, for all intents and purposes, lost control of the containment process."[29] When TEPCO provided this information, they also informed us that "by the way, it would no longer lie about how severe the situation truly was"[30]

This sizable leak makes it likely that fish swimming through the waters near Japan, and perhaps much farther out into the Pacific, will become contaminated. As a result, South Korea announced in early September of 2013 that they had banned fish from NE Japan. This ban "applies to a total of eight prefectures [states] with a combined coastline of more than 700 kilometers (430 miles), regardless of whether the fish pass safety standards or not."[31]

> The latest leak is so contaminated that a person standing half a meter (1 ft. 8 inches) away would, within an hour, receive a radiation dose five times the average annual global limit for nuclear workers.
>
> After 10 hours, a worker in that proximity to the leak would develop radiation sickness with symptoms including nausea and a drop in white blood cells.
>
> "That is a huge amount of radiation. The situation is getting worse," said Michiaki Furukawa, who is professor emeritus at Nagoya University and a nuclear chemist.[32]

The United States imported something like 150 million pounds of food in 2010 from Japan. "Imports from Japan included nearly 600,000 pounds of crab and anchovies and nearly five million gallons of bottled water, soft drinks, and other non-alcoholic beverages containing water, products that may be potentially higher risk if contamination continues to spread to the ocean and fresh water sources."[33]

The impact of this event has not yet been fully assessed. The extent to which sea life, and not just off the coastal waters of Japan, will be affected is unknown. In the meantime, U.S. agencies such as the FDA have been quiet on the issue. How dangerous is this threat?

> In 2006, the National Academies of Science issued a definitive report on radiation exposure that concluded that even low levels of radiation can cause human health problems, including cancer, heart disease, or immune disorders.
>
> The United States imports around 80% of its seafood as well as an increasing share of its fruits and vegetables. Unfortunately, the FDA inspects less than 2% of these imports, leaving consumers at risk to a host of foodborne issues, which now includes potential radioactivity.

Radioactive emissions from Japan have been detected throughout the United States, from California to Colorado and as far east as Massachusetts. Monitors in the Carolinas have detected the presence of radioactive iodine, the first time this material had been detected there since the Chernobyl accident twenty-five years ago.[34]

The Fukushima leak is anticipated to continue for years, and there remain possibilities at the time of this writing of yet another explosion.

"There are still reactor buildings we haven't gotten into yet," Fujimoto-san said. "So there's always the possibility of another explosion, and if that were to happen, we—the workers—would be the first victims.[35]

Should the FDA do something now about Fukushima? Should there be more proactive steps taken to ensure the safety of our food and water? Or will we wait sixty years (as with the arsenic in chicken meat) before we learn better?

A Mouth Full of Mercury

The entire world is aware of the health hazard mercury potentially poses to the public, and yet, did you know that dental amalgam fillings are, in fact, more than 50% mercury?

It turns out that "amalgam fillings" are intentionally and deliberately misnamed for the express purpose of misleading consumers. Those fillings are actually more than 50% mercury, and once installed in mouths, they give off a gas mercury vapor, which is then inhaled by the patient, entering the bloodstream and causing permanent cellular damage to heart, kidneys, liver, and brain.[36]

Recently the city council of Berkeley, California, voted to keep hidden the fact that dental amalgam fillings contain mercury. "This decision to keep consumers in the dark was, of course, supported by dentists and doctors . . ."[37]

How's that for a gotcha?

SV40

Is the Centers for Disease Control (CDC) trying to cover up facts about SV40 in the polio vaccine? Did the vaccine industry researchers intentionally hide the presence of the cancer-causing agent SV40? "The chief, if not the sole, cause of the monstrous increase in cancer has been vaccination," said Dr. Robert Bell, former VP International Society for Cancer Research at the British Cancer Hospital."[38]

> (The CDC) quietly admitted that SV40—a simian virus—had tainted polio vaccines, which the CDC estimates were administered to between ten to thirty million Americans between 1955 to 1963. Luther reported about how this was done in an informational fact sheet published online with otherwise little fanfare.[39]

The page originally posted by the CDC on the Internet making this announcement disappeared shortly after the news broke in the media. That said, investigators not only found and archived the original page, but a CDC FAQ page regarding SV40 was also recovered. If you're interested in checking this out for yourself, here is the URL: **web.archive.org/web/20120503021608/www.cdc.gov/vaccinesafety/updates/archive/polio_and_cancer.htm**.

In September 2013, I came across this headline: "Merck vaccine developer admits vaccines routinely contain hidden cancer viruses derived from deceased monkeys."[40] The article went on to disclose why some vaccine researchers lie to the public and protect one another.

> Decades ago, one of the most prominent vaccine scientists in the history of the vaccine industry—a Merck scientist—made a recording where he openly admitted that vaccines given to Americans were contaminated with leukemia and cancer viruses.
>
> In hearing this admission, his colleagues (who are also recorded here) break into laughter and seem to think it's hilarious. They then suggest that because these vaccines are first tested in Russia, their side effects will help the U.S. win the Olympics because the Russian athletes will all be "loaded

down with tumors."

For the record, this is the same vaccine that was given to tens of millions of Americans and promoted by the government. To this day, people still carry these hidden cancer viruses which have proven to be a boon to the cancer industry.[41]

The complete transcript of this recording is mind-boggling to the uninitiated. The participants include some of the leading vaccine scientists at the time. When you read this transcript, it is easy to conclude, as many have, that a significant number of today's diseases have vaccines as their source. I strongly urge you to check out the transcript.

Vaccines

Nothing is as important to parents as protecting their children. My wife and I went through the throes of "to vaccinate or not to vaccinate" ourselves. The information out there is both controversial and confusing, and there is no doubt that mistakes have been made and covered up. Still, the question to be answered is more about, is there more potential for "good" than "harm" as a result of vaccinations?

Unfortunately, I think that question must be answered individually. My wife and I delayed vaccinations while we searched the data banks, reviewing hundreds of studies and weighing even more opinions, professional and lay alike. In the end, we gave both of our sons their vaccinations but on a very delayed schedule. Rather than doing the full courses within our sons' first two years, we started vaccinating them at around age five or six and did not complete the courses until they were about twelve. Of course, we will never know if this was the best choice; all we know is that it was the best choice for us at the time. That said, there are a number of things that you should know about vaccines that have not been covered here until now.

We know that scientists have fabricated lab results in order to win approval for drugs. We know that mercury is still used in vaccines, and the CDC admits it. Here are some other important facts that you should be aware of.

In nearly every outbreak you hear about these days, the majority of the children affected by the outbreak have already been vaccinated against the virus! For example, outbreaks of whooping cough routinely involve children who have already been vaccinated against whooping cough. This is yet more proof that vaccines do not confer immunity.

The claimed history of vaccine "successes" against polio and other diseases is a pure fabrication. This is discussed and exposed in great detail in the powerful new book, *Dissolving Illusions* by Dr. Suzanne Humphries.

The vaccine industry refuses to conduct scientific tests on the health outcomes of vaccinated children vs. unvaccinated children. Why? Because these tests would no doubt show unvaccinated children to be healthier, smarter, and far better off than vaccinated children in terms of behavioral disorders, allergies, and even autoimmune disorders. Check the people you know: Don't you routinely find that the most heavily vaccinated kids are the ones who get sick all the time? Meanwhile, groups like the Amish who largely refuse to vaccinate their children have near-zero rates of autism.

The U.S. Supreme Court has already declared that the secret "vaccine court" is a higher power than the Supreme Court. The so-called "vaccine court" is granted extraordinary powers to operate utterly outside the Constitution, the Bill of Rights, and completely outside the rules of due process and law. The court itself—which isn't even a court of law—is a violation of law and a violation of basic human rights.[42]

Right to Withhold Vaccines

There is a world of controversy over vaccines. Some of it is actually not much more than fear-laden paranoia, but some of it has merit. Separating the wheat from the chaff is always the issue when it comes to matters like this. That said, we have already discussed the issue with the polio vaccine, so even the most ardent defender of the status quo cannot dismiss the legitimacy of this sort of inquiry.

Where I find the research in this matter to be very challenging, what I find really disturbing is the extent of intimidation and

outright bullying that people must go through when they question the establishment. Take this case, for instance:

New York vaccination rights attorney Patricia Finn was threatened with criminal charges and the loss of her license to practice
law in 2012 if she refused to surrender the names of all of her
clients. Finn is one of many attorneys across America who special-
izes in defending parents' rights to withhold vaccinations from
their children. Among the charges she is facing is that of "threatening the public interest."

> This is not merely a gross violation of attorney/client
> privilege; it's also a thinly veiled attempt by the New York
> judiciary to terrorize the parents who have sought legal help
> in opting out of dangerous vaccines.[43]

We all have heard stories about what can happen when the
state decides to send social workers to your home to investigate
your parenting. If Finn is a threat to the public interest of the
state of New York, then how much of a threat is each parent who
engaged her services? These are probably incompetent parents,
right? As such, they are unable to properly care for their children, so the state must place them in responsible homes, where
vaccinations will most assuredly follow. Does that disturb you?

Stolen Custody

If you thought the last story was troubling, how about this
one? Imagine that your child is diagnosed in the hospital with a
genetic disorder that could lead to muscle degeneration. Indeed,
let's just say that your daughter is diagnosed with mitochondrial
disease, but by the time she is a teenager, there is no sign of the
disease having any impact on her. She is a healthy, active young
woman, and as a caring parent, you have made certain to keep
her informed about the disease and to provide her with her own
psychologist so she has every opportunity to adjust to the possible outcome that may lie in her future. You're a caring parent,
and you have diligently followed the advice of your doctors when
dealing with your daughter's health. Then one day she gets a
cold. It appears to worsen, so you take her to the hospital where
her regular doctors can diagnose and treat her.

Once in the hospital, however, a different team of doctors takes over, and they have security throw you out of the hospital. How can that be? What is happening? Do we need to fear custody battles over our children when we take them for health care? Surely, if this happened there must be something else involved—right? It would appear not.

It has been a bitter custody battle, and nine months after it started, it's still going on.

In December 2012, Justina Pelletier was an active fifteen-year-old girl who would go ice skating, laughed, and spent time with her family.

But just two months later, her family says their nightmare began.

"[Exhales] It's beyond any wildest nightmare that you could think of," says Justina's father, Lou Pelletier.

Her longtime West Hartford psychologist has also been following the case.

"It's the most bizarre situation … I've ever been involved with," says Dean Hokanson, the clinical psychologist who has worked with Justina the past five years.

Justina was diagnosed with mitochondrial disease a few years ago. It's a genetic disorder that can cause loss of muscle coordination and weakness.

Despite that diagnosis she lived a normal life.

But last February, she also got the flu and was admitted to Boston Children's Hospital to see her specialist.

Almost immediately, a different team of doctors delivered a different diagnosis, questioning the original diagnosis of mitochondrial disease.

"They came in, and they said we cannot take Justina out of the hospital. They called DCF," says Linda Pelletier, Justina's mother.

They said Justina had "somatoform disorder."

In short, they were saying she suffered from a mental illness, not mitochondrial disease.

Her parents, Lou and Linda Pelletier, were escorted out of the hospital by security, and within four days, they had lost custody of Justina.

In addition to working with Justina, Dean Hokanson also testified at one of the court proceedings.

"They were actually being accused of being too active in pursuing healthcare matters for their child," says Hokanson.

"It is kidnapping," says Lou Pelletier.

Boston Children's Hospital refused to comment about the case, but internal discharge documents obtained by Fox CT provide insight into why the hospital called DCF.

An April report written by a Boston Children's physician shows that the hospital pulled Justina off many of her prior medications when she was admitted.

It reads:

> "Due to concerns regarding Justina's regressive behavior changes around her family, the multiple medical procedures and care episodes she has been through … and both parents' resistance towards recommended treatment plans for Justina … a child protection team was convened."

Before entering Boston Children's Hospital, Justina was on several medications and had undergone complex surgeries. The Pelletiers say Boston Children's accused them of "overmedicalizing" their daughter.

But the family showed Fox CT proof that every procedure and prescription was sanctioned by doctors, including Tufts Medical Center specialist Dr. Mark Korson.

Tufts wouldn't let Korson talk to Fox CT, but the Pelletiers did provide an email that Korson sent to their attorney, referring to Boston Children's Hospital, their team of doctors, and the somatoform diagnosis.

"I am dismayed. … It feels like Justina's treatment team is out to prove the diagnosis at all costs. … The team has demanded that Justina be removed from the home. … This represents the most severe and intrusive intervention a patient can undergo … for a clinical hunch," writes Dr. Korson.

Dr. Amel Karaa, who works at Massachusetts General Hospital, says conditions like mitochondrial disorder commonly lead to confusion for health care providers.

> "A lot of social cases have been reported where the children were taken away from their parents by social services and the hospital because the medical team thought that the parents were causing this to their child," says Dr. Karaa.[44]

I hope you noted the final comment within the report, "A lot of social cases have been reported where the children were taken away from their parents by social services and the hospital because the medical team thought that the parents were causing this to their child," and on a hunch! For Justina, this hunch triggered a nightmare that ended up lasting 16 months.

There's no doubt that we need to have protective services for children and others; however, should there not be some remedy attached to the wrongful action by folks who rush to judgment and yank children out of homes? If you make a false police report, it is a crime. How about a statute that protects parents, not just providing some possible civil remedy such as a lawsuit, but a criminal penalty for wrongfully acting in a way that interrupts parental custody of the child? That way, social workers, doctors, neighbors, and the like would exercise a little extra judiciousness in their assertions, for most of them are protected against criminal complaints, and a lawsuit is something the hospital or the insurance company and so forth deal with. What are your thoughts on this, and how would you like it if this happened to you? And what about those parents who lack the resources to hire attorneys and pursue the return of custody? What protects them?

Health Records

Health records are used for many things today, including, of course, insurance rates. While they are supposed to be confidential, don't count on it. The world has already seen that privacy may well be no more than a popular illusion. Still, how about the state grabbing children's medical records without the permission of the parents? Should that concern us?

The Virginia Department of Health did just that to one mother who did not submit a record indicating whether her children had been vaccinated.

32

When the mother contacted the school's director, even she was confused. The director informed her that the state of Virginia has built a website that allows schools to access children's health information, including what pediatrician they see and any insurance claims that have been made.

The distraught mom contacted the Virginia Immunization Information System (VIIS) and was informed that the site's purpose is to provide children's health information and allow it to be easily accessed by health officials.

According to the Virginia Department of Health's website, the "VIIS is a free statewide registry system that combines immunization history for persons of all ages from both the public and the private sector. Immunization information is accessible to authorized users only."[45]

Is this the way of the future? Should our medical records be as open and public as driver's license information?

Labeling of Children

Many professionals today believe that we overmedicate our children. Let a child appear to be somewhat unruly, overly energetic, and so forth, and it is likely they will be diagnosed with an attention disorder. That diagnosis solves the problem for the teacher because the medication quiets the child. A quiet child is easier to govern, so many parents find this approach equally satisfying. The fact is, though, labels of this sort can leave permanent marks on our children and be entirely wrong—and not just wrong but abusive! We could be labeling a genius as dysfunctional in some way and thus retarding the realization of the child's talents. Labels tend to place children in the subclass of fellow students, and that can lead to their ostracism from the group. The so-called out-group, punished by their fellow students for being different, can become tomorrow's criminals.

The fact is that the "stigmatization" is coming from those who benefit from people being labeled/stigmatized with mental disorders that have no medical/biological evidence. Case in point, if you are rebellious, you are "stigmatized" with the label "oppositional defiant disorder." If your kid acts like a kid, he is "stigmatized" with the label "ADHD." If you are sad, unhappy (even temporarily), you are "stigmatized" with the label "depressive" or "bipolar disorder." If you are shy, you are "stigmatized" with the label "social anxiety disorder." Moreover, you or your child are now stigmatized for life as this label, which is based solely on opinion, is now part of your permanent medical record, despite the fact there is no medical evidence to prove you are "mentally ill."[46]

And the really scary part of this is in the operative word, *proof!* Experts agree, there is no such proof!

"Psychiatry makes unproven claims that depression, bipolar illness, anxiety, alcoholism, and a host of other disorders are, in fact, primarily biologic and probably genetic in origin . . . This kind of faith in science and progress is staggering, not to mention naïve and perhaps delusional."—Dr. David Kaiser, psychiatrist

"There are no objective tests in psychiatry—no X-ray, laboratory, or exam finding that says definitively that someone does or does not have a mental disorder." Allen Frances, psychiatrist and former DSM-IV Task Force chairman.[47]

There is another deeply disturbing aspect to this sort of labeling. Our systems are set up in such a way as to provide for some truly gruesome practices by healthcare professionals when it comes to dealing with those labeled as "disturbed."

Consider this example: Until recently a special needs school in Canton, Massachusetts, the Judge Rotenberg Center (JRC), used electric shock to deal with unruly children. The school's practice was to deliver shocks even to children committing minor offenses.

A non-verbal, nearly blind girl with cerebral palsy was shocked as part of her behavioral plan for making a moaning sound and for attempts to hold a staff's hand (her attempts to communicate and to be loved).

In 2002, 18-year-old Andre McCollins was strapped down and shocked for hours at the JRC. He begged for the shocks to stop, and when they did, he was left in a catatonic state for days, which resulted in permanent damage. Video of Andre's shock treatment was sealed until recently. You can view it here: **youtube.com/watch?v=aAj9W0ntUMI&fe ature=youtu.be**

The JRC's founder, Dr. Matthew Israel, resigned after being charged with misleading a grand jury by destroying video footage of other students being shocked.[48]

This is not an illegal practice, and at the time of this writing, although there is a petition to stop the school and to involve the state's legislative body, aside from some embarrassment by management of the school and at least one resignation, there is no assurance that this practice is not still going on, not just at JC, but elsewhere as well.

Pesticides

There is a lot of concern of late regarding pesticides and herbicides and their effect on the honeybee population. Both have been linked to the serious depletion of our much-needed pollinators, and this in itself could become our next national disaster. That said, are you aware that pesticides have been linked as the cause of polio? In fact, the historical data suggests a positive correlation between the decline in use of DDT and the decline in the incidence of polio. In other words, when the use of DDT was outlawed, polio disappeared.

According to a report compiled by the Secretary of the Interior that was presented before the 85th Congress back in 1958, polio really only became a problem after the 1940s, when chemical companies began to produce large amounts of DDT, heptachlor, dieldrin, tetraethyl pyrophosphate (TEPP), malathion, benzene hexachloride (BHC), and other pesticide chemicals for use on agricultural crops. Prior to that time, polio was not nearly as virulent or problematic as many people believe it was.

As DDT and other pesticides were eventually phased out, cases of polio also began to decline, which suggests that vaccines may not have been primarily responsible for eradicating polio. Improvements in sanitation, which are hardly ever mentioned by mainstream health authorities, also played a major role in eradicating polio.

Many people during the 1950s became ill as a result of pesticide-contaminated milk, much of which ended up having to be quietly pulled from store shelves in subsequent years. This contaminated milk was also known to be a primary carrier of polio, and was directly responsible for spreading the disease until the contaminating pesticides were eventually phased out, and the milk supply effectively remediated.

Interestingly, milk-induced disease outbreaks were responsible for the later creation of milk pasteurization mandates. But it was the pesticides and their tolerance of polio virus, not the fact that milk was raw, that was responsible for spreading disease. And yet the belief that raw milk is inherently dangerous is still prevalent today, while few have any real understanding of the role pesticide-tainted milk played in spreading disease, and particularly polio.[49]

The population of honeybees has shrunk dramatically in the recent past, as we have said, and pesticide combinations have been shown to be one factor behind this. Two new studies have shown how these combinations can seriously affect the bees' ability to learn.

The researchers found that the pesticides, used in the research at levels shown to occur in the wild, could interfere with the learning circuits in the bee's brain. They also found that bees exposed to combined pesticides were slower to learn or completely forgot important associations between floral scent and food rewards.[50]

The article went on:

Dr. Geraldine Wright said, "Pollinators perform sophisticated behaviours while foraging that require them to learn and remember floral traits associated with food. Disruption in this important function has profound implications for honeybee colony survival because bees that cannot learn will not be able to find food."[51]

How much do we need to learn about the chemicals in use today before we decide that there must be further limitations? What would happen if we lost our honeybees?

Moral Irrelevance

As controversial as the subject may seem, right to life is about more than abortions. A recent article published in the *Telegraph* reported that a group of medical ethicists at Oxford University concluded that, "Parents should be allowed to have their newborn babies killed because they are 'morally irrelevant,' and ending their lives is no different to abortion."[52]

The *Telegraph* was reporting on an article published in the *Journal of Medical Ethics*. The *Journal* piece argues that, "Newborn babies are not 'actual persons' and do not have a 'moral right to life.'"[53] They reasoned this way:

> "The moral status of an infant is equivalent to that of a fetus in the sense that both lack those properties that justify the attribution of a right to life to an individual."
>
> Rather than being "actual persons," newborns were "potential persons." They explained: "Both a fetus and a newborn certainly are human beings and potential persons, but neither is a 'person' in the sense of 'subject of a moral right to life.'"[54]

"What is a life" is suddenly a question between potential life and actual life. If that is our operating definition, then it calls into question our practice of maintaining lives for those who fail to meet the standard.

We take "person" to mean an individual who is capable of attributing to her own existence some (at least) basic value such that being deprived of this existence represents a loss to her.[55]

Under this definition, it is only a slight slip on the slope and folks who have lost cognitive control over their lives also fit into this category. Perhaps they are those who suffer from Alzheimer's or those encephalitic lethargic patients Oliver Sacks told us about in his book *Awakenings*.[56]

The idea of "afterbirth abortion" may become acceptable in some countries in the future. After all, the ethicists have insisted:

> . . . Parents should be able to have the baby killed if it turned out to be disabled without their knowing before birth, for example, citing that "only 64% of Down's syndrome cases" in Europe are diagnosed by prenatal testing.
>
> Once such children were born there was "no choice for the parents but to keep the child," they wrote.
>
> "To bring up such children might be an unbearable burden on the family and on society as a whole, when the state economically provides for their care."[57]

Is this what we want? Do we want it to be okay to decide what lives have more potential than others? Changes like this occur slowly over time. Think of it as erosion—say the erosion of the earth that eventually becomes a great canyon. At first the damage is so slight as to go virtually unnoticed. Then one day what remains is so much less than what there was that the very nature of the topography is redefined. Moral values are like that as well. Where are we headed, and again, is this what you want? If not, what are you doing about it? Or, I guess it's fair to ask, have we already gone too far?

In my book *What If?* is a thought experiment dealing with some of the inconsistencies in our legal system that already exist regarding abortion. There are states where a mother can legally kill her child after birth so long as the umbilical cord is still attached when she does so. There are also states where late-term abortion is legal, but should you kill a pregnant woman, even a "barely" pregnant woman, you are guilty of a double homicide. Sadly, from my perspective, perhaps the canyon is already too deep to reverse the course of the erosion.

Now I'm not arguing that all abortions should be illegal. No, indeed! Since my days at Weber State College, where I was required to do a research paper on abortion, I have favored legalized abortion under certain conditions. That said, abortion as a means of birth control, especially beyond the first trimester, is nothing more or less than the erosion of our traditional Western values. Whether the erosion leads to a spectacular Grand Canyon or a nasty slit in the earth that promotes flash floods has yet to be seen.

Alive or Dead?

Dead or alive? That's a question, not a bounty ad. When is it okay to pull the plug? When is a vegetative state truly a vegetative state? We like to think that people are alive when their brain functions at a level sufficient to produce consciousness. If we're not conscious, not dreaming, and not asleep, when our brain wave activity meets the legal definition of vegetative, then conventional wisdom for years has suggested that it's okay to unplug persons from life support because, after all, they're really no longer in their body. There have been many famous cases where the plug was pulled despite outcries from loved ones and even Congress, as in the 2005 case of Terri Schiavo.[58]

What do you do when you learn that the vegetative state is not a state where the person is gone at all? Recent findings have shown the world just that. For example, headlines around the world like this one from the BBC have shouted a different story, "Scott Routley says, 'I'm not in pain.'"

> A Canadian man, who was believed to have been in a vegetative state for more than a decade, has been able to tell scientists that he is not in any pain.
>
> It's the first time an uncommunicative, severely brain-injured patient has been able to give answers clinically relevant to their care.
>
> Scott Routley, thirty-nine, was asked questions while having his brain activity scanned in an fMRI machine.
>
> His doctor says the discovery means medical textbooks will need rewriting.[59]

Until those textbooks, and perhaps even the laws, are rewritten, what then?

EMF

What do we do when we learn that an entire infrastructure

essential to our way of life, to the very undergirding of our economy, is potentially a killer?

Years ago I wrote about the dangers of electromagnetic fields. In my book *Thinking Without Thinking*, I discussed the early research that demonstrated that sixty cycles of electric current coursing through a room (your overhead lighting) could cause a mutation in the DNA molecule. I was so sensitized to this issue some twenty years ago that when my wife and I were looking for a new home, we walked away from several otherwise perfect homes because of their proximity to high-voltage power facilities.

EMF issues have only intensified since then. Our cell phones and cell towers, electric appliances and now electric cars, our computers and monitors, and so forth, all represent a potential hazard to our health.

Nearly 8 million people worldwide die from cancer on an annual basis. Cardiovascular disease is the number one cause of death, killing almost 17 million people in 2011; both of these statistics are spiraling out of control. Now three top scientists, Dr. Panagopoulos of the University of Athens, Associate Prof. Johansson of the Karolinska Institute, and Dr. Carlo of the Science and Public Policy Institute, are sounding the alarm bell.

Leaders in their respective fields, Panagopoulos, Johansson, and Carlo, claim electromagnetic field (EMF) exposures significantly below international safety levels exposures are destroying the public's health and well-being.

This latest study concluded the present standard of measuring EMFs, Specific Absorption Rate (SAR), to be totally inappropriate. SAR measures the heating effect of EMF based technologies like microwave ovens, cell phones, cordless phones, Wi-Fi and the like. But countless studies have brought to light adverse biological effects at radiation levels significantly below levels where a thermal effect is detected.

Dr. Carlo points out the life-threatening consequences of using SAR as an exposure metric in establishing the outcomes of EMF studies:

- "Studies which show 'no effect' are likely 'false negatives.'"

- "Studies that show an effect are likely under-reporting the true risk."
He goes on to say "this imprecision . . . shakes the foundation of the science that we are using to sort out the full range of non-ionizing radiation health effects."
At this point the real debate is moving beyond whether or not EMFs harm health and threaten public safety. Even the International Agency for Research on Cancer (IARC) has classified EMF exposure as a possible carcinogen (Group 2B carcinogen).[60]

In one Greek study, EMF was shown to negatively affect regions in the brain. The study was published in *Electromagnetic Biology and Medicine*. The study "found that 143 proteins in the brain were negatively impacted by radio frequency radiation over a period of eight months. A total of three hours of cell phone exposure were simulated over the eight-month time period, and the results showed that many neural function related proteins' functional relationship changed for the worse."[61]

A Russian study showed that children's cognitive abilities were negatively impacted, leading to a "long-term cognitive decline in children."[62]

One fact that many are unaware of with respect to today's must-have smart phones (cell phones) is that the World Health Organization has stated that, "Cell phones are in the same cancer-causing category as lead, engine exhaust, and chloroform."[63]

Counter measures can be used to minimize the influence of EMF. Should the FDA be looking into the many devices offered for this purpose and labeling those that are most effective? I mean, if you Google the subject, you find more than enough gadgets and gizmos to stock an entire store, and it's not likely that they are all effective, judging from the presentations I've seen. Also, amateur inventors make many of these devices and, while their hearts may be in the right place, it does not necessarily follow that their equipment performs as advertised.

It appears to me that instead of waiting until the bomb drops, we should be preparing to neutralize the effects of EMF the best we can. If our agencies ignore the issue, then it's up to us. I have taken precautions. How about you?

Big Pharma

Big Pharma is a term that everyone relates to today. It expresses the consumers' frustration with the lock pharmaceutical companies have on the development of new drugs. In a wonderful film, *Burzynski, the Movie,* we learn of the plight of one man fighting the establishment to bring a cancer cure to the public. The film copy describes the conflict this way:

> You will be placed into the turbulent journey of how the industry utilizes its now usurped regulatory agency to both block Antineoplastons' Phase 3 clinical trial process—and orchestrate a group of "information hit men" (also known as an "Astroturf Campaign") to pollute all channels of public information in an effort to confuse the public over the truth behind Antineoplastons. This international Astroturf group also engages in the intimidation and harassment of prospective and current terminal cancer patients under Dr. Burzynski's care.[64]

There are a number of stories such as this one. They all have in common the theme that money is power, power controls decisions, and decisions make money. It is this very circularity that should alarm us. How do we separate the money from the motive if we define the motive to be the benefit of all?

Friends in High Places

The very nature of our lives depends on various government agencies operating with our best interests in mind. It is therefore disconcerting when we learn that a significant appointment to some agency overseeing our food, water, and drugs has been given to some favored friend who has been or is still affiliated with a commercial company that the agency is supposed to oversee. This is the fox guarding the hen house, and it happens with every administration.

As mentioned earlier, what do you think when a former Monsanto executive is appointed to an agency that may well have the power to make decisions on matters that Monsanto has spent hundreds of millions of dollars lobbying about? Who then are we to trust? Is this good old boy form of corruption acceptable to you? If not, what are you doing about it? Have you just conceded that there is nothing you can do and let it all go, hoping for the best?

A very interesting chart available on the Internet shows the number of people Monsanto has on their payroll, people who are also members of Congress and serve in important governmental roles, including deputy director of the FDA. You will find not only this graphic at **GEKE.US/** but also many others, such as the same sort of interface between big tobacco and big oil.

A concern shared by many regarding GMOs includes the uncontrolled spread of GMO seeds and vegetation. Of course, there are many who insist this is both an unreasonable and unwarranted objection. But is it?

Barbara Peterson reported this story in September 2013.

> Following on the heels of the GM wheat contamination incident in Oregon, GM-contaminated alfalfa has now been found where it wasn't supposed to be in the state of Washington, only this time it was of the "approved" variety of GMOs.
>
> Agriculture officials in Washington state are testing samples of alfalfa after a farmer reported his hay was rejected for export because it tested positive for a genetically modified trait that was not supposed to be in his crop.[65]

GMOs

Genetically engineered food is now part of our mainstream diets. It has been estimated that Americans unknowingly eat their weight each year in GMOs, and the fact is, no long-term health study has ever been conducted to demonstrate the safety of GMO consumption.[66]

> "If you were planning on eating your body weight of anything in a year or feeding that much food to your family, wouldn't you first want to know if long-term government studies and monitoring have shown it to be safe?" asked

Renee Sharp, lead author of the report and the director of EWG's California office.[67]

GMO foods have been banned in many countries; partial and complete bans exist in Japan, Australia, New Zealand, Germany, Ireland, Austria, Hungary, Greece, Bulgaria, Luxembourg, France, Switzerland, India, Madeira, and Thailand.[68] Do these countries know something that Americans do not? What do you think of the headline, "Human genes engineered into experimental GMO rice being grown in Kansas"? My initial reaction when I saw this headline? Oh, come on, that couldn't be true! The facts differ.

Unless the rice you buy is certified organic, or comes specifically from a farm that tests its rice crops for genetically modified (GM) traits, you could be eating rice tainted with actual human genes. The only known GMO with inbred human traits in cultivation today, a GM rice product made by biotechnology company Ventria Bioscience is currently being grown on 3,200 acres in Junction City, Kansas—and possibly elsewhere—and most people have no idea about it.

Since about 2006, Ventria has been quietly cultivating rice that has been genetically modified (GM) with genes from the human liver for the purpose of taking the artificial proteins produced by this "Frankenrice" and using them in pharmaceuticals. With approval from the U.S. Department of Agriculture (USDA), Ventria has taken one of the most widely cultivated grain crops in the world today and essentially turned it into a catalyst for producing new drugs. *[69]

The article goes on to point out a couple more important facts:

"This is not a product that everyone would want to consume," said Jane Rissler from the Union of Concerned Scientists (UCS) to the *Washington Post* back in 2007. "It is unwise to produce drugs in plants outdoors."

Though receiving tens of thousands of public comments of opposition, many rightly concerned about the spread of GM traits, the USDA approved open cultivation of Ventria's

GM rice anyway. This, of course, occurred after the U.S. Food and Drug Administration (FDA) had refused approval for Ventria's GM rice back in 2003.

"These genetically engineered drugs could exacerbate certain infections, or cause dangerous allergic or immune system reactions," said Bill Freese, science policy analyst at the Center for Food Safety (CFS), who published a report back in 2007 about the dangers of Ventria's GM rice.[70]

What caused the FDA's policy change? Do you have an idea? When you learn of these things, does it increase your trust in Big Brother?

While we're discussing GMOs, did you know that Syngenta, a biotech giant, has been charged criminally with hiding the fact that their own research showed that cows died from eating its genetically modified corn?

The charges follow a long struggle for justice by a German farmer whose dairy cattle suffered mysterious illnesses and deaths after eating Bt 176. They were grown on his farm as part of authorised field tests during 1997 to 2002. By 2000, his cows were fed exclusively on Bt 176, and soon illnesses started to emerge. He was paid 40,000 euros by Syngenta as partial compensation for 5 dead cows, decreased milk yields, and vet costs. During a civil lawsuit brought against the company by the farmer however, Syngenta refused to admit that its GM corn was the cause, claiming no knowledge of harm. The case was dismissed and Gloeckner remained thousands of euros in debt.

But in 2009, the farmer learned of a feeding study allegedly commissioned by Syngenta in 1996 that resulted in four cows dying in two days. The trial was abruptly terminated. Now Gloeckner, along with a German group called Bündnis Aktion Gen-Klage and another farmer-turned-activist Urs Hans, have brought Syngenta to the criminal court to face charges of withholding knowledge of the U.S. trial, which makes the company liable for the destruction of the farmer's 65 cows. Syngenta is also charged with the deaths of cattle in the U.S. trial and on Gloeckner's farm, which should have been registered as "unexpected occurrences." Most seriously, the German head of Syngenta Hans-Theo Jahmann, is charged for withholding knowledge of the U.S. study from the judge and from Gloecker in the original civil court case.[71]

Stealth GMOs

There are genetically modified organisms by way of recombinant DNA, and then there is the stealth GMO. A stealth form of GMO is developed using a form of mutagenesis.

Genetic engineering means changing the genetic material of a living plant, fungus, or animal. What we've been fighting is merely one type, recombinant DNA, in which the gene from one species is transplanted into another. But it isn't the only way to change genes. Another technique has been developed and patented, technically called oligonucleotide-directed mutagenesis (ODM), but branded Rapid Transit Development System (RTDS) by Cibus, of San Diego, California.

A type of rapeseed has already been developed using this technique. The UK's Advisory Committee on Releases to the Environment (ACRE), a part of the Department for Environment, Food, and Rural Affairs (Defra), reviewed this product back in 2011 and concluded:

ACRE considers that herbicide-tolerant (HT) oilseed rape plants produced by Cibus LLC have been developed using a form of mutagenesis. It considers that this technique does not involve the use of recombinant nucleic acid molecules. Consequently, the HT oilseed rape plants could be excluded from the GMO Deliberate Release legislation in accordance with Annex 1B of Directive 2001/18/EC.

In other words, an organism that's been genetically mutated by ODM/RTDS is not being treated by the government as a genetically modified organism! This technique is sliding around the concerns of genetically engineered plants and animals by using a technique different from recombinant DNA.[72]

The end result is that governments around the world are allowing this form of GMO to go without oversight, and it will enter our food stream without notice of any kind. In fact, the result of this decision allows food processors to label these products as "natural."[73]

The Trans Pacific Partnership

The leading producer of GMOs is Monsanto. We have already discussed the GMO controversy, but there may be a hitch that few are aware of. Some at the time of this writing are reporting about a scheme designed to eliminate GMO labeling worldwide. The Trans Pacific Partnership (TPP) is a trade pact in negotiation that would outlaw labeling. The countries participating at the moment include the United States, Canada, Australia, Japan, Malaysia, Brunei, Mexico, New Zealand, Peru, Vietnam, and Singapore.

What is especially alarming about this trade agreement is its secrecy, given that companies like Monsanto, Walmart, and Big Pharma have been given a major influence in framing the conditions of the trade pact.

The TPP is so secret that members of Congress do not have access to it; however, the agreement is reported to contain sanctions against countries should they violate its terms, some of which include the following:

1. Eliminating "fair use" rights with respect to copyrighted material.
2. Closing down generic drugs.
3. Minimizing the standards regarding pesticide and herbicide use on food growers.
4. Dropping all GMO bans, and more.[74]

The TPP is the brainchild of the executive branch of our government. No one from Congress has any input in this pact. There is absolutely no transparency, and indeed the entire document has been classified as secret. When a congressman did see a copy of the document, he was threatened if he leaked any of it.

"This is astounding, given that the U.S. Constitution

provides Congress exclusive authority over trade policy," writes Wallach in the *Bangkok Post.*

This idea of total secrecy with zero oversight from Congress or the public is so offensive to the fundamental ideas of democracy that 132 members of Congress signed on to this letter demanding transparency over the language of the TPP. The letter was utterly ignored by the Obama administration, once again proving it is willing to sell out the American people for corporate interests.

"While the agreement could rewrite broad sections of nontrade policies affecting Americans' daily lives, the administration also has rejected demands by outside groups that the nearly complete text be publicly released," write Lori Wallach and Ben Beachy in a *New York Times* op-ed.

"This covert approach is a major problem because the agreement is more than just a trade deal. Existing and future American laws must be altered to conform with these terms, or trade sanctions can be imposed against American exports," they add . . .

After years of attempts by members of Congress to even see the TPP, finally one congressman was able to review only a few select sections of the agreement. That congressman's name is Alan Grayson.

He immediately characterized it as an "assault on democratic government."

The Obama administration threatened Grayson if he tried to release any of the information he saw by calling the TPP "classified" information . . . When the government doesn't want the public to see something it's doing, it simply slaps the "classified" label on the project and proceeds to engage in wild, runaway criminality with absolutely no repercussions.

"What I saw was nothing that could possibly justify the secrecy that surrounds it," Grayson said. "It is ironic in a way that the government thinks it's all right to have a record of every single call that an American makes, but not all right for an American citizen to know what sovereign powers the government is negotiating away."[75]

Now just to be clear here, I am neither arguing for or against the merits of the TPP. Rather, I am bringing to your attention the secretive nature of a program that would have a huge impact on us all, combined with the fact that the only people with any say in this matter are those who already have too much power by way of their financial influence. Surely a program with such far-reaching consequences as this should be open for public debate, and should most certainly be debated by our elected officials. What do you think?

When we encounter this kind of story, we once again see the absolute necessity for "whistleblowers." Everything I am reporting on in this book has already been leaked. You just have to wonder how many other such stories have yet to see the light of day.

Chemtrails

I battled with myself over whether to include this item. I finally decided that I should at least mention it. The fact is, I am uncertain what to believe regarding chemtrails, those long streams of vapor you see in the sky when some planes fly over. I do have a hard time believing they are only water vapor caused by the jet engines of aircraft. I know that when I was younger, these trails were much shorter and disappeared rather quickly; today it's not uncommon to see one reaching from horizon to horizon and lasting from sunup to sundown. So what is it if it is not just water vapor?

There are those who argue that oxides of metals, particularly aluminum oxide, are sprayed into the atmosphere to manage the environment, or more precisely, the weather. A geo-engineering patent exists for precisely that purpose.[76]

Is this possible? Quite a bit of evidence suggests the feasibility of this sort of thing, and a few claim that they have actually loaded this cargo aboard U.S. Air Force planes and others who have, under the promise of anonymity, come forward to share important details confirming the practice.[77]

Many potential problems may arise as a result of this practice, if it is true. And I'm sorry, but the denial by the military regarding something like this just means nothing to me. The reason? I had a very good friend and colleague by the name of William

(Bill) Bashore. On one mission during the Vietnam War, he led a team following a weapons smuggling operation. After hitting the weapons smugglers, Bill ordered a defoliant. Agent Orange was delivered by aircraft while Bill and his team waited. Bill was sprayed so heavily with Agent Orange, that he had to remove his shirt to dry his face.

Agent Orange was, of course, safe, or so the military insisted. A few years later, Bill was diagnosed with leukemia. He applied for medical benefits, but most were denied. Today we know that Agent Orange was largely DDT, and the military knew this at the time. Its use was outlawed in the U.S. because of known health risks, including leukemia. By the time the military got around to acknowledging the use and the risk, many if not most of the veterans who were exposed had died. Bill was one of those veterans.

As with Agent Orange, there are factors that we know about aluminum oxide. It is absolutely associated with a number of diseases, including Alzheimer's. The substance can cause irreversible neurological damage.[78]

Horizontal Gene Transfer

Before leaving the subject of chemtrails, I should also point out that there are reputable sources insisting that chemtrails and GMOs are giving rise to lateral or horizontal gene transfer in human genetic material. "Horizontal gene transfer is the transfer of genetic material from one organism to another organism that is not its offspring; this is most common among bacteria."[79]

Horizontal gene transfer is something our genetic engineers use in the laboratory. In a startling article appearing in several publications, including *Farm Wars,* we are invited into a world where genetic engineering has gone seriously amok. Drawing upon existing issues and present technology, these articles disclose the use and potential use of geo-engineering aerosols, including heavy metals, such as barium, and how they lead to abiotic stress (the negative impact of nonliving factors on the living organisms in a specific environment), such as heat shock. Linking horizontal gene transfer to Monsanto's patent covering abiotic stress leads to a connection between GMOs and chemtrails.

The *Farm Wars* article argues thus:

> Once GMOs are unleashed in the environment, there is absolutely nothing to stop the natural occurrence of horizontal gene transfer to non-GMO organisms, especially considering GMOs' increased tendency to do so. And what this process produces is anyone's guess. There is a reason for the limits nature places on this type of thing, and we've long since passed those limits.
>
> So, we are faced with the ever-increasing genetic pollution of almost all organisms on planet Earth from GMOs, and if that isn't enough, the horizontal gene transfer process, which is spreading these mutations far and wide throughout a host of divergent species, is being helped along by the pollutants being released into our atmosphere by geo-engineering programs.[80]

If chemtrails are real, if our government is once again lying about its activities, then we will undoubtedly as a society pay the price. You should know, however, and that's why I have included chemtrails and the GMO connection here.

Genetically Modified Insects

Several times during the three years I spent researching and writing this book, I came upon information that blew me away. This story is just one of those.

> Just when you thought genetically modified mosquitoes and mutated dinner entrees were the extent of biotech's hunger to manipulate the genetic coding of the planet, scientists have now unleashed a plan to launch thousands of 'frankenfly' style insects into the wild in order to combat pests.
>
> And just like we saw with the release of genetically modified mosquitoes, the altered insects are actually being pushed as a 'green alternative' to the use of chemicals. You see, British scientists claim that mutating the genetic code of the insects is actually a way of substituting for the use of chemical pesticides. Chemical pesticides used to lower the population of olive flies in Britain. The reality here, how-

ever, is that you are taking something damaging like chemical pesticides and replacing it with something far worse.[81]

Perhaps this is an alarmist attitude or the result of watching too many science fiction flicks, but why aren't there public hearings and the like before engineered seeds, chemicals, and insects are released into our world? Do we need to regulate technology tighter? Do we need a special department of government overseeing and regulating genetically engineered everything? And if we had such an agency, do you think it would be any different from the agencies we currently have protecting us?

Disappearing Male

Researchers have noted that births of male children are on the decline. Among heavily industrialized countries, this decline has persisted steadily for thirty years, resulting in an estimated "three million fewer baby boys."[82]

In the documentary film *The Disappearing Male,* a case is made that this phenomenon is due in large part to the ubiquitous chemicals present in these heavily industrialized countries, chemicals said to be in everything from shampoo to sunglasses and from meat and dairy products to cosmetics and baby bottles. The film documents a number of observed facts:

- The number of boys born with penis abnormalities and genital defects has increased by 200 percent in the past two decades.
- Boys have a higher incidence of attention deficit hyperactivity disorder, learning disabilities, Tourette's syndrome, cerebral palsy, and dyslexia.
- Boys are four times as likely to be autistic.
- The average sperm count of a North American college student today is less than half of what it was 50 years ago.
- The quality of sperm is declining. 85 percent of the sperm produced by a healthy male is DNA-damaged.
- Damaged sperm have been linked to a 300 percent increase in testicular cancer—a form of cancer that affects young men in their 20s and 30s.

- The chemical industry has developed more than 90,000 man-made chemicals in the last sixty years. Eighty-five percent of them have never undergone testing for their impact on the human body.[83]

The principal chemicals allegedly contributing to this situation are bisphenol A (BPA) and phthalates. Who is protecting us from these hazards? There are several things you can do to protect yourself from our chemical-driven country, and I recommend checking them out here: **articles.mercola.com/sites/articles/archive/2013/08/31/disappearing-male-documentary.aspx**

As disturbing as this assertion may seem, I would be remiss if I left the subject without pointing out two things. First, there are those who say the film is a pinch of science and a pound of speculation, but you can see it for yourself online, free, here: **smh.com.au/tv/health/the-disappearing-male-4260801.html**

Secondly, and much more controversial, some researchers have argued that these chemicals can actually be gender-bending in their effect:

> The diverse systems affected by endocrine-disrupting chemicals likely include all hormonal systems and range from those controlling development and function of reproductive organs to the tissues and organs regulating metabolism and satiety.
>
> Effects on these systems can lead to obesity, infertility or reduced fertility, learning and memory difficulties, adult-onset diabetes or cardiovascular disease, as well as a variety of other diseases.

The article goes on to say:

> "The prevalence of paediatric asthma has more than doubled over the past 20 years and is now the leading cause of child hospitalisations and school absenteeism," it said. "Certain birth defects, such as those of the male reproductive organs, are on the rise. The incidence of paediatric leukaemia and brain cancer has risen, as has the incidence of testicular cancer. These are stark health statistics."[84]

Defense Production Act

Executive Order 13603 of March 16, 2012, entitled National Defense Resources Preparedness, amends the Defense Production Act of 1950. The order provides that the president alone has the power to take control when appropriate "to promote the national defense." This includes:

> The power to seize control and take over these resources is delegated to the following government authorities:

> 1. the Secretary of Agriculture with respect to food resources, food resource facilities, livestock resources, veterinary resources, plant health resources, and the domestic distribution of farm equipment and commercial fertilizer;
> 2. the Secretary of Energy with respect to all forms of energy;
> 3. the Secretary of Health and Human Services with respect to health resources;
> 4. the Secretary of Transportation with respect to all forms of civil transportation;
> 5. the Secretary of Defense with respect to water resources; and
> 6. the Secretary of Commerce with respect to all other materials, services, and facilities, including construction materials.[85]

The phrase "to promote national defense" is somewhat ambiguous, in my opinion, and it certainly fails to provide any cushion of comfort that ensures our freedoms will remain in place. Are you comfortable with this phrase "to promote national defense"? Remember how important the promotion of fear is in encouraging people to give up their freedoms!

Labor Department

Big business has taken over most of the small farms of yesteryear. Those that remain are largely family businesses. I attended grade school at a time when some schools recessed at harvest time to allow the young people to help out on the farm.

Times change. Today the Labor Department is in contest with some states over its attempt to prohibit children under 18 from performing many farm chores. In Tennessee, for example, the House has passed a bill that prevents state enforcement of the Child Labor Law.[86]

What exactly is the effect of this proposed lack of enforcement? Not too positive, according to the publication, *The Farmer-Stockman.*

> If you've been following the dialogue about the new proposed regulations that the U.S. Department of Labor wants to impose on youth potentially working on farms or in so-called hazardous ag settings, you know that if the proposal becomes a final rule, children under the age of 18 would be severely limited as to what they could do as a farm employee. For some activities it's 16, but to drive a tractor, a young person would now need to be 18.
>
> You've probably also figured out that the exemptions for your own children could be wiped out if you farm in a family corporation, or if you farm with a brother or your father, and they take care of the grain and you don't. In that case, notes Megan Ritter, national policy specialist with Indiana Farm Bureau, Inc., the young person might still not be able to drive a tractor on the farm until they're 18 even if it's your own farm!
>
> If you've followed the dialogue, you've probably already concluded by now that to most farm families, these proposed rules may fall somewhere between restrictive and ridiculous. You're also likely aware that unless Big Brother is going to watch your farm 24 hours a day, enforcing these regulations could be next to impossible. If that attitude is preventing you from commenting on the law, with the comment period ending tomorrow, Ritter says you need to rethink the situation. She urges you to submit comments if you find the current proposal unsuitable, rather than just assuming it will go away or not be enforced.[87]

Is this a protective act really designed to protect children, or is it another land grab that works by making it even more difficult for the small family farm to survive? Remember, many of these smaller operations are the very ones who resist Monsanto and other corporations of that ilk. For those of us who visit local farmers markets, this may change the very nature of what we can buy that is locally grown. Am I being an alarmist? You decide.

Gattaca

In 1997 a futuristic world appeared on the big screen as a genetically inferior man pretended to be a genetically superior man in order to pursue his fantasy as a space traveler. Genetics decided the fate of people in this interesting movie. We may be approaching that same sort of thing in the real world today. Scientists are now able to identify some 3,500 "genetic faults" in an unborn child. Should these faults lead to abortions? Will our children blame us one day for not engineering them more perfectly?

> A team has been able to predict the whole genetic code of a foetus by taking a blood sample from a woman who was 18 weeks pregnant, and a swab of saliva from the father.
> They believe that, in time, the test will become widely available, enabling doctors to screen unborn babies for some 3,500 genetic disorders.[88]

What are the ethical ramifications of this screening? As with many technological advances of the day, including such things as cloning, the technology has outpaced the ethical inquiry. We therefore find ourselves very often running full speed ahead without anything more than a backward glance or a flicker of consideration whether we should be proceeding. As Dr. Malcolm in the movie *Jurassic Park* puts it, "Just because we can does not mean we should," and this might be an advisable motto for all to remember.

Scanners

The new world of global security has led to the development of many technologies that have impact in areas other than defense. Ignoring objections from the scientific community and forgoing tests of the devices on the long-term health of the population, full-body scanners were introduced as the answer to protecting us all from terrorism. Well, how about this for a dose of terror?

They've been approved all over the world and marketed as the next greatest airport scanning technology. The U.S., U.K., Russia, Australia, Europe, and Canada have all installed airport body scanners, which have potentially devastating health effects.

Many of these scanners are reportedly using terahertz (THz) waves, the radiation that fills the slot in the electromagnetic spectrum between microwaves and infrared. Evidence suggests that although the forces generated are tiny, resonant effects allow THz waves to unzip double-stranded DNA, creating bubbles in the double strand that could significantly interfere with processes such as gene expression and DNA replication.

As the path toward rolling out wider use of whole-body scanners in U.S. airports ran through the White House, Obama expedited their deployment because the Department of Homeland Security (DHS) and Transportation Security Administration (TSA) didn't need legislation from Congress to start using the devices at any of the 560 U.S. airports . . .

A watchdog group called the Electronic Privacy Information Center (EPIC) obtained over 100 of the images and states on its website that, "The images, which are routinely captured by the federal agency, prove that body scanning devices store and record images of individuals stripped naked." The group has filed a lawsuit to suspend the deployment of body scanners at airports.

EPIC also discovered that the TSA actually specified to manufacturers that the machines have the ability to send and store images. The TSA says that these functions are only for testing and training and insists on its website that the airport body scanners are delivered to airports with storage and recording functions disabled.[89]

Are we to trust the TSA? Must we check and double check the government to ensure that we are being told the truth, or is there a time when you just come to the conclusion that they are not to be trusted? For what it's worth, I am of the opinion today that we can no longer trust. I used to believe we could. By the time you finish reading this book, you may no longer have as much trust in the government as you might have had to begin with.

CONCLUSION

When I started this chapter, I found the stacks of material in my research piles terribly daunting. I decided to cull the information and organize it according to what I found most relevant. Unfortunately, that meant that more than 50 percent of files on my desk were passed over. Once I thought the book was done, I sent it to my editor, but the data kept coming in. The files piled ever higher. By the time one publisher told me to reduce the book by more than 50 percent, I had another 50 percent to add. To make a long story short, I added small parts, removed none, and yet the piles grow ever higher in my office today.

My point is simple: We must be vigilant about nearly every aspect of our lives, taking nothing for granted. If there was ever a time for 'mindful living,' it has never been more acutely appropriate than today! It's important for all of us to become aware and to speak up. I think the best way we can turn things around is by taking some small amount of time every day to do something proactive to bring about change—perhaps it's a letter, a petition, a post on your social networking page, an idea offered at a PTA meeting, and so on. What can you do? I think that is the question for all of us. What do you think?

They Start With Our Children

The greatest obstacle to discovery is not ignorance—
it is the illusion of knowledge.
~Daniel J. Boorstin

Misconception*: Most believe that sending their children to school will provide them with knowledge and skills to think, reason, and thereby succeed.*
Fact*: Our educational system is designed primarily to indoctrinate our children while maintaining a three-tier caste system, limiting most.*

During all of my research, nothing has touched me more than the realization that our children have repeatedly been held as property belonging to the nation. But first, it may surprise you to know that one of the most important starting points in any discussion of mind manipulation has to be our education system. By way of background, the first public compulsory education system originated in Prussia in 1819. The system was divided into three levels. The three levels, or tiers, afforded three different types of education for three different classes of children. According to retired schoolteacher and author John Gatto, tier one was for those who would become the rulers, tier two for those who would become the rulers' assistants and professionals such as doctors, lawyers, and the like, and tier three for those who were to be ruled—that's most of us. While this information may not ring true to you, think on this:

> There are over 500 colleges and universities in the United States, yet out of all of these numerous institutions of higher learning, we seem to have an over-representation of the same select few schools when it comes to the presidency. Of the 44 U.S. presidents, 15 of them (34%) have attended one of the eight Ivy League schools [Dartmouth, Harvard, Brown, Yale, Columbia, Princeton, Penn, and Cornell]. When you include three other prestigious institutions (Georgetown, Stanford, and William & Mary) that number increases to 20 out of 44 presidents (45%). Harvard alone lays claim to 8 presidents (John Adams, John Quincy Adams, Rutherford B. Hayes, Teddy Roosevelt, Franklin D. Roosevelt, John F. Kennedy, George W. Bush, and Barack Obama).[1]

And this picture is only getting worse. From 1988 to 2012, there have been seven presidential elections, so there have been 14 presidential nominees. Of these 14, 12 attended an Ivy League school!

Quoting from *Mind Programming,*

> [Those who were to be ruled] would receive the necessary education to guarantee obedience to the authority (rulers). The subjects constituted more than 90 percent of the population.[2]
>
> This lower class, the ruled, would be educated, but it would be led away from thinking and reasoning. Variations on curriculum and methods would expose the masses to math, social sciences, hard science, language, and art—but once again, in a manner that created what I've called "in-the-box thinking," and I use the word *thinking* loosely, for this really isn't thinking at all.

Think about it—how much of your education was dedicated to rote memory work? We were taught names and dates, and we were taught "right" answers, but how much time was spent teaching us how to think?

Over time, this system was copied and exported to many other countries. By the late 1800s, it had fully arrived in America, and under the tutelage of a few, it prospered. One of the most influential men of the period, philosopher John Dewey, believed that the purpose of public schools was to "take an active part in determining the social order of the future . . . according as the teachers align themselves with the newer forces, making for social control of economic forces."[3]

Another influential individual in the history of American public education was Edward Lee Thorndike. For Thorndike, teaching was:

> . . . the art of giving and withholding stimuli with the result of producing or preventing certain responses. In this definition, the term stimulus is used widely for any event which influences a person . . . for a word spoken to him, a look, a sentence which he reads, the air he breathes, etc. etc. The term response is used for any reaction made by him . . . a new thought, a feeling of interest, a bodily act, any mental or bodily condition resulting from the stimulus. The aim of the teacher is to produce desirable and prevent undesirable changes in human beings by producing and preventing certain responses. The means at the disposal of the teacher are the stimuli which can be brought to bear upon the pupil . . . the teacher's words, gestures, and appearance, the condition and appliances of the schoolroom, the books to be used, and the objects to be seen, and so on through a long list of the things and events which the teacher can control.[4]

Power of the Teachers College

It's clear that the opportunity to control/train the thinking of students is present and that at least some of the most notable and influential of those involved in the creation of our educational system intended for schooling to socialize rather than educate. They even thought that it should sub- jugate the student to a philosophy that emphasizes a social- order doctrine over the development of intellectualism. It's also worth noting that men like Dewey and Thorndike were instrumental in establishing the direction of the Teachers College, part of Columbia University, and according to Jim Keith, author of *Mind Control, World Control*: "By the 1950s, the Teachers College was indisputably the most powerful force in education in America, with approximately one- third of all school presidents and deans, and one-fourth of all American teachers accredited there."[5]

The next time you drop off your child at school, think about this: When you buy your child pencils and so forth and learn that they were collected by the teacher, together with those of other students, and placed in one common holder for everyone to use, ask yourself, *Why?* Does this promote individuality and property rights or . . . ? The next time you hear of some seemingly outlandish this or that going on in a school, you might ask yourself, *What am I doing to see that that does not go on in schools near me?* The next time you hear that the Pledge of Allegiance will be recited omitting certain words, ask yourself, *What will the Pledge be like in years to come?*[6]

Propagandizing Apology

Parents, students, and members of the faculty of a Wisconsin school complained about a 1940s-style German propaganda ap- proach used when the school played a video featuring celebrities proselytizing for President Obama during a school assembly.

At one point in the video, Red Hot Chili Peppers singer Anthony Kiedis says, "I pledge to be of service to Barack Obama," and at the end of the video, Demi Moore states, "I pledge to be a servant to our president . . ."

"It looks a little bit 1940s Germany," one person told a KMSP reporter during a man-on-the-street interview.

The reporter explained to another person that "in other words, we pledge to our country, to our flag, but we don't pledge our allegiance to the man, the president. It's like, he's not a king. He's the president. He serves us."

After outrage, the school was forced to issue some apologies, saying the district is non-partisan and didn't mean to promote allegiance to Obama.[7]

Black History Month

"He's our man—yes, we can," were some of the lyrics taught to kindergarten children in 2012 as part of the celebration for Black History Month at a Tipps Elementary School in Houston, Texas. A team chant was developed and passed around to teachers to share with their students, and believe it or not, in public schools where prayer is banned, where politics do not belong, where we send our children to learn the 4 Rs, the lyrics abandoned even common sense:

The Barack Obama Song

Who is our 44th President?
Obama is our 44th President
Who is a DC resident?
Obama is a DC resident
Resident, President

Who's favorite team is the Chicago White Sox?
Obama's favorite team is the Chicago White sox
Who really thinks outside the box?
Obama really thinks outside the box
Outside the box, Chicago White Sos
Resident, President

Who really likes to play basketball?
Obama really likes to play basketball
Who's gonna answer our every call?
Every Call, Basketball
Outside the box, Chicago White Sox
Resident, President

Who's famous slogan is Yes we can?
Obams's famous slogan is Yes we can
Who do we know is the man?

63

GOTCHA!

Barack Obama is the man
He's our man, Yes we can!
Every Call, Basketvall
Outside the box, Chicago White Sox
Resident, President
Who won a grammy for "Dreams of my Father"?
Obama won a grammy for "Dreams of my Father"?
Now can you guess who's a famous author
Barack Obama is a famous author

Famous Author, Dreams of my Father
He's our man, Yes we can!
Every Call, Basketball
Outside the box. Chicago White Sox
Resident President

Who wants to go to college at Yale?
Malia & Sasha will go to college at Yale
Who'll make sure they won't fail?
Barack & Michelle know they won't fail

They won't fail, they're going to Yale
Famous Author, Dream of my Father
He's our man, Yes we can!
Every Call, Basketball
Outside the box, Chicago White Sox
Resident, President[8]

Please note: this chant has been reproduced exactly as two teachers sent it to the parents of their kindergartners. According to one of our editors, there are 33 spelling and grammatical errors in this piece. How many can you find? More important, where do you think these teachers' priorities are in what they were teaching our children?

One person responded with a letter that says it all:

Dear Principal Redd,
Hi there . . . my name is Joe Pagliarulo . . . I go by Joe Pags on the radio. I had a listener contact me today . . . with the attached document. I'm confused. How exactly

is holding this president up on high—indoctrinating little children to believe what YOU want them to believe about this president a good lesson for Black History Month . . . What's said in the document is nothing less than proselytizing YOUR feelings for the president. You can love him. You can vote for him. You can be proud that he's the first black president—which would be appropriate for this month's program. But, you DO NOT get to tell the taxpayers who pay your salary that their kids have to genuflect to the altar you've clearly built to this president. I'd LOVE to have you on my show. I'd LOVE for you to explain to those who pay your salary why YOUR political beliefs are the ones THEIR kids have to get in lock-step with.

Really looking forward to hearing from you.

Regards,

Pags[9]

Should we be concerned? In my view, it's not about the party you do or do not belong to; it's really all about the principle. How on earth is educating our children in this fashion fundamentally different from the schools for Hitler Youth?

The Hitler Youth was a logical extension of Hitler's belief that the future of Nazi Germany was its children. The Hitler Youth was seen as being as important to a child as school was . . .

Nazi education schemes partly fitted in with this, but Hitler wanted to occupy the minds of the young in Nazi Germany even more.[10]

Limits

I started this chapter with my deep concern regarding our children. What are the acceptable limits for training our young people to behave according to approved standards? What are approved standards? Exactly what is considered to be good and bad behavior? Is it bad behavior for a youngster to wear a shirt with a picture of the American flag on it? Is it unacceptable behavior for a student to bless their food before eating in school? Is it wrong for a child to ask questions? Should a child remain silent when something is said that is contrary to the teachings of their parents? Should a child always behave like the adults in school?

Well—the answer is, and should be, it depends! There are so many horror stories of children led astray by adults, that a responsible parent today must caution their children about who, what, and when to obey the so-called authority. Enter this story from New Zealand.

Headline: "School Plans to Tag Students with Microchip Bracelets to Encourage 'Good Behavior.'" Now what do you think of that? The story continues:

> In a move that sounds like something out of a frightening dystopian fiction, a school in New Zealand has come under intense criticism from parents for attempting to introduce a scheme to tag children with microchips in order to promote good behavior.
>
> Fairfax Media reports that Swannanoa School in North Canterbury plans to attach chipped bracelets to students to track their behavior. Many parents were not notified of the scheme, only finding out about it via minutes from a Parent Teacher Association meeting.
>
> When the local media investigated the proposal, the school finally sent out notifications to parents. A letter from the principal suggested that the plan was more efficient than alternatives such as ID cards, which could be misplaced.
>
> The school has even gone as far as measuring up the wrists of children in preparation for the plan, which it says will cost $7000 to set up.
>
> Under the proposal, the devices locked to kids' arms would allow teachers to use portable scanners in order to add reward points to a student's good behavior record, stored on a database. Students would be rewarded points when they did something teachers determined to be positive, and incentives would be enhanced with the promise of prizes for reaching a certain amount of points.
>
> The chips would contain information, including names, points tally, and the schoolhouse that students belonged to. The school claims that the devices would not have a GPS tracker.[11]

Have we gone too far when we begin to monitor our children with microchip bracelets? Or not—for after all, college professor and MSNBC host Melissa Harris-Perry, professor of political science at Tulane University where she is founding director of the Anna Julia Cooper Project on Gender, Race, and Politics in the South, said, "We have to break through our private idea that kids belong to their parents or kids belong to their families." Kids belong to whole communities, she insists, and once we realize this we'll make "better investments" in government indoctrination of children.[12]

Could it be true? Do your children belong to the government? Research together with precedent suggests that indeed they do. The fact is, the government can step in as they have in the past on a federal, state, and local level, and take your children. A quick search of records shows some really inane reasons for seizing children as though they were the property of drug dealers. Take this instance, for example. A couple was charged with reading the Bible to their children without training, and for this their children were taken.[13]

"What!" you might say. We have already discussed the case of Justina Pelletier, kidnapped by the hospital she was taken to by her parents according to the instructions of the girl's primary physician. In other words, the parents did exactly as their doctor told them to do, and the state stepped in and took their daughter for doing so. Sure they eventually had their daughter returned to them, but not until the parents exhausted every foreseeable remedy, spent a personal fortune, and invested more than a year in getting their daughter back.

So, what do we do if the state decides to use microchips in schools to monitor our children? The Affordable Care health bill contains a piece that calls for medical tagging, microchips, allegedly to eliminate health care errors. Are we really too far behind New Zealand's proposal to use micro chipping for monitoring purposes? I am so reminded of Orwell and *Animal Farm*! To quote Mr. Orwell, "If liberty means anything at all, it means the right to tell people what they do not want to hear."[14]

That goes for all people, teachers, principals, politicians, and so on! How can anyone consider themselves to be truly free in a world of microchip monitoring? As Abe Lincoln stated, "Those who deny freedom to others, deserve it not for themselves."[15]

Absurd

The famous educator Noam Chomsky, professor emeritus from MIT, has come right out and called our education system absurd. In his words, "The intellectual tradition is one of servility to power, and if I didn't betray it I'd be ashamed of myself."[16] Chomsky has also made it clear that our system is one of indoctrination as opposed to education. Again, in his words, "The United States is unusual among the industrial democracies in the rigidity of the system of ideological control—'indoctrination,' we might say—exercised through the mass media."[17]

So let's turn to the media, staying with Professor Chomsky, who describes indoctrination as propaganda, a term perverted from its original meaning to mean today the nasty business of brainwashing, this way: "Propaganda is to a democracy what the bludgeon is to a totalitarian state."[18]

CONCLUSION

We cannot afford to blindly trust that our public school system has the best interest of our children in mind. Indeed, our children may well be seen as pawns in a larger scheme and not one that we necessarily approve of. We must all become involved if we are to have a chance at ensuring our children receive from their schooling what we send them to school to learn! And as for our children being properties of the state, well there too we must actively engage. Children do need protection from abusive environments, but in my view, when someone in authority makes a mistake and a child is taken from the family, the parties to the mistake should have some legal liability, civil and/or criminal. What are your thoughts?

Behaviorism

*People will always prefer black-and-white over shades of grey,
and so there will always be the temptation to hold overly simplified
beliefs and to hold them with excessive confidence.*

~Thomas Gilovich

Misconception: *You may have thought that you make your own decisions freely and with full conscious attention to those choices.*
Fact: *We have all been engineered and conditioned to think and behave in certain ways that have become automatic by definition, unless we pause and question.*

For a long time, behaviorism was the dominant theory in psychology. In the strict sense, behaviorism insists that human psychology is nothing more than an organized hierarchy of conditioned learning. Behaviorism assumes that mental states are subjective and irrelevant, and only observable behavior should be systematically studied. The term behaviorism comes from its founder, John Watson. Watson believed that behaviors can be conditioned, molded, and otherwise trained. Watson's work *Psychology as the Behaviorist Views It* is often now called *The Behaviorist Manifesto*. Watson's somewhat controversial statement within this text on page 82 pretty well sums up his position:

Give me a dozen healthy infants, well-formed, and my own specified world to bring them up in, and I'll guarantee to take any one at random and train him to become any type of specialist I might select—doctor, lawyer, artist, merchant-chief, and yes, even beggar-man and thief, regardless of his talents, penchants, tendencies, abilities, vocations, and race of his ancestors. I am going beyond my facts and I admit it, but so have the advocates of the contrary, and they have been doing it for many thousands of years.[1]

Conditioning

Conditioned behavior? One of Watson's experiments is still considered to be among the most unethical psychological studies in history, but it nevertheless is tutorial in our context. It is known as the Little Albert study.

The goal of the experiment was to show how principles of, at the time recently discovered, classical conditioning could be applied to condition fear of a white rat into "Little Albert," an 11-month-old boy. Watson and Rayner conditioned "Little Albert" by clanging an iron rod when a white rat was presented. First, they presented to the boy a white rat and observed that he was not afraid of it. Second, they presented him with a white rat and then clanged an iron rod. "Little Albert" responded by crying. This second presentation was repeated several times. Finally, Watson and Rayner presented the white rat by itself, and the boy showed fear. Later, in an attempt to see if the fear transferred to other objects, Watson presented Albert with a rabbit, a dog, and a fur coat. He cried at the sight of all of them. This study demonstrated how emotions could become conditioned responses.[2]

Following in Watson's steps was the man who put behaviorism at the forefront of psychological theory and research, B.F. Skinner. His publications were prolific, and some of his experimental designs were truly novel.

As he experimented with rats, Skinner noticed that the responses he was recording were influenced not only by what preceded them but also by what followed them. The common behavioral approach at the time was influenced by the work of Pavlov and Watson, both of whom focused on the stimulus-response paradigm. Their form of classical conditioning focused on what occurred prior to a response and how these stimuli affected learning. Skinner, however, focused on what occurred after a behavior, noting that the effects or repercussions of an action could influence an organism's learning . . .

A basic assumption of his was that all language, including private, internal discourse, was a behavior that developed in the same manner as other skills. He believed that a sentence is merely part of "a behavior chain, each element of which provides a conditional stimulus for the production of the succeeding element." The probability of a verbal response was contingent on four things: reinforcement, stimulus control, deprivation, and aversive stimulation. The interaction of these things in a child's environment would lead to particular associations, the basis of all language.[3]

Social Engineering in the Hive

For both Watson and Skinner, the idea of individual consciousness and its innate priority when viewing the human condition was simply and completely rejected! Consciousness as we think of it today was simply the result of conditioning—period. Full stop. This construct makes it very easy for some to think of the human condition in terms of drones, worker bees, and the like. Mankind as a species wrongly arrogates a conscious life to itself as a matter of psychological needs having to do with evolutionary adaptation and conditioning. The particular relevance to our concern in this context is well said in this piece by Christine Rosen:

> American psychologist John B. Watson, the founder of behaviorism, described his vision simply: "It is the business of behavioristic psychology to be able to predict and to control human activity." Building on Russian physiologist Ivan Pavlov's pioneering work on classical conditioning in dogs, Watson spent years performing animal studies that demon-

strated the powerful effects of reward and punishment on learned behavior. By 1913, when he published his ground-breaking essay, "Psychology as the Behaviorist Sees It," Watson was determined to create a new kind of psychology, one that actively applied to the real world knowledge gleaned from laboratory research. To Watson, the behaviorist was not merely a psychologist; he was a social engineer whose expertise would help design a better world.[4]

Shaping Elections

Think back for a minute now and reflect on an earlier chapter where we discussed the use of these social psychologists to shape the outcome of elections. Indeed, again quoting Rosen:

> When Barack Obama won the presidential election in November 2008, observers credited the extraordinary effectiveness of his grassroots organizing with helping him to achieve his historic victory. But Obama had another unacknowledged ally on his side: behavioral science. A team of behavioral scientists, including at least one Nobel laureate, advised the campaign on everything from honing his message to fund-raising techniques to voter turnout tactics.
>
> After the election, Obama appointed several members of this behavioral brain trust to prominent positions in his administration. In areas such as health care, environmental regulation, and the economy, Obama is relying on these experts to launch one of the most ambitious behaviorist-style policy projects in American political history.[5]

Do you feel that you have been conditioned to behave in ways that go beyond the classical imprinting we all experience during maturation? Or, alternatively, is the entire imprinting process something that never ends? Are we being conditioned today to approve and disapprove according to someone else's priorities? Are we conditioned to consume regardless of our economic ability to handle the debt? Are we conditioned to strive all of our lives chasing the proverbial carrot, only to serve the wealth-building class commonly thought of as the elite? It is true that the rich get richer and the poor get poorer according to the data, so again, have we just been conditioned to behave like worker ants?

When you take everything into consideration that we have examined to this point, what conclusions do you draw? Are you conditioned to reject the possibility that all of the dots add up to something other than the obvious? Conditioned to see this all as just another tin foil hat piece of nonsense?

I must admit that I do not want the dots to connect in ways that say what I think they are saying. Perhaps the real conspiracy is one of creating a conspiracy by manufacturing all of the history and evidence disclosed to now. Wow—imagine the herculean effort it would take to create a conspiracy that there was a conspiracy of an elite few that really pulled the strings from behind the scenes. That boggles my mind. So what does all of this mean?

Is it possible that, as with the ink blot test, I find the evidence that supports a preconceived idea, and that's all that I include herein? I suppose that I could be blind to that possibility and actually be acting out in some conditioned, unthinking, unconscious way—but I seriously doubt it. Still, that's up to you decide. What do the dots suggest to you?

CONCLUSION

Only by showing up informed and aware, truly mindful of our every action, can we hope to avoid the conditioning of our culture. Only by constantly questioning ourselves can we hope to uncover the extent and nature of the engineering that continues to exert an interest over the way we think and what we believe. How much of our own thinking and behavior do you think has been influenced this way? What are some of the things that you can think of to eliminate undesirable conditioning? Do you think social engineering is both necessary and good? I encourage you to examine your own past actions and present attitudes with a fresh eye and a resolute determination to be fully aware and mindful of the conditioning in our culture.

CHAPTER FIVE

Curtailing Freedom

If you don't control your mind, someone else will.
~John Allston

Misconception: *You probably believe that mind control is only a science fiction movie or some far-fetched conspiracy theory.*
Fact: *True mind control is not only possible—it has actually been achieved on more than one occasion.*

Despite the fact that it is public knowledge, very few people are aware that after World War II, our Office of Strategic Services (OSS) recruited Nazi scientists who had experimented on humans in order to gain their psychological insights. Many of those recruited were, in fact, war criminals.

> U.S. military and intelligence agencies protected some war criminals in the interest of obtaining technical or intelligence information from them, or taking part in ongoing intelligence or engineering (e.g. Operation Paperclip). Multiple U.S. intelligence organizations were involved (the Central Intelligence Agency was not created until 1947 and in control of its clandestine services until 1952). The relationships with German war criminals started immediately after the end of the Second World War, but some of the Japanese relationships were slower to develop.[1]

Let me give you a brief list of some of the programs that were implemented, supposedly very successfully, by the U.S. government and military.

Project Midnight Climax

Is it possible to wipe a mind clean and reimprint it at will? Can one combine electric shock, drugs, hypnosis, psychic traumas, and more, to accomplish this feat? What could you produce if you were allowed to do anything you could think of to control the actions of another? What if you employed a pornographer to work with you, and then you systematically exposed subjects to arousal stimulation while they were drugged, hypnotized, or were affected by any combination of mind-altering techniques known to man? Would the U.S. government ever actually permit this kind of research?

Operation Midnight Climax was an operation initially established by Sidney Gottlieb and placed under the direction of Narcotics Bureau officer George Hunter White under the alias of Morgan Hall for the CIA as a sub-project of Project MKUltra, the CIA mind-control research program that began in the 1950s.

The project consisted of a web of CIA-run safehouses in San Francisco, Marin, and New York. It was established in order to study the effects of LSD on unconsenting individuals. Prostitutes on the CIA payroll were instructed to lure clients back to the safehouses, where they were surreptitiously plied with a wide range of substances, including LSD, and monitored behind one-way glass. Several significant operational techniques were developed in this theater, including extensive research into sexual blackmail, surveillance technology, and the possible use of mind-altering drugs in field operations.[2]

The Manchurian Candidate

James Jesus Angleton of the CIA, chief of the CIA's counterintelligence section, defined three goals for their Manchurian Candidate Program. And, yes, this really was a government program and not just the title of a movie and book! The goals for this program involved research with hypnosis: "(1) the speedy hypnotic induction of unwitting subjects; (2) the ability to create long-lasting amnesia; and (3) the implanting of long-lasting, useful hypnotic suggestions."[3] Using these techniques it was shown that "men could be, contrary to popular wisdom on the topic, hypnotized to commit acts that violated their own moral codes, not to mention military codes."[4]

In one experiment, hypnotized soldiers were told that an officer in the room was actually an enemy infiltrator. "Without exception, on command the soldiers violently attacked the officer."[5]

Project Bluebird

The aim of Project Bluebird was to research ways in which disposable assassins could be created. Here are just some of the goals for this project, as provided in the declassified CIA document.

- Can we obtain control of the future activities (physical and mental) of any given individual, willing or unwilling, by application of SI [sleep induction] and H [hypnosis] techniques?
- Can we create, by post-H control, an action contrary to an individual's basic moral principles?
- Can we in a matter of an hour, two hours, one day, etc., induce an H condition in an unwilling subject to such an extent that he will perform an act for our benefit?
- Could we seize a subject and in the space of an hour or two by post-H control have him crash an airplane, wreck a train, etc.?
- Can we, by H and SI techniques, force a subject (unwilling or otherwise) to travel long distances, commit specified acts and return to us or bring documents or materials?
- Can we guarantee total amnesia under any and all conditions?
- Can we "alter" a person's personality?
- Can we devise a system for making unwilling subjects

into willing agents and then transfer that control to untrained agency agents in the field by use of codes or identifying signs?

- Is it possible to find a gas that can be used to gain SI control from a gas pencil, odorless, colorless: one shot, etc.?
- How can sodium A or P or any other sleep-inducing agent be best concealed in a normal or commonplace item, such as candy, cigarettes, liquor, wines, coffee, tea, beer, gum, water, aspirin tablets, common medicines, coke, tooth-paste?
- Can we, using SI and H, extract complicated formulas from scientists, engineers, etc., if they are unwilling?[6]

In this document, there is an interview with a person whose name has been redacted. The entire interview is eye-opening, but the following question and answer is the most shocking:

Q: Can individuals be made to do things under hypnosis that they would not otherwise?

A: Individuals could be taught to do anything, including murder, suicide, etc. I do believe that you could carry out acts that would be against an individual's moral feelings if they were rightly, psychologically conditioned.[7]

For those of you interested in reading the full text of the CIA documents, you can do so here: **wanttoknow.info/mind_control/ foia_mind_control/19520101_140401**

Project Artichoke

Project Artichoke evolved from Project Bluebird and was run by the CIA in an effort to research interrogation methods using drugs. While there is a lot of information available on the Internet regarding Project Artichoke, I chose to cite information from a CIA memorandum that was written on January 31, 1975. In this document, it stated that these "special interrogation methods have been known to include the use of drugs and chemicals, hypnosis and 'total isolation,' a form of psychological harassment."[8]

In reading through this document, it did become apparent to me that a lot of information was either lost or hidden. However, what little information there was certainly verified some of the techniques that were used in this project:

> In the case of XXXX, XXXX operation in XXXX drugs were utilized in the interrogation, which took place XXXX. Again, details for the operation were not available. However, an interview with the Office of Security representative who participated in the interrogation revealed that a form of LSD was used in this instance. In this case, approval was granted by headquarters for the ARTICHOKE interrogation. A memorandum dated 6 July 1960, signed by Mr. XXXX, deputy director of Security, reflected that approval for use of drugs in this case was granted at a meeting of the Drug Committee on 1 July 1960 and cabled to XXXX.[9]

One specific incident is worth sharing with you here as it indicated the use of these techniques on civilians:

> Although it was not clear from file information whether or not the incident occurred under the auspices of Project ARTICHOKE, the incident did involve use of LSD in an experimental exercise. One Frank Olson, a civilian employee of the Department of the Army, committed suicide a week or so after having been administered LSD by an agency representative. . . . it appears that the drug was administered to several unwitting subjects by a Dr. Gottlieb, at that time a branch chief in TSS (now OTS). A short time after the LSD was administered, the subjects were told that they had been given LSD. On the day following the experiment, Olson began to behave in a peculiar and erratic manner and was later placed under the care of a psychiatrist. A few days later, Olson crashed through a window in a New York hotel in an apparent suicide.[10]

Again, you can read this full report here: **gwu.edu/~nsarchiv/ NSAEBB/NSAEBB54/st02.pdf**

MKUltra

MKUltra was the CIA's program of research into behavioral modification. In the Joint Hearing Before the Select Committee on Intelligence and the Subcommittee on Health and Scientific Research of the Committee on Human Resources United States Senate Ninety-Fifth Congress (August 3, 1977), it was stated that the purpose of the hearings was to review "past events in order to better understand what statutes and other guidelines might be necessary to prevent the recurrence of such abuses in the future."[11] The report also stated that they were looking at events that had occurred between 12 and 25 years ago. While some could say that this is evidence of the government taking care of us by making sure these kinds of atrocious experiments no longer take place, I tend to see this as just more evidence for how long governmental agencies can get away with denying these kinds of acts.

The report goes on to state that:

> ... the Senate Health Subcommittee heard chilling testimony about the human experimentation activities of the Central Intelligence Agency.... Universities and institutions were involved in an "extensive testing and experimentation" program which included covert drug tests on unwitting citizens "at all social levels, high and low, native Americans and foreign." Several of these tests involved the administration of LSD to "unwitting subjects in social situations.[12]

If you choose to read the entire report for yourself, you will see that there were attempts made to cover up a lot of this information, with the then-CIA director ordering all MKUltra files destroyed in 1973. What we do know for certain, according to the Supreme Court, was that MKUltra was:

> ... concerned with "the research and development of chemical, biological, and radiological materials capable of employment in clandestine operations to control human behavior." The program consisted of some 149 subprojects, which the agency contracted out to various universities, research foundations, and similar institutions. At least

80 institutions and 185 private researchers participated. Because the Agency funded MKULTRA indirectly, many of the participating individuals were unaware that they were dealing with the Agency.[13]

At the beginning of this book, I cautioned against falling prey to the "That's just conspiracy talk" kind of thinking. For me, this is just evidence of once again of, "There is many a good argument to be found under the so-called tin foil hat."

HAARP

HAARP, the High Frequency Active Auroral Research Program, is said to be an ionospheric research program jointly funded by the U.S. Air Force, the U.S. Navy, the University of Alaska, and the Defense Advanced Research Projects Agency. Its purpose is supposedly to analyze the ionosphere and investigate the potential for developing ionospheric enhancement technology for radio communications and surveillance. Based in Alaska, HAARP appears to have provided plenty of fodder for conspiracy theorists who believe it is capable of modifying weather, disabling satellites, and exerting mind control over people, and that it is being used as a weapon against terrorists.[14] But are they just conspiracy theories?

According to two colleagues of mine, author and inventor Pat Flanagan and independent researcher and author Nick Begich, HAARP has the potential to entrain the brain waves of the population, slowing them down to the point that the brain releases neurochemicals that lead to a relaxed, melancholy-like feeling. Additionally, HAARP allegedly has the ability to cause earthquakes and, because it "punches" the ionosphere, it also heats the ionosphere. [15]

It may be that we will never find out the truth regarding HAARP as the facility was shut down in June 2013—or perhaps, as with MKUltra, we may discover the answers 25 years from now. At present, all we are being told is that the project is out of money and will come back on line if/when this situation changes.[16]

The Ugly and the Uglier

Obviously, any clandestine experiment carried out on U.S. citizens without their consent, or even knowledge, is an infringement on their rights. By the time you have read this far, you may have your doubts. You either doubt the veracity of what I have shared, or you have serious questions about your government and what you believe. So, let me now add something that must be weighed, especially when you question what else or how far they would go.

Investigative reporter Jon Rappoport informs us in *U.S. Government Mind Control Experiments on Children* just how far some of these so-called Intel folks can go:

> I now have it all, including many pages submitted to the committee that will likely never be released as part of their final report. Only a small percentage of the pages were read aloud at the hearing. Included are corroborating statements from other therapists around the country and several of their patients. I have now released all of this testimony as a book, *U.S. Government Mind-Control Experiments on Children*.
>
> When the sickening shock starts to wear off, deeply disturbing questions flood one's mind: just what was this CIA program? How extensive was it? What was its purpose?
>
> From what I have been able to discover so far, many American children, as well as children from Mexico and South America, were used over a period of about 40 years, starting around 1948. In fact, the program may still be going on. Doctors and agents who administered it wanted to obtain control over the minds of these children, ostensibly to create superagents who wouldn't remember even what missions they carried out because of hypnotically induced amnesia (which could be removed by their controllers and reinstalled at will).[17]
>
> Children were trained as sex agents, for example, with the job of blackmailing prominent Americans—primarily politicians, businessmen, and educators. A great deal of filming was done for this purpose. Eventually, people from the inner core of the CIA program filmed each other, and some of the centers where children were used as sex agents

got out of control and turned into CIA-operated sex rings. Some children were considered expendable and simply murdered.

One person who states that he was in this program as a child said, off the record:

"They tried out their brainwashing techniques on the kids from Mexico and South America. They were considered expendable. But on another echelon of the program, they went after the best and the brightest American kids. Making perfect agents to combat the Soviets wasn't, I don't think, their ultimate objective. I can't remember what that was."[18]

In all likelihood you are as shocked at this information as I was. Why would anyone, let alone our own government, think up such heinous experiments? For most people reading this information cold, that is, with no knowledge of such things as MKUltra, etc., it is very tempting to just disbelieve it. However, now that you have read this far, what do you think? Based on what we now know, this account is not only possible, but also highly probable. And that just makes me feel sick!

Mind Manipulation

I'm no conspiracy expert, nor do I indulge in secrecy and mind-manipulation theories. My work has at times led me to people and places that are much better informed on some of these matters than most. What I can say with certainty—and what should be clear to you after this little tour through such ideas—is that certain facts are worth bearing in mind.

First, as with the advertising world, a lot of research has been designed and carried out to determine how and under what circumstances human behavior can be best manipulated as well as what ends this can be used for. Second, the technical capacity exists to control people using a variety of methods, ranging from the direct and overt to many covert possibilities. Third, there remains a lot of secrecy around all of this research. Indeed, in some instances, much of it has come to light only during investigations as the result of a whistleblower or an internal agency leak. Fourth, the experts disagree about what's known and what can be done. Certain information has been declassified, but the blacked-out areas on those documents, together with everything that remains sealed in secrecy, leave room for an awful lot of discomfort. Add this all up, and there are definitely the makings of several conspiracy theories.

CONCLUSION

Later you will learn about a 1956 memorandum regarding Communist brainwashing that was written by Allen W. Dulles, Director of the CIA to J. Edgar Hoover, Director of the FBI. As the epigraph to this report, Dulles chose a quote from Jules Romains' Verdun, in which he says, "We now know that men can be made to do exactly anything . . . It's all a question of finding the right means."[19] As you have seen in this chapter, learning how to deal with American's who had been subjected to 'Communist brainwashing' was only a small part of the interest in this subject. The fact is, this country has carried out some extremely ugly research, supposed for the sake of security and protection. Most people are totally unaware of this sort of activity and our history teachers rarely discuss it. Why?

Yet again we discover that knowledge leads to power, for how else will this sort of thing ever be curtailed? We need to ask questions like, "Whose brain is being manipulated today and why?" How far are we willing to go in the name of security? I hope you will join me on my blog, **www.eldontaylor.com/blog**, and stay current with the many issues that we face as a society and as individuals today.

Fortunately, most of us will never become a subject in some clandestine study such as those described in this chapter. However, on a larger scale, we may already be unwitting participants in research designed to use what has been learned about human nature to guide our actions. It is fair to question just how much of our freedom has been covertly captured, or more appropriately, unconsciously surrendered. When research is aimed at altering personalities, changing memories, creating killers, and so forth, we must ask ourselves, "If it's okay to do this to 'them,' then why would it not be okay to do it to us?"

What are your thoughts on this? Now that you know these old rumors and stories are not the dribble of some conspiracy nut, what do you think should be the reaction of American citizens? What can any of us do? I suggest that you begin by becoming involved in the world of politics. Begin to voice your concerns and stay informed. Share the information and help others understand the dangers. Do what you can do and then turn the rest over. Remember, this information is to empower you, not distress you, so use it like a fuel to motor down the highway of life with your lights on—not as a combustible property that goes boom.

Giving Our Rights Away

Those who deny freedom to others deserve it not for themselves.
~Abraham Lincoln

Misconception: *If you're like most, you believe in a just world, one where actions eventually receive their punishment or reward.*
Fact: *Perhaps we need to believe in a just world, but this may just be a fallacy, a fictional requirement in order to endeavor to persevere.*

I have presented a lot of information and evidence, and processing it all may take you a while. In relation to that processing, let me point out a very interesting set of experiments that is instructive here. Martin Seligman showed us that animals, when convinced there is nothing they can do about a situation, just quit trying.[1]

I have enjoyed many conversations with people of all walks of life while writing this book. In almost every single case, the person I was conversing with accepted that the individual issues discussed in this book were beyond their ability to do anything about. In an acquiescing gesture, they generally lower their shoulders, some thereby admitting that every cell of their body feels helpless to do anything about any of it. Most will even shrug and say something that suggests they believe in the *Just World Hypothesis,* something we'll get to in a bit.

Martin Seligman showed us that, even when an escape route or resolution opportunity exists, learned helplessness will prevent us from acting.

> While conducting experimental research on classical conditioning, Seligman inadvertently discovered that dogs that had received unavoidable electric shocks failed to take action in subsequent situations—even those in which escape or avoidance was, in fact, possible—whereas dogs that had not received the unavoidable shocks immediately took action in subsequent situations. The experiment was replicated with human subjects (using loud noise as opposed to electric shocks), yielding similar results. Seligman coined the term 'learned helplessness' to describe the expectation that outcomes are uncontrollable.
>
> Learned helplessness has since become a basic principle of behavioral theory, demonstrating that prior learning can result in a drastic change in behavior and seeking to explain why individuals may accept and remain passive in negative situations despite their clear ability to change them. In his book *Helplessness* (1975), Seligman argued that, as a result of these negative expectations, other consequences may accompany the inability or unwillingness to act, including low self-esteem, chronic failure, sadness, and physical illness.[2]

Bottom line, this psychological state assumes that we cannot control the situation. Have you ever felt that way when it comes to matters of government? Have we been conditioned to believe that our fate is up to someone else, our legislative representatives, law enforcement, the courts, and the like? Have "we the people" become "we the sheeple?"

Just World Hypothesis

There is a popular idea that essentially argues for a just world. We want to believe, for many psychological reasons, that evil will be eventually punished in some way and that good deeds will eventually be rewarded. The problem is that this just world hypothesis is really a fallacy—a cognitive bias.

The fallacy popularly appears in the English language in various figures of speech, which often imply a negative reprisal of justice, such as: "You got what was coming to you," "What goes around comes around," and "You reap what you sow." This phenomenon of this fallacy has been widely studied by social psychologists since Melvin J. Lerner conducted seminal work on the belief in a just world in the early 1960s. Since that time, research has continued, examining the predictive capacity of the hypothesis in various situations and across cultures, and clarifying and expanding the theoretical understandings of just world beliefs.[3]

Melvin Lerner studied these beliefs and compared some of his findings to the work of Stanley Milgram and the obedience factor. Milgram, as we have discussed, is famous for his experiments in which subjects delivered what appeared to be lethal levels of electric shock to confederate participants despite the confederates' feigning of incredible pain and sobbing pleas to stop.[4]

Lerner reports that much of his motivation to research social norms, particularly victimhood, was based on his observation of how people blame others for their situation. "They got what they deserved." "What you sow is what you reap." "It's karma." Sayings of this nature evidence the popular idea that people are exactly where they are supposed to be.

In 1966, Lerner and his colleagues began a series of experiments that used shock paradigms to investigate observer responses to victimization. In the first of these experiments conducted at the University of Kansas, 72 female subjects were made to watch a confederate receiving electrical shocks under a variety of conditions. Initially, subjects were upset observing the apparent suffering of the confederate. However, as the suffering continued and observers remained unable to intervene, the observers began to derogate the victim. Derogation was greater when the observed suffering from shock treatments was greater. However, under conditions in which subjects were told that the victim would receive compensation for her suffering, subjects did not derogate the victim.[5] Lerner and colleagues replicated these findings in subsequent studies, as did other researchers.

To explain the findings of these studies, Lerner theorized the prevalence of the belief in a just world. A just world is one in which actions and conditions have predictable, appropriate consequences. These actions and conditions are typically individuals' behaviors or attributes. The specific conditions that correspond to certain consequences are socially determined by the norms and ideologies of a society. Lerner presents the belief in a just world as functional: it maintains the idea that one can impact the world in a predictable way. Belief in a just world functions as a sort of "contract" with the world regarding the consequences of behavior. This allows people to plan for the future and engage in effective, goal-driven behavior. Lerner summarized his findings and his theoretical work in his 1980 monograph *The Belief in a Just World: A Fundamental Delusion.*

Lerner hypothesized that the belief in a just world is crucially important for people to maintain for their own well-being. However, people are confronted daily with evidence that the world is not just: people suffer without apparent cause. Lerner explained that people use strategies to eliminate threats to their belief in a just world. These strategies can be rational or irrational. Rational strategies include accepting the reality of injustice, trying to prevent injustice or provide restitution, and accepting one's own limitations. Non-rational strategies include denial or withdrawal, and reinterpretation of the event.[6]

CONCLUSION

Is it possible that our psychological need to feel as if we are in control of our lives gives rise to surrendering our real power? Why take on City Hall? After all, you can't win. Is it a matter of engaging only where we can feel safe about controlling the outcome? Do you really believe that your best efforts are better left to someone or something else? Do you believe that bad things happen to good people? Is it dissonant to also believe that they somehow deserved it? Worse, is it wise to trust that when you give no effort to righting a wrong, someone or something else will see that it is justly dealt with?

CHAPTER SEVEN

Propaganda: From the Beginning

"We become slaves the moment we hand the keys to the definition of reality entirely over to someone else, whether it is a business, an economic theory, a political party, the White House, Newsworld, or CNN."

~B.W. Powe

Misconception: *You probably believe that you are too smart to be fooled or taken in on truly important matters.*
Fact: *You believe in a whole host of "facts" that are indeed false-to-fact, and have trusted many sources and authorities that have intentionally deceived you!*

The story of propaganda must begin with Edward Bernays. Interestingly enough, a great many defend Bernays as a genius who pioneered modern communication methods. In fact, not long ago I was on a plane with a fellow who had just sold several radio stations. Our conversation meandered into the area of propaganda, and when I brought up Bernays he became very defensive. Now, I don't happen to be a fan of Bernays, but that notwithstanding, I was unaware of just how deeply some people can feel about this man. So let me tell the story like a *Dragnet* setup, "The facts, only the facts!"

Edward Bernays was the nephew of Sigmund Freud. Freud

was busy advancing his theories of the unconscious replete with the well-known constructs of ego, superego, and id. These three aspects of the self became, essentially, the skeleton on which the flesh could be hung. From there the ideas of a Thanatos urge (the urge to quench the fear of our own inevitable death), the Oedipus complex, defense strategies, and mechanisms could all begin to fill out the muscle and fiber of this model of humanity. One could fairly conclude that Freud conceived of the human being as fundamentally operating like a machine, a biocomputer of sorts. After all, he was a devout atheist who once proclaimed that religion was nothing more than a sugar-coated neurotic crutch, so why would one in his shoes think otherwise—Homo sapiens were nothing more than a meat machine, in today's parlance. Evolutionary forces and mechanisms had shaped the human consciousness just as they had shaped everything else in nature.

Neuromarketing

The importance of Freud's work will become obvious as we now turn to his nephew Edward Bernays and the ultimate development of what today is known as neuromarketing.

Bernays theorized that according to Freud, people could be tweaked in ways out of range of their conscious mind by stimulating their unconscious. In other words, by appealing to unconscious fears and desires, one could motivate persons or cause them to reason in ways that ordinarily would not occur. Today we see this kind of marketing on a daily basis. For example, draping a scantily clad, pretty woman over an automobile, and men view the automobile not only as more desirable but also faster. In fact, studies have demonstrated that even when this result is pointed out to subjects whose choice of fast car changes as you move the woman around, the men will deny that the woman had anything to do with their decision. Their denial is accompanied by a host of rationalizations intended to convince the experimenter, but most important, it appears they themselves believe their own stories.[1]

Bernays took Uncle Freud's ideas and began to deploy them in the real world. He is often considered today to be the father of spin, as he combined the ideas of Gustave Le Bon and Wilfred Trotter on crowd psychology with the psychoanalytical ideas of his uncle. Bernays openly announced his conviction that a civilized society, in order to avoid tyranny, must manipulate the masses, and one way to do that was via propaganda. That said, except for his book *Propaganda*, Bernays typically avoided the word and preferred instead the term *public relations*.

Now let's get a little context here. Edward Louis Bernays was born on November 22, 1891, and died on March 9, 1995. He was born to Jewish parents in Vienna, and his family moved to New York when he was a year old. He graduated from Cornell University in 1912, and although his degree was in agriculture, he took up journalism. By 1919 his ideas had taken hold among many of the influential of the day, including President Woodrow Wilson. Bernays is generally credited with coming up with the justification for America's involvement in World War I, expressed in the slogan "Bringing democracy to all of Europe."

Responsibility of the Informed

As the account goes, Bernays himself was surprised at how effective this simple slogan was and wondered if such lines could be effectively used during peace time. Bernays states in his book *Propaganda* that the people are not to be trusted, and further, without proper guidance, in a democracy they may make the wrong choice and vote for the wrong candidate. As such, it was the responsibility of the informed to guide the masses.[2] Bernays' daughter, Anne, referred to her father's ideas regarding this guidance as "enlightened despotism."[3]

It wasn't just the world of governance that Bernays was interested in. He wrote, "If we understand the mechanism and motives of the group mind, is it not possible to control and regiment the masses according to our will without their knowing about it? The recent practice of propaganda has proved that it is possible, at least up to a certain point and within certain limits."[4] He thought of this approach as the 'engineering of consent.'[5]

95

Lights Golden Jubilee

Now that we've introduced the man, let's look at some of the ideas and campaigns he was behind. My favorite example of his influence on everyone was the Lights Golden Jubilee in 1929. The reason I chose this one is that still today, teachers everywhere in America inform their students that Thomas Edison invented the light bulb. It may come as a surprise to you, but without Bernays' campaign revamping the invention of the light bulb, we would know that, in fact, it was invented by the Englishman Joseph Swan. To promote the value of light bulbs, however, it was more convenient to have an American icon as the inventor—voilà, Thomas Edison.

Overthrowing Government

The revamping of the invention of the light bulb, however, although perhaps amusing, is certainly not the most important of Bernays' work.

> Bernays' most extreme political propaganda activities were said to be conducted on behalf of the multinational corporation United Fruit Company (today's Chiquita Brands International) and the U.S. government to facilitate the successful overthrow of the democratically elected president of Guatemala, General Jacobo Arbenz Guzman.[6]

So, from fictional inventions to the overthrow of a government, Bernays was a busy man. In 1920 he hosted the first National Association for the Advancement of Colored People (NAACP) convention, for which he later received an award. The convention was deemed a success because there was no violence attached to it.

Israel

There are many stories about Bernays and his Jewish heritage, including his possible involvement in what eventually led to the establishment of Israel. Jeff Jacoby, columnist for the *Boston Globe*, writes:

Though cluttered with books, awards, and mementos, Bernays' rambling home near Harvard Square is free of any Jewish influence. Early in the century, he "helped some of the Jewish charities in New York," he remembers, "but I was never particularly active in them." Nor has he visited Israel. "But I helped the fellow who started it," Bernays claims. Asked whom he means, the name eludes him, but his autobiography, *The Biography of an Ideal* (1965), offers this clue: "In those days (the late 1920s), we had often entertained Chaim Weizmann, then a prime minister without a country, who was touring the United States to raise money to further the Zionist cause.

"I had turned down a provisional offer to be foreign minister of a country, Israel, not yet in existence. I greatly respected Weizmann, but I was not in sympathy with his goals."

Bernays insists that his differences with Weizmann stemmed from concern about the vulnerability of small countries. "At the time, any small state . . . was in great danger. What they did around that time was just to raid them. All these small states wanted to exist, but large states took them over."

Asked if he would take on the government of Israel as a client, he answers, "Sure!" And here, gratis, is some public relations advice for Israel from the man who invented the game:

"What I would do, which apparently Israel has not done, is to establish much closer relationships with the democratic countries of the world and get those countries to make much more visible in the public mind how much they support Israel and how much they believe in freedom of religion, just as the democratic countries believe in freedom of the press, freedom of assembly, freedom of petition.

"Israel should appoint an international public relations committee, made up of all the best public relations people in the democratic countries of the world England, France, Germany, Italy, even Spain." [7]

Marketing

While working for the tobacco industry, Bernays spawned an idea to break the taboo against women smoking. He sent a group of young paid models to New York to march in a parade as women's rights advocates. He informed the press "that a group of women's rights marchers would light 'Torches of Freedom.' On his signal, the models lit Lucky Strike cigarettes in front of the eager photographers. The *New York Times* (1 April 1929) printed: "Group of Girls Puff at Cigarettes as a Gesture of 'Freedom.'"[8]

Bernays made notable contributions to other product lines. For example, his advertising campaigns on behalf of Ivory soap established it as a medically superior soap, and his work with AL-COA led to recruiting the American Dental Association to support the fluoridation of water as both safe and beneficial to human health.[9]

Drums of War

During the many years that Bernays worked at engineering consent, the science of measurement advanced greatly. From the early era of what became known as scientific marketing, whereby the use of gross physiological measurements reported on how potential consumers responded to various stimuli, to today's application of fMRI technology in which the activity in the brain is watched live in real time, Bernays is credited with leading the movement to plumb the depths of human consciousness in order to gain consent without the subject's conscious awareness of the manipulation that leads to the consent.

Where has this technology, now called *neuromarketing*, led us? Well, today we know things about behavior that allow those in the know to shape your vote, and you'll never know that it is being done. Obviously, slogans like the one used by Bernays in World War I with the Wilson administration, have a huge influence, and we will discuss later the many principles in play with this slogan, including the manipulation. However, the technology is now so much more sophisticated that psychology researcher and professor Dr. Robert Epstein recently told PBS, "We've discovered that search engine rankings can be manipulated in ways that dramatically change voter preferences."[10]

Before continuing with the Bernays story, we should be reminded that Bernays was not alone in selling the public on the idea of entering World War I. No, President Woodrow Wilson hired George Creel, and the Creel Commission had a significant role in selling the war to the public as the "duty of America to protect democracy around the world." Sound familiar?

The Creel folks told such outright lies as children being bayonetted by German soldiers to ignite the rage of the American people. This same sort of thing goes on today. In the first Gulf War, stories were manufactured about babies being pulled from incubators. The story was used to instigate fervor among Americans. It, too, was a lie!

In October, 1990, a 15-year-old Kuwaiti girl, identified only as Nayirah, appeared in Washington before the House of Representatives' Human Rights Caucus. She testified that Iraqi soldiers who had invaded Kuwait on August 2nd tore hundreds of babies from hospital incubators and killed them.

Television flashed her testimony around the world. It electrified opposition to Iraq's president, Saddam Hussein, who was now portrayed by U.S. President George Bush not only as "the Butcher of Baghdad" but—so much for old friends—"a tyrant worse than Hitler."

Bush quoted Nayirah at every opportunity. Six times in one month he referred to "312 premature babies at Kuwait City's maternity hospital who died after Iraqi soldiers stole their incubators and left the infants on the floor," and of "babies pulled from incubators and scattered like firewood across the floor." Bush used Nayirah's testimony to lambaste Senate Democrats still supporting "only" sanctions against Iraq—the blockade of trade which alone would cause hundreds of thousands of Iraqis to die of hunger and disease—but who waffled on endorsing the policy Bush wanted to implement: outright bombardment. Republicans and pro-war Democrats used Nayirah's tale to hammer their fellow politicians into line behind Bush's war in the Persian Gulf.

Nayirah, though, was no impartial eyewitness, a fact carefully concealed by her handlers. She was the daughter of one Saud Nasir Al-Sabah, Kuwait's ambassador to the United States. A few key congressional leaders and reporters knew who Nayirah was, but none of them thought of sharing that minor detail with Congress, let alone the American people.

Everything Nayirah said, as it turned out, was a lie.[11]

Syria

In 2013 there was a buildup toward war in Syria. A so-called red line was crossed, and the U.S. and its allies began to prepare their citizens for yet another war. To that end, apparently, the BBC decided to stage its own chemical weapons piece for propaganda.

A video of a BBC interview with a doctor in Syria in the aftermath of a napalm-style attack appears to have been artificially dubbed to falsely make reference to the incident being a "chemical weapons" attack, a clip that represents "a stunning bit of fakery," according to former UK Ambassador Craig Murray.

The news report was first released on August 29, just days before an attack on Syria seemed inevitable, and served to further the narrative that military action was necessary to halt atrocities being committed by President Bashar Al-Assad's forces.

The first clip is from the original interview with British medic Dr. Rola Hallam from the Hand in Hand for Syria charity. She states;

> " . . . It's just absolute chaos and carnage here. We've had a massive influx of what looks like serious burns, seems like it must be some sort of, I'm not really sure, maybe napalm, something similar to that . . ."

However, in the second clip, which is from the exact same interview, her words are slightly altered.

> " . . . It's just absolute chaos and carnage here.

We've had a massive influx of what looks like serious burns, seems like it must be some sort of chemical weapon. I'm not really sure . . ."

The second clip seems to have been artificially dubbed to characterize the event as a "chemical weapon" attack rather than an incendiary bomb attack. Hallam's mouth is hidden by a mask, making the dub impossible to detect without referring to the original clip.

The clip has sparked frenzied analysis by numerous Internet users, who point out that the background noise in the clip that uses the "chemical weapon" quote is different from the original. The BBC has been asked to explain the discrepancy but has so far not responded.

"I suspect the motive in this instance and others by the BBC is propaganda intended to affect public opinion in the UK in such a way as to congregate support and underpin an offensive against the Syrian government," writes one user who closely analyzed the audio.[12]

Fair Elections

Propaganda always fills the airwaves during times of election. During the 2012 U.S. election, some $6 billion was spent on ads. Everywhere we turn today there are ads, video news releases, television specials, documentaries, media pundits, would-be newsrooms, and even movies selling a perspective, sometimes a value, sometimes a platform, sometimes a product, and sometimes more of all of them in the guise of entertainment. Often the news you will hear about tomorrow was written days ago, and that's apparently what happened in the country of Azerbaijan in October of 2013:

Azerbaijan's big presidential election, held on Wednesday, was anticipated to be neither free nor fair. President Ilham Aliyev, who took over from his father ten years ago, has stepped up intimidation of activists and journalists. Rights groups are complaining about free speech restrictions and one-sided state media coverage. The BBC's headline for its story on the election reads "The Pre-Determined

President." So expectations were pretty low.

Even still, one expects a certain ritual in these sorts of authoritarian elections, a fealty to at least the appearance of democracy, if not democracy itself. So it was a bit awkward when Azerbaijan's election authorities released vote results—a full day before voting had even started.

The vote counts—spoiler alert: Aliyev was shown as winning by a landslide—were pushed out on an official smartphone app run by the Central Election Commission. It showed Aliyev as "winning" with 72.76 percent of the vote. That's on track with his official vote counts in previous elections: He won ("won"?) 76.84 percent of the vote in 2003 and 87 percent in 2008. [13]

For now we trust that such things happen only in developing countries, but is that always a fair assumption?

Time and again we find voter fraud throughout America. How prevalent is it in America? Here are some, just some, of the startling statistics:

- To date, 46 states have prosecuted or convicted cases of voter fraud.
- More than 24 million voter registrations are invalid, yet remain on the rolls nationwide.
- There are over 1.8 million dead voters still eligible on the rolls across the country.
- More than 2.75 million Americans are registered to vote in more than one state.
- True The Vote recently found 99 cases of potential felony interstate voter fraud.
- Maryland affiliates of True The Vote uncovered cases of people registering and voting after their respective deaths.
- This year, True The Vote uncovered more than 348,000 dead people on the rolls in 27 states. California: 49,000; Florida: 30,000; Texas: 28,500; Michigan: 25,000; and Illinois: 24,000.
- Twelve Indiana counties have more registered voters than residents.

- The Ohio Secretary of State admitted that multiple Ohio counties have more registered voters than residents.
- Federal records showed 160 counties in 19 states have over 100 percent voter registration.
- The Florida New Majority Education Fund, Democratic Party of Florida, and the National Council of La Raza are currently under investigation for alleged voter registration fraud.[14]

Freud

Okay, back to our story. Bernays owed much to his Uncle Freud, and understanding a little about Freudian psychology will be helpful later when we examine some of the more common techniques deployed to smooth down the gotchas.

As I outlined in my earlier book *Mind Programming*, Freud associated psychological development with sexual energy (psychosexual). According to him, as our sexual energy changed, so did our psychological development. Three of Freud's stages of development are oral, anal, and phallic.

Underlying this is the theme of polymorphous perversity, the ability to find erotic pleasure from any part of the body. During these stages, the child finds pleasure in ways that would be considered perverse in an adult. The first stage is oral. During the first two years of his life, the infant is focused on oral gratification. The second stage is thought of as the anal period, which is associated with toilet training and which a child experiences during years two and three. The third stage is the phallic stage, when a child experiences pleasure in his or her own sexual organs, generally between ages three and six.

If development is arrested early, then the child could remain stuck at one of the levels into adulthood. For Freud, stage-one problems in adults are a need to smoke or overeat. These could represent an incomplete oral stage, such as early weaning, punishment that accompanied nursing (perhaps a slap when a teething child bites), or prolonged nursing that lasts in some cases into the third level. Stage-two problems usually arise as a result of punishment during potty training. This is where the idea of being anal-retentive originates. In stage-three development, Freud believed that the child saw the parent of his or her own sex as a rival for attention from the parent of the opposite sex, and that's where the notions of the Oedipus and the Electra complexes come from.

Further, according to Freudian theory, the personality is structured into three components: the *id, superego,* and *ego.* The id is instinctive and primal, seeking to maximize pleasure and minimize pain. It's thought to comprise both the life force and the death instinct. It also drives sexual desire because propagation is a part of the life force. Freud's notion of the libido arises here, and because this notion of the libido includes both life and its opposite, libidinal impulses can contain death urges.

The superego is the authoritarian inner voice of our enculturation. It's the home of our socialized "ought to" notions. The superego seeks to impose morality and speaks to us through our conscience.

The ego mediates between the id's hungry drives, which often conflict with social mores, and the superego's urge to repress them. The ego gives rise to what most think of as finding the socially acceptable way. For example, sexuality is expressed through marriage instead of in a more beastlike manner, assuming a socially adjusted normal human being.

When intense conflicts between the id and the superego occur, the ego may employ any of several defense strategies to move the event out of consciousness, but the conflict still exists in the subconscious.

The ego is a construct of mind. For all intents and purposes, it puts down strong roots in each of us during our individuation process, normally at or around two years of age. Scientific literature is full of stratifications for various activities that are thought to occur or exist in the mind.

Bernays sought to evolve a form of communication that, to borrow his terminology, could be used to control the dumb masses. To do this, he advanced Freud's theories in ways that modern psychology is still catching up with. Bernays' approach was to apply the insights of Freud in a scientific manner. He employed behavioral scientists to study human reactions to various stimuli. Groups were tested for their response to certain words, images, and more. From this sophisticated analysis, advertisements were built and new tests were conducted. Needless to say, his methods were very successful.

In short, Bernays revolutionized the world of advertising, merchandising, and public relations. This man, who died in 1995, was widely acclaimed as the "father of public relations." His influence spanned more than 70 years, and his clients included elite Fortune 500 companies, politicians, and publicists.

Edward Bernays wasn't popular with everyone, however. He changed the meaning of the word *propaganda,* formerly meaning "truthful disclosure designed to confront ignorance and disinformation," to its present-day meaning, which most people view with appropriate suspicion. His arrogance and disregard for "the little guy" also led to some public condemnation. Most important, from our perspective, Bernays managed to meld social science and marketing in ways that sometimes led to more effective psychologists with marketing degrees than counselors with psychology degrees.

According to attorney and author August Bullock, by the end of the 1950s, "an estimated billion dollars a year was invested in motivational research and another $10 billion a year was spent on advertising in general . . . enormous expenditures considering that at the time a loaf of bread cost 17 cents."[15] In his engrossing book, *The Secret Sales Pitch,* Bullock illustrates how some of this motivational research was done. A quick look at some of the questions asked by researchers reveals their interest in unconscious reasons for the consumption of various things. For example, researchers asked such questions as, "What is your earliest memory regarding a cookie?" and "How does eating a cookie make you feel?"[16] Further, as Bullock points out, "These sessions were often filmed and analyzed by teams of researchers."[17]

Not everyone could afford Bernays. His fees were steep. He used a variety of tools to accomplish his aims, including targeted mailings. This was a pioneering strategy in 1949 when first employed on behalf of a Fifth Avenue hotel. Indeed, Bernays may well have been one of the first to mine data for a client. He used Dun and Bradstreet to get details on clients who had paid the hotel with credit cards and compared the data with that obtained from neighboring hotel competitors. [18]

Walter Lippman, in his book *Public Opinion,* points out that it is impossible to win a rational argument when dealing with an unreasoning public. It is therefore necessary to educate the public, to engineer consent. He closes his book on a note of optimism, "But you cannot despair of the possibilities that could exist by virtue of any human quality which a human being has exhibited."[19]

CONCLUSION

Whether it is the engineering of consent or, as Walter Lippman termed it, *the manufacture of consent,* the point remains the same. Those involved in engineering or manufacturing consent share a common philosophy: the majority is simply incompetent. In Bernays' own words, "It [mind control of the masses] constituted the very essence of the democratic process." What do you think of this? How does this make you feel? Once again, though, knowledge is power. It is only when you understand what propaganda is really about, that you have a much better chance of sifting out the truth from all of the dross.

Indoctrination via the Media

Whoever controls the media, controls the mind.
~Jim Morrison

Misconception: *You probably believe that an Orwellian America is impossible—just another nut case theory.*
Fact: *We are rapidly approaching a place in history where only the intent of our leaders separates us from Big Brother!*

Indoctrination is how some might describe our modern use of television. For years I have been pointing out that the flicker rate used by television to put those images on your TV screen actually entrains the brain. The research is solid, and I have pointed it out in great detail in my book, *Mind Programming.*[1] That said, for our purposes here, let us understand that when we sit down to watch television, we are visiting our resident hypnotist. That hypnotist lives in our TV.

The human brain typically operates in normal consciousness between 14 and 30 cycles per second. When persons enter hypnosis, their brain wave state slows down to between 8 and 14 cycles per second. In this state of consciousness, people can imagine a burn and a blister will rise; they can remember what has been lost to conscious attention; they can undergo surgery without chemical anesthetic, and so on. Indeed, the possibilities are very well-documented and rather mind-boggling to the uninitiated. (For more details and a complete how-to on hypnotizing yourself, see my book, *Self-Hypnosis and Subliminal Technology*.)[2]

Now imagine that you go to your local hypnotist for whatever reason, let's say to stop some nasty habit. While you are in hypnosis, the hypnotist suggests that you will become ill in the very near future. Because of that illness, you will come back to him for another session so that you can be healed of your illness. What would you think of the ethics of a hypnotist who behaved that way?

How often have you been in front of your television when a commercial came on that advertised not only that flu was coming to town but also the cure, a trip to the pharmacy to buy XYZ? I have long thought of this as selling sickness.

Many other ideas are sold through the media, and particularly television. In my view, one of those that is most pernicious leads to the systematic desensitization of our threshold of arousal.

Systematic Desensitization

It is a fundamental fact that for us to be entertained, our threshold of arousal must be teased out. That is, if we fail to be excited, to laugh or to cry, to become angry or happy, sad or thrilled, and so forth, we find the entertainment boring.

Boring is the buzzword of the younger generation. They have been raised on a 24/7 diet of stimulation. TV, computers, smart phones, pads, and the like have trained them to always be attending to more than the simplicities of the moment. It's not at all uncommon today to find young couples sitting across from each other in a coffee shop, but instead of looking at each other and having a conversation, they are texting or using their devices in some other fashion, occasionally looking up to acknowledge the other person or to make some short comment before lowering their head and returning to the device. All this stimulation seems to be required or they are bored!

I remember well when such events as Marilyn Monroe's skirt being raised by an updraft beneath her were titillating. Today that is hardly risqué. No, today we have prime-time nudity and soft porn. Characters show off major parts of their bodies while grinding with each other under the disguise of some partial hiding of this or that portion of their act and anatomy. Everyone gets the picture, though, and there's no doubt about what's happening. More sex is needed to meet the arousal requirement than years ago, and that's all there is to it!

And it's not just TV or movies where this is true. The trend in magazines is to increase advertisements using sex. The fact is, sex sells![3]

I'm perhaps dating myself somewhat here, but I remember when certain cartoons were considered violent and when viewers were warned about horror films because they might show some blood. Then along came movies that depicted so much gore that the viewer could witness the appearance of flesh being chewed into the chain of a chain saw and spewed out, splattering on virtually everything. The raw depiction of violent acts is so totally in your face that you either become conditioned to tolerate it or you turn your head away in horror and shock. And this is true in several forms of entertainment including video games. It's also not uncommon today to hear some young people goading the virtual perpetrator of violence with remarks like, "Get her! Rape her. Kill him. Do it!" and so forth. Once again, the threshold of arousal has been raised, and more is now better!

All of this desensitization does indeed influence us. For example, one study showed that sexual content exposure from popular movies is predictive of adolescent sexual behavior.

> "Adolescents who are exposed to more sexual content in movies start having sex at younger ages, have more sexual partners, and are less likely to use condoms with casual sexual partners," (Ross) O'Hara explained.
>
> Why do movies have these effects on adolescents? These researchers examined the role of a personality trait known as sensation-seeking. One of the great dangers of adolescence is the predisposition for "sensation-seeking" behavior. Between the ages of ten and fifteen, the tendency to seek more novel and intense stimulation of all kinds peaks. The wild hormonal surges of adolescence make judicious thinking a bit more difficult.[4]

Adolescents are not the only stimulation seekers. Adults, too, seek stimulation of one kind or another. Indeed, remove stimulation, as is done in sensory deprivation chambers, and some really disturbed folks emerge in a real hurry! Solitary confinement is but one means of turning against a person the human need for sensation and stimulation.

Another study dealing with video games and aggression showed that, the more time spent playing, the more aggression. Indeed, this study showed an accumulated effect, contradicting arguments that not everyone who plays video games is violent, and therefore violent video games cannot be charged with leading to violent behavior.

> Although other experimental studies have shown that a single session of playing a violent video game increased short-term aggression, this is the first to show longer-term effects, said Brad Bushman, co-author of the study and professor of communication and psychology at Ohio State University.
>
> "It's important to know the long-term causal effects of violent video games, because so many young people regularly play these games," Bushman said.
>
> "Playing video games could be compared to smoking cigarettes. A single cigarette won't cause lung cancer, but smoking over weeks or months or years greatly increases the risk. In the same way, repeated exposure to violent video games may have a cumulative effect on aggression."[5]

In my opinion, another factor that should be looked at is the psychology of the individual. For example, if we think of degrees of aggression/nonaggression on a scale of 1 to 100 (with 1 being dangerously aggressive and 100 having no aggressive tendencies at all), and playing a violent video game moves the gamer's desire for violence by, say, 10 points, that would not be a problem if the gamer started at 80. If, on the other hand, the score at the beginning was 55 and moved to 45 afterward, then that would, of course, be dangerous.

In yet another study, violent video games were shown to create a risk factor for criminal behavior. Indeed, this study demonstrated a very high correlation between juvenile delinquency and aggressive behavior.

Matt DeLisi, a professor of sociology, said the research shows a strong connection even when controlling for a history of violence and psychopathic traits among juvenile offenders.

"When critics say, 'Well, it's probably not video games, it's probably how antisocial they are,' we can address that directly because we controlled for a lot of things that we know matter," DeLisi said. "Even if you account for the child's sex, age, race, the age they were first referred to juvenile court—which is a very powerful effect—and a bunch of other media effects, like screen time and exposure. Even with all of that, the video game measure still mattered."[6]

If you're a parent, then you know how hard it is to keep your children, especially your male children, from that sort of play. The following research finding may therefore be of assistance to you in deciding which games to allow and which to ban in your home. We have learned that shooter games are less likely to lead to violent behavior if the shooting that takes place is not of humans. In fact, one study showed that, "Video games that pit players against human-looking characters may be more likely to provoke violent thoughts and words than games where monstrous creatures are the enemy."[7] This is something that law enforcement learned many years ago. Shooting bullseye targets on the range failed to prepare an officer for a real-life shooting encounter. Today police ranges all use targets that feature human figures.

Marvin Zukerman and his colleagues observed something interesting in the 1960s about sensation seekers while conducting experiments with sensory deprivation. They found that many of their participants were actually high-sensation seekers, and it was the excitement about what happens with the deprivation of the senses that drove them to volunteer as subjects in this experiment. In the end, Zukerman developed the scale used today to evaluate sensation seeking, but the bottom line is, we all seek sensation of some kind at some time. No one seeks out boredom for boredom's sake alone.[8]

This desensitization has even spread to our books, or so it would appear. In a report appearing in *Science Daily,* the headline read, "Fear Factor Increases, Emotions Decrease in Books Written in Last 50 Years." The article went on to point out that the use of emotional words had substantially decreased during the past century. (By emotional words, the authors are considering words that produce feelings of empathy, not words that lead to sexual arousal.) However, the authors of this study caution resisting interpreting their findings.

> While the trends found in this study are very clear, their interpretation is still open. A remaining question, the authors say, is whether word usage represents real behavior in a population, or possibly an absence of that behavior which is increasingly played out via literary fiction.[9]

War Movies

A wonderful book that discusses Hollywood's role in image making, particularly when it comes to the drumbeat of war, is *Hollywood Goes to War: How Politics, Profits and Propaganda Shaped World War II Movies* by Clayton R. Koppes and Gregory D. Black. It details how the sometimes conflicting views between Washington and Hollywood can lead to an uneasy relationship between the two. That said, there is a veritable list of movies that have been made to support war efforts. A quick look reveals it all began with World War I:

> A propaganda organization had also been formed by the Americans soon after America's declaration of war, the Committee on Public Information (CPI). America had made a considerable leap from its isolationist stance to war combatant, and a home propaganda campaign was needed to explain to Americans what they were fighting for and to control the information delivered to them in order that they might continue to support the war. The CPI was originally wary of films as a propaganda medium, but eventually created a Division of Films on 25 September 1917, handling films taken by Army Signal Corps cameramen . . . issued [were] three main features from the material, *Pershing's Crusaders, America's Answer,* and *Under Four Flags.* [10]

By the beginning of World War II, America knew the power of movies to promote strong feelings of patriotism and to, in other ways, persuade the public, or, as the process is often called today, "win hearts and minds." The Unites States and its allies produced more than thirty full-length motion pictures between 1939 and 1947, all as war propaganda films. [11] Indeed, the fervor could be said to be so high that it's no wonder a crackdown occurred on anything and everything that failed to smell of the purity of true American pride. Thus it should have been fully predictable that such events as the McCarthy hearings, which were supposedly designed to expose ties to communism, would follow.

The backlash against Joseph McCarthy is well known. Some might argue that Hollywood's love of the liberal perspective today has its roots in the censorship and punishment that many Hollywood figures endured during that part of American history.

Today things are different, or are they? We still see films packed with propaganda, and some of them are the direct result of collaboration between the government and Hollywood. What's more, we find ardent supporters of certain political ideologies using entertainment to conceal their persuasive form of consent engineering.

The West Wing

My son Roy Kenneth insisted that I watch *The West Wing*. He is a political science student and very active in Democrat grassroots efforts. Since regular television is something I generally avoid, the series had ended before we ordered it from Netflix. While I thought the show was well made and very enjoyable, it was nevertheless obvious to me that it was also pure propaganda designed to influence the voters.

I checked the Internet. Surely others could see what I saw. Rob Waring, writing in a USFCA (University of San Francisco, California) publication, echoed my feelings:

> The tangled web of soft money groups that influence voters' perceptions about candidates and issues just got thicker. A broadcast of the NBC show, *The West Wing*, on the

Wednesday preceding the November 2000 election, seemed an unprecedented, indirect effort to use a dramatic television series to influence the vote . . .

I don't yet know how we sort through this newest, thorny problem of corporate (owners of the networks) influence on elections, but I do know that it isn't going to go away.[12]

Numerous articles, including scholarly ones from such institutions as Cambridge, address the influence of *The West Wing*, or lack thereof, on elections. Where the information is mixed, most tend to agree with this observation by Doug Mataconis:

> Nonetheless, it's undeniable that *The West Wing* did have an influence on people who were involved or interested in politics at the time it aired. For Democrats in the '90s and 2000s, it strikes me that it represented an idealized version of the perfect Democratic presidency. For Republicans, and yes, there were and are Republican fans of the show, I would suggest it represented a Democratic presidency they could admire if not support, sort of a mix between John F. Kennedy and Harry Truman. [13]

This analysis indicates to me that right-leaning independents would have plenty of idealized reasons to change their stance and become left-leaning independents as a result of watching *The West Wing*. And those already firmly on the side of the left would become fanatical in their support of Democrat ideologies.

Even entertainment commentaries addressed the show's honesty.

> All but the show's most fervent fans will admit *The West Wing* is hardly an honest depiction of how politics is practiced in the White House. Watching any one episode is enough to make that clear: Everyone involved genuinely seems to be working towards some idea of a greater good, even if those greater goods occasionally clash. Even the "villains" of the piece—usually, but not exclusively, Republicans, with the religious right popping up as bonus boogeymen when needed—have their own internal moral compass that protects them from the outright demonization.

I can only imagine what the show looked like to someone who wasn't on board with *The West Wing* over-arching message that government was a great thing, and the more government, the better; even when Republicans were brought into the series to offer alternate viewpoints, they would eventually surrender or change their minds if they stuck around long enough. The show's viewpoint came to win over any attempt at being fair and balanced just as Fox News was popularizing the term.[14]

The series clearly had its bias, and any open-minded person could see it! It would be interesting to learn if some novel study could demonstrate the effect of the *The West Wing* on voters, like the one carried out at Adelphi University demonstrating that Bush's infamous RATS ad did influence voters in the Gore/Bush election. [15]

TV School

Public opinion is persuasive! Research has repeatedly demonstrated the power of a group. The classic example of that comes from studies that show when a subject is surrounded by people who choose differently—as when a shorter line is chosen to be the longest line by several others—that the subject will begin to agree by denying his or her own senses. Television shows can have that same power. Through the guise of entertainment, we are convinced of positions and viewpoints because we see the alternative fail. Of course, we are watching a show that is fiction, but who acknowledges that?

Neighbors' lawn signs, public opinion polls, and even a conversation in the next restaurant booth can affect how people vote in an election, suggests a new University of California, Davis, study. But it all depends on how far away the election is.

"Research like this highlights the fact that we are social creatures," said Alison Ledgerwood, assistant professor of psychology at UC Davis and author of the study. "We clearly use other people to help us make our decisions, but what this research shows is that we rely on different people's

115

opinions for near-future and distant-future events."[16]

Somewhere I read an interesting comparison. It went something like this: Why do so many people believe they are seeing, learning, how Washington works from *The West Wing*? Do we really think we can learn law by watching *Perry Mason* or medicine by watching *House*?

Just as an aside, when my wife read the preceding paragraph, she, too, had her "aha" moment. "Of course I know I can't learn law from *Perry Mason* or medicine from *House*. But even with my right-leaning tendencies and 20 years of extensive conversations with you on mind programming—even I have stated how much I learned as a result of watching *The West Wing*!"

Newsroom

Aaron Sorkin is an Emmy-award winning American screenwriter, producer, and playwright, whose works include *A Few Good Men, The American President, The West Wing,* and *The Newsroom,* among others. Sorkin insists that he has no political bias and yet, as with *The West Wing*, the TV series *The Newsroom* reveals a different story.

What unfolded, beginning with the very first episode, was in my mind soft money advertising. The show was a promotion of Democrat values, ideas, and the like, and if not a vilification of core Republican positions, a fictional portrayal of their weakness. The main character says he is a Republican, but most of the time his conscience forces him to support the Democrat view. It is a classic portrayal of the caring, compassionate ideology (Democrat) versus the greedy, religious ideology (Republican). This series remains a perfect example of the kind of films that contain elements of modern propaganda. And they call this entertainment?

I remember a college writing class in which the professor made it very clear that writers do best when they write from experience. For the entire quarter we wrote short papers that drew on our own personal experience, but each one drew us further away from our actual lives. For example, we might have been asked to write something about our first visit to a country we never wanted to visit and to describe feelings we experienced doing things we did not want to do.

When such writers as Sorkin turn out characters and stories like those we encounter in *The Newsroom* and *The West Wing*, to claim they have no political bias is ducking the fact that obviously *you* have a bias! You may call this bias many things, including experience, and avoid thinking of it as a political bias, but when it aligns itself so perfectly with a political platform—then please, give us a break!

How many times have we thought back on a conversation, wishing we had said things differently? It is easy to think of the perfect arguments in retrospect (even though they rarely go as planned when we can have a replay). Sorkin has the perfect platform, however. He can create the perfect situation, to present the perfect argument, making sure the opposition does not do or say anything to ruin the punch line.

The Newsroom, like *The West Wing,* has a strong liberal bias. Even President Obama acknowledges that.

> President Barack Obama gushed about *The Newsroom* creator Aaron Sorkin last night at a fundraiser in Westport, Connecticut, promptly earning him some slamming from conservatives and journalists who hate *The Newsroom.*
>
> Per the pool report, here are Obama's remarks thanking Sorkin for hosting the event, which came at the opening of his speech to supporters:
>
> "Aaron Sorkin, who writes the way every Democrat in Washington wished they spoke. (Laughter and applause.) Aaron, thank you."[17]

Writing in *NewsMax,* Lowell Ponte describes *The Newsroom* this way:

> Sorkin's new drama claims it is "speaking truth to stupid," with stupid portrayed as conservatives and Republicans.
>
> The show's star character is a network anchor who metamorphoses from a Republican-in-name-only worm into a

liberal butterfly who spews Obamacrat views.

"I'm too old to be changed by fear of dumb people," says this shiny butterfly with two left wings.

This is one of Sorkin's favorite strawman stereotypes: the "good" Republican with the courage and smarts to repudiate troglodyte right-wing individualism, capitalism, small governmentism, and American exceptionalism. Liberal Alan Alda played this literal RINO Republican in *The West Wing.*

(Critics share the contempt). "I can't imagine that the people who intend to watch *The Newsroom* really need basic liberal talking points parroted back at them as if they were startling new insights," writes *The Atlantic's* reviewer Richard Lawson.

The New Yorker's Emily Nussbaum writes that *The Newsroom* scores points only "if you share its politics," which she describes as "artificial intelligence," and "full of yelling and self-righteousness . . . like a sanctimonious 'Zelig.'"

As in *The West Wing,* writes Nussbaum, Sorkin's *The* Newsroom "deck stays stacked" to make liberals look brilliant and conservatives stupid to such an unbalanced degree that she found herself rooting for "all those flyover morons."[18]

Nussbaum is a Republican, and this fact really highlights the full impact of Sorkin's work. Even where she fully recognizes the tactics in play, she *still* finds herself rooting for the hero.

NBC recently purchased a show that follows the format of *The West Wing,* and already some are asking, "Will this show lead to the United States giving up sovereignty to the United Nations?"

Inundated By Media

A recent *Science News* headline caught my eye. The headline read, "We live our lives within our media, rather than simply with it." The article detailed a study carried out by Mark Deuze of Indiana University. Deuze's conclusion, "Media are to us as water is to fish. This does not mean life is determined by media—it just suggests that whether we like it or not, every aspect of our lives takes place in media."[19]

Could that be true? And if so, what does it mean?

"In terms of what media communicate, it is tempting to point to governments, companies, and corporations for pushing an unrelenting, ever-accelerating stream of content and experiences into our lives," he said. "However, most mediated communication comprises work done by you and me: through our endless texts, chats, and emails, with our phone calls from anywhere at any time, and through our online social networks that function as the living archives of social reality.

"With the majority of the world population owning a mobile phone, telecommunication networks spanning almost every inch of the globe, sales figures of any and all media devices growing steadily worldwide, time spent with media up every year, and any and all media by default integrated into an always-on, real-time, live mode of being, an almost complete mediatization of society seems a somewhat self-evident observation."

Rather than our being "addicted" to our tablets, mobile phones and video game players, Deuze said we have a "profoundly emotional relationship that we have with our media and through our media with other people."[20]

If this is true, it flags an important element answering the questions about how and why our media gains such an influence over our lives.

Orwellian America

I recently read a truly informative piece by commentator and macroanalyst Gordon T. Long. Indeed, I suggest checking out his many articles at **www.gordontlong.com**. This article was titled, "An Orwellian America." The article began by referring to the competition between Orwell's *1984* and Huxley's *Brave New World*. I read both of these books when I was a teenager. *Brave New World* was written in 1931, and *1984* was written in 1948; each had a different perspective about where we as a society might end up.

Long's article contrasted these differences by opening with something he had read by Chris Hedges of TruthDig.com:

The two greatest visions of a future dystopia were George Orwell's *1984* and Aldous Huxley's *Brave New World*. The debate, between those who watched our descent towards corporate totalitarianism, was who was right. Would we be, as Orwell wrote, dominated by a repressive surveillance and security state that used crude and violent forms of control? Or would we be, as Huxley envisioned, entranced by entertainment and spectacle, captivated by technology and seduced by profligate consumption to embrace our own oppression? It turns out Orwell and Huxley were both right. Huxley saw the first stage of our enslavement. Orwell saw the second.[21]

Think about it: In the USA there are approximately 30 million surveillance cameras, and the use of domestic drones is on the rise. There are stories like the policeman who pepper sprayed students at UC–Berkeley and other examples of police brutality. Yes, these actions have been condemned, but others like them still go on. We have also learned that large corporations have been forced to give up our private information to the government. And have you stopped to think about the impact of the recently released iPhone with its fingerprint access? What a great way to get everyone's fingerprint into the system! Or what about the Obamacare provision that would have us all microchipped, supposedly to reduce medical errors?

Long summarizes it this way:

> We have been gradually disempowered by a corporate state that, as Huxley foresaw, seduced and manipulated us through:
> - Sensual gratification
> - Cheap mass-produced goods
> - Boundless credit
> - Political theater
> - Amusement
>
> While we were entertained:
> - The regulations that once kept predatory corporate power in check were dismantled
> - The laws that once protected us were rewritten

- We were impoverished

Now that:
- Credit is drying up
- Good jobs for the working class are gone forever
- Mass-produced goods are unaffordable
- . . . we find ourselves transported from *Brave New World* to *1984*.

The state, crippled by massive deficits, endless war, and corporate malfeasance, is clearly sliding toward unavoidable bankruptcy. It is time for Big Brother to take over from Huxley's feelies, the orgy-porgy, and the centrifugal bumble-puppy.[22]

Have we really devolved that far? Are we living in a form of statism? If we have, what can we do to reverse the trend? Are we concerned and smart enough to do anything about it? Or will this information fall on the proverbial deaf ears and be rationalized or denied away?

I suppose as equally relevant is the question, "Does it matter?" I mean, as long as you're in a place that feels safe and secure, or you are benefiting in some way by the current direction of the country, or you find some other motive, does it really matter? If it's true, does it matter to you?

The sad fact is, there have been many, many conversations about all of this. Americans have declared their outrage over the NSA and Snowden's revelations, but what, if anything, is being done about it? How do we get beyond the protests to making sure action is taken? Why do most people feel the protest and then return to their comfortable homes with their televisions and other forms of entertainment? Is there any hope out there?

Who Owns the Media?

When we think about the possibility that either corporations or the government or both, joined in some unholy wedlock, may exert so much control over our lives that we face the possibility of being reduced from individuals to something more akin to a member of a hive in service to the queen (the elite), then the *who* behind the entertainment, news, and so forth becomes extremely important. The fact is, media conglomerates control the dissemination of information, and they break out this way.

According to a recent Fortune 500 list, the top five in terms of revenue are the following:

Walt Disney Company
News Corporation
Time Warner
CBS Corporation
Viacom

Other well-known major conglomerates include the following:

NBC Universal
Sony Corporation of America
Together, these giants control 95% of all the traditional media we receive every day.[23]

The next time you are tuned into any show, ask yourself what its agenda might be. Is it only to capture the largest audience and thereby increase revenue through advertising, or is there still another bias? I mean, it's impossible to miss Fox's slant toward the conservative Republican perspective or MSNBC's slant toward the liberal Democrat view? Similarly, when an entertainment piece is one-sided, it is one-sided for a reason!

Later we will revisit the influence of television, particularly comedy, on voters. For now, suffice it to say that the hard numbers show that these programs sway the votes and thereby continue to engineer consent.

CONCLUSION

This has been a chapter designed to bring to our attention a method of thinking. As an investigator, I was always looking for MOM. **M**otive, **O**pportunity, and **M**eans (MOM) will invariably lead a path to your perpetrator. Today we live in a world where nothing is more critical than to become somewhat suspect of motive. What is their agenda?

Perhaps the agenda is as innocent as profit, like television ratings. Perhaps the agenda is power, as with political campaigns. Whatever the agenda, realizing the power that is in the hands of so few informs us of our vulnerability. I, for one, believe we should begin to seek out independent sources and verify everything. It's not easy, but living awake demands it. As Eleanor Roosevelt said, "In the long run, we shape our lives, and we shape ourselves. The process never ends until we die. And the choices we make are ultimately our own responsibility." I would add, remember that to not choose is a choice by default!

Physiology/Psychology

I cannot make the universe obey me.
I cannot make other people conform to my own whims and fancies.
I cannot make even my own body obey me.

~Thomas Merton

Misconception: *You probably believe you know yourself and under-stand why you believe what you believe, and how and why you partici-pate in this world as you do.*
Fact: *You are simply hardwired in ways that you cannot escape and seldom understand, as well as programmed with biases and attitudes that often fail to serve truth.*

    As human beings, we are made in ways that offer ample op-portunity to those who would prey on our weaknesses to take advantage of us in almost innumerable ways. As you will see, the science of controlling our responses, shaping our attitudes, winning over our beliefs, and so forth is indeed quite advanced. Whether it's a matter of compliance principles or a nuance of in-formation processing, we remain vulnerable. Take, for example, our so-called hardwiring.

Willpower

A fair question has to do with free will and therefore also will-power. Since approximately 90 percent of our decisions are made in our unconscious, and since an fMRI technician can know what we will decide several milliseconds before we ourselves do by simply watching the brain,[1] how can we say we have free will? Is it possible that free will is only an illusion, nothing more than the complex result of genetics, experience, and sensory input? I mean, is it indeed true, as argued by one study after another, that all "actions precede conscious decisions to perform them"?[2]

> [In] Alex Rosenberg's, *The Atheist's Guide to Reality*, Rosenberg bases his claims [regarding the illusion of free will] on documented experiments, such as those by Lüder Deecke and Hans Helmut Kornhuber in 1964. . . . For example, Rosenberg argues, in his discussion concerning neural time delays, that a simple action like flexing a wrist can't be done at the instant one consciously thinks of doing so. Instead, there's an inevitable time delay of about 200 milliseconds from conscious willing to wrist flexing and finger pressing. He adds that the cortical processes responsible commence 500 ms before that! The obvious implication: Consciously deciding to do something is not the cause of doing it.[3]

What happens when free will is subtracted? So goes the fate of willpower. What does that mean in this context?

If our actions are the result of the information stimulation we have processed in a sort of biocomputer way, then that old saying by computer programmers that insists Garbage In—Garbage Out (GIGO) is absolutely true of humans as well. What's more, this principle translates directly to the power the manipulators have when it comes to programming us in ways we are unconscious of. For if I am conscious of an attempt to mold my consent and of the ways and means employed to do so, I can at least resist them. In fact, just realizing a technique or tactic is being used usually gives me the power to disarm its effect. However, when I am unaware of the many subtle forms of mind control, then I find myself choosing to act and think just as the controllers wish me to. This will soon become abundantly clear to you.

Hardwired Givers

It may surprise you to learn this, but there is evidence suggesting that we are all hardwired for religious experience. Indeed, there is an area in the brain that when electrically stimulated gives rise to a religious experience.[4] Some might argue that this is simply an evolutionary throwback, left over from a time when religion was needed by the species and that we are outgrowing that need today. I am not one of those. Neuroscientists have also found and measured discrete chemical changes that occur in the brain during a religious event. These chemicals produce feelings substantially similar to those reported with meditation. Some insist that feelings govern our minds, and thus we believe in spite of reason. According to proponents of this position, the evolutionary advantage of these kinds of feelings exists in the fact that "these practices help us to improve our mental state."[5]

We are also wired in such a way that when we go to the aid of someone in need, we are bathed with those good-feeling chemicals—reward chemicals such as endorphins, the body's own natural opiates. Indeed, one study carried out by Michael Norton of Harvard Business School, showed that *giving money* makes one feel better and sense a higher state of happiness than *receiving money*.[6]

In an article titled "Five Ways Giving Is Good," authors Jason Marsh and Jill Suttie point to the research demonstrating just how hardwired we are for service to others. The bottom line is this: Service makes us feel better, it is good for our health, it promotes cooperation and social cohesion, it evokes gratitude, and it is contagious.[7]

Remember this the next time you hear of a tragedy and are called upon to donate. I don't mean this as a warning to put you off charities but rather as an alert to how this natural aspect of human nature can be preyed upon, how you can be taken advantage of not just in giving but with your emotions. Think for a moment about the emotional investment we all make when we hear of a genuine tragedy. We can be mobilized against a perceived enemy, we can be motivated to join or resist ideas, we can marginalize another group or person, and on and on. Manipulating feelings can be about a lot more than mere money.

Nuances to Our Physical System

It always seems to amaze my audiences when I ask them to raise one leg, move their foot in a clockwise fashion, and then use a finger to draw the number six in the air. To their amazement, they find their foot changes direction. Well, this is only one of many ways in which we are built that deceives our perceptual processes. I have provided many examples of this phenomenon in my book *Choices and Illusions*, but for our purposes here, I will simply point out how real illusions can seem and how magic seems to trick us every time. In part, this is due to the way your perceptual processes work. For example, research has demonstrated that when a magician moves his hand in a curved motion, the audience will follow the trajectory of the hand from beginning to end. This little trick makes it possible for the magician to make use of his other hand in ways that go entirely unnoticed while the audience remains fixed on the curved movement.

> [Researchers] also found that the different types of hand motion triggered two different types of eye movement. The researchers discovered that curved motion engaged smooth pursuit eye movements (in which the eye follows a moving object smoothly), whereas straight motion led to saccadic eye movements (in which the eye jumps from one point of interest to another).
>
> "Not only is this discovery important for magicians, but the knowledge that curved motion attracts attention differently from straight motion could have wide-reaching implications—for example, in predator-prey evasion techniques in the natural world, military tactics, sports strategies, and marketing," says Martinez-Conde.[8]

The Pinocchio Effect

Researchers from the University of Granada in Spain discovered that when you tell a lie, your nose temperature increases.

Using thermographic measurements, they found a jump in body temperature accompanied a deceptive action. They also discovered that subjects' body temperature drops when they are anxious or asked to perform difficult mental tasks.[9]

Interdependence

Do you know that interdependence undermines our motivation to act? According to a study published in *Psychological Science*, Americans are bombarded with messages featuring the idea of interdependence. The messages may be about global warming, recycling, public health scares, and so forth, but the data shows that marketing messages this way may well backfire.

> "Appeals to interdependence might sound nice or like the right thing to do, but they will not get the job done for many Americans," says (researcher MarYam) Hamedani.
>
> A better strategy for motivating action among European Americans, according to Hamedani and her colleagues, may be to encourage individual effort for the good of the team or collective, urging each individual to "be the change YOU want to see in the world."[10]

Body Parts and Brain Differences

According to a study published in the *European Journal of Social Psychology*, both men and women process men as people and women as body parts. Images of men were processed more globally while those of women were processed more locally, and this was true for both sexes. Participants were more able to identify the women they had seen from pictures only of their body parts.

> "We always hear that women are reduced to their sexual body parts; you hear about examples in the media all the time. This research takes it a step further and finds that this perception spills over to everyday women, too," Gervais said. (Sarah Gervais is assistant professor of psychology at the University of Nebraska–Lincoln and the study's lead author.) "The subjects in the study's images were everyday, ordinary men and women . . . the fact that people are looking at ordinary men and women and remembering women's body parts better than their entire bodies was very interesting."[11]

129

The point not to be missed here is that our brains are wired in ways that predispose how we process information. We have many built-in biases, and that is true of all of us. (See the Implicit Association Test from Harvard for some insight on yourself: **implicit. harvard.edu/implicit**). Our wiring, our attitudes, our expectations, and so forth can predispose what we see. The tendency to fear can be a strong political influence. Our emotions and biases can prescribe what we see and believe. Indeed, our brains often fail to notice key words that can mean a difference in the meaning of a sentence. Sometimes we see what we want to see, reading into the sentence the outcome we desire. Sometimes we are victims of what is called semantic illusions. One such sentence might ask, "After a plane crash, where should we bury the survivors?" Obviously, we are not actually going to bury the survivors, but many people will see and interpret this sentence by insisting upon the location where they should be buried. In one study carried out by Professor H. Leuthold at the University of Glasgow, using EEG measurements, it was determined that when people are fooled by this sort of meaning error, their brains are totally unaware of it.[12]

Personality Scale for Advertisers

Advertisers of all sorts, political and otherwise, are more effective with their ads when they know the personality characteristics of their target audience. Ideally, they would have an actual personality scale to work from, but think of the information we ourselves put out there, in places such as social networking sites, that inform advertisers all about us.

The University of Missouri School of Journalism has developed a personality scale for precisely this sort of application. It is specifically aimed at assisting online advertisers in more efficiently using their advertising dollars. It is called the "Mini-Motivation Activation Measure" or Mini-MAM.

In her study, (Heather) Shoenberger surveyed people about their use on Facebook and then asked them to take the Mini-MAM test to determine their personality type.

Those who leaned toward high-risk activities were labeled as "appetitive," while those who were more reserved in their activities were labeled as "aversive." She found that both personality types used Facebook frequently, but she found significant differences in how they use the social media site.

"If you're highly 'appetitive' or lean toward high-risk activities, you're more likely to want to engage with media that are more exciting, whereas those who are higher in the 'aversive' trait tend to enjoy safer and more predictable media experiences," Shoenberger said. "Identifying these individuals using the motivation activation measure can give advertisers an advantage over their competitors and bring some order to online advertising."[13]

Indeed, while we're talking about advertising of this nature, are you aware of these facts? According to studies on visual attention, you are more likely to choose products or people in the center of a visual display. "Consumers had a tendency to increase their visual focus on the central option in the final five seconds prior to a decision, and this determined which option they would choose. Consumers did not accurately recall their choice process and were not aware of any conscious visual focus.[14]

Sincerity Trumps Facts

The near-scandalous lies that are a daily item on the Internet are so pervasive that a number of sites have cropped up just to fact-check stories. One of my favorites is **www.factcheck.org/**. The site regularly reports on prominent political issues and personalities as well as many the campaign ads that appear. However, as we will see, this approach really does not work for changing people's opinions.

Pundits are very aware that what matters most is how convincing they are, not how factually accurate they are. To be convincing, they must come across as passionate and sincere. They can have their facts wrong, but it is their emotion that sticks most with the audience. In other words, credibility is often measured by how truthful we feel the pundit is, and truthfulness seems to be at least partially based on the energy of sincerity.

131

Holding On to False Beliefs

We should also be aware that false beliefs may persist even after corrections are made. This is especially true among people who want to believe the falsehood. One often cited example of this phenomenon has to do with President Barack Obama's birth certificate. The idea that he was not born in America has been tenaciously held by those who wish it were true, despite its having been thoroughly debunked.[15] The possibility of spreading lies through the Internet is both obvious and tempting, but while some work at creating instant "fact checkers/correctors," Kelly Garrett and Brian Weeks at Ohio State University conducted a study to see the effect these "corrections" had on opinions.

> Garrett said the results of this study cast doubt on the theory that people who believe false rumors need only to be educated about the truth to change their minds.
>
> "Humans aren't vessels into which you can just pour accurate information," he said.
>
> "Correcting misperceptions is really a persuasion task. You have to convince people that, while there are competing claims, one claim is clearly more accurate."
>
> Garrett noted that, while instant corrections were slightly more effective than delayed corrections, the problem is that instant corrections actually increase resistance among those whose attitudes are supported by the falsehood.[16]

Emotional Biases

One of my favorite Facebook (FB) inquiries, designed to test how much attention people actually pay to issues requiring mental discernment versus emotional biases, came when I read an article stating that forensic investigators had determined Obama's online birth certificate was a fraud. The piece crossing my desk had the headline, "BOMBSHELL: Document Examiner Tied to Obama Defense Attorney Says Birth Certificate Is 100% Fraud." [17]

I searched and found that the document expert making this claim spelled out exactly how the document failed to meet the criteria necessary to be deemed authentic. I posted on my FB page the criteria used. The document examiner in question is a well-respected expert by the name of Reed Hayes. His opinion was this: "Based on my observations and findings, it is clear that the Certificate of Live Birth I examined is not a scan of an original paper birth certificate, but a digitally manufactured document created by utilizing material from various sources. In over 20 years of examining documentation of various types, I have never seen a document that is so seriously questionable in so many respects. In my opinion, the birth certificate is entirely fabricated."[18]

I posted the details behind the examiner's findings, providing only the information allegedly used to support the claim that the certificate was a fraud, and I asked for comments. They poured in from both sides of the issue. Interestingly, however, no one commented on my question: "What do you think of the examiner's *methods* for coming to this conclusion?" Rather, in a sometimes vitriolic diatribe, folks shouted hate or praise at me for posting such a thing. Most had very strong opinions about the matter, but no one had an opinion about the forensic tools used to come to the conclusion.

Think about the ramifications of that for a minute. Instead of looking at the question objectively, everyone responded according to their political interest. It's as if they failed to see the question. All that was seen somehow either fit into their view or scheme of things, or it directly threatened their opinions and ideas, and that is how they all responded. Pure, unguarded emotions poured out, somehow ignoring reason altogether.

By now, you have some insight into how and why this can happen. Has it happened to you? Is this another *gotcha?* Have your perceptions been so managed? Have you given up free will in favor of sound bites, convincing falsehoods, implicit biases, and so forth? Let's pursue some of the other areas that form a basis for what I think of as the many thefts of our free will.

Spiritual Attitude

Contrary to many of the stereotypes we hear pundits going on about, the so-called religious right may not be as far "right" as you might think. True, they may hold rather tenaciously to the tenets of their scriptures, especially in the area they think of as morality, but the fact is, research shows that moments of spirituality can induce strong liberal feelings. The catch may be in distinguishing between "religious" and "spiritual."

In one study, researchers made just such a distinction.

> "There's great overlap between religious beliefs and political orientations," says one of the study authors, Jordan Peterson of U of T's [University of Toronto's] Department of Psychology. "We found that religious individuals tend to be more conservative and spiritual people tend to be more liberal. Inducing a spiritual experience through a guided meditation exercise led both liberals and conservatives to endorse more liberal political attitudes."
>
> "While religiousness is characterized by devotion to a specific tradition, set of principles, or code of conduct, spirituality is associated with the direct experience of self-transcendence and the feeling that we're all connected," says lead author Jacob Hirsh of U of T's Rotman School of Management.[19]

The researchers conducted three studies examining this difference and the resulting attitudes. They concluded that a spiritual experience made you feel more connected to others and therefore more liberal, or tolerant, in your views. You should note, however, that this study differentiated among religious people by selecting those who have the "truth" and believe that their scripture is literal and infallible. In other words, by definition, the religious group is less tolerant of people and ideas outside of their community of views, or they are already, strictly speaking, conserving their beliefs. This group was then compared to a group of people who remained open to seeking. Ergo, it is a given, without the need of a study, that those who are more open are more likely to be flexible with regard to their beliefs and attitudes. That said, the three studies definitely provide an insight into yet another means by which we can influence large groups and perhaps even find room for compromise.

> "The conservative part of religious belief has played an

important role in holding cultures together and establishing common rules. The spiritual part, on the other hand,
helps cultures renew themselves by adapting to changing
circumstances," says Peterson. "Both right and left are necessary; it's not that either is correct, it's that the dialogue
between them produces the best chance we have at getting
the balance right. If people could understand that both
sides have an important role to play in society, some of the
unnecessary tension might be eliminated."[20]

Generic or Name Brand?

Just as an interesting aside, research shows that conservatives
and liberals differ on more than politics. The fact is they make
different choices at the supermarket, too. Buying behavior—the
sorts of products they choose to consume—differ between the
two groups. "Psychological research has shown that conservatives
and liberals differ on basic personality traits such as conscientiousness, tolerance for uncertainty, and openness to new experience."[21] Conservatives tend to prefer name brands and familiar
products, whereas liberals are more open to generic products
and also to trying out new items.

Wired to Cheat

I have often cited research that shows how we are hardwired
to give. Reward centers in the brain light up, to use the terminology of some neuroscientists, and the brain releases "feel good"
chemicals when we give. But we are also apparently hardwired
to cheat. A study published in the *Journal of Personality and Social
Psychology* discovered that people can enjoy cheating as long as
they feel no one was hurt as a result.

> We know that lying may have some relationship to brain
> anatomy. A study by University of Southern California psy-
> chologists, published in the British Journal of Psychiatry
> in 2005, found that people who habitually lie, cheat, and
> manipulate others actually have structural differences in
> their brains.
>
> MRIs showed that they had 22 percent more prefrontal

white matter—essentially, wiring of the brain's network—than a control group, which the researchers suspected gave them more sophisticated verbal skills, and added capability for juggling the complexities of a deception. At the same time, chronic liars also had 14 percent less gray matter, the material that enables the mind to, among other things, process moral issues and make judgments.[22]

Some believe that the ability to lie and cheat is an evolutionary adaptation, perhaps even a necessary one. Successful cheaters do appear to experience a sort of high, according to fMRI findings.[23]

The Honest Truth about Dishonesty

In Dan Ariely's book *The Honest Truth about Dishonesty*, we learn that mild cheating can be much more harmful than outright fraud and that people often create states of "wishful blindness," the state wherein we conveniently miss the signs of inappropriate conduct. Indeed, Ariely, the James B. Duke Professor of Psychology and Behavioral Economics at Duke University, shows facts derived from the hard data that convincingly demonstrate how dishonest we all are! This is a really important book for anyone interested in understanding why we do what we do and how we can live more mindfully.[24] In 2012, I had the opportunity to interview Professor Ariely, and you can hear that interview by going to: **provocativeenlightenment.com/wp/2012–1211-the-honest-truth-about-dishonesty-how-we-lie-to-everyone-especially-ourselves-with-dan-ariely/**.

Intelligence

Is it a fair question to ask whether our population is smart enough to take part in a democracy? I mean, when people sign petitions to legalize such bizarre things as the mandatory euthanasia of senior citizens,[25] you do seriously need to wonder. Is it possible that an intelligence test should be required in which voters must demonstrate a certain level of proficiency before being allowed to enter the polling booth? A new research study examined this idea.

The democratic process relies on the assumption that citizens (the majority of them, at least) can recognize the best political candidate, or best policy idea, when they see it. But a growing body of research has revealed an unfortunate aspect of the human psyche that would seem to disprove this notion, and imply instead that democratic elections produce mediocre leadership and policies.

The research, led by David Dunning, a psychologist at Cornell University, shows that incompetent people are inherently unable to judge the competence of other people or the quality of those people's ideas. For example, if people lack expertise on tax reform, it is very difficult for them to identify the candidates who are actual experts. They simply lack the mental tools needed to make meaningful judgments.

As a result, no amount of information or facts about political candidates can override the inherent inability of many voters to accurately evaluate them. On top of that, "very smart ideas are going to be hard for people to adopt, because most people don't have the sophistication to recognize how good an idea is."[26]

Before leaving the idea of intelligence as a basis for a democracy to properly operate, there is an idea called geniocracy that may interest you. The idea is simple. The main principle is that "only those of above average intelligence have the right to vote, while only geniuses are eligible to govern."[27] What are your thoughts on government of the people, for the people, by the geniuses? I don't know about you, but that is as frightening to me as government by the ignorant and uninformed.

CONCLUSION

It is a fair question to ask what the global implications are for us as individuals. Do we deserve to be given the power of choice? Some of our hardwiring makes great givers out of us, and some of our training can lead to great injustices. None of us are immune from holding onto false beliefs for it is common to simply fail to recognize them. Still, I believe in the greatness of the human being. For me, all of this information simply brings to my attention the many ways I can positively impact my world. I hope you remember to use what you learn to empower your life and not to rob you of optimism, for blind optimism is only denial—no more and no less!

CHAPTER TEN

Pushing the Boundaries

"Of all tyrannies, a tyranny sincerely exercised for the good of its victims may be the most oppressive. It would be better to live under robber barons than under omnipotent moral busybodies. The robber baron's cruelty may sometimes sleep, his cupidity may at some point be satiated; but those who torment us for our own good will torment us without end for they do so with the approval of their own conscience."

~ C.S. Lewis

Misconception: *You probably believe you would do the right thing in a situation where someone needed help for you are, after all, a good person.*
Fact: *You are subject to psychological effects that lead to conformity, obedience, and can suspend ethical action.*

An area we need to examine arises from the fact that our moral responses are predisposed by the situations and circumstances we find ourselves in. Is that something else that is used against us?

Most are familiar with the Genovese Effect, or the bystander effect. Where there is a crowd about us, we are inclined to expect someone else to deal with the matter at hand and thereby turn our backs on it all. The name Genovese comes from the case of Kitty

Genovese, who was brutally murdered while neighbors looked on.[1] Similar kinds of videos have surfaced over the past few years, for example, a video of a man who is hit by a car and people circle and take pictures but do nothing, or the woman in the emergency waiting room who is obviously dying, but no one does anything.

Bystander Effect

Research has repeatedly shown that the bystander effect is a characteristic of humanness, not a fluke, however unfavorably we look upon it. For example,

> In a series of classic studies, researchers Bibb Latane and John Darley found that the amount of time it takes the participant to take action and seek help varies depending on how many other observers are in the room. In one experiment, subjects were placed in one of three treatment conditions: alone in a room, with two other participants or with two confederates who pretended to be normal participants.
>
> As the participants sat filling out questionnaires, smoke began to fill the room. When participants were alone, 75% reported the smoke to the experimenters. In contrast, just 38% of participants in a room with two other people reported the smoke. In the final group, the two confederates in the experiment noted the smoke and then ignored it, which resulted in only 10% of the participants reporting the smoke.[2]

Researchers at the University College London investigated the bystander effect using virtual reality. What the researchers discovered has surprised some. Participants in the study were far more ready to intervene if they identified with the same group as the person being attacked.

> Interestingly, this work could go far beyond telling us more about the frailties of the human mind. It has already attracted attention from the police and the Ministry of Defense to help train their personnel in diffusing confrontational situations. The technology could even be used to help evaluate a prisoner's likelihood of violent re-offending, and a pilot study has already yielded promising results.[3]

Conformity or Obedience

Social identification may be the fulcrum on which unspeakable acts are motivated, argues a new study published in *Perspectives on Psychological Science*. In an interesting study design, researchers sought to determine if it was obedience or social identification that caused people to behave as they did in the study carried out by Stanley Milgram in which electric shock was used to punish students who failed at their appointed purpose.[4] Social identification may well be a better explanation for atrocities committed in history as well.

The researchers hypothesized that the willingness to perform these acts was a "reflection not of simple obedience, but of active identification with the experimenter and his mission." Their findings confirmed their hypothesis.

> According to the authors, these new findings suggest that we need to rethink obedience as the standard explanation for why people engage in cruel and brutal behavior. This new research "moves us away from a dominant viewpoint that has prevailed within and beyond the academic world for nearly half a century—a viewpoint suggesting that people engage in barbaric acts because they have little insight into what they are doing and conform slavishly to the will of authority," they write.
>
> These new findings suggest that social identification provides participants with a moral compass and motivates them to act as followers. This followership, as the authors point out, is not thoughtless—"it is the endeavor of committed subjects."[5]

The Lucifer Effect

Dr. Philip Zimbardo identified several less-than-moral characteristics that humans share. In his seminal work on the psychology of evil, he exposes the innumerable ways in which good people can be moved to do bad things. A focal point of his book is the research he carried out at Stanford in what is known as the Stanford Prison Experiment. His first-person account of the transformation of good people taking on the roles of inmates and guards is alarming, for it shows that given a context, and all contexts contain certain expectations, the individual would assume a role and act in aberrant ways.[6]

His work includes a review of research dealing with obedience, including the classic study carried out by Stanley Milgram mentioned above. Additionally, Zimbardo examined research in the areas of conformity, authority, dehumanization, deindividuation, role-playing, and moral disengagement. Where matters of obedience to authority are concerned, it's important to point at research employing fMRI technology, where it was discovered that areas of the brain in charge of discrimination and decision making shut down in the presence of an authority. We have become so conditioned to accept the power of authority as somewhat absolute that we fail even to process information given by them in the same way we process information from a nonauthority source. What does that tell you?

Zimbardo lays out "the groundwork for the rest of the book by vivid descriptions of torture in the Inquisition, in the massacre in Rwanda, the Rape of Nanking, and other venues where human nature has run amok . . . (and he) helps us make sense of corporate malfeasance, of 'administrative evil,' and most particularly, the abuse and torture of prisoners by American military police in Iraq's infamous Abu Ghraib prison."[7]

Monster Study

Psychological research is dotted with what has been termed "evil" studies. In the *Monster Study* (carried out in 1939), Wendell Johnson and his student Mary Tudor experimented on orphaned children, dividing them into two groups. First psychological pressure was applied in ways that led the youngsters to stutter. Tudor then provided speech therapy to both groups, after which one group was praised and the other derided repeatedly. The consequences of this study led to what some claim were long-term negative psychological effects for the children in the ridiculed group.[8]

Forced Sex Change

This next study shows just how perverse the so-called psychologically healthy can be.

South Africa's apartheid army forced white lesbian and gay soldiers to undergo 'sex-change' operations in the 1970s and the 1980s, and submitted many to chemical castration, electric shock, and other unethical medical experiments. Although the exact number is not known, former apartheid army surgeons estimate that as many as 900 forced 'sexual reassignment' operations may have been performed between 1971 and 1989 at military hospitals, as part of a top-secret program to root out homosexuality from the service.

Army psychiatrists aided by chaplains aggressively ferreted out suspected homosexuals from the armed forces, sending them discreetly to military psychiatric units, chiefly ward 22 of 1 Military Hospital at Voortrekkerhoogte, near Pretoria. Those who could not be 'cured' with drugs, aversion shock therapy, hormone treatment, and other radical 'psychiatric' means were chemically castrated or given sex-change operations . . .

. . . Dr. Aubrey Levin (the head of the study) is now clinical professor in the Department of Psychiatry (Forensic Division) at the University of Calgary's Medical School. He is also in private practice, as a member in good standing of the College of Physicians and Surgeons of Alberta.[9]

Top Ten Unethical Psychological Studies

There are many other examples of the immoral and decadent actions of researchers and subjects alike, as well as the general public acting in a manner totally immoral and unacceptable by the standards of civilized society. Indeed, although not within the scope of this work, it is well worth examining the top ten unethical psychological experiments, if for no other reason than to acknowledge how universal this propensity is with our species. I would recommend that you take a look at **brainz.org/10-psychological-experiments-went-horribly-wrong/.** Now you may say that this kind of thing could not happen again as research studies now need to be approved by human subjects committees. However, you should also realize that with the earlier unethical psychological studies, an "expert" had defined reasons for why the study was important and necessary.

Moral Values

But let's get back to situations we can all relate to. A study published in *Science Daily* in May 2012 reported on how individuals' moral values could change from situation to situation and do so without their awareness. Researchers focused on persons who held two jobs. They discovered that ethical decisions changed with the role the person assumed. Lead author Keith Leavitt explained:

> When people switch hats, they often switch moral compasses. People like to think they are inherently moral creatures—you either have character or you don't. But our studies show that the same person may make a completely different decision based on what hat they may be wearing at the time, often without even realizing it . . . What we consider to be moral sometimes depends on what constituency we are answering to at that moment. For a physician, a human life is priceless. But if that same physician is a managed-care administrator, some degree of moral flexibility becomes necessary to meet their obligations to stockholders.[10]

CONCLUSION

You might ask: What does this sort of research have to do with the theme of this work? Where is the gotcha? The answer is a straightforward: EVERYTHING! Understanding the human condition, its propensities and proclivities, both the angelic and the demonic side, is essential, for it is this human nature that manipulators take advantage of. Additionally, although most of us are not likely to be the subject of some unethical research, knowing that it has been done and done recently, even by the American government in the case of MKUltra (from the early 1950s to the early 1970s), is equally important if you are to approach your world wide-eyed and awake.

In a world that is becoming smaller every day, the connections between us all have never become more apparent. We are One People, and as such, we have an obligation to make sure that others are treated with the same respect and dignity that we believe we deserve.

Information Processing

No matter where you go or what you do,
you live your entire life within the confines of your head.

~Terry Josephson

Misconception: *Most people believe they are in charge of their own decisions and that they alone know what they really think.*
Fact: *The conscious mind can only guess at what's in the unconscious mind and yet the unconscious will make more than 90 percent of our decisions and do so before the conscious mind even knows what has been decided.*

We are continually processing information in parallel ways. While our conscious mind goes about our daily business, a part of it goes about the automatic processes involved in what we do. So as I typed this part of my manuscript, I became aware that my fingers do their thing automatically while my mind works on the sentence structure, thought, form of expression, and so forth involved in writing. All this time, operating in the background, is another form of consciousness interested in the somatic operation of my body. It sees to my breathing, my heart rate, blood pressure, and so on. And all the while this is being processed at some level of the mind, myriads of other operations are being carried out. Some part of my mind is attending to my vocabulary and the memory of my favorite movie, another part is dedicated to paying attention to the stimuli around me, and with the quietest mention of my name, my full attention will be brought to bear upon the direction from which the sound emanated. And there is much more going on in the brain, including the attention given by my subconscious to matters of the ego, self-preservation, and subliminal input. Indeed, every aspect of our lives could be said to happen at one of two levels, conscious and/or subconscious, and that there is not always an absolutely clear line or threshold between the two. Of equal importance is the depth of operation for both and the nature of our selective awareness with regard to what we give our attention to.

System One and System Two

Today we generally think of our cognitive system as being divided into two different systems. Daniel Kahneman, professor of psychology emeritus at Princeton University and Nobel Memorial Prize winner, advanced this idea, suggesting that system one delivers us the fast operation we think of as quick decisions, intuitive reactions, and the like while system two is the slower, more deliberate type of rational reasoning, mathematical calculations, and self-control. Obviously, most of our lives function from system one. System two, on the other hand, seems to handle only one type of demand at a time. Give it a detailed physical task involving concentration at the same time you attempt to resolve some mathematical abstraction, and never the two shall be done together.

And performing one type of System 2 thinking makes us less able to perform a subsequent System 2 activity in the period immediately afterward—even if one is physical and the other is cognitive or emotional. Furthermore, when the mind is actively focused on a System 2 activity, it results in System 1 having greater influence over our behavior:

It is now a well-established proposition that both self-control and cognitive effort are forms of mental work. Several psychological studies have shown that people who are simultaneously challenged by a demanding cognitive task

and by a temptation are more likely to yield to the temptation. Imagine that you are asked to retain a list of seven digits for a minute or two. You are told that remembering the
digits is your top priority. While your attention is focused
on the digits, you are offered a choice between two desserts:
a sinful chocolate cake and a virtuous fruit salad. The evidence suggests that you would be more likely to select the
tempting chocolate cake when your mind is loaded with digits. System 1 has more influence on behavior when System 2
is busy, and it has a sweet tooth.[1]

In *Thinking Fast and Slow,* author Daniel Kahneman describes
what has been called "ego depletion." Imagine that you have decided to get your body into shape, so you challenge yourself to
give up sweets and begin exercising. That evening you attend a
party with your spouse, and repeatedly you are offered the most
succulent sweets imaginable. Each time you turn one down, you
"deplete" your reserve of turn-down capabilities, so to speak.[2] As
Dan Ariely puts it, "Eventually, when we've said "no" to enough
yummy food, drinks, potential purchases, and forced ourselves to
do enough unwanted chores, we find ourselves in a state called
ego-depletion, where we don't have any more energy to make
good decisions."[3]

This has real-world consequences, especially when you consider the 24/7 media cycle full of advertisements and fear-laden
"news." And then, on top of the ego depletion, there are further
limits to our self-control.

The Limited Resource: Self-Control

I remind you of our discussion regarding free will and will-
power, but I have to say also that scientists believe there is a limit
to self-control. In other words, like a limited resource, you can
use up whatever self-control you may have. "A study by University of Iowa neuroscientist and neuro-marketing expert William
Hedgcock confirms previous studies that show self-control is a
finite commodity that is depleted by use. Once the pool has dried
up, we're less likely to keep our cool the next time we're faced
with a situation that requires self-control."[4]

149

Subliminal Input

Research has repeatedly demonstrated how powerful a subliminal stimulus can be. I have written several books on subliminal communication, and have appeared as an expert witness on the matter. This much is absolutely certain: We process subliminal cues, and they can affect our behavior. Period. Full stop. Some studies have shown that masked information can provoke mathematical calculations in the subconscious even when the exposure to the subliminally masked information is as short as 600 milliseconds.[5]

As we have already seen, our subconscious minds play more than a minor role in our lives. It is the subconscious that makes approximately 90 percent of our decisions. It is the subconscious that prioritizes much of our lives. As we have seen with marketing, the real force and effect of subliminal messages are well understood by those who would own our thoughts. Researchers have proven that subliminal content can persuade a vote, win over an attitude, move a value norm anchor point, motivate an action, ameliorate such conditions as depression and ADHD, and even facilitate the remission of cancer and affect other bodily conditions. As such, this technology is and remains as American political journalist, author, professor, and world peace advocate Norman Cousins once remarked, "potentially the most dangerous technology ever developed."

Over the past thirty years I have seen the opponents of subliminal information processing take a variety of positions. Initially, there was no such thing, and anyway, the public did not need to worry about it because it didn't work and no one would use it because it didn't work. This last statement was one often bandied about during attempts at creating legislation designed to require informed consent should someone decide to use subliminal information processing in their music, retail establishment, etc. It was always the first defense of the advertising agencies. (For the hard evidence on how subliminal is used in advertising, please see my book *Mind Programming*.[6])

These positions have changed over time. First came the admission that subliminal information is processed, but it never-theless is not acted upon. It can't change behavior. That, too, is false to fact. Today most professionals admit that subliminal information can and does influence behavior, but now the issue is for how long. (For a truly in-depth review of the literature, see Bornstein's Meta analysis.[7])

Understanding the importance of this technology is critical when it comes to evaluating some of the tactics that have been used on the public, and for that matter, by such agencies as the CIA when it comes to effectively brainwashing a subject. Could it be used on TV? Could you have been subliminally programmed while in a light hypnotic state and know nothing of it? Is television honest, or should I say, honestly what?

Brain Wave States

I have pointed out in several of my books the interesting fact that we know the flicker rate generated by television alters states of consciousness, or brain wave activity. It actually takes wide-awake brain wave states, known technically as beta waves, and slows them to what is called alpha waves. Indeed, it can slow them even more. This slowed brain wave activity—the alpha state—is associated with hyper states of suggestibility. Subjects experiencing hypnosis are in these slower states of brain wave activity. The point should be obvious: When you sit down in front of the television, you are beginning to participate in the most perfect mechanism yet developed for covert brainwashing.

When I was a boy, I trusted the TV news. Today, I have had to recalculate many of my views in light of the propaganda I was subjected to. Back then my trust in the news led me to believe that Barry Goldwater (a U.S. Presidential nominee in 1964) would start a nuclear war, and other preposterous notions. But then, I also trusted the government. Why?

The National Anthem

Here's a story you may find too incredible to believe, but no one has been able to debunk it. What's more, video evidence exists that clearly supports its veracity. In the 1950s and 1960s, television stations signed off at night. There is a film on YouTube of a sign-off segment that I remember seeing. This video is of the "Star Spangled Banner" with the flag waving and interspersed shots of various American scenes. The words to the national anthem appear on the screen, ostensibly to assist us in both singing along and learning the lyrics. I encourage you to check out this video. You can find it here: **truthstreammedia.com/1960s-subliminal-video-of-national-anthem-hides-mkultra-message-to-obey-government/**

What's of particular import here is the use of subliminal technology, something we'll look at in more depth in a bit. The video has been slowed down and the subliminal messages have been rendered more visible as a result. Now this is a video made in the days of MKUltra and other clandestine operations carried out by various departments within the government to experiment on the public with means and methods of mind control[8]

What were the subliminal messages in the video? If you stopped reading to view the video, then you're probably as shocked as I was when first this came to my attention. I remember seeing the movie *They Live*. In the movie a pair of sunglasses suddenly reveals to the wearer the hidden messages everywhere ordering consumption and obedience. Is this just far-fetched science fiction? Well, here are some of the messages in that national anthem sign-off:

> Obey Government
> Trust the U.S. Government
> God Is Real God Is Watching
> Believe In Government God
> Rebellion Will Not Be Tolerated
> Obey Consume Obey Consume

If that doesn't disturb you, it should! Is this video real? Could this really have happened? Is it still happening? We do know that President Bill Clinton apologized to Americans for the experiments carried out on the public during the days of MKUltra and its ilk.

I am uncertain about the authenticity of this video because

chiefly, I still want to believe in this country and its leadership, even though I am aware that my bias absolutely predisposes me to take this position. Is the video only an elaborate hoax? Has someone taken the old anthem signoff and doctored it? This much we know for certain, however: The technology was available, and it was deployed in covert operations designed to determine the limits of possibility when it comes to brainwashing or mind control. And this we also know for certain: In a memorandum on brainwashing that was sent to J. Edgar Hoover, Director of the FBI, Allen W. Dulles, Director of the CIA thought it appropriate to use as an epigraph the following quote from Jules Romains:

> "We know now that men can be made to do exactly anything . . . It's all a question of finding the right means. If only we take enough trouble and go sufficiently slowly, we can make him kill his aged parents and eat them in a stew."[9]

Subliminal Communication

I have repeatedly discussed subliminal communication, its dangers and advantages, in all of my books since at least 1984. I have appeared as an expert witness on the subject, and I have patented a technology to deliver subliminal content. I have conducted numerous studies employing subliminal methods, including the first-ever study of its kind with an incarcerated population. I have assisted or participated in a number of additional studies, both clinical and double blind in nature. All of my research has pointed to at least five obvious conclusions:

1. You absolutely process subliminal information.
2. Subliminal content absolutely can influence behavior.
3. Subliminal information is often prioritized.
4. Subliminal information can influence our value norm anchor points.
5. Subliminal communication can therefore "change our minds" and mold our "beliefs."

There are many misconceptions about subliminal technology and the law. The bottom line comes down to this: You are not protected against the use of subliminal technology. There are no laws protecting you. There is a much-touted FCC codification that essentially threatens to take a station's license if it "knowingly" broadcasts subliminal content. However, when the DNC pursued George W. Bush's people for including the subliminal message "RATS" in a campaign ad during the Bush/Gore presidential contest, they were unable to obtain relief. What chance, therefore, do you think you would have? And by the way, just for the record, research at Adelphi University demonstrated that the now infamous "RATS" ad did in all probability influence the outcome of the election.[10]

Subliminals in the Media

With all of this talk about subliminal communication, it is important to ask how common is subliminal insertion in our media? I have written several books on the influence of subliminal messages, the technology, and the legal issues surrounding it, but let me cover just a couple of additional matters here.

A quick search of the Internet for subliminal messages in ads or movies turns up quite a bundle of good finds. They range from such Disney movies as *Lion King* to content of *Comedy Central*. With today's technology, such as the common use of a DVR, viewers are able to slow films down and review them for subliminal content. Doing so has led many viewers to discover what one UK Comedy Central viewer reported in January 2013. Flashing very quickly across the screen was an odd bit that this viewer replayed. When our viewer replayed the section containing the flash, the still image below appeared:

ANOTHER VESTIGE OF OUR PAST HAS BITTEN THE DUST. HIS MASTER'S HAS FALLEN SILENT. THE NATION'S MOST-FAMOUS RECORD STORE IS GOING DOWN. IT'S NOT SURPRISING, BUT IT'S A SHAME. AFTER ALL, WHO HASN'T FOND OF GOING INTO THEIR LOCAL BRANCH AND BROWSING THROUGH THE RECORDS, TAPES, CDS, VIDEOS AND DVDS? THAT EXCITING WEEKEND TRIP ARMED WITH FRESHLY-GIFTED VOUCHERS OR HARD-EARNED SAVINGS BRIMMING WITH MAGICAL PROMISE OF AN EXCHANGE THAT WILL ADD TO THE POURING OVER ALBUM ARTWORK ON THE BUS HOME, ONLY FUELLING FURTHER THE IMPATIENCE TO GET BACK AND ENGULF THE SENSES IN THE LATEST RELEASE BY A FAVOURITE BAND OR SINGER, WILL IT BE AS GOOD AS THEIR LAST ONE? WHAT IF IT'S WORSE? RELIVING THE OF SEEING A FILM THAT BLEW YOUR MIND IN THE CINEMA BUT IN THE COMFORT OF YOUR LIVING ROOM, YEAH IT'S GREAT WE CAN INSTANTLY BUY EVERYTHING WE WANT AT THE CLICK OF A BUTTON, DELIVERED STRAIGHT TO YOUR DOOR, BUT IT'S NO LONGER A SHARED , THERE WAS A PRECIOUS COMMODITY IN BUYING STUFF FROM SHOPS IN THOSE DAYS: YOU WERE PART OF A TRIBE. FOR MANY, A TRIP TO THE RECORD SHOP WAS AN EVENT. HELL, FOR SOME IT WAS A PLACE JUST TO HANG OUT. BUT YOU CAN'T FIGHT CAN YOU? AND SELLING CDS FOR UP TO EIGHTEEN QUID IN 2013 PROBABLY DIDN'T HELP. SO FAREWELL HMV, THE HIGH STREET WON'T BE THE SAME WITHOUT YOU.

The words highlighted above are thought to be one way to see the message since they are capitalized. Those words are VOICE, MEMORIES, COLLECTION, JOY, EXPERIENCE, and PROGRESS. Not everyone viewing this still is of the same opinion, however. In disinfo.com, we find this:

> A hoax? Subliminal HMV advertising? Or the passing of a ciphered message? It's anyone's guess. *Who Forted?* writes:
>
> A television viewer thought he noticed something odd flash across the screen last evening, and lucky for us, his DVR was running and he was able to post the strange capture . . . a "very weird subliminal message."
>
> The flash, which was broadcast on Comedy Central during a commercial break, contains a huge block of text impossible to read unless paused, with several of the words highlighted as though important. Even weirder is that it seems to be an ode to financially troubled record store HMV. The highlighted words are VOICE, MEMORIES, COLLECTION, JOY, EXPERIENCE, and PROGRESS.
>
> Some [believe] the bits could be part of a modern-day "numbers station," a sort of updated version of the radio signals used by spies to relay information to those who knew how to decipher it.[11]

While I have discussed subliminal communication in a number of my books, one obvious oversight on my part is its application as a method to encrypt spy messages, as suggested above. This possibility adds still another dimension to matters of subliminal information processing. However, although it is not the scope of this work to explore the many nuances of subliminal technology, I would still encourage you to do so.

CONCLUSION

What were your thoughts when you learned that the information in your subconscious was employed somehow to make decisions without the involvement or knowledge of your conscious mind? Does that information make you realize just how important the "stuff" you put into your mind becomes? I hope it does! In a sense, perhaps the only free will any of us potentially have is in choosing what we put into our mind. My advice is: Choose wisely!

Be careful of those sound bites and rush-to-judgment condemnations. Think through issues before settling on an opinion. Pay attention to the entertainment and the implicit messages contained therein. Exercise caution about the media you choose to allow access to your mind, saturating your thoughts even when you're not paying attention to it. Don't allow the television to become a babysitter for your children or grandchildren. Monitor your thoughts and question the origin of those mental images.

CHAPTER TWELVE

Some of What "They" Have Learned

A lot of times you're just conditioned by what's around you.
~Ruben Blades

Misconception: *Most people believe they are already awake and aware and not much gets by them.*
Fact: *The fact is, simple primes alter our judgment, influence our decisions, and mobilize our drives—covertly maneuvering our entire psychology.*

A huge number of individuals, universities, and institutions are focused on researching human behavior. Most of us tend to see the results of this kind of research as just being interesting— it is fascinating to learn how the human animal works! However, there is a great deal of potential for the misuse of this information when it is in the "wrong" hands. By that I mean anyone who has an interest in manipulating others for his or her benefit. When you have a real idea of the amount of information out there on human behavior, I believe you, too, will view it in a different light.

Waitress in Red

I like to think of the various ways and means by which we respond to subconscious stimuli as the Waitress in Red simply because one silly little fact, unknown to us consciously, can have

---

much power over our behavior. A fascinating study showed that patrons would regularly leave larger tips to a waitress dressed in red. You should note that this higher tip did not come from male patrons alone. Female patrons increased their tips as well![1]

Now, here are a number of other such snippets of information. I would ask you not only to think of each snippet on its own merits but to think also of the ease with which your free will can be manipulated or subverted into making someone else's choices when subconscious stimuli are used against you.

Full or Empty?

Imagine you're on a bus with an empty seat next to you. Are you inviting someone to sit next to you, or are you using some tactic to keep the seat empty? In all probability, your choice would be to have an empty seat next to you. A novel study carried out by Esther Kim of Yale University showed that people go to great lengths to avoid having someone sit next to them. They use such tactics as avoiding eye contact, pretending to be asleep, placing a bag or a coat or other items on the seat next to them, and so forth. "This all changes, however, when it is announced that the bus will be full so all seats should be made available," Kim observed. "The objective changes, from sitting alone to sitting next to a 'normal' person."[2]

Counterintuitive

And just when you think that our intuitive abilities might at least inform us accurately of how others experience pain, research shows us that the brain processes the pain of villains more carefully than of people we like.

> While one might assume that we would empathize more with people we like, the study may indicate that the human brain focuses more greatly on the need to monitor enemies closely, especially when they are suffering.
>
> "When you watch an action movie and the bad guy appears to be defeated, the moment of his demise draws our focus intensely," said Lisa Aziz-Zadeh of the Brain and Creativity Institute of the USC Dornsife College of Letters,

Arts and Sciences. "We watch him closely to see whether he's really down for the count because it's critical for predicting his potential for retribution in the future."[3]

Robot Sympathy

What would you say if you discovered that humans display as much sympathy for a robot being injured as they do for a human being in the same situation? Well, toy and doll makers know this very well. One study utilizing fMRI observed the brain while subjects were shown images of robots being treated with either affection or violence. Subject's brains showed the same activity as subject's viewing similar situations with human beings.

> Participants were presented videos showing a human, a robot, and an inanimate object, again being treated in either an affectionate or in a violent way. Affectionate interaction towards both, the robot and human, resulted in similar neural activation patterns in classic limbic structures, indicating that they elicit similar emotional reactions. However, when comparing only the videos showing abusive behavior, differences in neural activity suggested that participants show more negative empathetic concern for the human in the abuse condition.[4]

Ritualistic Reasoning

Supernatural reasoning seems to many to be somewhat oxymoronic, since by definition, the supernatural is not subject to reason. Nevertheless, research suggests that supernatural reasoning is often employed to describe the world around us, and all that happens to us. Would it surprise you to know that repetition over time intensifies the effect of a ritual? In a clever experiment, researchers developed a ritual to test this idea with 162 Brazilians. They discovered three elements that gave the rituals more power in the minds of the subjects: the number of items involved, the length of time, and the number of steps required to complete the ritual. Then the researchers tested how rituals were perceived across cultures, testing sixty-eight U.S. respondents. The results: "Similar to the Brazilians, they [U.S. respondents] were more inclincd to believe in rituals involving numerous repetitions and steps. For example, they gave a higher rating for this sadness-curing ritual, which involves numerous steps and repetitions."[5]

An example of the better rituals went like this. "In a metal container, put the leaves of a white rose. After that, set fire to the leaves. Get the remaining ash from the leaves and put it in a small plastic bag. Take the small plastic bag and leave it at a crossroad. Repeat the procedure for seven days in a row."[6]

Now ask yourself this. Are there any rituals you find beneficial that meet the criteria of this study? Remember, not all rituals are religious, mystical, or magical per se. Some rituals are as common as the pledge of allegiance or the national anthem at a ball game. Since rituals act to "synchronize emotional, perceptual-cognitive, and motor process within the central nervous system of individual participants,"[7] something as seemingly innocent as a repeated chant (such as the famous "Yes, we can" chant during the Obama campaign of 2008), effects the body rhythm and thereby serves to incorporate our feelings into our cognitions generating stronger feelings of belonging and loyalty. I believe that all rituals are likely to have their effectiveness judged similarly, and we certainly have a lot of rituals in our society.

Firsts

Are you aware that people consistently prefer firsts? We are all more likely to choose our first option.

> In three experiments, when making quick choices, participants consistently preferred people (salespersons, teams, criminals on parole) or consumer goods presented first as opposed to similar offerings in second and sequential positions. The authors say their findings may have practical applications in a variety of settings including in consumer marketing.
>
> "The order of individuals performing on talent shows like *American Idol*. The order of potential companies recommended by a stockbroker. The order of college acceptance letters received by an applicant. All of these firsts have privileged status," says Carney. "Our research shows that manag-

ers, for example, in management or marketing, may want to develop their business strategies knowing that first encounters are preferable to their clients or consumers."

The study found that especially in circumstances under which decisions must be made quickly or without much deliberation, preferences are unconsciously and immediately guided to those options presented first. While there are sometimes rational reasons to prefer firsts, e.g. the first resume is designated on the top of the pile because that person wanted the job the most, Carney says the "first is best" effect suggests that firsts are preferred even when completely unwarranted and irrational.[8]

How many important decisions have you made on the basis of first? How many times do you think you have been manipulated into making a buying choice this way? In a subsequent chapter, we'll examine what compliance principles are, and then I know you will discover instances where you have been taken advantage of.

To Receive or to Give

On a brighter note, are you aware that thinking about giving motivates people to help others? In fact, our brains are hardwired in such a way as to reward us chemically for going to the aid of someone in need. Research has shown that simply writing a check to a charity we care about leads to the release of endorphins. That said, advertisers and charities are aware that motivating you to give should be about giving and the reward you feel for doing so. In years past, some thought that pointing out to you how lucky you were and how much you had received would work to motivate you to give more—but this line of reasoning has been proven to be false.

Researchers Adam Grant and Jane Dutton put that hypothesis to the test.

As the researchers hypothesized, the fundraisers who wrote about giving for just two or three days increased their hourly calls by more than 29% in the following two weeks. The fundraisers who wrote about receiving, however, showed no change in the number of hourly calls made.

(In a second study) participants who reflected on giving were significantly more likely to donate (46.15%) than those in either the beneficiary (21.43%) or control condition (13.33%).

"Helping, giving, volunteering, and other actions undertaken to benefit others play a critical role in protecting health, promoting education, fighting poverty and hunger, and providing disaster relief," the researchers write.

This new research suggests that self-reflection about giving can be a powerful tool for motivating helping and volunteering behaviors that benefit individuals and communities. When we reflect on positive experiences, it may be worthwhile to think about what we've given to others—not only what we've received.[9]

I believe in charity, and I like helping people. Indeed, much of my career and definitely nearly every high point of it have come as the result of what I have called that warm, fuzzy feeling we get when we know that we have made a difference, that we have helped someone in some way important to them! That said, each of these discoveries and all that follows help to lead those who would pull your strings to know exactly when, where, and how to do that. And again, not to be cynical, but the only defense against this form of manipulation is foreknowledge of the same information that can be used against us.

First

Later on we will discuss compliance principles, and you will learn about the need for consistency. At this juncture, however, it is important to add another kernel of knowledge into our mix. Social psychologists and marketing experts well know about consistency. Of particular relevance here, however, is our need to maintain the appearance of consistency over time. Let's say we make a choice about how we will vote, so the choice is about a candidate. Research shows that no matter how disappointed we may become with the performance of our candidate, we will defend our choice years later. That concept is equally true of the merchandise we choose. And it is equally true that our choice can influence our future choices for some time to come, shaping our preferences.

To test whether a sense of agency over the decision makes a difference for choice-induced changes in preference, the researchers looked at participants' preferences when the participants made the choices themselves and when a computer instructed the participants' choices.

The results suggest that the act of choosing between two similar options can lead to enduring changes in preference. Participants rated vacation destinations as more desirable both immediately after choosing them and again three years later. This change only occurred, however, if they had made the original choice themselves. The researchers observed no change in participants' preferences when the computer instructed their choices.

(Tali) Sharot and her colleagues argue the fact that this effect is robust and enduring has implications for a diverse array of fields, including economics, marketing, and even interpersonal relationships. As Sharot points out, for example, repeatedly endorsing a particular political party may entrench this preference for a long period of time.[10]

Using Brain Waves to Test Prices

Get this one: A German scientist is working on the development of a way to measure brain wave activity that will provide "feel good" feedback on consumers' attitudes toward pricing.

The brain researcher is also a sales professional. Müller used to work for Simon, Kucher and Partners, a leading international consulting firm that helps companies find suitable prices for their products. But he soon lost interest in the job when he recognized that "classic market research doesn't work correctly." From the scientist's perspective, research subjects have only limited credibility when they are asked to honestly state how much money they would spend for a product.

Instead, Müller is searching for "neuronal mechanisms," deeply buried in the human brain, "that we can't just deliberately switch off." In fact, there is a center in our gray matter that monitors proportionality independently of reason. This brain region functions according to simple rules. For instance, coffee and cake makes sense, while coffee and mustard triggers an alarm. Experts recognize the unconscious defensive reaction on the basis of certain waves that become visible with the help of electroencephalography (EEG). Do these graphs also reveal something about consumers' willingness to pay for products?

Using the example of a small cup of coffee, for which Starbucks charged €1.80 ($2.45) in Stuttgart, Müller tried to get to the bottom of the question. He showed subjects the same pot of coffee on a screen several times, but with different prices in each instance. At the same time, an EEG plotted the subjects' brain activity.

Especially in the case of extreme offers, strong reactions appeared in the brain within milliseconds. Prices that were either too low or too high, such as 10 cents or €10 per cup, were unacceptable to the brain's control mechanism. "When the brain was expected to process unexpected and disproportionate prices, feelings of shock, doubt, and astonishment manifested themselves," Müller reports.[11]

This finding indicates that it makes more sense for prices to be increased gradually rather than sharply. Think about that for a moment. In 2008, the price of gas at the pump spiked from around $1 per gallon to $4 per gallon. The public cut back on driving, and many people drove slower. The price of gas returned to a level that was still higher than before the jump but closer to what most of us thought as normal. Then slowly the price began to creep up again. Gas prices have reached the $4 per gallon mark several times since then, but there has not been a similar widespread public reaction.

Human Behavior Stranger Than Fiction

Many peculiarities about the human psyche operate quite counter to our intuitive guidance. For example, as I have reported earlier, fMRI scans have revealed that when smokers are shown the Surgeon General's warning, they actually want to smoke more. Well, it turns out that warnings in general may increase sales of a product.

> Drug ads often warn of serious side effects, from nausea and bleeding to blindness, even death. New research suggests that, rather than scaring consumers away, these warnings can improve consumers' opinions and increase product sales when there is a delay between seeing the ad and deciding to buy or consume the product.[12]

The delay effect is of particular interest because agencies that work to protect the public do not allow for it.

> According to Ziv Carmon of INSEAD in Singapore and his colleagues, the warnings backfired because the psychological distance created by the delay between exposure to the ad and the decision to buy made the side effects seem abstract—participants came to see the warning as an indication of the firm's honesty and trustworthiness.
>
> In fact, participants evaluated drugs for erectile dysfunction and hair loss that had potentially serious side effects more favorably, and as more trustworthy, when they were told the products weren't on the shelves yet.
>
> "This effect may fly under the radar since people who try to protect the public—regulatory agencies, for example—tend to test the impact of a warning shortly after consumers are exposed to it," says Carmon. "By doing so, they miss out on this worrisome delayed outcome."[13]

So it is possible for an organization to be totally upfront, airing all of their "dirty laundry," so to speak, and still manage to get the general public to believe in them or their products.

Likes and Dislikes and Movement

Have you ever watched politicians you did not like and found their movements, perhaps the way they walk, to be annoying or displeasing? There were many who commented on George W. Bush's "cowboy" walk, for example. Bush himself remarked on this, stating that, "Some folks look at me and see a certain swagger, which in Texas is called walking."

The data shows that whether we like someone or not bears

directly on how our brains process movement. In a study carried out by researchers at USC, the brains of participants were watched while they viewed films of people they liked and of people they had been conditioned by the researchers to dislike. Differing brain responses convinced the researchers that "even something as basic as how we process visual stimuli of a movement is modulated by social factors, such as our interpersonal relationships and social group membership," said Mona Sobhani, lead author of the paper and a graduate student in neuroscience at USC. "These findings lend important support for the notion that social factors influence our perceptual processing."[14]

How often have we seen politicians who are running for office, particularly presidential nominees, bounding up onto the stage, sleeves rolled up, no tie, and their top shirt button undone? Isn't that the image we have of the hard-working, down-to-earth person we love and trust? Al Gore had a difficult time with creating this persona when he ran for office against George Bush in 2000, and Mitt Romney never quite pulled it off in 2012. On the other hand, Barack Obama does it perfectly. Sometimes members of his audience even swooned!

Communication

As I have already indicated, I often use my FB pages to test ideas. When a new study reported in a headline that "Mitt Romney's Face Looks Different to Republicans and Democrats" and went on to describe the study this way, "The study of Ohioans immediately before and after the 2012 presidential election showed that people's mental representation of Republican candidate Mitt Romney's face differed based on their political persuasion,"[15] I had to post it.

The paper continued: "'That our attitudes could bias something that we're exposed to so frequently is an amazing biasing effect,' said Russell Fazio, professor of psychology at the Ohio State University and senior author of the study. 'It suggests that people may not just interpret political information about a candidate to fit their opinion, but that they may construct a political world in which they literally see candidates differently.'"[16]

I posted the piece on my FB page with this lead: "It isn't any longer a matter of, 'what you see is what you get,' it's rather what you expect to see is how you perceive what you get." Now the remarks at first were pretty neutral, and then came this one from someone I will just call Poster. The result was a very telling exchange, so let me share it with you in its entirety:

> **Poster:** You mean it's my liberal filter that sees Mitt Romney's face as a weasely, dishonest Machiavellian reptile?
> **ET:** Such self-disclosure.
> **Poster:** Yes, I'm an open book, Eldon.
> **ET:** A hateful, judgmental one? Those are very harsh words. I like Peale's quote here, "Watch your manner of speech if you wish to develop a peaceful state of mind. Start each day by affirming peaceful, contented, and happy attitudes and your days will tend to be pleasant and successful."
> **Poster:** Eldon, I have a peaceful state of mind, but I know an archetypal politician when I see one. Romney is exactly what Jon Huntsman said he was, "a perfectly lubricated weathervane." And that was from a fellow Republican Mormon. And yes, we do need a third party, led by the likes of Noam Chomsky or Ralph Nader.
> **ET:** What do you do when you meet someone who has substantially similar views, but about Barack Obama? Someone who strongly supported Romney? Do you end up slinging words at each other like stones? My point is as much about the ability to communicate with each other as anything else. When you attack with hateful speech, you lose the ability to even establish a basis of communication, and that's 99% of the problem in this country today, at least in my opinion.
> **Poster:** By the way, a lot of my peace of mind comes from the space created for it by the likes of Werner Erhard, Deepak Chopra, Thich Nhat Hanh, and many other great ontologists. I critique Romney fully realizing that he wasn't being true to his best self. Politics is my passion, and I recognize a panderer better than most.
> **ET:** Dropping names and calling names is not a substantial answer to my last comment.

> **Poster:** People who are very close to me don't like
> Barack Obama, and he's not the messiah. I try to look to
> the example of James Carville and Mary Matalin, a married
> couple who are political advisors to presidents of opposing
> parties. I get along with everybody.
> **ET:** Really, including the person who seriously opposes
> your harsh rhetoric and meets it in kind?
> **Poster:** Admittedly I have a long way to go. I'm not sure
> I'd like to run into Louis Gohmert or Michelle Bachmann
> or Sarah Palin. I can only aspire to be Christlike. We're all
> on our own paths, and I might be a bit lagging. It may take
> a few incarnations for me.
> **ET:** Maybe that's true for most of us so you're in good
> company.

As you can see from this exchange, one of the problems with
all of this brainwashing and propaganda is that it can create some
very strong polarization, which leads to a breakdown in our ability to communicate.

Hearing Hemispheres

Our hearing is a very important perceptual processor. Are
you aware that what you hear may depend upon what your hands
are doing? Our brains have two hemispheres, which we hear of in
popular parlance as the left and right brains. Both hemispheres
have their specializations, although they are amazingly redundant. They are also crosswired in our bodies in such a way that
the right brain is involved with movement on the left side of the
body, while the left brain works with the right side, except for our
eyes, which are wired to both hemispheres.

Research shows that just as with the famous Stroop test (in
which the color of the letters making up the printed name of the
color is different from the name itself, thus causing confusion
when we try to read the "color of the word" instead of reading the
word itself) moving our hands in a cross-brain way can interfere
with what we hear. (To try the Stroop test for yourself, please visit
eldontaylor.com/gotcha.)

(Peter) Turkeltaub and his team hid rapidly and slowly

changing sounds in background noise and asked 24 volunteers to simply indicate whether they heard the sounds by pressing a button.

"We asked the subjects to respond to sounds hidden in background noise," Turkeltaub explained. "Each subject was told to use their right hand to respond during the first 20 sounds, then their left hand for the next 20 sounds, then right, then left, and so on." He says when a subject was using their right hand, they heard the rapidly changing sounds more often than when they used their left hand, and vice versa for the slowly changing sounds.

"Since the left hemisphere controls the right hand and vice versa, these results demonstrate that the two hemispheres specialize in different kinds of sounds—the left hemisphere likes rapidly changing sounds, such as consonants, and the right hemisphere likes slowly changing sounds, such as syllables or intonation," Turkeltaub explains. "These results also demonstrate the interaction between motor systems and perception. It's really pretty amazing. Imagine you're waving an American flag while listening to one of the presidential candidates. The speech will actually sound slightly different to you depending on whether the flag is in your left hand or your right hand."[17]

Too Many Choices

Did you know that when provided with a multiple choice, too many choices may lead to riskier behavior? According to researchers, "This means that, when faced with a large number of choices—each having outcomes associated with different probabilities of occurring—people are more likely to overestimate the probabilities of some of the rarest events."[18]

A study demonstrated that when given a few choices, people are more likely to consider all of the information and gather the facts pertaining to each choice, whereas when they were provided with many choices, they estimate gains without investing the energy to make the best decision.[19]

In 'text speak' is the expression */sigh*, which is most expressive at this juncture. I, like most people, find human behavior to be fascinating, but while the snippets covered in this chapter have fulfilled their 'fascinator' role, a much larger picture is emerging. For those in positions of power and influence, knowledge of this research makes it easier to hold onto their power.

CONCLUSION

Please recall an earlier statement where I explained the many piles of research on my desk that are not included in this book. What I have just shared with you is not even the tip of the iceberg; it's more like a hint provided by the ripple of water as it passes. There are so many devices that the informed can employ to direct us, while we believe we are following own ideas, that a volume of books could be written about them, and for that matter, have been. I encourage you to explore more of this information, and once again I invite you to join me on my blog (**eldontaylor. com/blog**). You can also Google keywords on this subject and find hundreds of books to immerse yourself in, and your local library will have many of them.

When I know that I am more likely to leave a larger tip if the waitress is wearing red, I can neutralize this unconscious bias. Understanding the scope of influence primes have, the psychological technology, the predispositions, and so forth can empower you, and once again I urge you to use this information in that way. Pay attention to how many of these influences you encounter in your daily life. Notice them and make a mental note cancelling their influence. Choose to make your own choices! Inform you family and friends. Make a game out of uncovering every technique and technology you encounter.

What else can you do? I hope this matters to you for if it doesn't, someone else will enjoy the labors of your life and you are likely to depart this world far less happy and fulfilled than you deserve. For as Stephen Jay Gould, paleontologist and educator at Harvard University, said, "When people learn no tools of judgment and merely follow their hopes, the seeds of political manipulation are sown." In my view, refusing to become informed, truly informed, is inviting the wolf in!

CHAPTER THIRTEEN

Pulling on Our Emotions

The emotions aren't always immediately subject to reason,
but they are always immediately subject to action.

~William James

Misconception: *Emotions are private and a well-balanced person can control them, especially when common sense and reasonable judgment so dictate.*

Fact: *Emotions are a significant controller of most people, often trumping our own best judgment, and there are many who know exactly how to take advantage of this.*

Continuing our exploration of techniques used in the subordination of our free will, it is now time to turn to our emotions. Can they too, be tweaked so that they serve another master?

Emotional Morality

Our moral judgments are often guided by our intuition rather than by well-thought-out reasoning. Our emotions give us a sort of "gut feeling" that leads to our determination—this is right, or that is wrong. However, research shows that a dampening effect can be imposed on our emotions and thereby increase the amount of reasoning involved in our judgments. This dampening effect has been termed "reappraisal." It works by turning our intellectual capacity on to understanding why we are experiencing the emotion, or the feeling of right or wrong.

Participants who reappraised the scenarios logically were less likely to make intuition-based moral judgments. These findings suggest that although our emotional reactions elicit moral intuitions, these emotions can also be regulated. "In this way," the researchers write, "we are both slave and master, with the capacity to be controlled by, but also shape, our emotion-laden judgmental processes.[1]

Violence

New research has demonstrated that babies who see violence show aggression later in life. Megan Holmes, assistant professor of social work at the Jack, Joseph and Morton Mandel School of Applied Social Sciences at Case Western Reserve in Cleveland, argue that children are not passive and unaware—they do indeed pay attention to what's going on around them.

Holmes analyzed the behavior of 107 children exposed to IPV [Intimate Partner Violence] in their first three years but never again after age 3. The outcomes of those children were compared to 339 children who were never exposed.

Those studied were from the National Survey of Child and Adolescent Well-Being (NSCAW), which included children reported to Child Protective Services for abuse or neglect. The children's behavior was followed four times over the course of 5 years.

Holmes' research examined the timing, duration, and nature of their exposure to violence and how it affected aggressive behavior.

Analyzing aggressive behaviors, Holmes saw no behavioral differences between those who did or did not witness violence between the ages of 3 and 5, but children exposed to violence increased their aggression when they reached school age. And the more frequently IPV was witnessed, the more aggressive the behaviors became.[2]

So, at an age when generally children are thought of as being unaware and unable to understand the world around them, they are in fact, most susceptible to conditioning!

Empathy and Analytical Thought

It is a normal matter of human nature to experience empathy. Everyone except the sociopath experiences empathic feelings, but did you know that empathy represses critical thought and vice versa? Think about that for a moment. If our empathy button can be pushed, our ability to entertain issues critically is lost. Conversely, if we are focused on critical thinking, evaluation, and the like, our empathy button is so desensitized as to not exist.

> At rest, our brains cycle between the social and analytical networks. But when presented with a task, healthy adults engage the appropriate neural pathway, the researchers found.
>
> The study shows for the first time that we have a built-in neural constraint on our ability to be both empathetic and analytic at the same time.
>
> The work suggests that established theories about two competing networks within the brain must be revised. More, it provides insights into the operation of a healthy mind versus those of the mentally ill or developmentally disabled.
>
> "This is the cognitive structure we've evolved," said Anthony Jack, an assistant professor of cognitive science at Case Western Reserve and lead author of the new study. "Empathetic and analytic thinking are, at least to some extent, mutually exclusive in the brain."[3]

Knowing this, framers of arguments are able to marshal convincing information to send our way. And it is not uncommon to find opposing sides of some moral or social issue treating the subject in opposing ways. While one side argues from critical thinking, the other may well argue from empathy, which has often been the case with such issues as abortion. How do you get both sides to come to the party at the same time, or can you? And if not, what then?

Sentient

While we're addressing emotions, are you aware of the new emotion detector that arguably could influence the outcome of elections? The detector is designed to provide the method and means to design a "tailor-made election campaign."[4]

The device is called Sentient, and it works by measuring variations of heart rate "and certain parameters deriving from it."[5] The device can be used to measure emotion in any environment, so it is as suitable for marketing a product as it for marketing a politician. As an emotion detector, it can provide immediate feedback on how a candidate or product is received as well as help sculpt the precise approach that leads to the most desirable outcome. In fact, "Sentient has been used in a neuromarketing study that measured the emotional response to a series of TV adverts pursuing one goal: to aid the debate on the convenience to focus publicity about social issues on positive or negative messages."[6]

Once again methods of extracting information from the audience is something we have all seen in action, most frequently during election debates. The ticker tape running at the bottom of the television screen provides instant ratings on the particular words or approach used on any topic. We find this interesting; researchers continue to explore ways to extract more information from us.

Guilt Proneness

Are you aware that anticipating feelings of guilt predicts ethical behavior? New research suggests that "guilt proneness," not guilty feelings per se, is a preventative of unethical conduct. Guilt proneness is the anticipation of guilt as a result of some unethical action, and it operates as your conscience to prevent unethical conduct.

> Across several studies, (researchers) have found that people who report higher levels of guilt proneness are less likely to make unethical business decisions, lie for monetary gain, or cheat during negotiations. People who are guilt

prone are also less likely to engage in counterproductive work behaviors, like showing up to work late without permission, stealing office supplies, and being rude to clients, even after taking into account other factors like gender, age, and interpersonal conflict at work.

All of this research suggests that it may be wise to keep guilt proneness in mind, whether we are looking for an ethical friend, an ethical lover, or an ethical employee.

The guilt-proneness scale has the potential to be "an important measurement tool for predicting which individuals are likely to behave unethically in their social interactions inside and outside the workplace," Cohen and her colleagues write. The researchers encourage additional research to examine whether GASP [Guilt and Shame Proneness scale] might be a useful and valid tool in high-stakes settings such as personnel selection.[7]

This is a new scale to measure guilt proneness. Perhaps, as researchers suggest, we should have it completed by our political candidates before they ask for our votes.

CONCLUSION

Wise men rush in when the heat of passion overwhelms them. Thinking that we control our emotions and can keep them in check is usually very naïve. I have never met a human being that has not, at some point in their lives, been overcome by emotion, casting good sense to the wind, and charging on. I have also never met a healthy human being who at some point in their life didn't feel guilty over something. Tweaking our emotions can be a powerful motivator. Once again, it is our awareness that arms us against this sort of manipulation. Edward Bernays stated, "The conscious and intelligent manipulation of the organized habits and opinions of the masses is an important element in democratic society." By contrast, Heather Brooke opined, "Public relations is at best promotion or manipulation, at worst evasion and outright deception. What it is never about is a free flow of information." Which is to you?

GOTCHA!

Throughout this book I have repeatedly urged you to be aware. My ambition with this work is and has been to empower as many as possible with the information necessary to live in our modern world as free of as much manipulation as possible. I truly believe in the incredible power that resides in each and every one of you, but I also know that this power will lie dormant in many throughout their lifetime. It is for that reason that I once again urge you to share what you have learned with everyone you come in contact with. Spread the word. Only by raising the level of public awareness can we hope to minimize the many covert schemes, surreptitious strategies, and selfish ambitions that onslaught our culture on a 24/7 basis.

The Power of Suggestion

A vacant mind is open to all suggestions,
as a hollow mountain returns all sounds.

~Chinese Proverb

Misconception: *Most people believe they are above the power of suggestion and indeed immediately recognize it for what it is.*
Fact: *The fact is, suggestion rules! Everyone is subject to suggestion, and those who understand this can use it to puppet almost anyone.*

The power of suggestion cannot be overstated, and I have written entire books on this subject. Suggestion is one of the most powerful tools in the arsenal of anyone who wishes to influence another, or themselves for that matter. The simple power of suggestion has led to mass hysteria, mass psychogenic illness, and so much more. The fact is, this is something that we all should know and something that is so obvious that I almost left it out of this work.

It is important not only to recognize the power of suggestion but also to acknowledge the influence it has over our behavior. Whether it is an old wives' tale, a superstition, or the alleged strength of a drug including the effect, or for that matter, the nocebo effect (a harmless substance that actually causes harm),

179

and on and on, suggestion can rule our behavior. Solid research has demonstrated this repeatedly. What explains this power in our lives?

> The answer lies in our 'response expectancies,' or the ways in which we anticipate our responses in various situations. These expectancies set us up for automatic responses that actively influence how we get to the outcome we expect. Once we anticipate a specific outcome will occur, our subsequent thoughts and behaviors will actually help to bring that outcome to fruition.[1]

There is another important aspect to suggestion that we should be very aware of, and that is something called the "unintentional suggestion." There are potentially many unintended consequences as a result of unintentional suggestions, and sometimes, the unintended suggestion is not a conscious one per se.

And the unintended effects of suggestion aren't just restricted to the laboratory—they cut across many real world domains, including the fields of medicine, education, and criminal justice. For example, converging evidence on eyewitness identification procedures demonstrates that the rate of false identifications is significantly higher when lineups are conducted by people who know who the suspect is than when the lineups are conducted by people who don't.[2]

Price and Expectation

Later on we'll take a look at issues involving food, water, and drugs, and placebos. Still, at this juncture it would be remiss of me not to draw the correlation between expectancy, based on suggestion, and drugs. It is well known that price plays a major role in our expectation of quality. We expect to pay more for the best. The same is true of drugs. Study after study has shown us that we assign value to drugs based on our perception of cost. A fancy package, a special color, and so forth all serve to convince us of the power of a drug, and our expectation, or this suggestion, becomes our reality more often than not. However, there is an interesting twist to this.

When consumers see lifesaving products at a lower price they tend to infer a greater risk of contracting the disease. In their rationalization as to why this lifesaving drug is inexpensive, they conclude that a higher need dictates the lower price and this gives rise to the idea that the higher need implies more people contract the disease. Voilà—consumers are more likely to contract the condition themselves.[3]

Talk about unintended suggestion—this is a rather astounding one. Does it translate into more people actually getting the disease?

Sleight of Hand

Lars Hall and Peter Johansson of Lund University, Sweden, reported on a truly novel research design. They sought to determine just how rigid the political opinions of voters were.

They first asked people to state their voting intentions for the upcoming election, and presented them with a political survey of wedge issues that separated the two coalitions in the race. The questions concerned familiar issues like income taxation, unemployment insurance, and environmental policies on petrol and nuclear power that traditionally divides the left and right wing.

The special thing about this survey was that the researchers used sleight of hand to secretly alter the responses of the participants, instead placing them in the opposite political camp, and invited them to reason about their attitudes on these reversed issues. Then the researchers created a summary score on the survey, and asked for the participants' voting intentions again (please see **lucs.lu.se/cbp** for a video illustration of the experiment).

What the results showed was that only 22% of the manipulated responses were corrected and that a full 92% of the participants accepted and endorsed the reversed political survey score. Furthermore, the final voter intention question indicated that as many as 48% (±9.2%) were willing to consider a left-right coalition shift. This can be contrasted with the established polls tracking the Swedish election, which registered a maximum of 10% of voters open to a swing across the partisan divide.

The authors conclude that political attitudes and partisan affiliations can be far more flexible than what is assumed by the polls, and that people can reason about the issues of the campaign with considerable openness to change. Commenting on the study, Lars Hall says, "It is comforting to know only $5 worth of paper and glue is required to make this point, rather than a billion dollar campaign industry. I believe our method is a terrific educational tool to dramatise the potential for political change."[4]

Knowing this, how long do you think it will be before someone is using the technique to manipulate voters?

Illusion of Understanding

Understanding the mind, and how and why people do what they do, is essential to successful propaganda. Indeed, the difference between good old scientific marketing methods using **GSR (Galvanic Skin Response)** readings, and modern neuromarketing methods employing fMRI (functional Magnetic Resonance Imaging), is only the state of technology.

As we learn more and more about human behavior, we gain the same sort of insight into questions of how and why as we do when we peer into the brain and watch it perform live in real time, as with fMRI (functional Magnetic Resonance Imaging). And quite often we gain this information as the result of surveys, psychological scales, and the like. Using online surveys as their tool, researchers at Leeds School of Business, University of Colorado, Boulder, sought to explore the elements that contributed to strong polarization in America today. What they learned was that extreme political views may stem from an "illusion of understanding."[5]

> "We wanted to know how it's possible that people can maintain such strong positions on issues that are so complex—such as macroeconomics, health care, foreign relations—and yet seem to be so ill-informed about those issues."[6]

The researchers asked subjects to explain their point of view.

As the researchers predicted, people reported lower understanding of all six policies after they had to explain them, and their positions on the policies were less extreme. In fact, the data showed that the more people's understanding decreased, the more uncertain they were about the position, and the less extreme their position was in the end.

The act of explaining also affected participants' behavior. People who initially held a strong position softened their position after having to explain it, making them less likely to donate bonus money to a related organization when they were given the opportunity to do so.

Importantly, the results affected people along the whole political spectrum, from self-identified Democrats to Republicans to Independents.

According to the researchers, these findings shed light on a psychological process that may help people to open the lines of communication in the context of a heated debate or negotiation.[7]

Now the question is, "How do we get people to explain their opinions in contrast to blindly arguing them?"

Hypermasculinity

As I have said before, sex and violence sell. The fact is, death, or the Thanatos urge, as Freud described it, plays a major role in the creation of ads. (If you wish to pursue this notion, the subject is thoroughly described, with actual examples from an advertising training manual, in my book *Mind Programming*.) For our purposes here, suffice it say that such daredevil activities as bungee jumping are death-defying acts some are driven to perform as their way of denying and even defeating death—the certainty we all live with but ignore as much as we can.

Now, new research shows us that aggressive attitudes are spawned in men as a result of aggressive advertising. It is believed that this occurs because some ads reinforce the idea of hypermasculinity, a term used for the exaggeration of male stereotypical behavior, such as an emphasis on strength, aggression, boldness, toughness, callous attitudes toward sex, and so forth. Studies of this behavior have shown a strong connection to such dangerous behaviors as driving while intoxicated, using drugs, fighting, and using violent behavior with women.

For the study, researchers analyzed ads in eight, high-circulation magazines marketed to men, from Golf Digest to Game Informer. Megan Vokey, a Ph.D. candidate at the University of Manitoba, and her colleagues considered only the ads where a photograph, picture, or symbol of a man was shown.

They then categorized these advertisements using the four components that constitute hypermasculinity.

They found that at least one of these hypermasculine attitudes was depicted in 56 percent of the total sample of 527 advertisements. In some magazines, this percentage was as high as 90 percent, according to the researchers.

Further analysis showed that magazines with the highest proportion of hypermasculine advertisements were those aimed at younger, less-affluent and less-educated men, according to the researchers.

The researchers argue that this is an "area of concern as young men are still learning appropriate gender behaviors, and their beliefs and attitudes can be subtly shaped by images" repeatedly shown in the mass media.

Additionally, men with lower social and economic power are more likely to use "a facade of toughness and physical violence as methods of gaining power and respect," the researchers note. The advertisements are thought to help reinforce the belief that this is desirable behavior, they add.

"The widespread depiction of hypermasculinity in men's magazine advertising may be detrimental to both men and society at large," the researchers conclude in the study, which was published in Springer's journal *Sex Roles*.

"Although theoretically, men as a group can resist the harmful aspects of hypermasculine images, the effects of such images cannot be escaped completely."[8]

The authors of this study suggest contacting advertisers and informing them of the negative possible effect of this form of advertisement. All I have to say about that is GOOD LUCK!

I may sound cynical, but in all my research, not once have I come across a finding that could be used to manipulate, motivate, and in other ways deliver compliance that actually went unused because it might have some negative effect.

Death Manipulations

Before leaving the subject of death, it's worth also mentioning that those behind the scenes who wish to own your thoughts, and who provide you with the sound bites you share around the water-cooler, know that our sense of mortality can lead us to change our political views. Indeed, contemplating our mortality can remind us of how important spirituality is in life and make us feel more grateful. "For instance, studies have shown that after people reflect on what will happen when they die, they become more nationalistic and defensive about their political beliefs."[9]

In one very interesting study, the intensity with which subjects sensed thoughts of death instigated a greater need to make larger donations to the needy. In this study, subjects unknowingly viewed subliminal primes. The primes varied in their emotional urgency by wrapping one death image in flames. This subliminal technique is now well known to those who might use it for their own purposes.[10]

It's not within the scope of this work to investigate thoroughly potential uses and abuses of subliminal technology. That said, it is worth pointing out that simple priming, the presentation of pictures or words at speeds so fast that the conscious mind fails to discriminate them, have been shown to influence attitudes towards countries and even move our values along some calculus of anchor points on a variety of subjects.

Gaming Effects

Many studies have revealed a positive correlation between some forms of gaming and an increase in aggressive behavior.

185

Computer games are no exception. There is a double-edged sword when it comes to computer games, however, as some studies have shown that playing these games increases hand-eye coordination and can lead to increased perceptual skills. Other computer games are designed to effectively increase various cognitive abilities ranging from memory to attention. For our context here, though, I'll address only first-person shooter games.

Changes in attitudes occur relatively quickly as a result of violent video games. In one study, attitudes toward alcohol, drugs, and car theft dramatically changed among young adults who played the game *Grand Theft Auto*.[11] In a 2012 study, inexperienced gamers showed their relative innocence in their shopping choices following game play. Termed the Macbeth effect, innocence has a "need to cleanse to keep moral purity intact."

> When participants were asked to select gift products after they had played a violent video game, inexperienced players selected more hygienic products, such as shower gel, toothpaste, and deodorant, compared to those who played violent video games more often. Inexperienced players also felt higher moral distress from playing violent games.[12]

In time, of course, this innocence becomes systematically desensitized, something we have already discussed.

Advergames

Now, while we are talking about video games, are you aware that some video games promote the consumption of unhealthy foods? Okay, we all know what an infomercial is, and most of us know what an advertorial is as well, but what about an advergame? That's right, an advergame is, in fact, a disguised advertisement for a product and is aimed specifically at children. These are usually free games promoted for the sole purpose of providing advertisers with new consumers.

> Not only do some online video games promote a less-than-active lifestyle for children, the content of some of these games also may be contributing to unhealthy diets. A team of Michigan State University researchers took a closer

look at what are called advergames and found they have a tendency to promote foods that are chock full of fat, sugar, and sodium.

An advergame is defined as an online video game that promotes a particular product, service, or company by integrating it into the game, and is typically offered for free.

The researchers located hundreds of advergames actively played by children on food marketer websites. For the study, they focused on 145 different websites and found 439 food brands being promoted through advergames on those sites.

What they found was that many of the games centered around high-fat, high-sugar, and high-sodium products.

"One of the things we were concerned about was that the majority of foods that received the most interest were those that tended to be energy dense—high in calories— and not high in nutrients," said Lorraine Weatherspoon, a co-director of the project and an associate professor of food science and human nutrition. "These foods typically included high-sugar snacks and cereals as well as instant or canned soups, sugar-sweetened beverages and several types of candy products."

The games are quick and easy to play. They use brand names, logos, pictures of the product, and even a spokescharacter as a part of the game.

"Compared to a typical TV commercial that would last maybe 30 seconds, these games are fun and engaging, and children can play them for much longer periods of time," said Elizabeth Taylor Quilliam, project co-director and assistant professor of advertising and public relations.

The researchers noted there are no consistent standards for what can or cannot be marketed to children and how the marketing should be done.[13]

CONCLUSION

We now see that the power of suggestion goes a lot further than simply our reactions to things we are told. The suggestive themes can be so subtle as to be almost subliminal, but suggestion still has great power to tweak our values, choices, and more. Oftentimes these suggestions can have far-reaching additional consequences that were never intended. But, as I said earlier, when has a proven motivational tactic not been used because of some negative side effect? Unlike food and drugs, no agency is responsible for policing the power of suggestion. It is up to each of us to be aware.

Does any of this surprise you? By now, you may find yourself expecting more nefarious means and schemes designed to 'aid' your every decision. What steps can you take to negate or minimize this influence? How often have you seen these tools deployed in advertising? How about in politics? How about in your own family or among your friends and peers? Robert Laing, the British psychiatrist, once wrote a book titled *Knots*. A line from the book sticks with me and seems appropriate at this moment. Paraphrased some, Laing said this: "I see that they are playing a game, but if I let them know that they are playing a game, they will not allow me to play." How do you end manipulation in your own family or among your friends and peers and still be able to play with them?

Participating in the world while still holding onto your own individuality can be a really tricky business, but the rewards are immense. Inner conflict is often the evidence that we are not being true to ourselves. Learn who you are and neutralize any attempts to turn you into mere automatons!

CHAPTER FIFTEEN

Attention

*Suspicions that the mind, of itself, gathers, are but buzzes;
but suspicions that are artificially nourished and put into men's
heads by the tales and whisperings of others, have stings.*

~Francis Bacon, Sr.

Misconception: *Most people believe they are above the power of suggestion and indeed immediately recognize it for what it is.*
Fact: *The fact is, suggestion rules! Everyone is subject to suggestion
and those who understand this can use it to puppet almost anyone.*

Did you ever wonder why some things on YouTube or some
ideas on the Internet get so much attention? The answer may
well be in ourselves, as shown by the results of a study that peered
into how the brain becomes interested in spreading an idea.

UCLA psychologists have taken a significant step toward
answering these questions, identifying for the first time the
brain regions associated with the successful spread of ideas,
often called "buzz."

The research has a broad range of implications, the
study authors say, and could lead to more effective public
health campaigns, more persuasive advertisements, and better ways for teachers to communicate with students.

"Our study suggests that people are regularly attuned

to how the things they're seeing will be useful and interesting, not just to themselves but to other people," said the study's senior author, Matthew Lieberman, a UCLA professor of psychology, psychiatry and biobehavioral sciences and author of the forthcoming book *Social: Why Our Brains Are Wired to Connect.* "We always seem to be on the lookout for who else will find this helpful, amusing, or interesting, and our brain data are showing evidence of that. At the first encounter with information, people are already using the brain network involved in thinking about how this can be interesting to other people. We're wired to want to share information with other people. I think that is a profound statement about the social nature of our minds."

"Before this study, we didn't know what brain regions were associated with ideas that become contagious, and we didn't know what regions were associated with being an effective communicator of ideas," said lead author Emily Falk, who conducted the research as a UCLA doctoral student in Lieberman's lab and is currently a faculty member at the University of Pennsylvania's Annenberg School for Communication. "Now we have mapped the brain regions associated with ideas that are likely to be contagious and are associated with being a good 'idea salesperson.' In the future, we would like to be able to use these brain maps to forecast what ideas are likely to be successful and who is likely to be effective at spreading them."[1]

And I wonder who will be the first to use this information for personal gain—or has it already been used? Barack Obama and his team are considered to be the masters of the grassroots campaign. During the elections in 2008 and 2012, there was no shortage of young people willing to pound the streets, even to the point of incapacitating blisters, in their fervor to spread a message they believed would help others.

Blinded by Attention

You may be familiar with the famous YouTube video of a group of people playing basketball. This video also includes a gorilla that goes unnoticed by almost all viewers. (If you haven't seen that video, I suggest visiting this website for more information as well as the video: **bigthink.com/videos/missing-the-200-pound-gorilla-in-the-room.**) Research refers to this form of attentional blindness as "inattentional blindness." In fact, researchers have shown that even when trained specialists are concentrating on something, they will fail to see anything they are not looking for.

> When engaged in a demanding task, attention can act like a set of blinders, making it possible for stimuli to pass, undetected, right in front of our eyes," explained Trafton Drew, Ph.D., post-doctoral researcher at BWH and lead author on this study. "We found that even experts are vulnerable to this phenomenon."
>
> "This study helps illustrate that what we become focused on becomes the center of our world, and it shapes what we can and cannot see."[2]

This tactic, too, is often used in politics. Drown the public with information on some supposedly critical subject while slipping something else past them!

Noise

Years ago I was asked to develop sounds for slot machines that would increase both the attraction and the time played. The more I worked on this project, the clearer it became that the sound of money spilling from the machines was the best. After all, that was exactly what the player was seeking. So the sound of coins falling into a metal bowl was the answer I settled upon.

My findings were confirmed in a study reported in the *Journal of Gambling Studies,* and a new twist was added: "Winning sounds on slot machines make gambling more exciting, according to a new study by Mike Dixon and colleagues from the University of Waterloo in Canada. Moreover, their work shows that sounds also cause players to overestimate the number of times they won while playing on slot machines."[3]

Music Animals

What would you say if you learned that sounds mimicking the vocalizations of animals in distress excited human attention? Indeed, at least one study suggests that the reason rock 'n' roll music is exciting is due to precisely this factor.[4]

The noise of animals in distress is a distortion in sound. While you may be familiar with David Koresh and the Waco, Texas matter, you're probably not aware that distorted music/sounds and subliminal messages were blasted at the Koresh compound by the FBI before the bloody massacre. Why do you think that tactic was used?

Background Noise

According to new research, moderate background noise "enhances creativity and makes consumers more likely to buy new and innovative products."

> "For individuals looking for creative solutions to daily problems, instead of burying oneself in a quiet room trying to figure out a solution, walking out of one's comfort zone and getting into a relatively noisy environment (such as a café) may trigger the brain to think abstractly, and thus generate creative ideas," write the authors [of the study].
>
> The authors also found that consumers were more likely to choose an innovative product over a traditional one when there was a moderate level of background noise. For example, consumers were much more likely to choose a pair of running shoes with new and innovative features over a standard pair at this optimal level of background noise.
>
> "A moderate level of noise not only enhances creativity but also leads to greater adoption of innovative products. In order to encourage adoption of new and innovative products, companies might consider equipping their showrooms with a moderate level of ambient noise," the authors conclude.[5]

Perhaps that is why most political rallies use loud, cheerful music. If you stop and think about it, many individuals running for office are a little older, at an age when most people prefer quieter, less energetic music.

CONCLUSION

Once again we learn of yet another sense that can be unconsciously tweaked, thereby motivating an action, eliciting an emotion, identifying a feeling that enlarges in a thought and predisposing our judgment.

Our every sense can lead to responses that infer meaning and influence judgment. Meeting a stranger holding a warm cup of coffee has been shown to lead to judging the person favorably while meeting a stranger with an iced coffee leads to judging the person less favorably[6] Why? Think about it. One is warm and the other is cold—warm coffee verses cold coffee. Something this simple and obvious to the trained person can lead to a determination based on the contrivance of who knows the most about manipulation. How does that make you feel? If you are unaware of the power of these mechanisms, then you are powerless against them. But that is the purpose of this book. Become aware and take back your own choices! Again, become proactive, informed, share the information, make the subject of this book the talk around the water cooler or the coffee table at home. You deserve to know your own machinery—that wonderful mind and body you presently inhabit. Your loved ones, friends, neighbors, and everyone else deserve to maximize their potential and not just serve the means of others intent on selling you a proposition, a product, or some political platform or candidate.

Conditioning

It is no measure of health to be well adjusted
to a profoundly sick society.
~ Jiddu Krishnamurti

Misconception: *Most people believe they are principled people and once they take a moral position, they stand by it.*
Fact: *Most people compromise their values and moral positions on a daily basis.*

Remember the classic conditioning method developed by Ivan Pavlov? He rang a bell as he dispensed food to the dogs, and after a certain number of repetitions, the dog salivated at the sound of the bell alone. The association is, of course, with sound. But did you know that you can be conditioned to a visual image as well?

Our visual perception is not determined solely by retinal activity. Other factors also influence the processing of visual signals in the brain. "Selective attention is one such factor," says Professor Wim Vanduffel. "The more attention you pay to a stimulus, the better your visual perception is and the more effective your visual cortex is at processing that stimulus. Another factor is the reward value of a stimulus; when a visual signal becomes associated with a reward, it affects our processing of that visual signal. In this study, we wanted to investigate how a reward influences activity in the visual cortex."

(Brain) activations were not spread throughout the whole visual system but were instead confined to the specific brain regions responsible for processing the exact stimulus used earlier during conditioning. This result shows that information about rewards is being sent to the visual cortex to indicate which stimuli have been associated with rewards.

Equally surprising, these reward-only trials were found to strengthen the cue-reward associations. This is more or less the equivalent to giving Pavlov's dog an extra treat after a conditioning session and noticing the next day that he salivates twice as much as before. More generally, this result suggests that rewards can be associated with stimuli over longer time scales than previously thought.[1]

Now, just to be certain I do not leave you with an ambiguity, I believe that this sort of conditioning can be achieved using operant conditioning methods (a type of learning in which an individual's behavior is modified by its consequences). The primary difference between the two, for purposes relative to this context, is that operant conditioning is aimed at voluntary behaviors whereas the classic conditioning focuses on involuntary behaviors.

Giving

Did you know that you are less likely to give, and when you do, to give less, when you are in a group than when you are alone? This effect is not unlike the Genovese Effect, discussed earlier, where a group of people ignored a brutal murder in progress, each expecting someone else to intervene, or choosing not to put themselves at risk if no one else would! Research has consistently shown that individuals are less likely to help when they are in a group, and the larger the group, the greater the "less likely" coefficient becomes.

In a study carried out at the University of Missouri, researchers found that,

Even when multiple individuals can contribute to a common cause, the presence of others reduces an individual's likelihood of helping. This research has numerous applications, including possibly guiding the fundraising strategies of charitable organizations.

"In our study, individuals who didn't want to share money tended to influence others to not share money," said Karthik Panchanathan, assistant professor of anthropology in the College of Arts and Science. "We don't know what psychological mechanism caused that, but perhaps potential givers did not want to be 'suckers,' who gave up their money while someone else got away with giving nothing. Selfish behavior in others may have given individuals an opportunity to escape any moral obligation to share that they might have felt."[2]

Irrational Group Behavior

Speaking of the power of groups and particularly the notion of selfishness—which fits well into the compliance principle known as scarcity, something we will discuss in greater detail later—what do you suppose happens when the perception of an individual is that something is extremely popular with the group and in limited supply? I'm sure you guessed correctly: The individual may pay more than an item is worth just because of this pressure. Enter a truly interesting finding:

> Web tools and social media are our key sources of information when we make decisions as citizens and consumers. But these information technologies can mislead us by magnifying social processes that distort facts and make us act contrary to our own interests—such as buying property at wildly inflated prices because we are led to believe that everybody else is. New research from the University of Copenhagen, which has just been published in the journal *Metaphilosophy*, combines formal philosophy, social psychology, and decision theory to understand and tackle these phenomena.
>
> "Group behavior that encourages us to make decisions based on false beliefs has always existed. However, with the

advent of the Internet and social media, this kind of behavior is more likely to occur than ever, and on a much larger scale, with possibly severe consequences for the democratic institutions underpinning the information societies we live in," says professor of philosophy at the University of Copenhagen Vincent F. Hendricks.[3]

Some of those consequences are already being exerted on the people of the world. Can you think of some examples?

Materialism and Work

Some of us are old enough to be able to see several decades of development in the United States and the changing attitudes toward many things, including good old-fashioned hard work. When I was a boy, hard work was valued. *Work* was a positive word. Work meant that you had a job, that you were earning your way, and that you had some buying power—you were worth your salt, so to speak. More and more today, *work* has become a negative word.

There are those who feel that hard work is beneath them: "We need immigrant workers to do those jobs." Many are convinced that they can visualize their wealth and it will appear—magically! People will believe almost anything if it fits with their desires!

Recently one young woman approached my company for a gift. In an unabashed way, she simply said she would like us to give her a $50 item because she has a website all about just asking. *Ask and you shall receive.* Now I have some knowledge as to how this sort of ploy can work on your psyche, so when my staff asked me about this request, I checked out the woman.

We regularly give to those in need, the poor and the helpless and those whose hearts have been ravaged by loss or disease. Indeed, there are programs that are free to anyone for the asking on one of my websites, **www.innertalk.com**, and they are all posted conspicuously under Free MP3s. One associate suggested that we simply point out to the woman that our donations are of a charitable nature and that she is not in need of charity. I considered the suggestion for a moment and then recommended that we ask the woman what she could do for us to pay for the item. How could she work off the price? I believe she simply chose to purchase the item!

Work is not a nasty word to me. It still has meaning, and my success, whatever that might be, has been a combination of those who believed in me and in my willingness to work twelve- to fourteen-hour days, seven days a week, if necessary.

In a study published by *Personality and Social Psychology Bulletin*, researchers Jean M. Twenge, a San Diego State University psychology professor, and Tim Kasser, a professor of psychology at Knox College, determined that there was an increasing gap between the willingness of teens to work and their growing materialistic appetite.

Compared to baby boomers graduating from high school in the 1970s, recent high school students are more materialistic—62 percent of students surveyed in 2005–'07 think it's important to have a lot of money, while just 48 percent had the same belief in 1976–'78.

Sixty-nine percent of recent high school graduates thought it was important to own a home, compared to just 55 percent in 1976–'78. Materialism peaked in the '80s and '90s with Generation X and has continued to stay high.

As for work ethic, 39 percent of students surveyed in 2005–'07 admitted they didn't want to work hard, compared to only 25 percent in 1976–'78.

The researchers also found that adolescents' materialism was highest when advertising spending made up a greater percentage of the U.S. economy.

"This suggests that advertising may play a crucial role in the development of youth materialism," said Twenge. "It also might explain the gap between materialism and the work ethic, as advertising rarely shows the work necessary to earn the money necessary to pay for the advertised products."

Understanding generational trends in materialism among youth is important because placing a strong priority on money and possessions is associated with a variety of problems, including depression and anxiety, according to earlier research performed by Kasser.

"This study shows how the social environment shapes adolescents' attitudes," said Twenge. "When family life and economic conditions are unstable, youth may turn to material things for comfort. And when our society funds large amounts of advertising, youth are more likely to believe that 'the good life' is 'the goods life.'"[4]

This finding can also help explain why politicians so often run, and win, on a platform based on what they will give you. Long gone are the days of John F. Kennedy and his famous words: "Ask not what your country can do for you . . . ask what you can do for your country."

Market Erosion of Values

What do you think when you hear of young children working ten-hour days in sweat factories turning out goods? How do you feel when you hear of animal cruelty in connection with farming methods? How do you respond when shopping and you find an item at one store that is $100 more than the same item is at another? Well, this next gotcha is worth including.

Many people express objections against child labor, exploitation of the workforce, or meat production involving cruelty against animals. At the same time, however, people ignore their own moral standards when acting as market participants, searching for the cheapest electronics, fashion, or food. Thus, markets reduce moral concerns. This is the main result of an experiment conducted by economists from the Universities of Bonn and Bamberg.[5]

How important is this sort of consistency to you? Or is it an acceptable form of dissonance that some of us choose to ignore?

CONCLUSION

What would happen if we stopped being swayed by the power of the group, if we all spoke our own truth and acted in a way that honored our highest self? Oftentimes unacceptable behavior becomes acceptable by the mere fact that 'everyone is doing it.' What could you change about the way you live that would make you feel happier about the person you are? For myself, I cannot help but smile when I think of the amazing good we could do as a country if everyone lived with honor and integrity. Are you up to the challenge of being the first to live this way in your community?

Perception

There are things known and there are things unknown,
and in between are the doors of perception.
~Aldous Huxley

Misconception: *Most people believe they are principled people and once they take a moral position, they stand by it.*
Fact: *Most people compromise their values and moral positions on a daily basis.*

Understanding the various nuances of our human nature could feasibly take a lifetime. If it's understanding ourselves, I am convinced that it is a lifetime journey, for we are not static individuals living in a vacuum—at least those of us who have our eyes wide open, so to speak, and have chosen to become fully awake to ourselves and to the world around us in which our lives unfold every day.

One of my favorite things to do is confuse an audience with the many ways in which they fail to understand their own perceptual mechanisms. I will often show illusions in which audience members see something that isn't there (or fail to see something that is there), or they report hearing something totally different from what was said, or that they see movement in a still picture. One of the studies I recently came across demonstrates that an impoitant element underlying perceptual confusion has to do with imagination. This study showed that imagination could change what we see and hear.

> "This is the first set of experiments to definitively establish that the sensory signals generated by one's imagination are strong enough to change one's real-world perception of a different sensory modality," says Professor Henrik Ehrsson, the principal investigator behind the study.[1]

I wonder how long it will be before this finding is used in marketing or politics?

Hunger

My mother told me never to go grocery shopping when I was hungry, and yours probably said the same thing to you. She was convinced that this behavior would lead to making unsound buying decisions—and from my experience, she is absolutely right! But what would you say if I told you that not only does hunger affect decision-making, but it can also impair our perception of risk? The fact is, when you are hungry, you are more likely to take certain types of risks than when your belly is full.[2]

Honest or Dishonest

Are you aware that the physical setting in which you find yourself can influence the likelihood of dishonest behavior? It has been demonstrated than an expansive environment, such as a large desk or a lot of room behind the steering wheel in your automobile, seems to increase an individual's sense of power. This sense of power can lead to feelings that increase the likelihood of such behaviors as those we see in white-collar crime: cheating, stealing, lying, and of course, traffic violations.

> "In everyday working and living environments, our body postures are incidentally expanded and contracted by our surroundings—by the seats in our cars, the furniture in and around workspaces, even the hallways in our offices—and these environments directly influence the propensity of dishonest behavior in our everyday lives," said Andy Yap, a key

author of the research who spearheaded its development during his time at Columbia Business School.[3]

Does this observation suggest that richer people are more likely to be dishonest because they are always surrounded by bigger things, or do they become immune to it? Would a poor person placed in a rich, expansive environment be more likely to commit a dishonest act? Or are we all more likely to be dishonest when out in the big wide world than when we are in our own homes and communities?

Seating Arrangements

Marketing people and public figures are very well aware of the effect of seating arrangements on the psychology of those attending a gathering. There are a number of websites and even software specially designed to assist in seating arrangements for everything from the private, personal gathering to the very public political event. And the seating arrangement does matter! For example, consumers feel a greater need to belong when they are seated in a circular as opposed to an angular layout.[4]

> "The geometric shape of a seating arrangement can impact consumers by priming one of two fundamental needs: a need to belong or a need to be unique. Consumers will be most favorable toward persuasion material (advertising) that is consistent with the primed need," write authors Rui (Juliet) Zhu (University of British Columbia) and Jennifer J. Argo (University of Alberta).[5]

The geometry of persuasion is important. Consider this observation:

> The professors performing the study took it a step further and wanted to find out how the participants would respond to promotional material while sitting at different shaped tables, and if there would be any difference in reaction. They found that volunteers who were sitting at the round or oval tables "reacted more favorably towards ads that conveyed a sense of belonging, showing groups of family members or friends," while volunteers at the angu-

lai tables "identified more with ads portraying go-getting individuals—'maverick' types."[6]

The next time you enter an event, look at the seating arrangement. Pay attention to the purpose of the meeting. What is intended? At the last one I attended, the seats were arranged in a circle, and the event sought donations from the group. I noted to myself, a group tends to diminish donation size and yet the circular arrangement tends to encourage belonging and identifying with the group's purpose. I doubt the organizers were really aware of these dynamics, but if you must raise money from a group, what better way to do it?

Search Engines

What if the information collected by search engines could determine an election? Would that, in turn, lead a democracy to prosper? I mentioned these questions earlier, but it is appropriate to provide some additional details here. The fact is, researchers have discovered that search engines can be manipulated in various ways to achieve desired objectives.

Dr. Robert Epstein, [who by the way was also a member of the President's Dream Team, which we will discuss later] senior research psychologist at the American Institute for Behavioral Research and Technology, (reported on) the latest study, which he will present at the Association for Psychological Science Convention in May.

"We've discovered that search engine rankings can be manipulated in ways that dramatically change voter preferences," Epstein told PBS NewsHour's Hari Sreenivasan in a Google Hangout on Friday.

In the study, Epstein and his team used a mock search engine, real material from Australia's 2010 prime ministerial election and three different test groups. When the study's participants looked up candidates on the search engine, one test group found search rankings favorable to candidate Tony Abbott, the second found rankings favorable to opposing candidate Julia Gillard, and the last group had rankings that didn't favor either candidate. Epstein found that the differing results could influence people to vote for one candidate over the other by margins of 15 percent or more. "What we are showing is . . . search rankings alone can shift people," he said.[7]

I, for one, find this last snippet particularly disturbing. How much manipulation has already occurred through the use of this technique? Here is a quote from the wonderful fiction book *Lexicon* by Max Barry that is particularly apropos as this point:

> The key to the Web is it's interactive. That's the difference. Online, someone visits your site. You can have a little poll there. It says, 'Hey, what do you think about the tax cuts?' And people click and segment themselves. First advantage right there. You're not just proselytizing, speaking into the void. You're getting data back. But here's the really clever part. Your site isn't static. It's dynamically generated. Do you know what that means?"
>
> "No."
>
> "It means the site looks different to different people. Let's say you chose the poll option that said you're in favor of tax cuts. Well there's a cookie on your machine now, and when you look at the site again, the articles are about how the government is wasting your money. The site is dynamically selecting content based on what you want. I mean, not what you want. What will piss you off? What will engage your attention and reinforce your beliefs, make you trust the site. And if you said you were against tax cuts, we'll show you stories of Republicans blocking social programs or whatever. It works every which way. Your site is made of mirrors, reflecting everyone's thoughts back at them. That's pretty great, right?"
>
> "It's great."
>
> "And we haven't even started talking about keywords. This is just the beginning. Third major advantage: People who use a site like this tend to ramp up their dependence on it. Suddenly all those other news sources, the ones that aren't framing every story in terms of the user's core beliefs, they start to seem confusing and strange. They start to seem biased, actually, which is kind of funny. So now you've got

a user who not only trusts you, you're his major source of information on what's happening in the world. Boom, you own that guy. You can tell him whatever you like and no one's contradicting you.[8]

CONCLUSION

From this chapter we discover and can infer at this point, that every tiny detail involving some events has been carefully choreographed. When next you attend or see a political rally, pay particular attention to how everything is staged. How many manipulative means can you identify? When your own perception can be confused and manipulated, it can be difficult to know what exactly you would have chosen under different circumstances. Research, ranging from the seating arrangement at an event to the placements in search engines, shows repeatedly how those with the knowledge can influence your choices. Having the knowledge of these kinds of persuasive techniques is the only way you can protect yourself from them. When you see through these tactics, you are in a much stronger position to make choices that are in line with your own values. If everyone were to do this, I wonder what effect this would have on the country. I tend to think we would all be happier as a result.

Political Strategies

I'm not upset that you lied to me,
I'm upset that from now on I can't believe you.
~Friedrich Nietzsche

Misconception: *Most people believe they are fair-minded and objective when it comes to weighing in on important matters.*
Fact: *The fact is, most people are strongly opinionated, and their emotions often get the best of them in expressing those opinions.*

Upton Sinclair dubbed Campaigns Incorporated (the first political consulting firm, founded in 1933 by Clem Whitaker and Leone Baxter) the Lie Factory after Sinclair lost his attempt to become governor of California in 1934. As he described the event, "They had a staff of political chemists at work, preparing poisons to be let loose in the California atmosphere on every one of a hundred mornings."[1]

It is often thought that political advertising is the child of merchant advertising, but it is more likely the other way around. Influence has always been about the story; propaganda creates the characters and frames their adventures. The public—well, everyone likes a good story, whether it's true or not!

GOTCHA!

News

Two well-respected early television anchors were Chet Huntley and David Brinkley, and their show, the *Huntley-Brinkley Report,* was on air from 1956 to 1970. During those years, television was still gaining a foothold in most homes in America, but agendas were as common then as they are now. Huntley and Brinkley had their agenda, and in a rare moment of candor actually confessed to having had a part in assisting President Lyndon Johnson to defeat Republican challenger Barry Goldwater in 1964. Author and constitutionalist Cleon Skousen wrote:

> As this reviewer watched this *Huntley-Brinkley Special Report,* it was difficult to understand why these dedicated employees of the power-complex media would admit how popular Goldwater had been and he would have won the election if their propaganda efforts had not been so effective. However, Brinkley explained toward the end of the program why it is important for the 'liberal, progressive' element of the country to appreciate that even though they had won the election, they had not changed the 'conservative mood' at the grassroots. He said President Johnson would therefore have an uphill pull to get many of his 'progressive' bills passed through Congress (just as the Democratic Congress had initially bucked President Kennedy's Socialist legislation) unless all the liberal-progressive element firmly united to overcome the conservative, grassroots resistance.[2]

Negative and Positive Freedom

Generally two types of freedom are discussed when it comes to the philosophy underlying our political establishment and the freedoms guaranteed by our Constitution, and for that matter, by the constitutions of free peoples around the world. Those two types of freedom are negative freedom and positive freedom. Distinguishing between the two goes back as far as Immanuel Kant, but for most modern purposes, it is the work of British philosopher Isaiah Berlin that draws attention. Berlin's writings during the 1950s and '60s discussed the two types of freedom as not only distinct from each other but competitive.

"Political liberalism tends to presuppose a negative definition of liberty; liberals generally claim that if one favors
individual liberty one should place strong limitations on the
activities of the state. Critics of liberalism often contest this
implication by contesting the negative definition of liberty;
they argue that the pursuit of liberty understood as self-realization or as self-determination (whether of the individual
or of the collectivity) can require state intervention of a
kind not normally allowed by liberals."[3]

According to Berlin, then, positive freedom provides for the
freedom to direct one's own life while negative freedom is based
on the idea of noninterference. Negative freedom involves acceptable limits on the levels and kind of interference the state
can put on the individual, whereas positive freedom is all about
what individuals can do by way of governing their own lives as opposed to restrictions per se.

Berlin and others often use examples to make this distinction
clearer. The examples typically call upon what you might think of
as the difference between a higher and a lower self. Let's say that
one self is driven to smoke cigarettes, and the other self feels tor-
mented and wishes to stop smoking. Positive freedom allows the
smoker to smoke despite the long-term negative consequences
inherent in this activity. Now let us assume a person is a heavy
drinker. The state allows the drinker to drink but puts limitations
on activities while intoxicated, such as drinking and driving. In
this example, there is a crossover between positive and negative
freedom. To ensure others' freedom from drunk drivers, the the
freedom of the drinker to drive while intoxicated is restricted.
Sometimes, however, these freedoms come into conflict. Assume
the state decides that a substance is too dangerous to consume.
Take marijuana as an example. A positive freedom would allow
the use of marijuana, perhaps subject to the same or substantially similar restrictions as those placed on the use and possession of alcohol. Negative freedom with respect to marijuana use
protects nonusers from interference in their lives, just as with
alcohol; others argue that the state has an interest in protecting

211

the health of the state's citizens (the state's role in public health, education, and welfare).

The conflict should be obvious. When the positive freedom to use tobacco fails to be in the best interest of the individual, perhaps then the state steps in and restricts that freedom in the name of a greater good. We are all faced with choices every day. Nations are likewise faced with choices. Should a dissenting person be treated as a traitor or as a whistleblower? Should a peaceful protest be allowed outside the convention hall of a political gathering or should it be broken up even if it means making arrests, thereby depriving protestors the right to assemble? I could go on, but the idea is clear: individuals and states alike make choices every day, presumably in their best interest.

When is it appropriate for someone, the state in most cases, to decide what is ultimately in the best interest of individuals or groups when values conflict? Should the smoker's higher self have the power to override the lower self's right to smoke? Many would say yes. We all recognize the priority of values here; however, not all conflicting values can be prioritized in so mutually agreeable a way.

Indentured Servitude

American philosopher Robert Nozik, for example, is famous for arguing that taxation is neither more nor less than a form of indentured servitude, or slavery. In 2013, fewer than 50 percent of the American population paid federal taxes, and yet the federal tax dollar is the primary support for most government aid programs. Does this mean that the hardworking, taxpaying citizens are slaves to those who benefit from these tax dollars? If so, why? Who makes this decision? We all would like to help the needy and those less fortunate than ourselves, but is that really where the tax dollars go? Consider this—the great food stamp binge:

> It was during an investigation into the record number of food stamp recipients that Fox News' John Roberts met Jason Greenslate, a surfer and rocker who is living the self-described "rat life" in California.

212

The 29-year-old signed up for SNAP and receives $200 a month in taxpayer money for food. He put it simply, "I don't got a paycheck coming in, so I qualify."

All he has to do is provide his birth certificate and Social Security card and fill out a form once a year.

In 1996, if you were an able adult with no family, you would only qualify for food stamps for three months every three years. President Obama wiped away those restrictions when he signed the 2009 stimulus bill. In 2010, the president used his regulatory powers to extend the suspension of the welfare-to-work requirements.

Greenslate is trained to be a recording engineer, but he told Roberts he has no paycheck because holding down a steady job isn't for him.

So, it was off to the gourmet section of the grocery store, as Greenslate purchased sushi and lobster with his EBT card. "All paid for by our wonderful tax dollars," he said, telling Roberts that's what he typically buys.

"This is the way I want to live and I don't really see anything changing," Greenslate said. "It's free food; it's awesome."[4]

How does that story make you feel? What sort of freedom is this? Is this sort of thing unusual? Have you heard about "free phones?"

The devices issued through the Lifeline program have often been referred to as "Obama phones" and critics have questioned whether the program is a good way to spend taxpayers' money.

Jillian Kay Melchior of the National Review has shed some light on the program after she says she received not one, not two, but three free cell phones through the program, despite clearly being unable to qualify.

She said she noticed that vendors are actively trying to sell "free phones" at locations where low-income residents can sign up for food stamps. Even though she said she was not on welfare, she was still able to sign up for a free phone eight times, and subsequently received three phones.

Melchior says FCC rules stipulate that you can only get one free phone per household, but the vendors are not following that rule.

"[The vendors said] 'Don't worry, it's okay, you can have one phone from every single vendor participating in the program,' and it turns out that's just not true," she said, pointing out that every person who uses a cell phone can look at their monthly bill and see a small "universal service" tax that goes to support the government's "free phone" effort.[5]

How much of our hard-earned and tax-sacrificed dollars are we talking about going to waste and fraud? Are these stories typical, or do pundits opposed to the present administration exaggerate them in the media?

"According to the report in 2011 the United States spent $1.028 trillion on welfare, which is more than the states and federal government spent on Social Security, Non-Military Defense, or Medicare. The federal spending on welfare entitlements now accounts for one-fifth of the federal budget and consumes over 5% of the GDP."[6]

Of this, the estimate for fraud is rather low in terms of percentages.

"If the fraud rate is only 2%-3%, how much money could it really be costing us? Well . . . these low rates would mean that roughly 785,000 to 1.2 million families are illegally receiving welfare benefits. At the average rate of $11,500 per year, this is costing the taxpayers between $9.0–$13.5 billion every year."[7]

Those who pay attention to matters of the budget on the news are probably surprised at this low number. The reason is that this number is usually inflated by those people/groups who would like to roll back welfare programs. The 2 to 3 percent number should not be the principal issue we consider, however. The real issue is, who decides to put working taxpayers in servitude to the programs non-taxpaying citizens take advantage of?

The competition between the types of freedom we have discussed spells opportunity for government to act in ways that may appear to be helpful while in reality they lead to the loss of more freedom. In that way, the question may well be more one of redefining freedom than one of the discussion between the types of freedom. Perhaps freedom will become an illusion perpetrated by propaganda, and meanwhile, I'll assume myself to be free because I will still be able to choose between working or surfing and be assured that I will not starve.

Global Warming

A number of hotly debated issues face the world's population today. One of them is the matter of global warming. Many scientists agree that global warming is man-made. A few argue that it is a natural cycle and will not last. Computer models rolled out several years ago indicated that the Arctic would be ice-free come the summer of 2013. In 2007, this forecast led to headlines around the world:

> Scientists in the U.S. have presented one of the most dramatic forecasts yet for the disappearance of Arctic sea ice. Their latest modelling studies indicate northern polar waters could be ice-free in summers within just 5–6 years. Professor Wieslaw Maslowski told an American Geophysical Union meeting that previous projections had underestimated the processes now driving ice loss.[8]

By 2013, however, there was a rather massive expansion of the ice in the Arctic. Indeed, it was an increase of more than 60 percent![9]

Those who objected to the notion of man-made global warming were quick to jump on this report and call the global alarmists hoaxsters with a hidden agenda, a political motive, and so forth. Those who defended man-made global warming theories countered with explanations of why the computer models failed. A new model was published to show that the warming effect caused the massive ice increase because the melt created cold-water plumes in the oceans.

> According to a new study published in Nature Geoscience, every year the edges of the Antarctic thaw, sending more and more melting ice out into the ocean. That melted water forms large cold-water plumes in the ocean, which,

according to the study, "shields the surface ocean from the warmer deeper waters that are melting the ice shelves." As temperatures drop in the winter, these cold-water plumes refreeze, adding to the ice in the Antarctic.

The study cautions that while the ice formation in the Antarctic seems to be increasing, the overall melt across the planet is still contributing to a rise in sea level overall. Additionally, the ice below the surface in the Antarctic is still melting as quickly as ever. Recent studies also indicate that while the ice may be increasing on one side, the other side of the Antarctic is decreasing, leading to a reduction in total mass overall.[10]

This issue is a perfect example of the conflicting information we must deal with in coming to conclusions about what is really going on in the world. Scientists are not infallible, nor are they above peer pressure and illicit motives. Ethical considerations aside, scientists can also have their own biases, and their psychology is not any different from yours: They are not immune to the many compliance principles and other subtle means known to have a powerful influence in engineering consent.

Some have documented how scientists who disagree with the establishment, those with government tax dollar support behind them, face ever-diminishing opportunities. Richard Lindsen, in *Climate of Fear: Global-Warming Alarmists Intimidate Dissenting Scientists into Silence,* wrote:

> Scientists who dissent from the alarmism [over global warming] have seen their grant funds disappear, their work derided, and themselves libeled as industry stooges, scientific hacks, or worse. Consequently, lies about climate change gain credence even when they fly in the face of the science that supposedly is their basis . . . In Europe, Henk Tennekes was dismissed as research director of the Royal Dutch Meteorological Society after questioning the scientific underpinnings of global warming. Aksel Winn-Nielsen, former director of the U.N.'s World Meteorological Organization, was tarred by Bert Bolin, first head of the IPCC, as a tool of the coal industry for questioning climate alarmism. Respected Italian

professors Alfonso Sutera and Antonio Speranza disappeared from the debate in 1991, apparently losing climate-research funding for raising questions.[11]

When dissenting views are marginalized in this way, there is no possibility of new ideas. Had that been the case in centuries past, we could still believe the Earth is flat or that the sun revolves around the Earth. And this demonstrates two problems: One is our desire to defend a belief in spite of contrary evidence, and the other is the ability of those in power to give us the beliefs they want us to have.

How do we ascertain whether someone is being correctly reprimanded for incorrect or inappropriate behavior, or whether it is the intent of a few to keep you believing the politically correct way?

Mean What You Say?

The science of political advertising holds some interesting information about how we respond to ads, both positive and negative. Typically, those positive ads showing the flag blowing in the wind, young mothers with their smiling babies, open-collared politicians hobnobbing in the local eatery, and so forth, tend to bring about short-term results. So a positive image-building ad might be counted on to bump that candidate's numbers for a week or so.

Now, despite how much complaining the public registers about negative ads, compare the results of a negative ad to the results of the positive ad. First, attack ads can break through party lines and even attract independents more than positive ads. Next, the effect of negative ads is much more long lasting. In addition, it gains traction when done properly by way of the word-of-mouth sharing that goes with it. Think about it: When was the last time you gathered at the water fountain with colleagues to discuss a positive ad? How many times have you cited a negative ad as a reason not to vote for someone?[12]

And there is another big payoff. A good attack ad can gain the attention of the media and thereby give a lot of free publicity to the candidate, even if it is a subtle tactic like placing a subliminal message in the ad. The now infamous RATS ad (mentioned earlier when we discussed the TV series *The West Wing*) is one such example. During the Bush/Gore campaign, the Bush people ran an advertisement that pulled the word RATS out of bureaucRATS, and bolded it above Al Gore's head, flashing it for but a fraction of a second. Researcher Joel Weinberger of Adelphi University conducted a replication study of the effect of this ad and the data robustly suggested that the ad made a difference in the outcome of the election.[13]

The masters of the art of advertising employ many subtle nuances. Billions, perhaps even trillions of dollars, have been spent since the advent of marketing research spawned by Edward Bernays and Ivy Lee (whom we will discuss in more detail later) to discover exactly how and why we can be influenced without our being aware. For example, in a recent study, researchers randomly selected students to fill out a questionnaire surveying their political attitudes.

> They found that the students endorsed more conservative attitudes when they stood next to a bottle of hand sanitizer or near a sign reminding them to wash their hands. In another study, published last year in *Emotion*, students who filled out a survey in a room with a noxious odor reported feeling less warmth toward gays than students in a normal-smelling room. That may sound like an unlikely result, but past research suggests that subtle reminders of contamination can trigger a knee-jerk fear of outsiders—a xenophobic disgust reaction that may have once served to protect people from diseases carried by other tribes.[14]

Another simple example of our more subtle context evaluations is this one by parents:

> Thinking of children can also make people lean conservative, according to research by Richard Eibach, Ph.D., a psychology professor at the University of Waterloo. In a 2009 study published in the *Journal of Experimental Social Psychology*, Eibach found that simply reminding parents of their children triggered harsher evaluations of people engaged in distasteful but essentially harmless behavior, such as a dwarf

who participates in dwarf-tossing events. Results from the 2006 General Social Survey provide dovetailing results, with parents judging premarital sex as more morally wrong than nonparents. "When you are a nonparent, you can afford to have a fairly lax attitude toward morality so long as someone isn't harming someone else," he says. "When you're a parent—or reminded of being a parent—you can't afford to ignore rude or uncivil or unpleasant behavior because it can potentially corrupt your children's character development."[15]

Values Vs. Issues

Ronald Reagan defied the wisdom of the day regarding voters. It had long been held that voters backed the man with the issues important to them. However, even when voters opposed some of Reagan's positions, they still wanted to vote for him according to polls. This led Richard Wirthlin, then chief strategist for Reagan, to investigate the reasoning behind this apparent contradiction. What Wirthlin learned can be distilled this way: Voters supported Reagan's values, and Reagan spoke about values rather than issues![16]

Values necessarily say little about the real world. Take, for instance, the Obama campaign slogan regarding change: "Yes we can!" How does that translate into a real issue? Is it change? Change what? Transparency? Cooperation between political parties? Opportunities? Now this is not to say that there were not real issues attached to the campaign. There were, just as there were for Reagan. What is worthy of note in our context is that the idea of values somehow trumps issues in voter's minds.[17]

Elections are often more about personalities than they are about substantive issues. "Politics is about values; it is about communication; it is about voters trusting a candidate to do what is right; it is about believing in and identifying with, a candidate's world view. And it is about symbolism."[18]

Such symbols as 'handouts' and 'laziness' were two elements Reagan successfully used against his "mythical Cadillac-driving 'welfare queen.'"[19] In other words, rather than voters paying close attention to the issues, they cast their ballot on their sense of identification with the candidate, *feeling* their way through elections. Because of this human response, the electorate becomes many times more vulnerable to manipulation.

Inside the Political Brain

One of the many leading researchers investigating why people behave as they do, particularly where politics and economics are concerned, is Dan Ariely of MIT. In a conversation with Ariely, I suggested that there was evidence linking anatomical differences in the brain to differing political biases, particularly conservative versus liberal. His response suggested that more research was needed before one could accept the strict difference drawn by some. So with this bit of a disclaimer, what are those differences and what is the evidence?

Researchers at University College London performed scans on 90 volunteer students who had completed a survey of political attitudes. The results varied from very liberal to very conservative.

> "Students who reported more 'conservative' political views tended to have larger amygdalae, a structure in the temporal lobes that performs a primary role in the processing and memory of emotions. On the other hand, more 'liberal' students tended to have a larger volume of grey matter in the anterior cingulate cortex, a structure of the brain associated with monitoring uncertainty and handling conflicting information."[20]

A functional difference was also observed in a novel way:

> A study by scientists at New York University and the University of California, Los Angeles, found differences in how self-described liberal and conservative research participants responded to changes in patterns. Participants were asked to tap a keyboard when the letter "M" appeared on a computer monitor and to refrain from tapping when they saw a "W." The letter "M" appeared four times more frequently than "W," conditioning participants to press the keyboard on almost every trial. Liberal participants made fewer mistakes

than conservatives when they saw the rare "W," indicating to the researchers that these participants were better able to accept changes or conflicts in established patterns. The participants were also wired to an electroencephalograph that recorded activity in their anterior cingulate cortex, the part of the brain that detects conflicts between a habitual tendency and a more appropriate response. Liberals were significantly more likely than conservatives to show activity in the brain circuits that deal with conflicts during the experiment, and this correlated with their greater accuracy in the test. The lead author of the study, David Amodio, warned against concluding that a particular political orientation is superior. "The tendency of conservatives to block distracting information could be a good thing depending on the situation," he said.[21]

Numerous interpretations exist for the data generated by the studies conducted so far on genetic differences and brain biases. Some insist that conservatives are more sensitive to fear, having larger fear centers in their brains, whereas liberals are greater risk takers. And here is another genetic difference:

In a study published in October, researchers at Harvard and UC-San Diego found that a variant of the DRD4 gene predisposes people to being liberal, but only if they had active social lives as adolescents. The "liberal gene" has also been linked to a desire to try new things, and other "personality traits related to political liberalism."[22]

Fear drives preservation, and so for many, the obvious conclusion is that conservatives are more sensitive to danger than liberals and thus the difference between them regarding such things as defense, debt, and traditional values. Liberals, on the other hand, are more inclined to experiment, to take risks, and to try the new and the novel. Some studies have gone so far as to suggest that conservatives are more likely to be concerned with their immediate neighbor's well being while liberals pay more attention to global matters.

Writing in *Scientific American Mind*, in an article titled "Calling a Truce in the Political Wars," author Emily Laber-Warren described the evidence as suggesting that, "Conservatives are fundamentally more anxious than liberals, which may be why they typically desire stability . . . (while) caring for people who are vulnerable, and fairness, which for liberals tends to mean sharing resources equally. Conservatives care about those things, too, but for them fairness means proportionality—that people should get what they deserve based on the amount of effort they have put in. Conservatives also emphasize loyalty and authority, values helpful for maintaining a stable society."[23]

Additionally, in research discussed earlier, it was shown that conservatives and liberals even make different choices at the supermarket. "Psychological research has shown that conservatives and liberals differ on basic personality traits such as conscientiousness, tolerance for uncertainty, and openness to new experience."[24] Conservatives tend to prefer name brands and familiar products, whereas liberals are more open to generic products and to trying out new items.

Framing

But let's get back to techniques used by those who wish to influence our choices, in particular *framing*. There are many different types of frames, such as surface frames, issue defining frames, deep frames, and message frames. Since the subject of this work is limited to the influence frames have on us, our discussion here will focus on that aspect of framing.

Framing is a perception-management tool that is used time and again. Over and over we learn that how something is said and the context in which it is framed become all-important to how information is perceived. My favorite context-framing proposition continues to be this one: If you think about the saliva in your mouth, you probably, like most, appreciate it. A dry mouth is no fun! However, if I change the context slightly and ask you to spit some of that saliva into a glass and then drink it, you're probably immediately disgusted by the thought. This is a simple and yet powerful example of context framing.

Words themselves often make the best frames. For example, if you want to redistribute wealth in America, talking about how much less the poor make than the wealthy is not the way to do it. Change the framing and instead address how rich the rich are and how much more they have than the poor have, and this new pitch is persuasive. Indeed, you can quite easily influence attitudes about wealth redistribution, as the researchers in a new study reported in *Psychological Science* illustrate.

The researchers recruited 79 U.S. adults to participate in an online survey about "people's views on income inequality in the United States." Participants in the rich-have-more condition were told that the top five percentile of wage earners make, on average, $111,000 more than the median wage earner (those in the 50th percentile). Participants in the poor-have-less condition were told that the median wage earner makes, on average, $111,000 less than the top five percentile. Participants in a control condition were not given any information about income inequality.

Next, the participants were asked to indicate their beliefs about why the rich are wealthy and why the poor are in poverty by completing a variety of internal- and external-attribution measures.

Participants then indicated their level of support for two redistributive tax policies: one that would create a new tax bracket for people with incomes over $1 million and one that would create a new tax bracket for people with incomes over $5 million.

Finally, participants indicated their level of political conservatism and reported their household income.

Conservatism was negatively associated with support for redistributive policies among participants in the control condition, confirming previous findings. This was also true for participants who were told that the poor make less than the rich. In these two groups, more conservative participants showed less support for redistributive tax policies.

But participants who were told that the rich make more than the poor didn't show a negative association between conservatism and policy support. These findings suggest that the rich-have-more frame may have reduced conservatives' opposition to raising taxes on the rich.[25]

Words Lost to Reframing

Many words have lost their original meaning as a result of framing. *Propaganda* is one such word. It used to mean, 'to correct errors'; today it is generally thought to mean 'a message with an agenda that is probably full of false information.' Another, and one that disturbs me, is the word *liberal.*

Liberal originally referred to freedom seekers, those very same folks who founded America. Liberals were behind women gaining the vote and slavery ending. Liberals have given much to America, including Social Security and Medicare. The hard right, however, portrays liberals as tax-and-spend pirates lacking fiscal discipline and seeking to end the free market. They are portrayed as unpatriotic because they resist war and entirely lack traditional family values.

Liberals are likewise guilty of such framing. They portray conservative as warmongers intent on caring for only the wealthy—to hell with the poor, the sick, and the elderly! Again, this framing is false to facts.

Voters, however, often respond to the frame rather than to the truth. Just as the saliva in the glass became vile, so goes the group once they accept the frame. Here are some frames to consider, and when you do, evaluate what they mean to you and why: Patriotism, national security, rule of law, family values, religious freedom, right to life, marriage, pro-choice, progressive, secularism, and cultural relativism.

Each of these terms is likely to elicit an emotional response of sorts when they are considered seriously. Why is that? What can we learn about ourselves with exercises of this nature?

Comedians

While we're on framing, let's address the influence the comedian has on our perceptions, particularly voters' attitudes. In a study conducted by Amy Bree Becker, assistant professor at Towson University, voters' attitudes were shown to become negative as a result of public ridicule of a presidential candidate. Harken back to Sarah Palin and false statements about her seeing Russia from her kitchen, and the like, or Mitt Romney and the dog on the roof of his car. Becker had this to say:

> "In reality, the critical comedy people are used to from programs like *The Colbert Report* and *The Daily Show* promotes negative attitudes toward the comic target, while self-directed humor may actually prove to be a very useful and strategic tool for candidates looking to appeal to voters. Moving forward, politicians will need to become more skilled at deflecting humor directed at them and also be able to tell a good joke."[26]

I don't know about you, but I have been absolutely astonished at the number of people who have based their political opinions on the words of comedians. Talk about Kool-Aid! This sort of reasoning is Kool-Aid on steroids!

Abstract Moderation

While we're on political preferences, are you aware that by simply answering three "why" questions you can be made to be more politically moderate? This study, led by Professor Jesse Preston of the University of Illinois and reported in the journal of *Social Psychology and Personality Science,* has some incredibly powerful ramifications when it comes to shaping the attitudes of society. It clearly shows that some of the most sacred political ideas are really quite malleable.

> The interventions were simple. In the first experiment the researchers established that, after viewing an image of an airplane flying into one of the World Trade Center towers, liberals and conservatives held opposing attitudes toward the ground zero mosque and community center.
> A second study repeated the first with new participants and included one minor—but significant—change. Before they gave their views on the mosque and community center, participants answered either three consecutive "why" questions or three consecutive "how" questions on an unrelated topic—in this case, about maintaining their health.
> "The *why* questions, but not the *how* questions, moved liberals and conservatives closer together on the issue of the Islamic center," Preston said.

"We observed that liberals and conservatives became more moderate in their attitudes," she said. "After this very brief task that just put them in this abstract mindset, they were more willing to consider the point of view of the opposition."

The researchers conducted a third experiment online to test the effects in a more diverse population. In this round, they asked participants to read an ambiguous "faux Yahoo! News" article that included multiple arguments for and against the Islamic center.

Those who viewed the article in an easy-to-read format remained polarized in their views, the researchers found. But those who read the same article after it had been photocopied and made harder to read were more moderate in their responses.

"Making the information harder to read induced abstract thinking," Preston said.

"It's a surprisingly powerful manipulation because people are thinking in a different way and putting in more mental effort while reading," she said.[27]

Using Facebook for Inquiry

You may find this interesting—I did. As I said earlier, sometimes I use my Facebook pages to investigate feelings and thought processes. I made such a post before the 2012 election and then discussed the post and some of the responses on my radio show, *Provocative Enlightenment*. Here is the discussion:

> I posted a new study that was reported in *Science News*: "This Is Your Brain on Politics: Neuroscience Reveals Brain Differences Between Republicans and Democrats." The research was carried out at the University of South Carolina, and the lead researcher was Roger Newman-Norlund. I made only this comment: "I have posted findings of this nature before, but here we have a new twist."
>
> The new twist was this, quoting from the article:
>
>> The results found more neural activity in areas believed to be linked with broad social connectedness in Democrats (friends, the world

at-large) and more activity in areas linked with tight social connectedness in the Republicans (family, country). In some ways the study confirms a stereotype about members of the two parties—Democrats tend to be more global and Republicans more America-centric—but it actually runs counter to other recent research indicating Democrats enjoyed a virtual biological lock on caring for others. "The results were a little surprising," Newman-Norlund said. This shows the picture is more complicated. One possible explanation for our results is that Democrats and Republicans process social connectedness in a fundamentally different way."[28]

To that posting one former FB friend (former because she subsequently unfriended me as a result of this post), left a quotation from Carl Rove suggesting that, "as people do better they vote Republican unless they have too much education." Now that's a thoroughly stupid gaffe by Rove. I responded by pointing out that both sides make gaffes, and I offered one by President Obama that he has apologized for, the infamous remark regarding small-town voters who are "bitter and cling to their God and their guns."

The following was our private exchange, and I share it only to emphasize this point: Remember what really matters!

She wrote, "You know, a very wise and very rich marketing genius with a 30 year, stellar reputation in the industry told a group of business owners, of which I was one, that if a person was in business, the most ignorant and damaging thing he could ever do was publicly make statements about politics or religion—that doing so would forever alienate the customer. That has never been more true than what I have seen from you, Dr. Taylor. I have a stack of your books. I have a stack of your CDs. I have bought your CDs and given them to friends and family. I have recommend cancer patients and war veterans suffering PTSD take a look at your work. I'm involved with a health and wellness group whose members number 5,000, and I've talked you up there and know a lot of sales of your products were generated by those group members. Because I have seen you be completely and totally wrong when it comes to political statements made, I have questioned your thinking, which in turn, makes me question your work. This statement just made to me by you really underscores the hatefulness I've seen coming from you. I have questioned myself using your work, based on how you obviously think. I told myself to ignore my misgivings, but you just set my thinking straight. All of your things that are in my bookcase are going in the trash, and I will not recommend you again. Goodbye."

"Well," I responded, "I am truly sorry to hear that. I posted a study. I offered no interpretations about that study. You responded. I offered back a gaffe from the other side, also not my statement, but one of President Obama's, since both sides say stupid things. I don't see how you get hateful out of any of this. It is, of course, your choice to escalate the matter, and I respect that. However, I will not compromise myself on the basis of money. Very many business people are speaking out on both sides of this election. Unfortunately, instead of agreeing to disagree, passion takes over reason with some and emotions rule. That said, I do apologize for offending you. Love and light to you and yours always, Eldon."

The point to all of this is simple. We are not alike. We all bring different talents, abilities, and perspectives to life. That is who we are. It would be silly to think that because I have dark hair, only dark-haired people can be my friends. It is equally self-limiting to go through life discarding those who do not agree with you. In fact, to make that point even clearer, we are sometimes much better off surrounding ourselves with people who do disagree with us. For example, research has shown that competing areas of the brain can limit our resources when it comes to decisions. Brain physiology limits the simultaneous use of both our empathetic and our analytic networks. As such, if you are analytical about a subject, in order not to miss the side of your decision involving empathy, you need someone near you who is focused on the empathetic nature of the problem. This is just one example, and there are many more.

I also recently posted a study that showed when we promote abstract thinking, we can bring opposing political sides together, making both more moderate.[29] The study clearly illustrates the influence of the deliberate *dumbing down* of our conversations, as when facts are replaced by cute sound bites, and shows how easy it is to promote real thinking by simply adding in three 'why' questions that promote analytic thinking.

My mother had a saying that went like this: "Don't cut off your nose to spite your face." I would encourage you to remember that our differences create our paths and purposes in life. Quoting from author and family physician Dr. Karen Wyatt, whom I interviewed on my *Provocative Enlightenment* radio show, "Aside from your goals and insecurities and desires and opinions and seeking and striving, you are only here to BE that which you already ARE."

So in the end, the fact that I posted a science study, not one I had conducted or funded myself, but simply a journal-published study, and then followed up by balancing a one-sided post made by a so-called friend on Facebook that implied Republican values were for lesser-educated people, with a like quote from the opposing side that implied that Republicans were folks angrily clinging to their God and guns, led one woman not only to throw out books and CDs (maybe she may even have burned them) but to deny providing valuable information to patients who could benefit from programs we make available free. That sounds very much like the nose-and-face analogy to me.

CONCLUSION

How is it that we can be so intolerant of opinions that differ from our own? Well, by now you should not only be clear on how, but why. The more divided we are the less control we have over the direction of our country and the politics that rule it, and as a consequence, the less control we have over our own lives. Every single piece of legislation, constitutional interpretation, executive action and so forth can directly affect our lives, our children, our food, our drugs—indeed, what part of our lives does it fail to influence in some way or another?

GOTCHA!

It is always advisable to hear out the other side and to pay close attention not to our emotional, knee-jerk reaction, but to what is being truly communicated. It is not possible to reach a compromise unless you understand the other side. No compromise and we either have gridlock or punishment by way of actions we object to or inaction all together.

Think about it—have you ever gone off at someone in your family, a friend, or colleague over some difference in politics or religion? Why? How did you become so invested in your beliefs that you could burn bridges over them and feel justified for doing so? If you haven't found yourself in that place before, then you're in the minority and great for you. Unfortunatley, most of us *have* experienced those moments when we couldn't stand it any more and we therefore unloaded our objections on those around us—but who or what did that serve?

If we are to ever maximize the opportunities of all, we are going to have to learn to work together. I would suggest that we begin by resolving to listen, to hear out the alternative views, to weigh carefully what's being said, to sincerely contemplate the other's position, and do all of this before we respond with vitriolic condemnation. Patience is a virtue and that's because it leads to understanding. What are your thoughts on this? How can you become a better listener? Can you see the importance of moderation in our remarks? Do you understand how just changing the context in minor ways can change the very nature of meaning? How would you instruct your children to deal with this sort of abuse? Context leads to definition and definitions matter. As I've stated in more than one of my books, remember that those who control the definition control the argument.

CHAPTER NINETEEN

Physical Control

Anything is better than lies and deceit!
~Leo Tolstoy

Misconception: *Most trust their government to be fair and just and impartially administer the law, alert to our constitutional rights and wary of treading on them except in dire instances of national security.* **Fact:** *The fact is, trust no further than you can verify! History advises the informed over and over again that those in power do what you can inspect, not what you expect!*

It's generally known that the real conspiracy theorists are members of various governmental defense and security organizations, such as the NSA and CIA. The 'gamers' in the Pentagon are continually coming up with scenarios, just-in-case models, to be prepared for contingencies in the world. As a result, we have attack plans for nearly every location on the planet.

War games are practiced, and sometimes they are practiced with our allies. Just as a fire department practices, so do our military. What sort of war game is being practiced when the U.S. Army invades an American town? In August 2013, Gillette, a small town in Wisconsin, saw a complete takeover by U.S Army Civil Affairs and Psychological Operations (CS & PSYOP). The command battalion practiced "joint control of a small town with local authorities in a 'realistic training exercise.'"[1]

We chose the city of Gillett for the first time this year because of the size, demographics, and municipalities offered within the city and surrounding area," said Sgt. First Class Patrick Leon, the noncommissioned officer in charge of the civil-military operations center. "It replicates what we may find in an overseas environment."

The article [released by the army[2]] later admits, however, that there are no future plans to deploy these soldiers overseas.

The soldiers also gathered information on community leaders "from hobbies, interests, and religion" as well as "daily activities," thus honing behavior profiling skills that could be useful to PSYOP teams in identifying "political dissidents."[3]

I'm not sure what to make of this myself. Civil Command is typically the good guy there to advise local government on how to get things done. This is very valuable in such places as Iraq during the Second Gulf War, but there we have Americans teaching Iraqis about American systems and methods. How does this work when it's in America? For whatever the purpose, the Command maintained control of Gillette for three days.

Bullets

A report by Paul Watson in August 2013 pointed out the planned acquisition of 3.5 million rounds of ammunition by the Transportation Security Administration (TSA). That is enough ammunition for their "agents to fire 9,400 rounds a day, every day of the year."[4] What is their plan? Is it fair to ask?

Car Cyberattack

In 2013, Michael Hastings, an award-winning journalist, died in an automobile accident under very strange circumstances. The man collided with a tree in a head-on accident, but his engine was somehow catapulted nearly 200 feet in the opposite direction because of the momentum of the automobile at time of impact. Was Hastings assassinated? Was his automobile under cyberattack? "Richard Clarke, a State Department official-turned-special advisor to several United States presidents, said the early morning auto crash last Tuesday was 'consistent with a car cyberattack,' raising new questions about the death of the award-winning journalist."[5]

According to an article by Paul Joseph Watson, Michael Hastings feared his Mercedes had been tampered with. Indeed, he asked to borrow a friend's automobile, telling her he was "scared and wanted to leave town." Unfortunately her car was having mechanical problems, so she was unable to help him.[6]

Some believe that Hastings was about to blow the whistle on CIA Director John Brennan. What did he know? That's still unknown at the time of this writing but there is some speculation. Others believe that it had something to do with Hastings bringing down General Stanley A. McChrystal.[7] I would not want to venture a guess. The reason you find this information here has to do with the technology. Just as you have seen in science fiction movies, the technology exists to take over an automobile and operate it remotely—and our intelligence agencies have this technology today.

Firefighters and police who were on the scene investigating the Hastings accident were ordered not to speak,[8]. What we do know is that, two days after the crash the coroner and the investigative reporter decided that drug intoxication was the cause, and this was widely reported on the news networks. However, the toxicology report that was released two months later said that, "Hastings didn't have enough drugs in his body to affect his driving."[9]

Remote Control

The ability to take control of vehicles without the operator's knowledge is very real. Indeed, a University of Texas team took control of a yacht covertly in a well-reported story appearing in August 2013.

> Led by Assistant Professor Todd Humphreys of the Department of Aerospace Engineering and Engineering Mechanics at the Cockrell School of Engineering, the team was able to successfully spoof an $80 million private yacht

using the world's first openly acknowledged GPS spoofing device. Spoofing is a technique that creates false civil GPS signals to gain control of a vessel's GPS receivers. The purpose of the experiment was to measure the difficulty of carrying out a spoofing attack at sea and to determine how easily sensors in the ship's command room could identify the threat.

The researchers hope their demonstration will shed light on the perils of navigation attacks, serving as evidence that spoofing is a serious threat to marine vessels and other forms of transportation. Last year, Humphreys and a group of students led the first public capture of a GPS-guided unmanned aerial vehicle (UAV), or drone, using a GPS device created by Humphreys and his students.

"With 90 percent of the world's freight moving across the seas and a great deal of the world's human transportation going across the skies, we have to gain a better understanding of the broader implications of GPS spoofing," Humphreys said. "I didn't know, until we performed this experiment, just how possible it is to spoof a marine vessel and how difficult it is to detect this attack."[10]

Hackable

You may not be aware that many of the things in your home and on your person can be hacked. Hackers have successfully turned on the camera in smart TVs and remotely viewed the television viewers. In fact, hackers can take remote control of your computer, your phone, your TV, your car, and more.

Charlie Miller and Chris Valasek with DARPA funding not only humorously demonstrated the takeover of vehicles using a laptop, but released tools and code with the goal of making it easier for researchers to develop monitoring and control applications to circumvent harmful attacks. They chose a 2010 Toyota Prius and 2010 Ford Escape for their parking assist feature that assigns some automated control over steering in addition to the usual braking and display controls.[11]

It's not just our personal items that are hackable. Our infrastructure itself is vulnerable.

Two teams of presenters at Black Hat demonstrated new ways our world's infrastructure could be one step closer to a chaotic scene from a sci-fi movie. After creating a demonstration oil pump, engineers used a series of attacks starting from susceptible Internet-facing servers and finally "pivoting" towards the programmable logic controllers (PLCs), hardware that actually controls oil pump function. The industrial protocols used were developed in the 1970s and are not only unencrypted but often too weak to even support encryption. In fact, the team, who in their day jobs install and support these oil pump systems, argued that it wouldn't take a government to cause an environmental catastrophe, but "script kiddies."

In a second demonstration, IOActive, the same company that presented the Prius and Escape hack above, showed that the wireless devices distributed by the top three developers of industrial network solutions were all subject to the same vulnerabilities. Not only did the team prove that false data could be injected into these systems with radio frequency transceivers, but that the companies involved had only the slightest concerns about security. Combined, this puts many oil, natural gas, nuclear, and petroleum companies at risk for catastrophic failures.[12]

Personal Tracking

A number of ways are available to track your activities, particularly your movements. Most of these are GPS-dependent. There is also at least one device that for a few hundred dollars can "track your every movement, activity, and interaction."[13] This device is known as CreepyDOL.

CreepyDOL is a network of sensors that communicates with a data-processing server. The sensor network runs on boxes about the size of a small external hard drive, with each node containing a Raspberry Pi Model A, two Wi-Fi adapters, and a USB hub. Previously developed by O'Connor, these are called F-BOMBs (Falling Ballistically-launched

Object that Makes Backdoors) and are sufficiently rugged to be thrown, or even dropped from a UAV [unmanned aerial vehicle]. Each F-BOMB costs just over US$50, giving a network of 10 a price of around $500 . . .

. . . The impact of CreepyDOL is that it eliminates the idea of "blending into a crowd." If you're carrying a wireless device, CreepyDOL will see you, track your movements, and report home, even if you aren't using it.[14]

Automobile Black Boxes

At the time of this writing, Senate Bill 1813 has cleared the Senate and is believed will easily pass in the House. This bill requires all vehicles built beginning in 2015 to have mandatory black boxes, or event data recorders (EDRs). So, not only can you be located using the onboard GPS, but your speed, your stops, your route, the time the car is parked, and so much more become another series of ones and zeros defining your life to those who peep. In fact, although a minimum amount of data is required, there is no limit to how much data the recorders can store. Concerns about privacy are obvious.

> The Electronic Frontier Foundation (EFF) urged the National Highway Traffic Safety Administration (NHTSA) today to include strict privacy protections for data collected by vehicle "black boxes" to protect drivers from long-term tracking as well as the misuse of their information.[15]

At the time of this writing, it is being stated that this black box will simply make road taxes easier and fairer as you will then be taxed according to the miles you have driven. However, as we all well know, a tax on gas already serves this function very well. How would replacing the tax on fuel with a tax calculated using the black box be more fair? Does the government really think we are that stupid? Probably—how many times has there been outrage over incursions into privacy that simply died down as individuals assume they can do nothing about it or expect someone else to do it for them?

Wi-Vi Uses Wi-Fi

Researchers at MIT have demonstrated technology that can see through walls, and your Wi-Fi system could be the doorway into your home.

Researchers at MIT's Computer Science and Artificial Intelligence Laboratory have developed what could become low-cost, X-ray vision. The system, known as "Wi-Vi," is based on a concept similar to radar and sonar imaging, but rather than using high-power signals, this tech uses reflected Wi-Fi signals to track the movement of people behind walls and closed doors.

When a Wi-Fi signal is transmitted at a wall, a portion of that signal penetrates through and reflects off any humans that happen to be moving around in the other room. Since only a tiny fraction of the signal passes through the wall, with the rest being reflected, the researchers had to devise a technology that could cancel out the arbitrary reflections, and keep only those reflecting from moving human bodies.

Dina Katabi, a professor in MIT's Department of Electrical Engineering and Computer Science, and her graduate student Fadel Adib have tuned a system that uses two transmission antennas and a single receiver. The two antennas transmit almost identical signals, except the second antenna's signal is the inverse of the first, resulting in interference.

This interference causes the signals to cancel each other out. Since any static objects that the signals hit create identical reflections, they are also cancelled out by this effect. Only the reflections that change between the two signals, like moving bodies on the other side of the wall, arrive back at the receiver, allowing the system to track the moving people.

Adib says, "So, if the person moves behind the wall, all reflections from static objects are cancelled out, and the only thing registered by the device is the moving human."[16]

Eye in the Sky

DARPA's (Defense Advanced Research Projects Agency) has a new 1.8 gigapixel camera capable of real time surveillance surpassing most of the expectations of even the most dyed-in-the-wool science fiction fan. From an altitude of 20,000 feet, the camera can survey an area 4.5 miles across and focus in, providing a close-up zoom of something as small as six inches.[17]

City Lights

Farmington Hill, Michigan, has some new outdoor lights that spy on the community. The lights are designed to curb crime, not so much by lighting the streets as by recording the events that fall under their glare.

> Farmington Hills just became the first city in America to host a state-of-the-art system of lampposts that make up something called the Intellistreets system. Farmington Hills native Ron Harwood worked over ten years to make the project a reality, and as of Friday his dream had fully come to fruition. For his neighbors that dream of a future where their every move won't be monitored, however, they might want to think about heading out of Michigan.
>
> Simply put, the Intellistreets project is a system of Internet-connected luminaries that communicate with one another across the city. In addition to lighting the area, they can broadcast verbal and written messages, monitor rainfall, and give directions.
>
> According to their own website, the system is also great for "data harvesting."
>
> Not only does Intellistreets offer information about the neighborhood and provide light, it also monitors the conversations of pedestrians, records video, monitors foot traffic, and counts heads—all of which is recorded and stored for possible analysis. And according to Harwood, the tiny 80,000-person community of Farmington Hills isn't going to be the only town using his technology—Detroit, Chicago, and Pittsburgh have placed orders, and the inventor claims that he is in talks with the Department of Homeland Security.[18]

Blind Faith

Speigel Online drew renewed attention to black helicopters in an article that appeared in August 2013 with this headline: "Black

Helicopters: Britain's Blind Faith in Intelligence Agencies."[19] *Speigel* is a German publication, and as such, they are perhaps more sensitive to the methods used to advance means that might lead to giving up individual rights.

Most in Britain seem unconcerned about the mass surveillance carried out by its intelligence agency GCHQ. Even the intimidation tactics being used on the *Guardian* this week [August 2013] have caused little soul-searching. The reason is simple: Britons blindly and uncritically trust their secret service.

The Snowden affair was actually going pretty well for British Prime Minister David Cameron. After the initial uproar, many of his fellow citizens quickly lost interest in the surveillance scandal and in the fact that the British intelligence agency Government Communications Headquarters (GCHQ) had launched what was presumably the most ambitious project ever to monitor global data communications. The opposition helped out by making itself largely invisible. And the Liberal Democrats, in a coalition government with the Conservatives, likewise did nothing despite the party's tradition of being champions of privacy protections.

The United Kingdom is not an authoritarian surveillance state like China. But it is a country in which surveillance has become part of everyday life. The cold eyes of the security apparatus keep watch over everything that moves—in underground stations and hospitals, at intersections, and on buses. The British Security Industry Authority (BSIA) recently estimated that there could be up to 5.9 million surveillance cameras in the country—or one camera for every 11 Britons.[20]

Brain Implants

Brain implants will soon be used to treat depression. By implanting electrodes, a sort of reset can be initiated by scientists that proponents say can reboot the brain. Hackers may be able to access the device remotely, however, and guess what. If you're not too trusting, you might also readily imagine many uses other than the treatment of depression, perhaps even a new version of *The Manchurian Candidate.*

"The more neurologists and surgeons learn about the aptly named deep brain stimulation, the more they are convinced that the currents from the technology's implanted electrodes can literally reboot brain circuits involved with the mood disorder," reports *Scientific American.*

Is this a potential scientific success story or the first step towards psychopharmacological dictatorship?

Hacker Barnaby Jack warned that medical implants like pacemakers could be remotely accessed by hackers and governments to "commit mass murder."

Jack was found dead just a week before he was set to present his research at a conference.[21]

Heart Attack Gun?

Those who have enjoyed a *007* movie have seen the many toys that James Bond brings to bear on his foes; however this one challenges even the Bond character. In 1975 the world learned of a dart gun developed by the CIA that can cause a heart attack.

"At the first televised hearing, staged in the Senate Caucus Room, Chairman Church dramatically displayed a CIA poison dart gun to highlight the committee's discovery that the CIA directly violated a presidential order by maintaining stocks of shellfish toxin sufficient to kill thousands," a Senate web page explains.

"The lethal poison then rapidly enters the bloodstream causing a heart attack. Once the damage is done, the poison denatures quickly, so that an autopsy is very unlikely to detect that the heart attack resulted from anything other than natural causes. Sounds like the perfect James Bond weapon, doesn't it? Yet this is all verifiable in congressional testimony," writes Fred Burks.

"The dart from this secret CIA weapon can penetrate clothing and leave nothing but a tiny red dot on the skin. On penetration of the deadly dart, the individual targeted for assassination may feel as if bitten by a mosquito, or they may not feel anything at all. The poisonous dart completely disintegrates upon entering the target."[22]

If you're interested, the testimony is available on You-Tube at this URL: **www.youtube.com/watch?feature=player_embedded&v=tzIw44w000w**

Of course, the knowledge that there is such a weapon often fuels rumors and theories about those who both are a thorn in the side of the government and who die suddenly of a heart attack despite no history of heart disease. Such are the rumors attached to the deaths of men such as Andrew Breitbart (a noted conservative activist, author, and publisher who died of an unexpected heart attack at age 43) and Mark Pittman (a reporter who challenged federal secrecy and died unexpectedly at age 52).

Is it possible that members of our government would order citizens killed? No trial, no arrest, no hearing—just a summary judgment: extreme prejudice!

> At the end of 2011, President Obama ordered the assassinations of New Mexico-born Anwar al-Awlaki and Samir Khan of North Carolina, both American citizens. With a drone strike in Yemen, the order was carried out and two Americans were dead, without charge, without trial, and without conviction.
>
> Waiving the rule of law as his personal authorization, it was the first time in American history that the president of the United States publicly ordered the assassination of American citizens.[23]

Drones

The use of drones in domestic America has increased exponentially in recent years. What is being spied on? Are the drones armed? The FBI has recently been under pressure from members of Congress on both sides of the aisle to explain their use of drones. Once again, we see the absence of citizen input with a decision that steals away citizens' liberties. Senator Rand Paul said, "I am disturbed by the revelation that the FBI has unilaterally decided to begin using drone surveillance technology without a governance policy, and thus without the requisite assurances that the constitutional rights of Americans are being protected."[24]

DC Chase

One argument goes something like this: When terrorists control our behavior, they have won, for we are then living in a 24/7 world full of the fear of terrorism. Do we find ourselves there now—constantly vigilant in different ways, ever aware of an imminent and certain threat?

Consider this: In October, 2013, a 34-year-old mother, Miriam Carey, accompanied by her one-year-old daughter, visited Washington, D.C. Miriam was a dental hygienist under professional healthcare supervision for postpartum depression. She had recently been taken off of medication and was considered to be doing well by everyone concerned, including two dentists for whom she worked.

Miriam became lost and came upon what appears to have been a temporary barricade set up for a security exercise. When five officers pulled guns on her, she panicked and attempted to flee. She was shot and killed in a flurry of bullets. Luckily her child was not also killed.

Miriam was unarmed. According to family members, she was not political, and contrary to some stories put out without an ounce of evidence, she was not delusional nor had she been hearing President Obama's voice in her head.

Miriam was an unarmed U.S. citizen visiting the nation's capital, and that is an indisputable fact. She was shot and killed, not stopped or detained. No doubt any number of other methods could have been used to arrest her. Capitol police received commendations for their actions from Congress.

Since when does law enforcement shoot first and ask questions later? When something like this happens, it's clear that the terrorists are winning![25]

CONCLUSION

Do you ever wonder what happens to those headline stories that just disappear without ever telling the end of the story? I have often puzzled over stories without ending such as when the then-Speaker of the House Nancy Pelosi accused the CIA of lying.[26] In a statement it was said, "The U.S. House Speaker Nancy Pelosi has accused the Bush-era CIA of misleading her about alleged torture of suspected terrorists and denied her failure to object to such tactics made her complicit." Where did this story go? Did the CIA lie to Congress, and if they did, why wasn't there a hearing and proper follow-through? If not, why didn't the CIA follow through? Remember that the then-director was a fellow Democrat newly appointed to the CIA, Leon Panetta. So what happened to the story? If it didn't matter, then why did we hear about it in the first place?

The bottom line is this: Many of the stories that we hear are actually press releases often designed to distract us or to create a talking point that has little or no substance. When a prominent politician makes an assertion, his tribe will naturally believe and repeat it. Repeat it enough times and it sticks, and subsequent information that falsifies the original assertion correcting the lie, fails to win the minds of most.

How often do you follow up stories you hear and believe? Are you like me? Have you too observed a pattern? Do you see the same old stories coming around every election cycle? Are there news commentators with agendas that you recognize on both sides of the aisle? How about so-called news reporters and anchors—can you spot those with their own biases and agenda?

Think of what you can do to help create a more honest environment. Is that important to you? How can each of us advance a world that resembles something more like a Utopia instead of *1984*?

Mind Control

All over the place, from the popular culture to the propaganda system, there is constant pressure to make people feel that they are helpless, that the only role they can have is to ratify decisions and to consume.

~Noam Chomsky

Misconception: *Most people think mind control is a work of fiction, and what's more, they're above the fray—it's something that might happen to someone else but not them.*
Fact: *Most people are already under the influence of many different forms of mind control, and they're oblivious of the fact.*

Brian Pasley, a neuroscientist at the University of California–Berkeley reported in February, 2012, that by linking sound patterns to thought activity, researchers had been able to "hear the thoughts of people."[1]

This technology has great promise with respect to assisting people who can no longer talk and, for that matter, perhaps many other individuals with special needs. It also contains the seed for another interrogation technique. Perhaps in the near future we will all need such training as transcendental meditation and yoga techniques to learn to control our every thought.

Pasley and colleagues enlisted the help of 15 patients with epilepsy or brain tumors who had electrodes attached to the surface of their brains in order to map out the source of their seizures. With electrodes in place, participants listened to about 50 different speech sounds in the form of sentences and words, both real and fake, such as "jazz," "peace," "Waldo," "fook," and "nim."

After mapping out the brain's electrical responses to each sound, the research team found that they could predict which of two sounds from the study set the brain was responding to, and they could do it with about 90 percent accuracy.

Decoding the brain's perception of sound in this way, Pasley said, is sort of like learning how a piano works.

"If you understand the relationship between the keys and their sounds, you could turn on the TV and watch someone perform with the sound off," he said. "And just by looking at what keys were being pressed, you could understand what sounds were being played."[2]

Computerized Mind Reading

Using fMRI scanners to derive images of the brain while employing a very sophisticated mathematical formula, researchers have successfully read letters directly from the brain.

Our approach is similar to how we believe the brain itself combines prior knowledge with sensory information. For example, you can recognize the lines and curves in this article as letters only after you have learned to read. And this is exactly what we are looking for: models that show what is happening in the brain in a realistic fashion. We hope to improve the models to such an extent that we can also apply them to the working memory or to subjective experiences such as dreams or visualizations.[3]

Neuroelectromagnetic Mind Control

It is one thing to read someone's mind, and quite another to actually control it. However, it seems that this, too, may have been done.

It was Dr. Michael Persinger, a neurologist at Laurentian University of Ontario, Canada, who discovered that stimulating different areas of the brain would give rise to different experiences. According to author and conspiracy theorist Glenn Krawczyk, Persinger was also later involved with Operation Black Beauty, which was an electromagnetic broadcasting device designed to be used during riots and other mass civil disobedience.[4] Jim Keith, author of *Mind Control, World Control*, stated that "The device is said to employ time-varying fields of extremely low frequency energy, broadcast at frequencies between 1 and 10 hertz, that cause vomiting in whomever the unit is trained on."[5]

If you think neuro-electric or neuro-electromagnetic weapons or mind-control methods are far out, consider this. If you Google "Voice-to-Skull device" the U.S. Army's website appears. However, when you click on the link, you discover that the page has been taken down. Still, a description remains on the Federation of American Scientist's website. The device is described there as:

> Nonlethal weapon which includes (1) a neuro-electromagnetic device which uses microwave transmission of sound into the skull of persons or animals by way of pulsed-modulated microwave radiation; and (2) a silent sound device which can transmit sound into the skull of persons or animals. Note: The sound modulation may be voice or audio subliminal messages. One application of V2K is use as an electronic scarecrow to frighten birds in the vicinity of airports.[6]

This microwave-sound transmission has another name: Medusa. This project was funded for a period by the U.S. Navy and designed to be a microwave-sound weapon. This type of transmission is a silent audio form that essentially puts noises in a person's head.[7] It's been suggested that it might be used at low power to produce a whisper that was too quiet to perceive consciously but might be able to subconsciously influence someone.[8]

Controlling the Brain

Technology has progressed to the point today that much of what formerly was science fiction is no longer fictional at all. For example, scientists have learned to read the thoughts of monkeys. They have decoded brain activity and have thereby been enabled to predict monkey movement before a muscle is moved.[9]

This sort of technology has advanced way beyond predicting monkeys' actions. Researchers have been able to manipulate neurons in the brains of worms and thereby take control of their behavior.[10]

In one study, fMRI was used to "see" the mental picture subjects had of others. This study demonstrated that it was possible to determine who someone was thinking about by viewing activated brain patterns.[11]

In another project, scientists at the Korea Advanced Institute of Science and Technology successfully controlled live turtles remotely.[12]

Another interesting development of this nature comes from the field of optogenetics, in which genetically programmed neurons can be triggered by light. Injecting tiny LEDs into the brain gives researchers the ability to direct the activity of those neurons. Some of the researchers in this area have advanced the art in recent days.

"These materials and device structures open up new ways to integrate semiconductor components directly into the brain," said John Rogers, the Swanlund professor of materials science and engineering at the University of Illinois. "More generally, the ideas establish a paradigm for delivering sophisticated forms of electronics into the body: ultra miniaturised devices that are injected into and provide direct interaction with the depths of the tissue."

Rogers believes the devices could provide neuroscientists with a new way of measuring and manipulating the brain and other living tissues. One obvious application is in optogenetics experiments, which involve genetically modifying neurons to make them fire in response to light.[13]

In another recent announcement, Harvard scientists reported human-to-rat, brain-to-brain control.[14]

Topping that came the announcement by researchers at the University of Washington who reported telepathy between humans in a human-to-human, brain-to-brain connection.

> By wearing an EEG cap that read his brain's electrical signals, UW computer scientist Rajesh Rao was able to use his thoughts to control the actions of Assistant Professor Andrea Stucco, who wore a transcranial magnetic stimulation coil that stimulates brain activity. A code was used to translate brain signals from EEG readings into brain commands.
>
> With both hands on his chair's armrests, Rao envisioned his right hand moving, as if he was clicking a "fire" button on a cannon-shooting video game. Across campus, Stucco had his back to the computer screen where the video game was playing out. Still, he involuntary moved his right hand and pushed his keyboard's space bar to fire the cannon.
>
> "It was both exciting and eerie to watch an imagined action from my brain get translated into actual action by another brain," Rao said in a university news release. "This was basically a one-way flow of information from my brain to his. The next step is having a more equitable two-way conversation directly between the two brains."[15]

Think about the possibilities inherent in this technology. As a former lie detection examiner, I can see interrogation headed this way soon. fMRI is already in use for the detection of deception, and according to one leading developer, Joel Huizenga, who spoke with me on my *Provocative Enlightenment* radio show, it is 100% accurate.[16]

Unconscious Emotions

One of the most intriguing studies I have reviewed in the past several years has a passage that really caught my attention: "Further complicating matters is that many emotional responses may not be consciously experienced."[17]

Think about that. Researchers were able to identify unconscious emotions using fMRI technology. The study was designed to analyze emotions and, in the process, researchers not only succeeded in identifying those emotions the participants were aware of but they also identified unconscious emotions. Think of how this discovery might be used. When we think of mind reading, we typically imagine that our thoughts will be read, but did you ever think that your unconscious might be read?

"Despite manifest differences between people's psychology, different people tend to neurally encode emotions in remarkably similar ways," noted Amanda Markey, a graduate student in the Department of Social and Decision Sciences [Carnegie Mellon University].

A surprising finding from the research was that almost equivalent accuracy levels could be achieved even when the computer model made use of activation patterns in only one of a number of different subsections of the human brain.

"This suggests that emotion signatures aren't limited to specific brain regions, such as the amygdala, but produce characteristic patterns throughout a number of brain regions," said Vladimir Cherkassky, senior research programmer in the Psychology Department.[18]

Artificial Memories

In September of 2013, scientists at UC Irvine succeed in creating specific memories by manipulating the brain.

Research led by senior author Norman M. Weinberger, a research professor of neurobiology & behavior at UC Irvine, and colleagues has shown that specific memories can be made by directly altering brain cells in the cerebral cortex, which produces the predicted specific memory. The researchers say this is the first evidence that memories can be created by direct cortical manipulation.[19]

Think about that. This is reminiscent of the Arnold Schwarzenegger movie *Total Recall*. Although this technology is exciting in terms of its potential therapeutic applications, it is also frightening when we consider how advanced technologies have been used by some of our clandestine agencies.

But while we're thinking about *Total Recall,* add this into the mix. On the same day that the science news headlined stories about artificial memories, this story appeared.

> Now, for the first time, scientists from the Florida campus of The Scripps Research Institute (TSRI) have been able to erase dangerous drug-associated memories in mice and rats without affecting other more benign memories.
>
> The surprising discovery, published this week online ahead of print by the journal *Biological Psychiatry*, points to a clear and workable method to disrupt unwanted memories while leaving the rest intact.[20]

So we now possess the technology to erase a memory and implant a new one, and you need not know that either has occurred. I can't help but wonder who will be the architects or mind managers in the future, deciding what should be erased and what new memories would be beneficial. Urgh!!!

The Lilly Wave

I would be remiss if I failed to inform you of both a mind-control technique reportedly perpetrated by electromagnetic means and also the alleged countermeasure for it. The Lilly Wave, as it is called, is an electrical current waveform that can stimulate animals via implanted electrodes. The wave can be passed through the brain for extended periods without causing either thermal or electrolytic damage. It is named for its finder, John Cunningham Lilly. It is believed to be a "carrier waveform that bypasses the mind's subconscious defense systems."[21]

I say "believed" because I have no firsthand experience with this technology, nor do I know anyone who has. Still, proponents of this sort of technology and the counter measures can be convincing.

> It has been monitored via oscilloscopes connected to homes' A/C ground and neutral of power lines. It can be used to transmit mind control via ultrasonic (1—10MHz) and electromagnetic wavelengths (600m to 1e-15m). Electromagnetic wavelengths transmit long/short/FM wave-

length radio waves, and TV/telephone/wireless signals or energies. They are also responsible for transmitting energy in the form of microwaves, infrared radiation (IR), visible light (VIS), ultraviolet light (UV), X-rays, and gamma rays (1996). The Lilly wave can be neutralized via pink or white noise generators connecting to the non-voltage A/C ground and neutral of the homes' power grid.[22]

Psychotronics

An entire field of information deals with the idea of transferring information directly from animal to animal or via a carrier such as a scaler wave. The scope of this information is broad and beyond the purpose of this book. I have covered this information in some depth in my book *Thinking Without Thinking*. For our purposes here, now-unclassified work from the former Soviet Union combined with the research of such American researchers as Russel Targ and Harold Putoff clearly shows that psychotronic weapons may be entirely possible, and "These weapons would be able to induce illness or death at little or no risk to the operator."[23]

9/11 and the Takeover of Civil Rights

According to Rense.com, Americans are the target of the largest brainwashing media effort in history. In a rather interesting article, they insist that the media, controlled by the "Anglo-American establishment" and run as a cartel, has used 9/11 as a terror device to stage the largest takeover of civil rights in history. They cite some interesting historical information.

> Cyrulik is part of a network of "thinkers" who seek to change all military doctrine to meet alleged 21st Century threats; in so doing, this network wants to activate psyops, including "covert warfare" such as assassinations. While we can't say that such people are directly responsible for what occurred on September 11, their assumptions about strategy, tactics, and the elevated value of psychological warfare, as well as the misdirection involved in their ascribing powers to "terrorist organizations" or "rogue states" fit nicely into the overall operation . . .

"God, this is just like a movie," exclaimed CBS anchor Dan Rather as the first of the World Trade Center towers collapsed. "Only, it's the real thing." Did you have the sense, as you were witnessing the horror of the WTC attack, that you, too, had seen this before? You probably had—and that is part of the brainwashing operation.

In the last five years, there have been at least a half dozen movies whose plots have centered on a terrorist attack on the United States. Hollywood statisticians have estimated that these have been viewed, both in movie theaters and home videos, by more than 100 million people. And, many of these movies, in the recent period, have portrayed "Arabs" or "Islamic fundamentalists" as being behind the terrorist assaults.

Each of these latter films has some "expert" advisor, usually a "former counterterrorism expert" and, in some cases, someone who has worked in the military. While it would be a leap to say that the movie production companies or the "experts" are necessarily witting accomplices in the current plot, the movies, with their "steered" scripts helped people believe that "Arab" terrorists might be capable of what was done on September 11 . . .

In Nazi Germany, Propaganda Minister Josef Goebbels boasted that the press was free to report whatever it wanted. But that press was "coordinated" through the operation of a "press trust," that encompassed all media. The Nazis planted stories in the press to suit their ends, and the trust dutifully reported them, with various spins that might give the appearance that not all media were receiving information from the same spigot.

While Americans might find it hard to believe, THERE IS NO PRACTICAL DIFFERENCE BETWEEN THE PROPAGANDA OPERATION OF THE NAZI PRESS TRUST AND THE ANGLO-AMERICAN MEDIA AND ENTERTAINMENT CARTEL. It is not hard to slant the coverage of any event to suit almost any purpose—as long as that purpose fits the needs of those elites that control the media. All it takes is the planting of a few key items of content, which are then flushed down through the media sewer pipes. Before you know it, the poor citizen is deluged. In a certain sense, the Nazi operation was less insidious because it was more overt; only fools would fail to realize that they were being fed the "line" by Goebbels and his crew. Here, the appearance of choice, the appearance of a flood of information, confuses the average citizen into believing that he MUST BE GETTING THE TRUTH, FROM SOMEWHERE.[24]

The Rense article concluded that our best defense, indeed, our only defense, came from recognizing the programming and our own level of brainwashing. In the alternative, the world as we know it ends—news at eleven.

It was the view of Trist and Emery (Eric Trist and Fred Emery, two leading Tavistock brainwashers and "experts" on the effects of mass media) in two works widely circulated among the networks of brainwashers and social psychiatrists associated with Tavistock, and among the psychological warfare operatives of the U.S. and Britain, that the process of watching television was itself a brainwashing mechanism. They cited their own studies, that regardless of content, habituated television viewing shuts down the cognitive powers of the mind and has a narcotic-like effect on the central nervous system, making the habituated viewer an easy subject for suggestion and manipulation; in addition, they found that such effectively brainwashed "zombies" would hysterically deny that there was anything wrong with them, or, even, that such manipulation of what they "thought" were possible.

In a chilling metaphor, Trist and Emery proposed that the terrorized, violent society of the Anthony Burgess book, *A Clockwork Orange*, made into a movie by Stanley Kubrick, was the logical societal outcome for an America that would, by the end of the century, have been subjected to more than 50 years of mass brainwashing by the "boob tube." Burgess's world is one of perpetual violence and terrorism, as a daily part of life; it is accepted that, if you go out at a certain time, or walk in a certain neighborhood, you will be attacked and/ or killed. There is no purpose to the violence—it is random and meaningless, and therefore all the more terrifying. The wealthy are protected; everyone else is told to go about their business with knowledge of the risk.[25]

(The Tavistock Institute developed the mass brain-washing techniques, which were first used experimentally on American prisoners of war in Korea. Its experiments in crowd control methods have been widely used on the American public, a surreptitious but nevertheless outrageous assault on human freedom by modifying individual behavior through topical psychology. A German refugee, Kurt Lewin, became director of Tavistock in 1932. He came to the U.S. in 1933 as a 'refugee,' the first of many infiltrators, and set up the Harvard Psychology Clinic, which originated the propaganda campaign to turn the American public against Germany and involve us in World War II.[26])

Popular Methods of Mind Control

To bring things all together, you should be aware that there are at least ten modern methods in popular use for mind control.

1. Education

When you think about it, education is of course the most obvious place to start when considering the different ways the public can be manipulated. This is such an important area that we will cover it in detail later.

2. Advertising and Media

By now, I think we are all very aware of the wholesale use of advertising and media in shifting the beliefs of the public at large

3. Predictive Programming

Predictive programming is a kind of pacing in which Hollywood offers us a vision of what could be in the future. For example, films like *Brokeback Mountain* have been credited with changing attitudes toward the gay population. Some argue that science fiction films prepare us for future events just as emotionally laden films tenderize our attitudes and ideas regarding many issues.

4. Politics, Sports, and Religion

You may find it strange that politics, sports, and religion are in the same category, but these all inform and manage our perceptions and expectations. Winners, for example, are always praised, and most of us are familiar with the famous line of Hall of Fame football coach Vince Lombardi: "Winning isn't everything—it's the ONLY thing!"

We also all know how divisive politics and religion can be, and that is precisely because they both have such a powerful influence on us. To nonbelievers, it is almost impossible to think that religious persons who believe in intelligent design are capable of passing a written driver's test—their intelligence, or lack thereof, is so dismissed. And for the conservative who is convinced that the world is a threatening place in need of advanced security, the idea of large reductions in military spending is simply foolish! You get the picture.

5. Food, Water, Air, and Drugs

The need for food, water, air, and drugs is something we have yet to discuss, but for now, just know that these also offer channels through which manipulation can occur. As a quick example, consider this gotcha: Suppose we are given an inoculation for polio, only to learn years later that it contained a cancer-causing agent? This is an important area and one I will cover in detail later, along with many other gotchas.

6. Addictions

Addictions are a very interesting method for mind control, as it doesn't really matter what you are addicted to, only that you are addicted. Once you are addicted, that very fact can be used against you. In America today, it is considered almost unheard of for a household not to own a television or phone, and most households have several of both! We have already covered the Obama phones, but I wonder how long it will be before televisions are also offered in the same way—as an entitlement. And then there is the more serious issue of drugs. There appears to be an effort to medicate most of the population, as can be seen in the increasing use of statin drugs and also in the wholesale use of such drugs as Ritalin for children. And of course, there is the issue of mass medications, such as fluoridating the public water systems.

7. Government and Military

As we have seen, our government and military have carried out a great deal of research on technologies that can entrain our brains or otherwise circumvent our discretionary decision-making processes. Consider such tools as HAARP and such methods as MKUltra that were discussed earlier.

8. Television, computer, and flicker-rates.

We have already seen that the physiology lends itself to being taken advantage of as well. For example, the flicker rate of television induces alpha consciousness, which in turn makes the viewer more open to suggestion. The computer screen has a different flicker rate from that of television, but studies have shown that blood flow to the brain is lessened with prolonged computer gaming.[27] With this kind of information, it is only a matter of time before those in power find a way to use it to exert control through this means.

9. Electromagnetic Spectrum

There is an ever-increasing electromagnetic spectrum that envelops us all. When you think about the Soviet Woodpecker signal or the U.S. Army's "Voice-to-Skull device," this has to be an area of concern, especially when you also consider the huge number of cell phone towers.

10. Implants

Lastly we have the world of implants, ranging from tags, such as those suggested in the Affordable Health Care Act (Obamacare) to identify medical histories and allegedly thereby eliminate many medical errors, to nanobots, which would run around inside our bodies for the alleged purpose of keeping us well. Any and all of these devices can be programmed for nefarious purposes as well as employed as sophisticated tracking devices.

When you're finished adding up the many ways we can be managed, it is reasonable to ask about the herd and the herders. Are we just part of the herd? If so, who is herding us where and for what purpose? Is it possible to leave the herd and go unnoticed? Or is it possible to change the course of the herd itself?

CONCLUSION

Did you ever think about addictions as a means of mind control? Have you given serious thought before to how much television all of us watch? Do you worry about the quality of food and water that you consume? Are you happy with the direction your food and water supply are going? Before reading this book, did you give any thought to the power our education system has on indoctrinating the public? Or how about textbook revisions—do you approve of this? What can you do in your local community to impact the abuse of these technologies? Do you think that letters to local television stations, newspapers, and legislators will make a difference? Many people don't, and by now you understand the psychology behind that as well. The fact is, you can make a difference, and it begins locally where your influence can easily be heard and magnified. There are indeed many examples of one person doing great things; think of Martin Luther King, Mahatma Gandhi, Nelson Mandela, and Mother Teresa. But you don't have to leave such a large footprint to be important. One person brought stevia to America. One person decided to form Doctors Without Borders. One person's ideas have often changed the world and we don't even know their names, but we do enjoy the benefits of their labors. Are you one who waits for someone else or are you one willing to rise up and do what you can to empower your neighborhood, your community, your city, your state, your country and your world? One person at a time is how the world changes. I urge you to be one of those who dares to boldly go where you can best effect the change that leads to the world we all envision—a world framed by our Bill of Rights!

CHAPTER TWENTY-ONE

Data Mining

We are moving rapidly into a world in which the
spying machinery is built into every object we encounter.
~Howard Rheingold

Misconception: *Most believe they have no misconceptions about data mining, as they are already suspicious of our intelligence agencies, their tools, tactics, and technologies.*
Fact: *Still we use our smart phones and otherwise comply with the many levels of added security imposed since 9-11 in our country.*

Many Americans, at least those who are moviegoers, are well aware that smart phones can be used to track people. Tracking is not the only thing that spy agencies can do with our smart phones, however. Indeed, in September 2013, the online publication *Spiegel* broke the news that a smart phone could be used to gain access to anything on it, contact list, emails, passwords, and the like. Despite the fact that Americans had been assured only months earlier that the NSA did not monitor private phone calls or spy on average Americans, one release after another through private contractor and whistleblower Edward Snowden have shown that assurance to be a falsehood intentionally told to the public to keep them asleep regarding the real activities of a spying government.

Michael Hayden has an interesting story to tell about the iPhone. He and his wife were in an Apple store in Virginia, Hayden, the former head of the United States National Security Agency (NSA) said at a conference in Washington recently. A salesman approached and raved about the iPhone, saying that there were already "400,000 apps" for the device. Hayden, amused, turned to his wife and quietly asked, "This kid doesn't know who I am, does he? Four hundred thousand apps means 400,000 possibilities for attacks."

Hayden was apparently exaggerating only slightly. According to internal NSA documents from the Edward Snowden archive that *Spiegel* has been granted access to, the U.S. intelligence service doesn't just bug embassies and access data from undersea cables to gain information. The NSA is also extremely interested in that new form of communication, which has experienced such breathtaking success in recent years: smart phones.[1]

iPhone 5S

In late summer 2013, Apple announced the release of its new iPhone 5S. This new smart phone is destined to be a real coup for law enforcement. Indeed, imagine a police state in which citizens volunteer all of the relevant information necessary to identify them wherever they might go, regardless of their disguise.

The new iPhone uses your fingerprint to identify you and unlock the phone. You can bet that many other smart phone makers will rush to copy the new iPhone features. Soon, as with Facebook, the people of the world will volunteer their most personal data, including their fingerprints, and the establishment is most certainly going to gather this information in some data bank, just as they are doing now with other so-called privacy-protected info.

Website Fingerprinting

A study heavily reported late in 2013 conducted by KU Leuven-iMinds discovered that 145 of the Internet's top websites grab user information and track their activities.

Device fingerprinting, also known as browser fingerprinting, is the practice of collecting properties of PCs, smart phones and tablets to identify and track users. These properties include the screen size, the versions of installed software and plugins, and the list of installed fonts. A 2010 study by the Electronic Frontier Foundation (EFF) showed that, for the vast majority of browsers, the combination of these properties is unique, and thus functions as a 'fingerprint' that can be used to track users without relying on cookies. Device fingerprinting targets either Flash, the ubiquitous browser plugin for playing animations, videos, and sound files, or JavaScript, a common programming language for web applications.[2]

Utah Data Center

The NSA's new data center in Utah is allegedly the largest domestic spy lab ever built. When finished, the center will provide one million square feet of total space at an estimated cost of $2 billion. In a revealing article appearing in *RT Question More* (the online newspaper for Russia TV mentioned earlier), we learn that everyone is the target of this data center.

"This is more than just a data center," an official source close to the project told the online magazine *Wired.com*. The source says the center will actually focus on deciphering the accumulated data, essentially code-breaking.

This means not only exposing Facebook activities or Wikipedia requests, but compromising "the invisible" Internet, or the "deepnet." Legal and business deals, financial transactions, password-protected files and inter-governmental communications will all become vulnerable.

Once communication data is stored, a process known as data-mining will begin. Everything a person does—from traveling to buying groceries—is to be displayed on a graph, allowing the NSA to paint a detailed picture of any given individual's life.

With this in mind, the agency now indeed looks to be "the most covert and potentially most intrusive intelligence agency ever," as Wired.com puts it.

William Binney, NSA's former senior mathematician-gone-whistleblower, holds his thumb and forefinger close

together and tells the online magazine:
"We are that far from a turnkey totalitarian state."[3]

The article then went on to inform us that nothing is safe (or private), stating that it is only a matter of time before the NSA is able to break the unbreakable!

> Now, the last hurdle in the NSA's path seems to be the Advanced Encryption Standard cipher algorithm, which guards financial transactions, corporate mail, business deals, and diplomatic exchanges globally. It is so effective that the National Security Agency even recommended it for the U.S. government.[4]

The center will intercept and handle data from around the world gathered by satellites and underground as well as underwater networks of both foreign and domestic origin.

The gorilla of a question in the room is, of course, have we slid into a surveillance state? If so, will we soon need to conform our speech and activities to those approved by the state? When the ACLU discovers that the FBI is illegally collecting information from churchgoers in order to use it to profile those likely to in some way harbor, assist, or become a terrorist, then perhaps the time has already come.[5] Consider visiting **aclu.org/national-security/foia-documents-show-fbi-illegally-collecting-intelligence-under-guise-community.**

Metadata

In June 2013, the world woke up to the news that the NSA had collected millions of phone records of average Americans and stored those records just in case they one day might need them. Initially we learned of Verizon and how the Justice Department justified the actions.

> The order, a copy of which has been obtained by the *Guardian*, requires Verizon on an "ongoing, daily basis" to give the NSA information on all telephone calls in its systems, both within the U.S. and between the U.S. and other countries.
> The document shows for the first time that under the Obama administration the communication records of mil-

lions of U.S. citizens are being collected indiscriminately and in bulk—regardless of whether they are suspected of any wrongdoing.

The secret Foreign Intelligence Surveillance Court (FISA) granted the order to the FBI on April 25, giving the government unlimited authority to obtain the data for a specified three-month period ending on July 19.

Under the terms of the blanket order, the numbers of both parties on a call are handed over, as is location data, call duration, unique identifiers, and the time and duration of all calls. The contents of the conversation itself are not covered.

Under the Bush administration, officials in security agencies had disclosed to reporters the large-scale collection of call records data by the NSA, but this is the first time significant and top-secret documents have revealed the continuation of the practice on a massive scale under President Obama.[6]

The information gathered is classified as metadata. The authority by which this dragnet action was justified is still classified. When the story regarding the data mining broke, the Administration declared that the data had been used to halt at least three attacks on America. That wasn't quite true.

Testifying before the Senate on Wednesday, National Security Agency Deputy Director John Inglis conceded that the bulk collection of phone records of millions of Americans under Section 215 of the USA PATRIOT Act has been key in stopping only one terror plot—not the dozens officials had previously said. Ahead of Wednesday's Senate hearing, the Obama administration released three heavily censored documents related to its surveillance efforts, but the White House has refused to declassify the legal arguments underlying the dragnet or the original rulings by the U.S. Foreign Intelligence Surveillance Court, on which the released order to collect phone records was based.[7]

NSA's Transparency/Truthfulness

Documents published by the *Washington Post* made it clear in 2013 that NSA officials lied when they claimed that they did not spy on U.S. citizens. Indeed, some 2,776 incidents appear in a quarterly report from 2012 alone.[8]

According to the *Post* article, the 2,776 incidents probably represent only a very small percentage of the real total.

> But the more serious lapses include unauthorized access to intercepted communications, the distribution of protected content, and the use of automated systems without built-in safeguards to prevent unlawful surveillance.
>
> The May 2012 audit, intended for the agency's top leaders, counts only incidents at the NSA's Fort Meade headquarters and other facilities in the Washington area. Three government officials, speaking on the condition of anonymity to discuss classified matters, said the number would be substantially higher if it included other NSA operating units and regional collection centers.[9]

How important is your privacy? What trade-offs are you willing to make to give it up? Could it be true that the objective of the government is to collect every bit of information and later determine if it may become useful? How do you feel about that? With all the technology available today, if we input the data available about all of us through the various means available to collect that data, out pops a pretty complete profile. It may be that some mainframe somewhere knows more about each of us than even our most intimate partner.

Banking

It should come as no surprise to anyone that government agencies monitor banking transactions, but did you know there is actually a branch of the NSA called, "Follow the Money"? Now it makes sense to follow the money in matters dealing with terrorists, but that's not the only data collected and kept on file for at least five years.

Indeed, secret documents reveal that the main NSA financial database Tracfin, which collects the "Follow the Money" surveillance results on bank transfers, credit card transactions, and money transfers, already had 180 million datasets by 2011. The corresponding figure in 2008 was merely 20 million.[10]

Not only is much of the activity by the NSA considered illegal in the U.S., but some of it also violates agreements that we have with allies. On September 16, 2013, the German publication *Spiegel* reported on the NSA's money targets this way:

The most politically explosive revelations, though, concern the agency's secret access to the SWIFT networks. Following extensive debates, in 2010 the European Union signed the so-called SWIFT agreement with the U.S. From its headquarters in Belgium, SWIFT handles international transactions for banks and other financial institutions. For many years following the 9/11 terrorist attacks, the U.S. lobbied for access to this international financial data, which SWIFT virtually monopolizes worldwide.

An initial agreement failed in early 2010 after it was vetoed by the European Parliament. A few months later, a slightly watered-down SWIFT agreement was signed with the express approval of the German government.

NSA documents from the archive of whistleblower Edward Snowden now show that the compromise reached with the EU is apparently being circumvented by the U.S. A document from the year 2011 clearly designates the SWIFT computer network as a "target." The secret data collection also involves the NSA department for "tailored access operations."

According to the documents, one of the various means of accessing the SWIFT information has existed since 2006. Since then, it has been possible to read the "SWIFT printer traffic from numerous banks."

In the wake of revelations that the NSA bugged the EU embassies in New York and Washington, the attack on SWIFT could be the next major stress test for relations between the U.S. government and the European Union. The NSA failed to comment on the latest allegations before *Spiegel's* printing deadline on Friday.[11]

It's probably a safe bet that if the information goes down in zeros and ones, someone other than the intended recipient either has the information or access to it. Snowden had access to a so-called lower level network. According to award-winning investigative journalist James Bamford, writing in his book *Body of Secrets: Anatomy of the Ultra-Secret National Security Agency*, the most secret of CIA and NSA networks, known as Intelink-PolicyNet, distributes supersensitive documents not available elsewhere. Access to this network is limited to the president, the vice president, the directors of the CIA and NSA, and a small number of other people.[12]

Many networks link various levels of government, agencies within the government, and foreign government agencies—and one can only imagine the information that may become visible one day. At the lowest end of the networks is what has been labeled as the largest data repository in the world, and it circulates unclassified and open source data. This network is called Intelink-U.[13]

When you Google "intelink," a variety of listings is found, each explaining something about the nature and purpose of a particular version of "intelink." For example, **www.intelink.gov/** asks us to "Please choose one of the following authentication options in order to access Intelink. Selection of an authentication method constitutes your acceptance of both." Contrast this to Intelink-U where we are informed:

> Intelink-U is a sensitive-but-unclassified network for information sharing and collaboration across many different federal, state, and local government agencies. They are continuing to expand their acceptance of HSPD-12 credentials. According to Intelink:
>
> "This eliminated unnamed user access to Intelink-U services, removed users' need to authenticate to individual Intelink-U services. Recognizing HSPD-12 credentials reduced Intelink-U accounts by two-thirds, and achieved

PKI authentication for almost 90 percent of active Intelink-U users. This simplifies user access and enhances access control by eliminating varied access methods."[14]

On the other hand, Google Intelink-C, the link between intelligence agencies in the U.S., Canada, the UK, and Australia, and you find a Wiki listing but no dot gov information.

The bottom line is this: Various data banks are storing, transferring, and otherwise holding information that we can only guess how many have access to, how many are known, or how many permanently store what. In this sense, George Orwell was definitely a prophet! In the words of Bamford, "The National Security Agency is the world's most powerful, most far-reaching espionage organization."[15]

Affordable Health Tracking

It's not news to report that the Affordable Care Act (Obamacare) is controversial in America, but here's something that may add to the controversy when it becomes widely known. When individuals enroll in Obamacare, their computer IP address is linked to their name, bank accounts, Social Security number, and even web-surfing habits. Reportedly the information is handed over to the NSA for storage in the new mega data center in Utah.

Armed with this information, the NSA can then link your seemingly anonymous online chats, comments, and posts with your Social Security number. Linguistic algorithms can "score" your online posts to create red flags that call for additional investigations of anyone using words like "liberty" or "patriot."

This information can then be turned over to law enforcement, as is found in the fine print of the Maryland Obamacare exchange, which states:

. . . we may share information provided in your application with the appropriate authorities for law enforcement and audit activities.

Thus, by enrolling in Obamacare, you are voluntarily

surveilling yourself and handing over the data to the government while also AGREEING to terms of self-incrimination.[16]

CONCLUSION

Fear has long been the tactic used to control the masses, and now 'convenience' is also becoming an effective tool. What happens when we give too much information away? By now, this answer should be pretty clear. The more 'they' know about us, the more they can 'persuade us' to make their choices! Sometimes, living an awake and aware life means looking at the big picture. Right now our freedoms are being taken away from us but we are not really aware of the effects, but what will the world be like for our children, or grandchildren? Are today's conveniences worth giving up our freedom and that of our children?

The best protection we have at this moment is simply that of caring. The fact is, it does matter that there is someone watching our buying habits, collecting our fingerprints, monitoring our health. When you speak up for your own freedoms, you are also speaking up for the freedoms of generations to come. Is there any incentive better than that?

CHAPTER TWENTY-TWO

Who Are They Protecting?

When truth is replaced by silence, the silence is a lie.
~Yevgeny Yevtushenko

Misconception: *Most believe that matters such as indefinite detention and sanctioned killings are the rubric of the movies.*
Fact: *The fact is, the evidence suggests that not only should we all be aware of this, but we should also be concerned about the alarming number of freedoms that are being surrendered on a regular basis.*

❖ ❖ ❖

As we have discussed before, the Pentagon plays war games in all parts of the world. Contingency plans exist for every imaginable possibility. So it should not surprise you to know that our government games its own people.

What would happen if there was an economic meltdown? What if there was a massive revolt by the citizens? How would government respond?

Many believe that one of the reasons behind all of the domestic spying is to maintain watch on those who may instigate such an event. And should there be a revolt by citizens, "DoD might be forced by circumstances to put its broad resources at the disposal of civil authorities to contain and reverse violent threats to domestic tranquility. Under the most extreme circumstances, this might include use of military force against hostile groups inside the United States. Further, DoD would be, by necessity, an essential enabling hub for the continuity of political authority in a multi-state or nationwide civil conflict or disturbance."[1]

Are there not supposed to be restrictions on how the U.S. military can be used against its own citizens?

> The U.S. military expects to have 20,000 uniformed troops inside the United States by 2011 trained to help state and local officials respond to a nuclear terrorist attack or other domestic catastrophe, according to Pentagon officials.
>
> The long-planned shift in the Defense Department's role in homeland security was recently backed with funding and troop commitments after years of prodding by Congress and outside experts, defense analysts said.
>
> There are critics of the change, in the military and among civil liberties groups and libertarians who express concern that the new homeland emphasis threatens to strain the military and possibly undermine the Posse Comitatus Act, a 130-year-old federal law restricting the military's role in domestic law enforcement.[2]

How does this make you feel? Are you more secure knowing that the military will suppress any interior uprising? How would this "use of the military against U.S. citizens" differ from what such other countries as Libya, Egypt, and Syria have experienced? Perhaps just trusting that our government would never take such harsh steps to put down a civil disturbance helps us rest well at night, but is that trust reasonable?

Of course, as with all the surveillance and increased "security," it is for our own protection. We willingly subscribe to that belief. At least most of us seem to. And every time I think about it, I remember Benjamin Franklin's famous words: "He who sacrifices freedom for security deserves neither."

Benghazi

There is little doubt that the American public was initially told a tall tale about what happened in Benghazi when our diplomatic compound was stormed and U.S. Ambassador J. Christopher Stevens and three others were killed. Very few people today still believe that the event was a spontaneous demonstration caused by an anti-Islamic YouTube video.

As of the time of this writing, the American public still does not know the full extent of President Obama and then-Secretary of State Hillary Clinton's involvement in the handling of the situation as it was unfolding. We do know that neither of them were in the situation room at any point that evening, that the president had only one half hour meeting with his defense officials, Defense Secretary Leon Panetta and Joint Chiefs Chairman Gen. Martin Dempsey, at 5pm (EST),[3] and that he made one call to Secretary Clinton right before 10pm (EST).[4] We also know that Ansar al-Sharia took credit for the event and that both President Obama and Secretary Clinton were aware of this at the time.[5] However, the narrative that the Obama administration chose to tell for two weeks after the attack was that this was all a spontaneous action as a result of a video that was airing on YouTube. There is also no satisfactory reason for why we failed to send support. However, according to attorneys Joe diGenova and Victoria Toensing, who represent Benghazi witnesses and others with knowledge of the attack, 400 surface-to-air missiles were stolen. Further, the administration's fear that those missiles might be used against our other embassies is what led to shutting down 19 of the embassies in August, 2013.

> DiGenova says he doesn't know if the missiles were physically at the CIA annex on the night of September 12—"but it is clear that the annex was somehow involved in the process of the distribution of those missiles." The CIA annex in Benghazi apparently was gathering the Libyan missiles to be sent to an unknown destination.[6]

Were we lied to in order to protect us? It is feasible to think that informing the world that we had lost 400 missiles could be a matter of national security. It is also possible that we were lied to for other reasons. Propaganda has come a long way. Or has it?

> Why did the Obama administration delay the entry of FBI investigators into Benghazi after four Americans, including Ambassador Chris Stevens, were killed that night?

271

DiGenova was asked.

"Because it happened before an election," he replied.

DiGenova said the theft of the missiles continues to have a ripple effect: "This is why we shut down the 19 embassies recently. They were afraid that there was going to be a missile attack on one of the embassies. Remember, you can take a shoulder-held missile and shoot it into an embassy, not just into the sky.

"What happened is, the reason they lied, about—in other words, remember the famous demonstration, and the phony video and all of that? That's what this was all about. That's why they're so worried."[7]

Whistleblower or Traitor

One tool of every successful propaganda machine is fear. How do you instill fear in those who might rat out your bad deeds? You call them traitors! You charge them with treason! In recent years we have seen several whistleblowers, or traitors, depending on your point of view, deliver information to the public that has embarrassed the government by disclosing their lies. Is that the act of a traitor? Treason is defined in the law as "The betrayal of one's own country by waging war against it or by consciously or purposely acting to aid its enemies."[8]

Manning

Bradley Manning is the U.S. Army private who was convicted of releasing the largest set of classified documents ever leaked to the public. Is what Manning did treason? Was Manning used to send a signal to all—do not mess with this administration? In other words, was Manning the example designed to shut up potential whistleblowers? I tend to think so, and it was probably effective. But should we be alarmed by actions of this sort?

The German publication *Spiegel* made the point this way:

> It was never an issue whether Bradley Manning violated U.S. law. Manning pleaded guilty to 10 charges at the beginning of his military trial. The maximum sentence for those charges was 20 years in prison—an intolerable sentence, but

unlikely to be the extent of his punishment.

That punishment could now be a 136-year prison sentence. Prosecutors have brought in the big guns—and invoked the Espionage Act, which was passed in 1917 in reaction to fears of German spies and saboteurs.

It is political despotism to use this act in a trial that has to do with neither espionage nor sabotage. It means the defense can no longer argue that the defendant harmed no one, that he acted in the public interest. It deprives Manning of the only basis to justify his actions and the opportunity to avoid a guilty verdict.

This is why the appropriate reaction to this verdict would be to reverse it. It would be overzealous, both from a legal and political standpoint, to pass judgment on Manning as a warning to other possible politically motivated offenders. The 25-year-old soldier, a man who is unconvincing as a heroic figure and burdened with complexes, is the most recent casualty in a hysterically prolonged "war on terror."[9]

Snowden

The same questions we ask regarding Manning also apply in the case of Edward Snowden. When the world learned of PRISM (Planning Tool for Resource Integration, Synchronization, and Management) and other intelligence activities, did that compromise the security of the United States under the definition of treason? As a citizen now aware of how much of your privacy may have been compromised and how many times agency personnel lied to Congress and the American people about their activities, do you believe Snowden simply ratted out the liars, or do you think his actions were treasonous?

Assange

Julian Assange is the founder of WikiLeaks. In 2010 Assange began publishing material regarding military and foreign affairs based on 251,000 diplomatic documents that had been turned over to him. It was Bradley (now Chelsea) Manning who delivered the documents to Assange. In November 2010 a European arrest warrant was issued for Assange. In a bizarre overreaction:

GOTCHA!

On 30 November 2010, Tom Flanagan, a former aide to the Canadian prime minister, Stephen Harper, called for Assange's assassination. Flanagan later retracted his comments, after a Vancouver lawyer filed a complaint with the Calgary Police against Harper,[10] and Canadian nationals filed complaint with the ombudsman of CBC News.[11]

On 1 December 2010, Republican Mike Huckabee called for those behind the leak of the cables to be executed,[12] a view partly supported by Kathleen McFarland, former Pentagon advisor under Nixon, Ford, and Reagan,[13] and current Fox News national security expert.

On 6 December 2010, during a segment of the Fox Business show *Follow the Money*, Fox News political commentator and analyst Bob Beckel stated, "A dead man can't leak stuff. This guy's a traitor. He's treasonous, and he has broken every law of the United States . . . And I'm not for the death penalty, so . . . there's only one way to do it: illegally shoot the son of a bitch." Other guests on the program agreed.[14]

Assange responded on the *Guardian* newspaper website to a reader's question about Flanagan's remarks, by contending that "Mr. Flanagan and the others seriously making these statements should be charged with incitement to commit murder.[15]

Now, you should note that just because most of us perceive politicians and news pundits as being experts, it really does not mean that they can actually separate fact from fiction. They are just as prone to mass brainwashing efforts as any of us. In fact, they are probably more prone, as they have already invested heavily in following a particular party line. Combining this investment with brainwashing ideals, and these experts can become the most dangerous weapon in the arsenal of brainwashing techniques. The more dangerous because they can speak with utter sincerity!

At the time of this writing, Julian Assange is in the Ecuadorian Embassy in London, England. In a statement released on the day of Bradley's sentencing, Assange had this to say:

. . . it should be remembered that Mr. Manning's trial and conviction is an affront to basic concepts of Western justice. On Mr. Manning's arrest in May 2010, he was immediately subjected to punitive incarceration by the U.S. government, which was found to be "cruel, inhumane, and degrading" by the U.N. Special Rapporteur on Torture, Juan Mendez, and even found to be unlawful by U.S. military courts.

Mr. Manning's treatment has been intended to send a signal to people of conscience in the U.S. government who might seek to bring wrongdoing to light. This strategy has spectacularly backfired, as recent months have proven. Instead, the Obama administration is demonstrating that there is no place in its system for people of conscience and principle. As a result, there will be a thousand more Bradley Mannings.[16]

ATF Whistleblower

Not all whistleblowers leak information. Some step forward and offer the information publicly to the press and other interested parties. Such is the case with ATF Agent John Dodson. He was recently denied permission to tell the story of the botched gun deal involving the Justice Department known as Fast and Furious. And the reason the public could not learn what Dodson had to say in his proposed book was that, "'It would have a negative impact on morale,' according to the very agency responsible for the scandal."[17]

After first trying to stop the operation internally, ATF Agent John Dodson went to Congress and eventually the media following the death of Border Patrol Agent Brian Terry in December 2010. Two guns found at the murder scene were sold through the ATF operation.

Dodson's book, titled *The Unarmed Truth*, provides the first inside account of how the federal government permitted and helped sell some 2,000 guns to Mexican drug cartels, despite evidence the guns killed innocent people.

Dodson, who is working with publisher Simon & Schuster, submitted his manuscript to the department for review, per federal rules. However, it was denied.

Greg Serres, an ATF ethics official, told Dodson that any of his supervisors at any level could disapprove outside employment "for any reason."

Serres' letter said, "This would have a negative impact

275

on morale in the Phoenix Field Division and would have a detrimental effect on our relationships with DEA and FBI."

The ATF said in a statement, though, that they did not actually block Dodson from publishing.

"ATF has not denied the publishing of a manuscript or an individual's First Amendment rights. We have denied Mr. Dodson outside employment which can be denied for any reason by a supervisor," the agency said. "While his supervisor stated morale and interagency issues for the denial, the fact remains no agent may profit financially from information gained through his federal employment while still an employee.

"This is not about First Amendment rights; this is about a current employee trying to profit financially from knowledge he has gained while currently employed as a special agent."

The national office of the American Civil Liberties Association is representing Dodson as he fights the decision. ACLU attorney Lee Rowland says the agency's restriction is overly broad.[18]

Indefinite Detention

An extremely interesting article titled "The Military Coup of 2012: Encroachment upon Basic Freedoms, Militarized Police State in America," by Frank Morales, begins by informing the reader that a fictional article by that title was a prizewinner in a competition sponsored by the National War College. The article then proceeds to interweave the fictional article with real world developments.

The ostensibly fictional work is written from the perspective of an imprisoned senior military officer about to be executed for opposing the military takeover of America, a coup accomplished through "legal" means. The essay makes the point that the coup was "the outgrowth of trends visible as far back as 1992," including "the massive diversion of military forces to civilian uses," particularly law enforcement.

Dunlap cites what he considered a dangerous precedent, the 1981 Military Cooperation with Civilian Law Enforcement Agencies Act, an act that sanctioned U.S. military engagement with law enforcement in domestic "support operations," including "civil disturbance" operations. The act codified the lawful status and use of military "assets" in domestic police work.[19]

The encroachment parallels only begin with the interface of military and police. The indefinite detention provision in the National Defense Authorization Act (NDAA) signed into law by President Obama is used to illustrate the extent to which we must all now "trust" our government.

While President Obama issued a signing statement saying he had "serious reservations" about the provisions, the statement only applies to how his administration ("you can trust me") would use the authorities granted by the NDAA, and would not affect how the law is interpreted by subsequent administrations. The White House had threatened to veto an earlier version of the NDAA, but reversed course (of course) shortly before Congress voted on the final bill, which the president signed on the 31st of December 2011, a day that will go down in infamy.

"President Obama's action today is a blight on his legacy because he will forever be known as the president who signed indefinite detention without charge or trial into law," said Anthony D. Romero, ACLU executive director. "The statute is particularly dangerous because it has no temporal or geographic limitations, and can be used by this and future presidents to militarily detain people captured far from any battlefield," according to Senator Dianne Feinstein. "Congress is essentially authorizing the indefinite imprisonment of American citizens, without charge," she said. "We are not a nation that locks up its citizens without charge." Think again.

Under the legislation, suspects can be held without trial "until the end of hostilities." They will have the right to appear once a year before a committee that will decide if the detention will continue. A spokesperson for Human Rights Watch implied that the signing of such a bill by a president would have once been unthinkable, noting that "the paradigm of the war on terror has advanced so far in people's minds that this has to appear more normal than it actually is." Further, "it wasn't asked for by any of the agencies on the frontlines in the fight against terrorism in the United States. It breaks with over 200 years of tradition in America against using the military in domestic affairs."[20]

Trust? If this doesn't concern you—it should! If you're not aware, you should be—this piece of legislation is in direct violation of the Fourth and Fifth Amendments to the Constitution.

We should recall, that the current attempt by the executive to designate American citizens for detention without trial; a naked violation of the Fourth and Fifth Amendments to the U.S. Constitution against unreasonable search and seizure and the guarantee of a trial, was preceded by the administration's "resolve" to assassinate at will Americans abroad, place them on a "kill list," and eliminate them. According to the New York Times "Secret 'Kill List' Proves a Test of Obama's Principles and Will," the president and his advisors have made it clear that they have the authority "to order the targeted killing of an American citizen, in a country with which the United States was not at war, in secret and without the benefit of a trial."

The Justice Department's Office of Legal Counsel rationalized such a move in "a lengthy memo justifying that extraordinary step, asserting that while the Fifth Amendment's guarantee of due process applied, it could be satisfied by internal deliberations in the executive branch." Accordingly, after a dubious period of "internal deliberations," Mr. Obama gave his approval, and the cleric Anwar al-Awlak was assassinated in September 2011, along with an associate Samir Khan, an American citizen who was not on the target list but happened to be traveling with Mr. al-Awlak. Apparently, campaign rhetoric and public demeanor to the contrary, when asked what surprised him most about Mr. Obama, Mr. Donilon, the national security adviser, answered immediately: "He's a president who is quite comfortable with the use of force on behalf of the United States."[21]

Posse Comitatus Act

The Posse Comitatus Act is the only piece of legislation that prevents the military from being used on citizens. Current acts and legislation have sought to undermine this act. Indeed, today the U.S. Army has a division trained to enter the domestic scene and interface with local law enforcement. As we have already discussed, this practice has already seen its first dress rehearsal with the Army taking over Gillette, a small town in Wisconsin.[22]

Secret Court Equals Secret Government

The FISA Court (FISC) operates in secret with one judge making the final rulings. According to material recently declassified, we have learned that the government is getting rulings that are used as precedents to circumvent or even trump the Constitution.

> Revelations about the secretive FISA "court" (FISC) have been trickling out in the wake of the Snowden NSA leaks. What has emerged indicates that the federal government believes it can secretly set precedents that amend the Constitution in a "court" that consists of a single judge acting in a process that allows no argument by opposing sides. The resulting opinion is then classified "Top Secret" and used as legal cover for government actions that are clearly in violation of the Constitution.
>
> This secret FISC issued a decision over the weekend extending "authority to collect telephony [electronic transmission of voice, fax, or data] metadata in bulk." We know about this secret decision only because DNI Clapper [Director of National Intelligence, James R. Clapper] "decided to declassify and disclose" it publicly.
>
> That same day, Congressman Jim Sensenbrenner, co-architect of the Patriot Act (R) publicly came out against the NSA's phone data dragnet calling it abusive, excessive, and un-American and saying it was time "to put their metadata program out of business."
>
> . . . The heavily redacted, "top secret" FISC opinion replaces Constitutional warrants from judges with "reason-

able, articulable suspicion (RAS) as determined by a limited set of personnel."

But don't worry, there are safeguards and oversight. The FISC decision "requires the government to notify the Court [remember it's really just a single FISA judge] in writing immediately concerning any instance of non-compliance.[23]

Just knowing that the government will notify the FISA court should provide a warm, cozy feeling of trust—right? I certainly hope not, considering the abuse of public trust we have been witness to following the whistleblower leaks of late.

Assembly

Many rules define lawful assembly, a right safeguarded for Americans by the First Amendment. Unfortunately, as with many other rights, there are some interesting ways around it. For example, HR347, also known as the "Federal Restricted Buildings and Grounds Improvement Act of 2011," makes it illegal to gather in protest anywhere the Secret Service is present. This bill was signed into law early in 2012. Some argue that this is but another step in the elimination of the First Amendment while the ACLU sees it as no big deal. The law makes it unlawful to gather anywhere the Secret Service is.

In 1998, Bill Clinton signed Presidential Decision Directive 62 establishing the National Special Security Events, or NSSE, a directive making the Secret Service responsible for security at designated events, including presidential nominating conventions. Other events under NSEE include summits of world leaders, meetings of international organizations, and presidential inaugurations. In other words, with the passage of this bill, it will now be a felony to protest the G20 and globalist "trade" summits and other neoliberal confabs where international banksters and their minions plot our future behind closed doors.[24]

These restricted areas include locations where individuals under Secret Service protection are temporarily located, and certain large special events like a presidential inauguration. They can also include large public events like the

Super Bowl and the presidential nominating conventions (troublingly, the Department of Homeland Security has significant discretion in designating what qualifies as one of these special events).[25]

Since events such as political gatherings are included in this regulation, it does appear to further erode the rights of Americans. We need only reflect on the many times a political gathering has drawn important assemblies, both supporting and protesting the event, to realize the potential impact of this new law. And unfortunately, if history is our tutor, selective prosecution will become the pattern when it comes to the enforcement of HR347.

Guns

Gun control has been an issue for many years. Many claims have been made on both sides of the issue, and they have strongly divided the American people. Winning consent begins with arguments that appeal to our emotions and biases. If you tend to be suspicious and fearful, then you probably oppose gun control. If, on the other hand, you tend to be more concerned about eliminating violence and finding peaceful solutions to problems, then you are probably for gun control. (Remember our earlier discussion of how the brain processes information and the physical differences between brains of liberals and of conservatives.) Given this difference, however, what happens when you decide to prove that guns are dangerous and the study you have run proves otherwise?

In a recent study orchestrated by the CDC [Centers for Disease Control] and carried out by the Institute of Medicine and National Research Council, it was found that individuals involved in violent crimes who defended themselves using techniques other than carrying a gun were more likely to be injured when compared to those who were carrying a concealed firearm.

All in all, the Obama-ordered report ended up finding more pros than cons in regards to the right to an open or concealed weapon. The report also reminds us of the numerous causes of gun deaths, citing that most gun deaths are at the hands of those who used a gun for their suicide—not homicide. The report highlights the poor state of America's suffering mental health. The report states that suicide by guns outweighs the amount of deaths caused by violent crimes by 61 percent.[26]

You had an opinion about gun control when you began reading this section. Are you still convinced of your position? Have you checked it out to assure yourself of all the facts? If your opinion remains the same, what would it take to change it? If nothing could change your mind, is it your thinking, rational mind that is doing the work here or something else?

In light of the many means by which government now can seize control of our lives, do you think that citizens should have a right to resist? After all, our founding documents give the people the right to revolution. How would that right ever be carried out today? Suggest such a thing, and you could be indefinitely detained as an enemy of the state.

Guns may not be the solution; I tend to think that they are not. That said, it disturbs me when I read that the guns of honest folks who registered them are being confiscated, and that's just what happened in Chicago.

There's a good reason that law-abiding gun owners don't want their names on a national gun registry—namely, registration leads to confiscation. Gun control advocates immediately spout that, "No one wants to take your guns" and other assorted platitudes designed to comfort gun owners about the prospect of being treated like sex offenders. And yet, from the city of Chicago comes a story of exactly that: registered gun owners having their guns confiscated . . .

In Illinois, gun owners are required to get a Firearms Owners ID card, or FOID. It's good for ten years, and then you need to renew it. But if you don't renew your card, or if you do something that displeases the powers that be, your FOID is NULL and VOID, which means you can't own guns legally.

Cook County police officers have become increasingly worried that when someone's FOID card is revoked, their guns aren't instantly confiscated. So they're doing exactly what gun control advocates have said that registration would never result in—door-to-door confiscation.[27]

This process may seem perfectly okay to some. I mean, look, these people failed to renew their license. Think of it this way, though. What would you think if your car was confiscated because you failed to renew your driver's license or the car's tags?

Sanctioned Killing?

Could it be true that the FBI planned to kill Occupy movement leaders? Such a plan was confirmed by a redacted document obtained by journalist David Lindorff under the Freedom of Information Act (I honestly wonder how much longer this act will continue to have full force and effect). The FBI has verified the document's authenticity.

> The redacted document obtained from the FBI in Houston states: An identified [DELETED] as of October planned to engage in sniper attacks against protestors (sic) in Houston, Texas if deemed necessary. An identified [DELETED] had received intelligence that indicated the protesters in New York and Seattle planned similar protests in Houston, Dallas, San Antonio, and Austin, Texas. [DELETED] planned to gather intelligence against the leaders of the protest groups and obtain photographs, then formulate a plan to kill the leadership via suppressed sniper rifles.[28]

This isn't the stuff I learned about law enforcement and America. I would like to believe that Lindorff has it wrong and that somehow the document is misunderstood. How about you?

Suspicion or Conspiracy Theory

When does trust devolve to distrust? How many apologies can be made before they become meaningless? How many lies do we hear before we no longer listen? I feel it important to bring something into focus now. As I have said before, I want to trust my government. I want to believe in our leaders. I want to think we live under the best system in the world. I have a big package of ethnocentric biases that causes me to dismiss the possibility that malevolent forces are at work in this great country. Unfortunately, my faith has moved away from the leaders per se and toward the people. "We the people" are at the core of what created the good old USA. What I have attempted to deal with in this book is both so complicated and complex that to do so in detail would lead to a veritable encyclopedia. Therefore, what I have tried to do is place some dots on the page. It is up to you to determine if there is a picture there when you begin to connect them. Perhaps you will find a picture that disturbs you, as it does me. If so, I encourage you to share the picture with others. It is up to us, for if not you, who? And if not now, when?

CONCLUSION

Today the various technologies for mind control and manipulation continue to evolve, becoming more and more sophisticated. In June 2013, the *Washington Times* reported a story under this headline, "Big Brother alert: Cameras in the cable box to monitor TV viewers." The story disclosed the desire of cable companies to collect information on how consumers react to different stimuli.[29] As a result of this technological development, Massachusetts Representative Michael Capuano, a Democrat, introduced the "We Are Watching You Act," with the intention of halting this sort of thing. Will it pass, or will Big Brother be watching you watch?

What are your thoughts on the evolution of this sort of technology? Are you comfortable preparing to live in a world where your whereabouts are always known because of a microchip embedded in your arm? Do you like the idea that merchandisers can buy your psychological profile from the data miners? Do you like the direction of the so-called protection acts that give agencies the power to arrest and hold you without due process indefinitely? Do you fear the misuse and abuse of these powers? If you do, speak up—and speak up loudly! Get behind the brave legislators like Michael Capuano and write your elected officials urging the support of ideas that return your freedoms and safe guard against abuses. You do have the power to make a differ-ence, because it takes just one person at a time!

CHAPTER TWENTY-THREE

What's a Gotcha?

If liberty means anything at all,
it means the right to tell people
what they do not want to hear.
~George Orwell

Misconception: *Most believe that we live in a nation that protects the free speech of honest Americans.*
Fact: *Today speech is seriously limited by political correctness, arguments of hate speech, and more. The fact is, your speech today must conform or you pay a price. You no longer can just express your opinion without being painted a racist, a homophobe, a bigot, etc. You must even be careful when you speak of the "terrorists" and their religious motivation. We are very close to Orwell's newspeak.*

In a typical book, much of the information that follows would have been presented earlier, much earlier. However, the purpose of this work is to make abundantly clear to you that most of your thoughts are not your own and that you have been programmed to think along very specific lines. But first you have to be open to these ideas. It is my hope that by this point you have given up the instinct to laugh or shrug things off as being just the domain of kooky conspiracy nuts and tin foil hat believers. The fact is, a great deal of information out there can be used to manipulate your thoughts, and many groups use this information tirelessly. If anything, having read this far, you should be aware that the greatest conspiracy is the one behind getting you to think that those who present this information are conspiracy freaks! I think of this sort of spin as a *gotcha*!

Dream Team

So, now, let us define in depth what constitutes a gotcha and discuss some the great variety of gotchas you are likely to deal with. Many of our gotchas nowadays are political in nature, and you should not find that surprising now, after having learned something more about the father of propaganda, Edward Bernays, and his history in government and politics. Indeed, the so-called Dream Team of social scientists was assembled by Barack Obama during the 2008 and 2012 presidential elections specifically to take advantage of every ounce of knowledge known about how and why we think and do as we do. These folks orchestrated everything from the major issues to what was said by the volunteers phoning in local jurisdictions to get out the vote. How would you feel if you discovered that the folks on the Dream Team had certain knowledge that could swing an election and you would never know that your decision to vote one way or the other had been manipulated? Would that be a gotcha?

This election season the Obama campaign won a reputation for drawing on the tools of social science. The book *The Victory Lab*, by Sasha Issenberg, and news reports have portrayed an operation that ran its own experiment and, among other efforts, consulted with the Analyst Institute, a Washington voter research group established in 2007 by union officials and their allies to help Democratic candidates.

Less well known is that the Obama campaign also had a panel of unpaid academic advisers. The group—which calls itself the "consortium of behavioral scientists," or COBS— provided ideas on how to counter false rumors, like one that President Obama is a Muslim. It suggested how to characterize the Republican opponent, Mitt Romney, in advertisements. It also delivered research-based advice on how to mobilize voters.

"In the way it used research, this was a campaign like no other," said Todd Rogers, a psychologist at Harvard's Kennedy School of Government and a former director of the Analyst Institute. "It's a big change for a culture that historically has relied on consultants, experts and gurulike intuition."[1]

Hypnotic

A paper on the Internet entitled "Obama's Use of Hidden Hypnosis Techniques in His Speeches" spells out the use of hidden hypnosis techniques in President Barack Obama's speeches.[2] It essentially begins by suggesting that Obama employs a technique developed by the famous psychiatrist and hypnotist Milton Erickson. The technique is known as conversational hypnosis.

Neuro Linguistic Programming (NLP) is based on Erickson's work. NLP can be a covert way in which one gains the trust and consent of another and was originally designed by Erickson for therapeutic purposes. Conversational hypnosis merges the tools of NLP with hypnosis to induce an altered state in an audience (trance), to pace and lead, anchor and bypass, reprogram responses, accomplish an emotion transference, hide secondary meanings, and create suggestions that work like post-hypnotic cues.

The paper is very well written, and I recommend it to everyone interested. The fact is, whether by premeditated design or not, President Obama is a master of elocution. His oratory skills are second to none, and his followers are devout, often totally ignoring facts that contradict the claims of Obama himself.

The press had a heyday, really a "pay day," with the crowds Obama pulled during his first campaign and the women who fainted from excitement. The crowds often did behave as though they were "tranced," or "blissed." *Blissed* is a term I encountered in a short-lived TV series entitled *V*, and the expression certainly seemed to fit the crowds who listened to Obama's speeches, especially when the statement, "There is no such thing as an honest politician" has been a well-known saying for a very long time! In the series *V*, aliens came to earth with malevolent plans disguised behind gifts. Earthlings who listened to the leader of the aliens were said to be "blissed" because they could see only the good in the aliens.

I have listened to and watched carefully many of the presentations made by President Obama. He does, in fact, use techniques that are from the conversation hypnosis strategy book, metaphorically speaking. I have also seen speeches delivered by other great speakers, including the infamous soapbox agitator Adolf Hitler. They all have certain commonalities, such as their use of a particular word count per minute, their tone and inflection, their hand engagement, the elevated podium that tips the head of the audience slightly upward, often leading to eye flutter and even closure, and so forth.

Now, I am fully aware that it is politically incorrect to allude to any commonality between President Obama and Hitler, so I really should make myself clear. In this comparison I am speaking *only* of their oratory skills. Is this an innate skill or something they each rehearsed?

Was Obama coached or taught to use these methods? I don't know. What I do know is that you can only begin to be immune to them if you know about them. I have written extensively about hypnotic tools, including subliminal hypnosis, and have provided a "how-to" guide for inducing self-hypnosis. I would recommend that you check out the PDF article for yourself and learn more about these techniques. In today's world, you either use them or are used by them! (You can find this article online by going to **pennypresslv.com/Obama's_Use_of_Hidden_Hypnosis_techniques_in_His_Speeches.pdf**.)

I can remember reading the book *Catch 22* by American author Joseph Heller, and musing over how it is possible to find yourself in a place where you are trapped by the proverbial "damned if you do and damned if you don't." I thought then, "That's a real gotcha!"

Many years have passed since I read the novel by Heller, and it sometimes seems as though each year I have learned of yet another category of gotchas. Today, there are gotchas everywhere. Some have to do with the news as it is delivered to us, and some with what we are not told. There are gotchas due to the manipulation of what you trust and gotchas that result because of the manipulation of your mind. There are many more categories of gotchas, but since the proverbial picture speaks much louder than discursive definitions, let's look at some gotchas.

Thought Squad

Engineering consent is accomplished with small nudges added to each other over time. The goal is a long-term objective. So what do you think of government creating a behavioral nudge squad?

The "Behavioral Insights Team" to be formed would work with the White House, as well as the Department of Health and Human Services and the Department of Agriculture, among others. The document, emailed by White House senior adviser on social and behavioral sciences Maya Shenker to a university professor, states, "Behavioral sciences can be used to help design public policies that work better, cost less, and help people achieve their goals."

The document names several behavioral changes brought about by British "nudging," including "sending letters to late taxpayers that indicated a social norm," resulting in higher tax receipts. Another British policy promoted "adoption of attic-insulation."[3]

At least no one is denying the ability to nudge (engineer consent) or the intent to do so.

Monsanto

Here's a gotcha for you. Somehow, you guess how, a former Monsanto scientist was appointed to a journal's peer review board that decides which papers will be published. The *Journal of Food and Chemical Toxicology* just added Richard E. Goodman, a former Monsanto researcher with close biotech industry ties, to its senior editorial staff. "Goodman was given the specially created position of associate editor for biotechnology," *Earth Open Source* said.[4]

Or how about this one? In HR933, a bill designed to prevent the financial collapse of the government, President Obama signed into law a rider attached to the bill that is known as the Monsanto Protection Act. "As a result, Monsanto was granted complete immunity from federal courts with regards to their experimental GMO crops—regardless of any scenario . . . This means that even if Monsanto were to go and plant a genetically modified crop variation that was admitted to cause cancer, they would still be immune."[5]

Fukushima

Here's another, a little more subtle but nevertheless a gotcha in my book. There is a lot going on in the world. How much of it is a distraction? The news carries endless stories of drawn out homicide trials but not a word about the Fukushima radiation effects expected on the shores of the U.S. very soon, at least at the time of this writing.

In August 2012, the Japanese government disclosed that they had found radiation levels in a fish caught off Fukushima Prefecture to be 380 times the standard safety level. Since then, no more reports, but tons of debris are still washing up on the Pacific coast, according to an article in the *Liberty Beacon.*[6]

So, is this an 'out of sight, out of mind' strategy suggesting that when it becomes a recognized problem something will be done, but until the population begins to have hair falling out and other forms of radiation poison become prevalent, why deal with it? Perhaps this strategy has worked in the past with everything from the so-called harmless Agent Orange to the doctor-recommended drug thalidomide.

American Government

The call for increased security due to terrorism has led to sweeping changes in our freedoms. We are now protected by the Patriot Act. (There's a gotcha in the title alone. Do you think the original patriots, the founding fathers, would have gone along with this?) During the most recent application of this act, we have seen great abuses. The IRS has targeted groups who hold ideologies opposed to those of the current administration. The Department of Justice has monitored the phone calls and activities of our so-called free press, often inhibiting their ability to obtain or maintain sources. The State Department has blocked the prosecution of members of its own staff. Congress has indicted the attorney general both criminally and civilly for obstruction of justice. The Department of Justice, headed of course by the lawfully indicted attorney general, has done nothing. The NSA and FBI have recorded every phone call and keystroke of millions of Americans and have them on record for future use. None of this is hypothesis or hyperbole—it's all happened circa 2013. The U.S. Constitution prohibits just this sort of invasion. Your rights guaranteed by the First and Fourth Amendments have been trampled. You sip your coffee and lament the direction of things, but after all, what can you do? You're just one person. And in swallowing that belief along with your coffee, you just also swallowed another gotcha!

Search Engines

The metadata collected by Google and others, including the NSA under PRISM, can be used not only to sell you products but to also sell you politics. As we have already said, but it is worth a reminder here, according to Dr. Roberts Epstein 15 percent of the population can easily be guided to cast a vote a certain way. Not only *can* that be done, it can be done without anyone knowing it was done! Elections are often won or lost by swing voters; 15 percent is a number that will win most elections. So what if a search engine determines an election? Is this another gotcha?

According to Epstein, "No company in the history of the world has had this kind of power to alter governments around the world!" Just as the telephone companies (at the time, primarily one company) abused their power by listening in on phone conversations, and just as the credit bureaus were abusing their power, government rightly stepped in, creating tight regulations for both. In a dramatically insistent manner, Epstein adds, "Government must tightly regulate search engines!"[7]

NSA Pays Tech Companies

The *Wall Street Journal* reported that documents released by Edward Snowden showed that the NSA paid Microsoft, Google, Yahoo, and Facebook for data requested based on "secret orders from the Foreign Intelligence Surveillance court under the same PRISM program."[8]

> The document, an NSA newsletter dated December 2012, says that the tech companies faced extensive costs for meeting new certification demands following a secret court ruling. The Obama administration Wednesday [August 21, 2013] declassified the October 2011 ruling, which found the agency violated the Constitution for three years by collecting tens of thousands domestic communications without adequate privacy protections.
>
> "Last year's problems resulted in multiple extensions to the certifications' expiration dates which cost millions of dollars for PRISM providers to implement each successive extension—costs covered by Special Source Operations," the document says, referring to a division of the NSA.[9]

How do you feel, knowing that your data, private emails, phone calls, shares with friends, search engine use, computer purchases, electronic filings whether for your child's school loans or your taxes, and so much more are all available to almost anyone in the NSA, including such reportedly low-level hired contractors as Edward Snowden? Does this anger you or give rise to feeling of helpless hopelessness?

Often this information is met with "It's okay. My life is boring. How can it hurt me if the government knows my favorite grocery store?" But by now, you should know better. They can use this information to make you a puppet . . . and they do!

Encryption Keys

It should not surprise you that the feds are working on obtaining the master encryption keys used by Internet operators to protect users' private info. Do they have the legal authority to demand them?

These demands for master encryption keys, which have not been disclosed previously, represent a technological escalation in the clandestine methods that the FBI and the National Security Agency employ when conducting electronic surveillance against Internet users.

If the government obtains a company's master encryption key, agents could decrypt the contents of communications intercepted through a wiretap or by invoking the potent surveillance authorities of the Foreign Intelligence Surveillance Act. Web encryption—which often appears in a browser with a HTTPS lock icon when enabled—uses a technique called SSL, or Secure Sockets Layer.

"The government is definitely demanding SSL keys from providers," said one person who has responded to government attempts to obtain encryption keys. The source spoke with CNET on condition of anonymity.

The person said that large Internet companies have resisted the requests on the grounds that they go beyond what the law permits, but voiced concern that smaller companies without well-staffed legal departments might be less willing to put up a fight. "I believe the government is beating up on the little guys," the person said. "The government's view is that anything we can think of, we can compel you to do."[10]

At the time of this writing, it is unclear whether the government has the legal right to these keys. However, if history is to be our teacher, whether they do have the right or not is somewhat academic, for they will eventually either usurp the right, even if by intimidation, or create some need for legislation that will provide them the legal basis to obtain the keys. Perhaps they will claim that a cyberattack will happen and use fear (once again) to take away more of your rights. Is this destined to be another gotcha?

Freedom of the Press

Even the freedom of the press, one of our most treasured freedoms and definitely a historical watchdog on government, has recently found itself compromised, threatened, and intimidated. *Spiegel Online* reported in August 2013 on one such event in what they referred to as a "blatant attack on press freedom."[11] U.S. citizen and lawyer-turned-journalist Glenn Greenwald received a cache of documents from Edward Snowden in June, 2013. Glenn's friend and colleague David Miranda was detained at Heathrow Airport in London under the Terrorism Act. Glenn and David had been reporting on the Snowden matter. The article in *Spiegel* is worth quoting here for it contains both first-hand information and powerful questions we should all be asking:

> We now know that David's detention was ordered at the highest levels of the British government, including the prime minister. We also know the U.S. government was given advance warning that David would be detained and interrogated.
>
> The NSA has special relationships with the spy agencies from the so-called "Five-Eyes" nations, which include Britain's GCHQ. Weeks before David was detained, agents from GCHQ entered the offices of the *Guardian* newspaper and oversaw the destruction of several hard drives which contained disclosures made by Snowden. This action was also authorized at the highest levels of the UK government. Included on those drives were documents detailing GCHQ's massive domestic spying program called "Tempora."
>
> This program deploys NSA's XKeyscore "DeepDive" Internet buffer technology, which slows down the Internet to allow GCHQ to spy on global communications, including those of UK citizens. Tempora relies on the "corporate partnership" of UK telecoms, including British Telecommunications and Vodafone. Revealing the secret partnerships between spy agencies and telecoms entrusted with the private communications of citizens is journalism, not terrorism.
>
> The UK government's destruction of material provided by a source to a news organization will surely be remembered as one of the most blatant government attacks on press freedom.
>
> As the hours went by on Sunday, *Guardian* lawyers searched to find where David was being held; the Brazilian ambassador in London could get no information; and

Glenn struggled with whether he should go public or work behind the scenes to make sure David would be released and not arrested. I have never been through a hostage negotiation, but this certainly felt like one. David was finally released after nine hours. He was forced to hand over all electronics.

Using border crossings to target journalism is not new to me. I experienced it for the first time in 2006 in Vienna, when I was traveling from the Sarajevo Film Festival back to New York. I was put in a van and driven to a security room, searched, and interrogated. The Austrian security agents told me I was stopped at the request of the U.S. government. When I landed in New York I was again searched and interrogated.

Since then I have lost count of how many times I have been interrogated at the U.S. border all because of my reporting on post 9/11 issues. I've had electronics seized, notebooks photocopied, and have been threatened with handcuffs for taking notes. I moved to Berlin to edit my next film because I do not feel I can keep source material safe in my own country.

At the moment I live in what used to be East Berlin. It feels strange to come to the former home of the Stasi to expose the dangers of government surveillance, but being here gives me hope. There is a deep historical memory among Germans of what happens to societies when its government targets and spies on its own citizens. The public outcry in Germany to the NSA disclosures has been enormous.

Because of the disclosures made by Edward Snowden, we have for the first time an international debate on the scope of government surveillance. Almost daily for the past three months citizens learn of new unlawful surveillance programs being secretly run by their governments. All of our reporting has been in the public interest, and none has caused harm. David's detention and the destruction of the hard drives in the *Guardian's* basement reveal one thing: Our governments do not want citizens to be informed when it comes to the topic of surveillance. The governments of the United States, Britain, Germany, and others would like this debate to go away. It won't.[12]

Spying on Reporters

The attack on the press became major news a few months earlier when it was discovered that the U.S. Department of Justice had collected two months' worth of phone records of reporters and editors:

> The Justice Department's spying on reporters is being called the latest in the Obama administration's war on leaks. 'The media's purpose is to keep the public informed, and it should be free to do so without the threat of unwarranted surveillance,' Laura W. Murphy, director of the American Civil Liberties Union Washington Legislative Office, said in a statement Monday.[13]

It's not just the NSA and the DOJ who are grabbing records. The FBI has its hands in the cookie jar as well, at least according to some reports. "The ACLU also published a report last week making the argument that recently obtained FBI documents suggest the agency reads emails without a warrant. The documents were obtained by the organization through a Freedom of Information Act request."[14]

Most famous among the many reporters to have their phone records seized is James Rosen. Rosen is the Fox reporter who reported on North Korea's intention to escalate their nuclear tests if additional sanctions were leveled at them. Harken back to the detention of David Miranda, and Glenn Greenwald, who reported on the Rosen case long before Miranda was detained at Heathrow.

> Glenn Greenwald explains what sets this apart from the Obama administration's other prosecutions over leaks:
> It involves the prosecution of State Department adviser Stephen Kim, a naturalized citizen from South Korea who was indicted in 2009 for allegedly telling Fox News' chief Washington correspondent, James Rosen, that U.S. intelligence believed North Korea would respond to additional

U.N. sanctions with more nuclear tests—something Rosen then reported. Kim did not obtain unauthorized access to classified information, nor steal documents, nor sell secrets, nor pass them to an enemy of the U.S. Instead, the DOJ alleges that he merely communicated this innocuous information to a journalist—something done every day in Washington—and, for that, this arms expert and long-time government employee faces more than a decade in prison for "espionage." . . .

This newfound theory of the Obama DOJ—that a journalist can be guilty of crimes for "soliciting" the disclosure of classified information—is a means for circumventing those safeguards and criminalizing the act of investigative journalism itself. These latest revelations show that this is not just a theory but one put into practice, as the Obama DOJ submitted court documents accusing a journalist of committing crimes by doing this.[15]

How comfortable are you that something like Watergate could ever make headline news now? Do you think the press is being bullied and intimidated or is the press colluding with the government? Is the clash between state and press really just a matter of the clash between freedoms—positive and negative?

Religious Freedom

You are constitutionally guaranteed the right to opt out of immunizing your children on religious grounds, and then one day the state Senate passes a bill that removes this option, still allowing for nonmedical exclusions but no longer on the basis of religion. That actually happened in Oregon in June 2013. Now maybe it doesn't matter to you today as you're not particularly religious and you don't have children. But what if, in five years' time, you have married, have a child, and have experienced a life-threatening event that has sparked a deep spiritual interest within you? You just handed yourself a gotcha!

ACLU and the FBI

Through the Freedom of Information Act, the ACLU has

uncovered a frightening fact about the kind of information the FBI is collecting. Much of the information is collected under the guise of a community outreach effort. In several releases, the ACLU points to the illegal collection of information by the FBI and violations of the Privacy Act. They have called for a Department of Justice inspector general to investigate.

"Except under certain special circumstances, the Privacy Act bars the FBI from maintaining records like these describing how Americans exercise their First Amendment rights to freedom of speech and association," said Nusrat Choudhury, a staff attorney with the ACLU National Security Project. "Congress passed this law to prevent records obtained by the government for one purpose from being used for another reason without a person's consent, but that is precisely what the FBI has done."[16]

One by one our "protected" freedoms are being taken away from us. Each time there is a brief hue and cry about it, but nothing is ever done. Soon the new restrictions are just a part and parcel of normal American life. If they do not impinge on us personally, we just let it go . . .until it is too late!

Transparencies

While we're on government gotchas, how about an administration that promises the greatest transparency in history? To live up to that promise, the president signed into law the following:

1. The National Defense Authorization Act, which makes it legal for citizens to be taken into custody without "due process."
2. The National Defense Resources Preparedness Act, which gives authorization to the president and Cabinet members to take over private companies and other crucial parts of the economy, not just in wartime but anytime deemed appropriate.
3. The Federal Restricted Buildings and Grounds Improvement Act, which restricts peaceful protest, there-

by depriving us of our fundamental rights to exercise free speech and the right to assembly.

4. A promise to introduce a "shield" bill to protect us from being spied on by the very administration whose IRS, NSA, FBI, etc. have been spying on us. Now that's a pretty good gotcha!

1984

There are many more gotchas in the world. Some of them might have come straight out of the pages of Orwell's classic work *1984*. For example, we have many instances of doublespeak (language that deliberately disguises, distorts, or reverses the meaning of words). *That* is exactly what we hear a lot of today, when labels provide the illusion of one meaning when, in fact, they have another. For instance, the Department of Homeland Security under Janet Napolitano proposed a new Domestic Extremism Lexicon in 2009. The publication was leaked, and we discovered that among the proposed extremists—and bear in mind these are groups of people to be watched closely by law enforcement everywhere—were returning soldiers from Iraq and Afghanistan, animal rights activists, pro-lifers, Second Amendment supporters, and so forth. In other words, this lexicon appeared to place on the list of marginalized Americans descriptions of groups that supported ideas and philosophies opposed to those of the current administration. So our heroes, returning veterans in this instance, were relabeled as potential extremists, as were many other patriots living law-abiding lives under the rule of law but supporting ideologies that contrasted with those of the establishment. There was a hue and cry over this, and the list was ultimately 'withdrawn,' but this is an example of a very deliberate attempt to frame arguments!

Referendum

Now here's a gotcha for you: As a free people living under a representative form of government, we come to expect our representatives to represent us, even though we all know they often don't. Among the constitutionally prescribed means by which we the people can take things into our own hands is a tool known as a referendum.

To call a referendum, the process entails creating a petition and circulating it until sufficient signatures are garnered. Once there are enough signatures, the matter is put before the voters in a referendum. The citizens decide if they like the idea or not and cast their votes. Let's assume the referendum wins. That means the voters have decided the law—right?

Wrong, or at least, not necessarily, according to the Supreme Court decision regarding same-sex marriage. In June 2013, the California law prohibiting same sex- marriage could not be heard by the court because the government of the state of California was not in court to defend the law.

Now this gotcha is not about gay marriage (as it happens, I support gay marriage), but that said, doesn't it mean that if we the people petition and successfully win a ballot to change or create a law and then cronies in government exert their influence so that the attorney general's office refuses to defend the new law, just as was done in California and also in New Mexico, then the voters, the "we the people," are shut out? What kind of deal is that? Another gotcha? In my mind, it's a rather big gotcha, despite the fact that I recognize the court did the right thing constitutionally. (To get technical, the U.S. Supreme Court deferred decision making to the Ninth Circuit Court, which upheld a lower court case that ruled Proposition 8 unconstitutional for violating the due process clause and the equal protection clause.) Still, the fact remains that a decision on the merits of the case was not made by the Supreme Court. Rather, the governor and the attorney general's office decided not to represent the voters of the state of California in the matter before the court. After all, how can a ruling be made for or against someone who is not represented in court?

Newspeak or Political Correctness?

Now, as for Orwell's Newspeak (a language created by the state as a tool to limit free thought), that may be exactly what retired surgeon and columnist Ben Carson describes as politically correct speech—speech designed to limit the expression of ideas. We can no longer express certain ideas because they are considered to be politically incorrect or even hate speech. In such circumstances, to speak out about Muslim extremists, for example, requires a guarded tongue. To address certain racial differences or even to refer to a race requires the use of specific language. Interestingly, however, it seems acceptable for a member of a race to refer to another member of his own race using a term acceptable among members of that race, but it is considered an outrage if used by someone of another race.

CONCLUSION

I am sure that by now, you too are thinking about and remembering many other gotchas. How do you stop all the *gotchas* in the world? Indeed, can you? If you can't stop them, know this: you can definitely limit their impact on your thinking when you recognize the *gotcha* for what it is. Only by becoming alert to the many ways in which you can be manipulated do we stand a chance in ending the control exerted over us. You can help everyone by becoming a part of the change—the real change!

CHAPTER TWENTY-FOUR

A Little History Continued: Public Relations

All the president is, is a glorified public relations man
who spends his time flattering, kissing, and kicking people
to get them to do what they are supposed to do anyway.
~Harry S. Truman

Misconception: *Most believe that 'public relations' is an honorable way to present the best side of an issue or person.*
Fact: *Historically, public relations experts have cranked emotions to lead us to war over falsehoods, to sell us lies, and even to cover up massacres.*

Now that you have some inkling of the size of and scope of the issue, it is time to go back and fill in some of the blanks.

Edward Bernays may well deserve the title "Father of Public Relations," but a close second would definitely be Ivy Lee. I recently reviewed a film titled *The Age of Lucidity*. A comment, somewhat paraphrased here, caught my attention: "The reality is a free nation or open society needs sophisticated forms of propaganda more than any other in order to orchestrate cohesion. Now, thanks to the help of people like Edward Bernays and Ivy Lee, propaganda has not only been refined and polished to the extent that people anxiously consume it, but it has become uber big business amounting to a $200 billion annual industry."

Two hundred billion dollars—wow! And all of this money is spent every year to own your thoughts, to prime your self-talk, to fill your mind with sound bites, to sell you everything from a moral position to a character trait, to position you over and over again, to provide you with acceptable options that, of course, you can choose between, to placate you with goods and promises, to relieve you of your need to think and reason, to fill the news with entertainment, to fill your heads with more "to get along you must go along" stuff, and to further intimidate you in ways often disguised as an essential matter of national security.

How much of this serves the public and how much serves some special interest? Well, let's take a look at a few historical examples. Perhaps that will assist in answering that question.

Since we have already introduced Edward Bernays, let's take a look at Mr. Ivy Lebetter Lee's contributions to the development of public relations, or at least some of the more notable ones. The most offensive of them was accepting payment by the Nazi regime to manage their image and portray them as a friendly regime. This he did despite his stated declaration of principles, one of which asserts: "In brief, our plan is frankly, and openly, on behalf of business concerns and public institutions, to supply the press and public of the United States prompt and accurate information concerning subjects which it is of value and interest to the public to know about."[1]

Public Be Damned

Another of Ivy Lee's notable clients was the Rockefeller family. John D. Rockefeller's public stance at the time was, "The public be damned." His reputation was that of a robber baron who had even ordered the killing of those who stood in his way. When Lee discovered that the Rockefellers had a sizable sum of money set aside for advertising, he convinced them to change their image by giving money to charitable organizations, colleges, hospitals, and the like. He, too, was ahead of his time.

> "Instead of limiting his role to writing press releases and public statements and arranging special appearances for

Rockefeller, Lee was soon advising Rockefeller on the public relations advantages of a broad range of business decisions and management policy that included mechanisms to redress workers' grievances, the selection of new plant sites, setting employee wages and working conditions, and negotiating contracts with suppliers and vendors. In many ways this presaged the interactive adjustment and mutual satisfaction approaches to public relations that weren't fully articulated until 70 years later."[2]

Historians differ on whether Lee was a saint or a sinner. He did raise over $400 million for the Red Cross during World War I, and he recruited millions of volunteers along the way. What he was certainly very good at was shaping the public image of those for whom he worked.[3]

Lee is credited by most as being the first of the crisis managers. He worked for the Democratic Party in an unsuccessful bid to win the presidential election against Theodore Roosevelt. In 1906, Lee issued what is considered to be the very first press release, following a train wreck in Atlantic City. His approach was proactive: provide the bad news before someone else does, and frame it in the most favorable light.

In his book *The Problem of International Propaganda,* originally delivered as an "address to a private group of persona concerned with international affairs in London, England," Lee argued for a propaganda of understanding. In his words, "the most tragic fact of our time is the failure of nations to understand one another's best side." Lee makes it clear in his presentation that the reason for a new propaganda is "the attainment of peace and the outlawing of war."[4] Who can object to that?

Video News Release

Of course, the task today has become the war of "winning the hearts and minds of a target audience." The news release idea ultimately inspired the video news release (VNR). The American government creates VNRs deliberately to be used in places like Iraq during the Second Gulf War. Indeed, under the direction of the Bush administration, more VNRs were created than under any prior president. Now, VNRs are purportedly not to be used on the domestic audience, Americans, but under the Bush people much of the content in these VNRs came back and was circulated by news stations at home.

A VNR by definition is designed to persuade a target audience to a point of view. Some of the brightest minds in social science and advertising are employed in the creation of these videos. The piece is made to look like a news release but is solely designed to shape opinion.

There are many examples of media events that have been orchestrated behind the scenes by PSYOPs groups (Psychological Operations). For instance, the toppling of the Saddam Hussein statute that aired everywhere in the world during the war with Iraq was engineered and staged by a PSYOPs team.[5]

Just as Edward Bernays sold Americans on World War I, so John Rendon (The Rendon Group) sold America the war with Iraq. "His firm, the Rendon Group, has made millions from government contracts since 1991, when it was hired by the CIA to help 'create the conditions for the removal of Hussein from power.'"[6]

A February 1998 report by Peter Jennings cited records obtained by ABC News, which showed that the Rendon Group spent more than $23 million in the first year of its contract with the CIA.[7]

Rendon publicly describes himself this way, "I am an information warrior and a perception manager."[8]

Following 9/11, Rendon was charged with managing U.S. public relations regarding the U.S. bombing of Afghanistan. The bottom line is this, the Bush White House created some 55 VNRs before and during the assault on Iraq.

Now, one other fact should be discussed before we temporarily leave our PSYOPs folks, and that is this: So-called psywarriors (PSYOPs personnel) were working for CNN during this period. They were from the Third Psychological Operations at Fort Bragg. According to Major Thomas Collins, U.S. Army Information Services, "PSYOPs personnel, soldiers, and officers, have been working in CNN's headquarters in Atlanta through our program, *Training with Industry*. They helped in the production of news."[9]

Governments are not the only ones using VNRs. Many corporations sell products this same way. Again, the sales pitch is disguised as a news story selling a product or an individual, including a politician. Is this ethical? Should it be legal? Or should some notice appear with the VNR as with print advertorials informing viewers that they are watching a video designed to look like news but it really is not—instead it is an advertisement.

The *New York Times* openly admitted that much of mainstream news is actually scripted by the White House.[10]

News or VNRs? Is there really a difference today?

War of Images

A piece appeared in *Spiegel* on August 13, 2013, headlining "Putin's Weapon in the War of Images," in reference to the cable TV channel, Russia Today. Of particular interest is the disclosure of the purpose of the channel that receives more than $300 million annually from the Russian government: to hurt America's reputation. Quoting from the article:

> A photo of Edward Snowden, the whistleblower the United States wants to bring home to face charges, is projected onto the studio wall. Then there is a report on the detention camp at Guantanamo, which has hurt America's reputation. Russia Today uses the source material America supplies to its rivals untiringly and with relish. Even Washington's relatively minor peccadilloes don't escape notice. For instance, the show also includes a story about Gabonese dictator Ali Bongo Ondimba, whom U.S. President Barack Obama supports.
>
> Many in the West are also interested in seeing critical coverage of the self-proclaimed top world power. Russia Today is already more successful than all other foreign broadcast stations available in major U.S. cities, such as San Francisco, Chicago, and New York. In Washington, 13 times as many people watch the Russian program as those

that tune into Deutsche Welle, Germany's public international broadcaster. Two million Britons watch the Kremlin channel regularly. Its online presence is also more successful than those of all its competitors. What's more, in June, Russia Today broke a YouTube record by being the first TV station to get a billion views of its videos.

The station was even more triumphant when it signed Larry King, a legend of American radio and TV journalism who began working for Russia Today this summer. Before that, King was the face of CNN for 25 years. His suspenders are even more striking than Abby Martin's lipstick antics. "America's best-known TV interviewer is defecting to the Russians," wrote the London-based *Times* in May.

King and his new colleagues have a simple assignment: They are to "break the monopoly of the Anglo-Saxon mass media," President Vladimir Putin said during a studio visit a few weeks ago. The Russians' recipe for success has three ingredients: sex appeal, which has been atypical for most news channel; a rigidly anti-American stance; and a never-ending flow of money from the Kremlin.[11]

So there is a blatant war of images being played right in our homes. I wonder how many people experienced a softening of their feelings toward Russia and its government as a result?

But then we come to the story of Crimea, which began in November 2013. There were reports that the U.S. was behind the ousting of a democratically elected president, and that this created the vacuum that led to Russia entering the Ukraine. Another free election then resulted in Crimea rejoining Russia. According to Western sources this was due to the occupation by Russian military forces and its implied duress. According to Russian sources, the election expressed the will of the people and further, Russia would not have entered Crimea if Russian citizens and loyalists were not in danger.

Now, all of a sudden, many in the Western media started comparing Vladimir Putin to Adolph Hitler. Is the press beginning to sound the drums for yet another world war? Putin has now outflanked Western leaders on Georgia, Syria, and Crimea.

The Russian Olympics together with some of Putin's other recent moves have generated a great deal of new ethnocentrism and pride among the Russian people. Is it any wonder that the media is now playing him off as the bad guy—the arch villain? Is he? Has your opinion changed at all about Putin and Russia since Crimea? The real question is this: how much of your opinion is based on unbiased factual data versus the sound bites authored by our mediaocracy?

Burson-Marsteller

At the time of this writing, there is great controversy around the world regarding genetically modified organisms (GMOs), and the chief proponent of GMOs is the Monsanto Corporation. We discussed GMOs earlier, but now let us focus on the representation of Monsanto by Burson-Marsteller, a PR firm with offices in 35 countries. They have represented tobacco companies, chemical companies, and so forth. Their chief officers have served both political parties. "At times [they] have also been the subject of protests and criticism for [their] use of smearing and doubt campaigns (to undermine concerns about passive smoking for Philip Morris in the 1990s[12] and anti-Google smear campaigning for Facebook in 2011)[13] and [their] work for regimes facing severe human rights criticisms (Argentina and Indonesia)."[14] And so far, in their PR work for Monsanto, they have successfully fought back many labeling attempts made by states, and they have apparently also won favor with President Obama.

> The Monsanto Protection Act, essentially both written by and benefiting Monsanto Corporation, has been signed into law by United States President Barack Obama. The infamous Monsanto Corporation will benefit greatly and directly from the bill, as it essentially gives companies that deal with genetically modified organisms (GMOs) and genetically engineered (GE) seeds immunity to the federal courts, among other things.
>
> The bill states that even if future research shows that GMOs or GE seeds cause significant health problems, can-

cer, etc., anything that the federal courts no longer have any power to stop their spread, use, or sales.[15]

There are some other interesting facts about this bill. CBS informs us:

> Food safety advocacy groups like Food Democracy Now, which collected more than 250,000 signatures on a petition calling for the president to veto the CR [continuing resolution], argue not enough studies have been conducted into the possible health risks of GMO and GE seeds. Eliminating judicial power to halt the selling or planting of them essentially cuts off their course to ensuring consumer safety should health risks emerge.
>
> Seeking a "balance" to the newly minted law, Food Democracy Now has shifted its tactics to encouraging supporters to sign and send letters to Mr. Obama, chiding him for signing the legislation despite the fact that refusal to do so would have expired the federal budget and triggered a government-wide shutdown this week.
>
> Part of the template for the letter reads: "In an effort to balance this violation of our basic rights, I am urging you as president to issue an executive order to require the mandatory labeling of genetically engineered foods, something that you promised farmers while on the campaign trail in 2007. It is urgent that the U.S. government rectify the 20 year-old politically engineered loophole and allow for open and transparent labeling of genetically engineered foods," the letter continues, "a basic right that citizens in 62 others countries already enjoy."
>
> Other groups have aimed their ire toward the more worthy target, criticizing Congress for slipping the language into a must-pass bill without review by the Agricultural or Judiciary Committees. The *International Business Times* reports that the Center for Food Safety is putting in the hot seat Senator Barbara Mikulski (D-Md.), chairwoman for the Senate Appropriations Committee, for not giving the amendment a proper hearing. According to Salon [the award-winning online news and entertainment website], many members of Congress who voted to approve the bill were unaware the language existed.

"In this hidden backroom deal, Senator Mikulski turned her back on consumer, environmental, and farmer protection in favor of corporate welfare for biotech companies such as Monsanto," Andrew Kimbrell, executive director of the Center for Food Safety, said in a statement, according to IBT. "This abuse of power is not the kind of leadership the public has come to expect from Senator Mikulski or the Democrat majority in the Senate."[16]

The Consumption Ladder

Merchandisers use many similar practices to win our hearts and minds, but one of the tools in their arsenal that is almost always present is the notion that we are somehow deficient. Paraphrasing Vance Packard from his book *The Status Seekers:* "Their job is to sell you on the idea that you are, in modern parlance, inferior and insufficient. This is a deliberate strategy by advertisers targeting the less advantaged with status symbols for consumption such as luxury automobiles. The strategy makes people feel as though they are climbing the social ladder when in fact, they're standing still."[17] And indeed, in our material democracy, there is an almost infinite number of goods to be consumed, and this furthers the strategy of social climbing.

The consumption cycle gives rise to many problems, and those relevant to our inquiry will become obvious as we continue. That said, it is important to note that the great American dream has become all about consumption. The model is one of how the poor can become rich, and this drives consumerism.

The facts are not quite that simple. Throughout history the rich have argued that the poor are poor because they are lazy—unwilling to work hard and endure self-sacrifice. The fact is, there is no level playing field for all Americans to participate in and therefore gain the riches and success that the very few achieve. The system actually works against that. Yet the strength of the consumption model has grown to the point that crazed shoppers will fight over merchandise, trample their fellow human beings to death in their need to buy an item, and even refuse to get out of line to allow EMTs to reach injured shoppers.[18]

Obedient Consumers

We will examine advertising in more depth later, but it is easy to see that what might have been a good idea has had some perverse applications. For what it's worth, I find Lee's work much more honest and worthy of a noble effort than that of Bernays. Uncle Bernie, as some called him, seemed to be more interested in his own objectives, which included gaining more and more power, than in the average person on the street. In fact, Bernays held that the average person was incapable of self-governance, and therefore it was the obligation of the elite to guide them, like a herder manages his livestock. Whether the aim of the various PR firms of today is to further the interest of the public or their clients becomes somewhat academic. Obviously the dollar will trump for almost all, if not all, the direction and aim of public relations and the ensuing propaganda!

Whether by VNRs or other means, the public has become so saturated with information presented 24/7 by the media that it's no wonder we walk the talk of the advertisers, buying their products, using their drugs, trusting the authority to care for us by protecting our food, guarding us against disease with inoculations, regulating our habits to keep us safe wherever we are, etc., etc., etc. We have collectively become obedient consumers excited about our next purchase, or vacation, or trinket of some kind, as though they represented the means to be happy. Blindly we march on in cadence to the drum of the Pied Piper of consumption, and there is never an end to things we want—more, more, more!

As we'll see, all of this consumer protection we're supposedly afforded is but a tool employed to keep us in line. Well, perhaps it is more than that, in honesty, but it's hard not to be cynical when you know what the protectors have actually done. When you have finished this book, let me know if you think the motives are never, sometimes, often, or usually altruistic—just looking out for us common folks.

So the fact is, these two men, Bernays and Lee, fundamentally changed the way communication between the people and the ruling forces in the world has been carried out ever since. Propaganda and public relations have become as the dictionary now defines them, "information, ideas, or rumors deliberately spread widely to help or harm a person, group, movement, institution, nation, etc."[19]

Ludlow Massacre

Arguably, the system is maintained by giving just enough people just enough to prevent people from engaging in open rebellion. The propaganda pundits insist that the reality of a free nation or open society needs sophisticated forms of propaganda more than any other in order to orchestrate cohesion. Thanks to the help of people like Bernays, Lee, and Rendon, propaganda has been refined and polished to the extent that people actually have come to love it! Perhaps even without it, America would have run seriously amok. Perhaps without some tune leading the masses in Pied Piper style there would have been riots and massacres, such as when the coal miners went on strike in Ludlow, Colorado. If you're not familiar with this event, and even if you are, for our discussion now it's worth reviewing:

> The Ludlow Massacre was an attack by the Colorado National Guard and Colorado Fuel & Iron Company camp guards on a tent colony of 1,200 striking coal miners and their families at Ludlow, Colorado on April 20, 1914.
>
> In 1914, when workers at Colorado mine went on strike, company guards fired machine guns and killed several men. More battling followed, during which 2 women and 11 children were killed and John D. Rockefeller Jr., the chief mine owner, was pilloried for what had happened.
>
> The massacre resulted in the violent deaths of between 19 and 25 people; sources vary but include two women and eleven children, asphyxiated and burned to death under a single tent. The deaths occurred after a daylong fight between militia and camp guards against striking workers. Ludlow was the deadliest single incident in the southern Colorado Coal Strike, lasting from September 1913 through December 1914. The strike was organized by the

United Mine Workers of America (UMWA) against coal mining companies in Colorado. The three largest companies involved were the Rockefeller family-owned Colorado Fuel & Iron Company (CF&I), the Rocky Mountain Fuel Company (RMF), and the Victor-American Fuel Company (VAF).[20]

The record shows that big money controlled government interests and deployed the same to massacre striking workers. Historian Howard Zinn described the Ludlow Massacre as "the culminating act of perhaps the most violent struggle between corporate power and laboring men in American history."[21]

Remember that it was Ivy Lee who reshaped the reputation and image of the Rockefellers following the Ludlow Massacre. Is it reasonable to think that free societies simply could not work without the Pipers playing their tunes? Is this another gotcha?

Tax-Exempt Foundations

There is no shortage of material available informing the public of how and why tax-exempt foundations were formed to manage the perception of the public. We have already discussed how Ivy Lee coached the Rockefellers and purportedly why they formed the Rockefeller Foundation. The tactic appears to have had a lasting effect, rewarding the Rockefellers with a generally positive public image.

Among the literature available regarding tax-exempt foundations is the investigation carried out between 1952 and 1954 by the United States Select Committee to Investigate Tax-Exempt Foundations and Comparable Organizations, also known as the Cox Committee and the Reese Committee after the two chairs, Edward Cox and B. Carroll Reese. Although the history of the committee's activities is dotted with political intrigue and power struggles, the net result of the findings as delivered in what is called the Dodd Report found that certain tax-exempt organizations were using subversive means to undermine government.

The final report was submitted by Norman Dodd, and because of its provocative nature, the committee became subject to attack. He began by listing criticisms of the Cox Committee, and then moved on to content.

In the Dodd report to the Reece Committee on Foundations, he gave a definition of the word "subversive," saying that the term referred to "Any action having as its purpose the alteration of either the principle or the form of the United States government by other than constitutional means." He then argued that the Ford Foundation, Rockefeller Foundation, and Carnegie Endowment were using funds excessively on projects at Columbia, Harvard, Chicago University, and the University of California, in order to enable oligarchical collectivism. He stated, "The purported deterioration in scholarship and in the techniques of teaching which, lately, has attracted the attention of the American public, has apparently been caused primarily by a premature effort to reduce our meager knowledge of social phenomena to the level of an applied science." He stated that his research staff had discovered that in "1933–1936, a change took place which was so drastic as to constitute a "revolution." They also indicated conclusively that the responsibility for the economic welfare of the American people had been transferred heavily to the executive branch of the federal government; that a corresponding change in education had taken place from an impetus outside of the local community, and that this "revolution" had occurred without violence and with the full consent of an overwhelming majority of the electorate." He stated that this revolution "could not have occurred peacefully, or with the consent of the majority, unless education in the United States had been prepared in advance to endorse it."

Although the promotion of internationalism and moral relativism by foundations concerned the committee, it saw their concentrated power as the more central threat. Even if benign, this power posed a threat to democratic government . . .

The report conceded that, with several exceptions "such as the Institute of Pacific Relations, foundations have not directly supported organizations which, in turn, operated to support communism." However, the report did conclude that

> Some of the larger foundations have directly
> supported 'subversion' in the true meaning of
> that term—namely, the process of undermining
> some of our vitally protective concepts and
> principles. They have actively supported attacks
> upon our social and governmental system
> and financed the promotion of socialism and
> collectivist ideas.[22]

What happened as a result of the report? The answer is nothing. Did you expect something else?

Advertising

As I said earlier, the common message in all ads today is simply this: You are deficient! You need this or that to be whole or perfect or better or—and on and on! The advertising world knows every pulley and string to motivate you to action. We have already discussed many, and more will be discussed later as we develop the story. You should be aware of some interesting means and methods used by marketing firms.

Consumers develop some genuinely complex relationships with celebrities and often construct identities formed around these relationships that lead to buying decisions. In one study that evaluated this relationship, researchers discovered that consumers use celebrities to build both their self-image and their self-esteem. Quoting from *Science Daily:*

> The interviews with all subjects revealed nine types of
> relationships young adults develop with celebrities. These
> relationships fit within three general categories—everyday,
> inspirational, and negative. Everyday relationships include
> "best friendship," "compartmentalized" and "childhood
> friendship." The inspirational category includes "aspira-
> tional," "admiration" and "illusory" relationships. Negative
> celebrity relationships include "antagonistic," "not for me,"
> and "guilty pleasures," all of which connote, as the name
> suggests, some kind of negative quality that motivates the
> consumer.[23]

Advertisers have learned that running slightly different versions of the same ad increases sales because it tends to build a feeling of familiarity with the audience.[24]

Full-Immersion Marketing

A new form of advertising is known as full-immersion stealth marketing. One target of this sort of marketing is our children. In the documentary *Consuming Kids,* the wholesale attempts to shape the consumption attitudes of our children is exposed, right down to how marketing research people have determined exactly how to prompt a tantrum from children and what kind of tantrum works best to push mom and dad into complying with the child's request. The idea is simple: "Children under 12 influence adult spending worth a staggering $700 billion a year, which equates to the combined economy of 115 of the world's poorest countries."[25]

The tactics employed are designed to increase the frequency that children request an item. How effective has this stealth immersion strategy become? Where is the regulation designed to halt marketing to children?

In the late 1970s, in the wake of rising concerns about sugary cereals and children's inability to understand the intent of advertising, the Federal Trade Commission (FTC) tried to ban all ads aimed at kids below the age of eight. After all, a young child cannot understand that an ad is not an impartial infomercial that tells the truth, the whole truth, and nothing but the truth . . . For this reason, advertising aimed at children is grossly underhanded, if not outright immoral.

Alas, Big Business stepped in and convinced Congress to block such attempts. Instead of banning advertising to children, Congress passed "The FTC Improvement Act," which strips the FTC of the power and authority to regulate marketing to children. The final blow came in 1984, when the entire industry was deregulated.

Before deregulating children's TV marketing, children's spending had risen at a modest four percent per year. After deregulation, children's spending skyrocketed to 35 percent per year, from $4.2 billion a year in 1984 to $40 billion a year today—an 852 percent increase in less than three decades.[26]

It's all about turning children into lifelong consumers, brand loyal ones at that, but first last and always, consumers who must have more, more, more! How does that make you feel? What about all the other possible repercussions from marketing aimed at children? Do we see a society where young adults expect to have everything their parents worked for years to get? Is the expectation of entitlement rather than "earning it for yourself" more prevalent today? And how about you? Do you find it a convenient stress-reduction method to go shopping yourself? Is buying a habit with you, something that feels good until the bills come in? Are you yourself perhaps partially a product of this sort of conditioning?

Neuromarketing

Using functional magnetic resonance imaging (fMRI), researchers are able to watch the brain in real time as it processes information. Today researchers use this technology to predict consumption behavior as much as to deal with wellness issues. In the first study to use this technology to predict how large populations would respond, researchers at UCLA gathered brain data to access the wisdom of the brain. Activity in the medial prefrontal cortex accurately predicted a winning advertisement, regardless of the conscious opinion of the subject. Surprised by this result, one researcher said, "We were hoping the brain data would add something to the self-reports of our participants," Lieberman said. "Given how different they were from one another, we were afraid our brain data might not end up predicting the real-world outcomes at all."[27]

> "If people are making decisions based on what focus groups tell them, here's an important brain region saying, 'No, spend your money a different way,'" (Matthew) Lieberman said. "If I were deciding on an advertising campaign, I would want to know which ads are activating this region the

most—that is where I would want to spend my money."

This new research represents "the first thing you could call a neural focus group," Lieberman said.

One reason focus groups can be misleading, he said, is that people often do not know what motivates their own behavior.

"Our brain is built to generate reasons for our actions," Lieberman said, "and we think the reasons we come up with must be true. We believe our own reasons with an intensity that is out of proportion to their accuracy. In this study, we are bypassing people's self-reports and getting at a form of hidden wisdom in the brain.

"We wanted to determine what kind of brain activity serves as the catalyst between people seeing a message and whether they actually change their behavior," he said. "This is the region we identified. We have tested it multiple times, and each time, it has been successful."[28]

One of the questions I would have to ask is this: Are they accessing the "wisdom" of the brain or the "programming"? Either way, this **study** does speak to the sophistication of the research going on to discover more effective ways to manipulate you.

Tweets

Technology is an intricate aspect of propaganda. The Internet is now a worldwide billboard for advertisers of all sorts. The use of the Internet to spread political misinformation and disinformation is well known. Where theoretically, perhaps, the Internet remains our most independent source for news, it also is full of pure unmitigated garbage! For many, this makes no difference. If what they read agrees with what they wish to believe, the game is on.

Researchers are well aware of how important the use of the Internet, and especially various social networking tools, can be to advancing their agendas. President Obama was one of the first politicians to truly take advantage of the Internet, and the Arab Spring demonstrated to the world how powerful this form of communication could be.

A recent study at Indiana University found that more tweets

translate into more votes, and it doesn't matter whether the tweets are negative or positive.

"Think of this as a measurement of buzz," said Fabio Rojas, an associate professor of sociology in the College of Arts and Sciences at IU Bloomington. "We call this the 'all publicity is good publicity' finding. Even if you don't like somebody, you would only talk about them if they're important."[29]

Media Control

The result of all of this PR is well summed up by Noam Chomsky in his book *Media Control:*

"The issue is whether we want to live in a free society or whether we want to live under what amounts to a form of self-imposed totalitarianism, with the bewildered herd marginalized, directed elsewhere, terrified, screaming patriotic slogans, fearing for their lives, and admiring with awe the leader who saved them from destruction, while the educated masses goose-step on command and repeat the slogans they're supposed to repeat and the society deteriorates at home."[30]

CONCLUSION

I doubt you will ever see marketing in quite the same way as you have in the past. It is clear that the herding of the masses, you and me, is often the target and goal of PR campaigns. Who, then, can we trust? What information is real and what has been spun to serve an agenda? How do we get to the truth? What are you going to do about this newly obtained knowledge? Know this, some will ignore it. Others will dismiss it in favor of an ideation that goes like this: "If I don't think about it, if I remain positive in my little world, it will never affect me." For this person, negativity exists only in the minds of those who perceive it.

I hope you're not one of either of these folks. I sincerely believe in the human potential, but I also know that it is all too easy to get on with our lives, go shopping, catch a movie, relax in front of the TV, dream about a new car or new home, and plan how we'll achieve our goals—but in doing that, those who would use you go right on doing so. Little by little the world changes and it becomes something we don't want for our children and something that is the opposite of what our veterans fought and sometimes died for. So once again, please get involved!

CHAPTER TWENTY-FIVE

The Human Vehicle: What "They" Know and Why Propaganda Works

A great deal of intelligence can be invested in ignorance when the need for illusion is deep.
~Saul Bellow

Misconception: *Most people believe that their defense mechanisms exist to serve and protect them.*
Fact: *Some of our defense mechanisms not only lead to self-sabotage but they can also easily be used to manipulate us.*

Over the years I have addressed tens of thousands of people. One of my favorite things to do when beginning a lecture is to point out to the audience how little they know about themselves and how they work. I do that by first exposing physiological nuances about their bodies that they are ignorant of. For example, I may begin a lecture by stating that I know more about how the machine they drive around in every day, that human vehicle we call a body, than they do. I may explain that by knowing this you can manipulate the expectation of an individual, and that in turn will provide the opportunity to manipulate their perception. Conversely, you can manipulate the expectation by managing the perception. At this point, I will ask the audience to raise their right foot off the ground while remaining sitting. Next they are to move that foot in a clockwise fashion. Then, with their foot moving clockwise, I tell them to use their right hand to draw the number 6 in the air. They are always amazed at the automatic response: Their foot changes direction and starts to move in a counterclockwise direction. Is it the dog wagging its tail, or the tail wagging the dog? Try it yourself.

The point of the exercise is simple. Very few people are truly aware of the many intricate operational opportunities a trained person can take advantage of, and therefore, they are amazed at suggestions, even the absurd ones, that might explain phenomena.

The Truth about Illusions

I next show audiences a variety of illusions. Now, almost everyone has seen illusions of different kinds, from the images that show one picture when viewed in a certain way only to show a totally new image when looked at differently, to the pair of lines that appear to be different lengths, but are in fact identical. If you would like to see more of these, a simple search on the Internet will bring up many. I shared some of my favorite illusions in my earlier book, *Choices and Illusions,* including the cogs that appear to move in a still picture, or the image of Jesus that can appear on a blank wall. However, the important thing to note here is that, while most people have experienced illusions of all kinds, very few of them stop to think about what this means. If your senses can feed you false information, what is it that you can really say that you know?

Manipulating Choices

What I like to do next is show how simple it is to manipulate your choices, how easy it is to guide you through possibilities in such a way that you become aware of the options I wish you to choose between. And in many instances, I really don't care what you choose, for I win regardless. It's sort of a heads-I-win, tails-you-lose scenario, only not nearly as obvious or crude. For example, I may show you how a hypnotist guides you to believe that he has taken control of your body or your mind and that you are now compelled to do his beckoning. As a suggestibility measurement, the hypnotist may call upon your imagination abilities. He/she may explain that everyone naturally enters the state of hypnosis rather easily once they understand what it is, except for very small children lacking an attention span and certain other mentally handicapped persons. After all, hypnosis is only an altered state of brain wave activity in the identical range with dream sleep and certain daydreaming states. Objectified, it exists at a brain wave state between 8 and 14 cycles per second, which may be somewhat lower for talented people, but generally in the area thought of as alpha brain wave activity.

I hope you have noticed the careful positioning involved in this simple introduction. Obviously you do not want to be thought of as mentally challenged or unable to maintain attention, like a tiny child, and you are, of course, bright enough to understand this simple explanation about brain waves, so you have readied yourself to comply—or you have been readied, however you prefer to see it.

Next, the hypnotist suggests that while you are sitting, you are to rest your arm on your leg with the palm of your hand facing upward so you can stare right into the palm. Then you are further asked to use just a little extra imagination and imagine a very powerful magnet in the palm of your hand. In fact, as if you were a cyborg, this magnet is part of your hand, wedded to the tissue, bone, nerves, muscles, and fiber. It is part of your hand.

Now the hypnotist continue: "I want you also to imagine that another very powerful magnet is attached to your forehead. You can feel the magnetic force between the two, and as a result you feel your arm lifting and rising, lifting and rising. Ever so gently at first, you feel, you sense, the attraction is strong, the magnetic force is pulling your hand up, lifting your arm, and your arm and hand are lifting and rising, pulled ever so powerfully and yet slowly toward your forehead, the two magnetic forces getting stronger and stronger as they get closer and closer. Now, I want you decide, is the magnetic force stronger from your hand to your head or from your head to your hand?"

GOTCHA!

This is something you too can play around with at home. You may want to try this little experiment in visualization and imagination. How powerful is your imagination? Do you have a good one? Are you sufficiently aware of yourself to actually generate the feeling of the magnetic force, or are you dumb to the sensation? Don't read any further! Try the magnet test now!

Forgive me, but that last paragraph was also positioning. It doesn't matter what your experiment yielded, because that's not really important. First, whether you decided the magnetic force was stronger from head to hand or hand to head does not matter. The fact is that once you made that decision, you recognized the presence of such a force, and that gave me power, as the hypnotist, to direct the two to touch and for you to enter hypnosis upon doing so. This indeed is a very effective induction tool because you see your body respond to the direction of the hypnotist.

"And as your arm lifts and rises, your mind lets go, allowing the deeper wisdom of the subconscious mind to come forward, so that we can address the issues of concern that brought you here to me today."

The second is that most of you will find that you have been positioned a second time, despite your having been warned against being so positioned just moments before. This second point is critical! We must know how these things work, or we are at the mercy of those who would take advantage of us in some way— and believe me, there are many who want to own your thoughts. That said, just knowing is often not enough. We must be vigilant to protect our thoughts, to guard against the pernicious, ever-present onslaught of manipulative techniques and practices deployed by those with something to sell you, a product, a service, an idea, a plank in a political platform, a candidate, etc. For as you will see, the vanguards of your thoughts in all likelihood belong to someone other than you.

Okay, with this introduction, let's take a tour and see what we can learn that those with an agenda to sell us something already know.

Why You Do What You Do

Earlier we spoke of President Barack Obama's *Dream Team*, the group of social psychologists and mind manipulators he relied on during the presidential campaigns. One of the members of this team was Dr. Robert B. Cialdini, president of Influence at Work and regents professor emeritus of psychology and marketing at Arizona State University. Cialdini's 1984 book, *Influence: The Psychology of Persuasion,* remains to this day mandatory reading for anyone interested in persuasion techniques; however, it is his work with compliance principles to which I wish to direct your attention. Again, this is something I cover in great depth in my book *Mind Programming,* so I will give you just a quick overview here.

Principles of Compliance

Compliance principles are those elements of our psychology that cause us to do certain things in order to fulfill an inner need. It is as though we have competing desires, and it is the needs of our inner self that win. Unfortunately, having drives that can push us so hard in a particular direction just means that they can also be used to manipulate us!

The 11 principles of compliance are:

1. Social Beliefs

Social beliefs are among the strongest principles of the individual, and they often conflict with personal desires. These tenets form the very fabric of society. Politicians and profiteers play these beliefs, longings, and their conflicts like musicians. Social beliefs, selfish interests, and the tension between them form the bedrock of compliance principles.

2. Reciprocity

Studies have shown that the act of giving produces the need to reciprocate. From the so-called warm handshake to inside information and the free things offered today, a gift extended implies that there should be a gift in return. Cialdini calls it "the old give and take . . . and take."[1]

3. Social Proof

Merchants enlist testimony after testimony from faithful, satisfied users in order to sell us their wares. Carnival hucksters seed their audiences with winners of the big stuffed toy. Merchants and politicians, like preachers, often sow the seeds of mass conversion by enlisting an army of stooges to "come forth at varying intervals to create the impression of a spontaneous mass outpouring."[4] We believe that if many people agree on something, it must be true; it must be good and desirable.

4. Association

Association seeks to link favorable feelings with a product or aim. We see politicians with apple pie, babies, and the American flag. We see stunning men and women in the most unlikely of places, wearing the most unlikely of apparel, just to connect their image with the product.

As with all of these principles, you can look beyond the obvious. Take, for instance, a project that sought to measure the influence of major credit-card logos on buying. In this study, carried out by researcher Richard Feinberg, it was found that subjects would spend 29 percent more on mail-order items when they could see a major credit card logo in the room. Another study by the same researcher showed that college students give money to charity more often with the credit card logo in the room. Only 33 percent of the students gave to charity where there was no credit card logo in the room, whereas 87 percent gave when the logo was present—and this was despite the fact that credit cards weren't accepted. Just the association increased spending.[2]

Don't discount even the most innocent of features that accompany a product or advertisement. The companies behind them spend billions annually on deliberately applying skillful knowledge to manipulate you.

5. Conditioning and Association

Some authors combine conditioning and association.[3] They tend to come as a pair. The credit card logo study assumes the association of credit cards with pleasure, a principle of conditioning, while prior negative experience with a credit card reversed the effects on spending.[4]

I separate these two principles because classical conditioning has been accomplished by subliminal stimuli. The principle of association implies at least some conscious recognition of the stimuli, but subliminal stimuli violate this assumption. In other words, although the stimuli are asso-

331

ciated with a response, as with classical conditioning, the stimuli themselves are unrecognized by the conscious mind.

For example, when subjects have pictures of people's faces repeatedly presented subliminally to them, the subjects become more comfortable with those in the images. The more frequent the subliminal exposure, the greater the liking for the individuals when they later met. This occurs even though the subjects had no conscious awareness of the subliminally presented faces.[5]

Many forms of association can bypass conscious awareness, and not all of them necessarily qualify as subliminal. We have perceptual defense mechanisms that figuratively blindfold us at times. As with the associations intentionally built into most advertisements, certain consciously undetected associations can operate on existing conditioning and pair with it to produce new conditioning.

6. Liking

The more we identify with and feel comfortable with someone else, the more we like the other person and the more often we comply with that individual's requests. Discussing anything so obvious may seem ridiculous, but the liking principle has nuances unfamiliar to most of us. It has mechanical features.

The science of neuro linguistic programming (NLP) often starts with the mechanics of rapport. It breaks the phenomenon into matching, pacing, and leading. Match by adopting an individual's speaking style, physical mannerisms, and so forth. Pace by continuing to do so, and lead by making a new gesture or by shifting your tone of voice. So long as others follow your example, you can continue to lead them. You have rapport.

NLP is a powerful technology now taught indiscriminately to anyone from healthcare professionals to sales organizations to political and religious groups. The latter have become the major market for books on the subject. This powerful technology can operate almost as mechanically as a knee-jerk reflex. (For more information, see books by Richard Bandler and John Grinder.) The ability to build rapport, increase liking, and so on is so enhanced by NLP techniques, which nearly every trained interrogator in the country has had some exposure to.

Liking often develops under conditions of cooperation. We all know that "politics make for strange bedfellows" and that there's a strategy to unite disparate groups by getting them to band together against a common enemy.

7. Authority

Everywhere we turn today, an authority instructs and informs—authority to which we come to trust our very lives. How did we survive before we had so many different experts? But the authority figure not only provides us with information we can trust, it can also override our better judgment.

Earlier we mentioned the study carried out in the 1960s by the social psychologist Professor Stanley Milgram. In the study, naïve volunteers received instructions to deliver electric shocks, up to 450 volts, to volunteer subjects (research assistants) who'd been tied to chairs with electric wires. The punishment would be given for failing some trivial task, such as a memory test. The subjects would protest the increasing voltage with cries of pain and warnings of a heart condition, but the volunteers, under the instructions of the authority figure, continued to deliver the shocks.[6]

As we said earlier, some believe that this study demonstrated the power of social identification rather than obedience. However, a 2009 study, led by professor of neuroeconomics and psychiatry, Gregory Berns, showed that "people will actually stop thinking for themselves when a person they perceive as an expert offers them advice or direction . . . It seems that receiving 'expert' advice shuts down the areas of our brains that are responsible for decision-making processes."[7]

8. Scarcity

Rare, scarce, and similar qualities equate to value for most people. Economic theory defines value as the relationship between demand and supply—that is, scarcity. An adage applies here: "The grass is always greener on the other side of the fence." We all want what we don't have until we have it. Of course, the greater the demand, the scarcer the product. We belief in social proof of value; the product has to be good to be so highly sought after, doesn't it?

Yet another tactic involving this compliance principle is the "no longer available" notion. Book publishers know that one of the best ways to sell books is for some group to ban the work.

9. Drives

Drives are the basic built-in needs of the species. In psychology, human drives are often referred to as the four *F's: fight, flight, feeding,* and *fornication.* I tend to think that we've evolved with the advent of modem merchandising and deferred payment. Consequently, my view incorporates five *F's,* or five forces. The fifth one is simple: *more!*

Add this to the first four elements and you see that no one has enough; everyone wants more. *More* has somehow become desirable in and of itself. Today, the word *more* equals power, prestige, status, peace of mind, and so on. It now means quality as much as it means quantity. Keep up with the Joneses.

Experts know how to tap into and use these drives with the principles of compliance. When compliance practitioners wish to persuade someone in a subtle way, they employ drive-related strategies that will invariably invoke vulnerability, nondominance, loyalty, and so on. If something is scary (flight), violent (fight), filling/fulfilling (food), and/or sexual, it sells. If two or more of the forces can be combined, sales soar!

If a product is really none of these things, then associating it with them will enhance sales and product image. In fact, Cialdini reports a study conducted by Smith and Engel in which "men who saw a new-car ad that included a seductive young woman model rated the car as faster, more appealing, more expensive-looking, and better-designed than men who viewed the same ad without the model."[8] These same men, when questioned about the ad and their response, denied the possibility that the seductive female had anything whatsoever to do with their rating of the automobile.

10. Justification

Justification is the principle that extenuating circumstances can call for radical action. Indeed, a tenet of our system of jurisprudence allows for just this. That is why there are such characterizations of a killing as justifiable homicide, self-defense, and so on. This principle is probably the most often overlooked tool of compliance. An excellent example of its power exists in an older television commercial. The viewer sees a woman performing the many tasks of an absolutely frantic day: shopping, cleaning, caring for children, banking, and so forth. At the end of the day, she (a very beautiful and seductive woman) relaxes in her bath covered by bubbles. The ad is for bubble bath, and it ends with the statement: "Let XYZ product take you away." It's an excellent commercial that employs more than one compliance principle. Still, it's the notion of justifying indulgence that makes this commercial so powerful. How else do you sell bubble bath?

History records bizarre events. From the German attempt to eradicate the Jewish people to the mass suicide of Jim Jones' followers, history shows people acting in crazy ways. Why? They all had a reason. Any reason will do. Can you think of anything flimsier than the excuse for torture in Milgram's authority experiment? Human beings need reasons to act, and that truth does have a good side. Victor Frankl, who survived a Nazi death camp, quotes philosopher Friedrich Nietzsche on the subject: "He who has a why to live for can bear with almost any how."[9] We must make our own reasons—our own why—or someone else will.

Informed Compliance

Being informed doesn't necessarily remove us from the power of these principles. They obtain most of their strength because they operate automatically. They don't happen as a result of thinking a matter over. Rather, Cialdini refers to the response as a mechanical one: "click, whirr."[10]

He and other social scientists regard this automation as necessary. Normally, we benefit from sticking with people we like, those who have done favors for us, who have authority, and so on. What would happen if we simply reversed all these patterns? Think about it: We use these responses in our lives because they work, and sometimes we need ways to react quickly and with incomplete information.

Defense Mechanisms

In addition to the compliance principles, we also have a host of defense mechanisms that can be exploited:

Denial is, simply, a mechanism of denying. We can see this at work when insincere compliments are accepted as genuine. Because each of us has a basic desire to be liked, we may deny that we're being flattered. People who think ill of themselves may even reject a sincere compliment. In either case, we can simply take the news and test the truth of it elsewhere.

Fantasy formation creates a perceived reality out of fantasy. Sometimes we can't satisfy ourselves in the objective external world. We can always play make-believe and create a perceived reality in a dream world. Much of our entertainment satisfies our desire for fantasies of adventure, affection, and security.

Introjection allows placement of blame upon oneself. Self-directed blame or punishment defends against disappointment, disillusionment, and insecurity. For example, when a parent pays no attention to a child, the child feels unworthy of attention. The child scarcely dares consider the possibility that the parent just doesn't care. Often, this mechanism perpetuates the acceptance of authoritarian guidance even when it has persistently erred in the past. A subtle yet pervasive form of this mechanism goes like this: "I'm not smart enough. I must have misunderstood something."

Isolation involves avoiding associations that produce anxiety. One set of data is isolated from an associated set: people isolate victory in war from suffering and death, nuclear arsenals from murderous horror. Think back to the model and the automobile reviews, where the men rated the car pictured with an attractive woman as being faster than the car pictured alone, yet denied being influenced by the model. The men rating the automobile had isolated the woman from the formation of their rating; to admit otherwise would feel threatening. This mechanism can also be used in associations that have no immediate relationship, such as birth and death.

Projection places our intention, attitude, blame, or responsibility onto another. Consider the numerous television clips in which an actress in a short skirt is able to enlist the aid of nearly every male passerby. What do you think their fantasy formation projected onto the actress had to do with their willingness to heft heavy packages for a great distance? A fine line divides normal and pathological projection. Many rapists have the attitude that the victim "really wanted it."

Regression involves returning to an earlier age, usually as a dependent, where one felt safe and comfortable. The individual returns to an earlier stage of development in which someone else assumed responsibility and where fewer, simpler, and more primitive demands existed. This mechanism commonly occurs during illness. The bubble bath commercial, where the overworked mother relaxes in the tub at the end of the day, and other similar approaches intimately involve this mechanism. It's also present in the ads for flu medications, as well as some gusto advertisements. (For those of you too young to remember the "go for the gusto" television ads, they were designed to sell you on the idea that you only go around once so make sure that you do so with maximum joy, zest, and gusto.) Pampering, spoiling, carefree desires, and other childish elements of ad campaigns appeal to this mechanism.

Repression censors or conceals memories, associations, and adjustments from conscious awareness. Like an invisible filter, this mechanism prevents the conscious mind from seeing painful memories and stymied motives. Personal experiences ranging from embarrassment to cruelty are often blurred under the lens of repression. Here again, social enculturation plays a significant role. For example, one of the reasons a person fails to see a large penis in a bourbon ad is probably related to the "dirty mind" argument. To see the penis means admitting, even if only to ourselves, to having a dirty mind. So we don't see it, or we at least repress the awareness of it.

Sublimation redirects basic drive mechanisms. It means substituting acceptable behavior to satisfy basic motives that might be met equally well in a primitive sense by some form of unacceptable behavior. Sports often sublimate aggression. This mechanism is most useful in associations, especially those of a sexual nature. A sports car, for example, can be made into a socially acceptable sexual expression.

Some theorists consider several miscellaneous escapes and defenses as contributing to these eight basic perceptual defenses. Each serves the purpose of concealing from us what we don't want—or can't psychologically afford—to know about ourselves and the world around us.

Compliance professionals are very aware of both the principles and the perceptual defenses. In fact, these experts are most often employed in the field of advertising for that very reason.

Ethics and Exploitation

This really is a huge subject and I have barely touched the tip of the iceberg here. If you would like to know more, then I would recommend that you read my book *Mind Programming*, where I also cover such things as consistency, tells, context/content and more. However, my purpose here is just to give you an overview of this area so you can gain some idea of how frequently you operate on automatic, and how this can be used to usher you into making choices that do not necessarily serve you.

Use of these techniques and principles is inevitable and valuable, although I oppose their misuse. To level the playing field, so to speak, I feel that the consumer, voter, or novice on the receiving end of the technique is entitled to the same knowledge that compliance professionals have at their disposal.

Defense mechanisms, like compliance principles, are essential and necessary elements in individual and social well-being.

How they're employed determines whether they're good or bad. An ethical imperative requires skillful and well-intentioned use.

Compliance principles are appropriate in marketing, provided there are no misrepresentations. Advertising moves products, which drives the economy, and that has given us the physical capacity to feed and clothe everyone on earth, however poorly we manage it.

Employing these concepts to sell products while surreptitiously using subliminal imagery that may increase hostility is unethical and irresponsible. Our sensitivity to violence has declined dramatically in this decade. I even argue that the continued tweaking of the psyche and manipulation of the human condition could eventually erode the very fabric of our social order. Do you think that you've never turned down the request of a friend because someone who felt like a friend took advantage of you?

CONCLUSION

All of this information adds up to a brief overview of the data available. It can facilitate our understanding of some manipulations and protect us from them. It can also suggest the ethical use of the patterns of compliance. The fact is there is a time and place for the correct use of the compliance principles. However, being manipulated in this way does not lead to any of us making the smartest decisions. Our only protection against this is the knowledge of how it works. When we can see clearly through these tactics, then once again we are empowered to live the life that suits us best.

CHAPTER TWENTY-SIX

Scandals

A lie has no leg, but a scandal has wings.
~Thomas Fuller

Misconception: *Most people believe they are open-minded and give others the benefit of the doubt, always prepared to change their mind if evidence justifies it, even when the reports about someone are from a trusted source.*
Fact: *We trust the sources that confirm what we already think. We resist the information that challenges our status quo. Once we make a decision, we defend it whether it is right or wrong. A wrongful accusation is never forgotten.*

There is no end to the scandals that are reported everywhere in the news. Often scandals are invented to brand, position, frame, or embarrass an opponent. Sometimes scandals are created to make people think, "Where there's smoke, there's fire."

One of the more interesting things about scandals is how the public responds. If, for instance, there's a scandal that involves someone you are invested in, the likelihood is you will defend the person and dismiss or justify the scandal to defend your investment. Let's see if that's true.

I love thought experiments—how about you? They tend to promote clarity when issues can otherwise seem ambiguous or when our defense strategies will not allow us to see ourselves. To that end I will provide a few thought experiments representing both sides of issues where the public is deeply divided and emotionally invested. Please understand that you may be provoked, but if that happens, be sure to check with yourself and ask the question, "Why does this disturb me?" Remember, the whole point is to experience what I meant when I said earlier: the most interesting thing about scandals is how we respond when we are invested. Do we indeed lose objectivity and react emotionally? Has our consent been engineered to the point that we have become pundits for the engineering?

Point of View

Imagine that you're a fiscal conservative and you're opposed to the Affordable Health Care Act. You own a small business, and you have seen your health care costs soar as much as 25 percent in the first two years since the act was passed by Congress. You are struggling with whether to continue to provide health care for your employees or to pay the federal fine set to be imposed if you do not. The fine is less than your health care costs, but you also care very much for your employees. For the moment, you are watching, uncertain of what will happen since the president has decided not to enforce certain portions of the law according to their original schedule. You like the idea of health care for those who cannot afford it but fail to find the correct solution in a bill Congress passed before they read it. Now, to really appreciate this, you must put yourself in these shoes.

You want to grow your business but are reluctant to hire more people until you can have some certainty about your overhead and direction with regards to the law. Struggling with this, you donate to your congressman, who states that he opposes the bill as it stands. He desires to see certain amendments added or something else implemented that will take care of the needy. As a reasonably successful person, you pay a fair amount of taxes, more than most by both number of dollars as well as percentages. You are not rich, but you are solidly placed in the so-called upper-middle class. You work seven days a week on most weeks and often twelve to fourteen hours a day. Your success has been hard-earned, and when you look at the annual Social Security reports showing your contributions for prior years, you note that there are several years that there was no contribution because you lived on borrowed money while trying to establish your business.

Then one day your youngest child comes home from school and informs you of the many advantages to the Affordable Health Care Act. As you inquire about the source of the information, you discover that it is being taught in his school. Chills go up your spine. You remember the days of the Cold War and some of the arguments against totalitarian states—regimes that specifically target children to be the carriers of their propaganda. You say nothing to your child, but you decide to look into the matter.

The next day your inquiries lead to the discovery that in Los Angeles, the place where you live, $990,000 of your tax dollars are being spent by the Los Angeles Unified School District (LAUSD) to train teens to sell their families on Obamacare.[1] It seems that LAUSD has received a grant from the state of California for this purpose, and what's more, this is just a part of $37 million the state is spending to get people to cooperate with Obamacare.[2]

Your tax dollars are working against your interest. Is this scandalous? How do you feel?

Now imagine that you are a single parent with four children at home. You have lost your job through no fault of your own—downsizing. Your savings are tiny, and your unemployment isn't enough to cover bare essentials. You have taken a part-time evening job to make ends meet. Suddenly your youngest is involved in a bike accident. He tried to jump a curb and failed. The bike catapulted end over end, and his face was smashed into the concrete. Fortunately he was wearing a helmet. Still, his nose is broken, his lip is partially torn away, his jaw needs stitches, and he has cuts and abrasions elsewhere on his body. He needs emergency care. Thank God—the new Obamacare will provide his much-needed care. You sigh in relief as you leave the hospital, your son's care having been mandated by an act of Congress. Now how do you feel? Is it still so scandalous?

There are always two sides to every argument. The art of compromise is in the ability of both sides to feel the needs of the other. Empathy will inevitably lead to solutions that propaganda will fail to achieve. The reason: both sides use propaganda to sell the public on the idea that it's in their best interest (self-interest) to accept or reject an idea, a piece of legislation, an argument, and so forth. Why then do we not have more thought experiments and fewer sound bites?

The Neutralize Option

Of course, one of the best tools yet to be deployed when it comes to true scandals is what I think of as the "neutralize option." This is how that works. Remember the IRS scandal about how agents were targeting the Tea Party folks and other conservative groups?

In this scandal the IRS targeted 292 Tea Party groups between May 2010 and May 2012. According to the *Washington Examiner,* "'At this point, the evidence shows us that conservative groups were not only flagged, but targeted and abused by the IRS,' said Sarah Swinehart spokeswoman for the Ways and Means Committee. As we gather the facts, we will follow them wherever they lead us. Chairman [Rep. David] Camp encourages all groups, regardless of political affiliation, that feel they may have been targeted to come forward and share their story."[3]

Now the neutralize button, one that many heard and then failed to follow any further, for I have heard it repeated over and over again since, went like this: "It wasn't only Tea Party groups; certain liberal groups were also targeted."

The facts are different. "Refuting Democratic suggestions that progressive groups were also swept up in the IRS probe of the tax status of Tea Party organizations, the Treasury Department's inspector general has revealed that just six progressive groups were targeted compared to 292 conservative groups."[4]

Is this a scandal? This is how the president addressed many would-be scandals, or real scandals depending on your point of view—scandals such as Benghazi, Fast and Furious, the IRS, the NSA and PRISM and other spying practices, and so forth.

"With an endless parade of distractions, political posturing and phony scandals, Washington has taken its eye off
the ball," Obama said in an economic address at Knox College in Galesburg, Illinois in July of 2013.[5]

In a piece published by the *WFC Courier*, the notion of dis-
missal was dismissed.

He could even be grateful there are so many Americans
have lost track of perhaps one of the most egregious of them
all. That would be Fast and Furious. This was a scheme in
which federal agencies allowed weapons from U.S. gun
dealers to "walk" across the border and into the possession
of Mexican drug dealers, with the intent of tracking them.
The ATF lost track of a good portion of those weapons,
which have been used in hundreds of crimes, including the
December 2010 murder of Border Patrol Agent Brian Terry.

Estimates of the number of Mexican nationals killed or
injured with these weapons have exceeded 300.

Attorney General Eric Holder became the first sitting
member of the Cabinet of the United States to be held in
contempt of Congress on June 28, 2012. Earlier that month,
Obama had invoked executive privilege for the first time in
his presidency over related documents.

We're left wondering: Why smother a "phony" scandal
with the executive privilege pillow?

Or have there been others since then?

—The Internal Revenue Service flap, where the IRS targeted American citizens based on their political ideology.

The IRS official who oversaw the agency's tax-exempt
office invoked her constitutional right against self-incrimination when questioned by Congress.

Why plead the fifth over a "phony" scandal?

—Benghazi. The attack on a foreign consulate in which
four Americans were murdered. If you want the definition
of phony, you might want to consider the changes that were
made to the talking points in order to suggest the attack was
motivated by an anti-Muslim video.

—Warrantless domestic spying by the National Security
Agency.

—The Justice Department's massive cull of Associated Press reporters' home phone records.

What's so problematic is that it is not even a series of scandals any longer; it's a pattern. Information gets to the public. The administration feigns ignorance and/or indignation. Move on.[6]

Now I would be remiss if I failed to include the latest at the time of this writing.

Even as the White House labels Benghazi a "phony scandal," a raft of new allegations and concerns is once again bringing the controversy back to the forefront in Washington.

Fox News has learned that at least five CIA employees were forced to sign additional nondisclosure agreements this past spring in the wake of the Benghazi attack. These employees had already signed such agreements before the attack but were made to sign new agreements aimed at discouraging survivors from leaking their stories to the media or anyone else.

CNN has also reported that dozens of people working for the CIA were in Benghazi on the night of the attack, and that employees are being intimidated into staying silent.[7]

Is this true? How do you find out? There has been pushback by the CIA, insisting that their agents are always free to talk to the press. Really?

The Art of Thinking

Now you must decide if these are matters that should be meaningful to you or not, but the fact remains that you must consider more than the information you want to believe or you deprive yourself inevitably of the full truth. If being someone's puppet pleases you, then discovering the truth is probably counterproductive.

CONCLUSION

By now, our adventure in examining the influence of public relations, propaganda, compliance principles, unconscious motives, definitions, and so much more, makes the material discussed in this chapter less and less important in the overall scheme of things. That is because you have come to understand that the system is designed in such a way today that our real education must be in *how* to find the truth rather than in memorizing names, dates, and places, as most of us were taught. Thinking is becoming a lost art for too many. In other words, it is only when our mind turns fully around on itself, examining not just its content but its operating system, that we stand a chance in realizing who we really are, let alone what we really believe. Have you yet made the commitment to yourself to do this?

CHAPTER TWENTY-SEVEN

What to Do if You Want to Subvert the System

What we must understand is that the industries, processes, and inventions created by modern science can be used either to subjugate or liberate. The choice is up to us.

~Henry A. Wallace

Misconception: *Most people believe conspiracy theories are the work of loons. They are convinced that if there were any truth behind them, the government would check it out publicly. Fair-minded people governed by elected fair-minded representatives with only a few bad apples, that's the state of affairs.*
Fact: *Many of the so-called conspiracy theories of the past have turned out to be representations of fact. A common technique used to discredit a theory is to throw in a bit of nonsense from a shill. Government can and has quickly discredited events by sending someone out to burn the flag in front of the cameras. We are subjects—the question is, are we about to be subjugated?*

Let's assume that you desire to subjugate the majority of Americans, or for that matter, the majority of people in free countries. What would you do? Could steps be taken to systematically bring this about?

The answer is yes. Indeed, there is a plan that was laid out years ago to accomplish this. It really is time to think back to that chapter on tin foil hats, for the information that follows has often been labeled in part or whole as one absurd conspiracy theory. True? False? You decide.

Debt

I'll begin with a man whom I met personally and for whom I have a great deal of respect. I am speaking of W. Cleon Skousen. Years ago I was handling a case that gave rise to my meeting with Cleon Skousen, then chief of police in Salt Lake City. He had been a special agent with the FBI, had earned his law degree many years earlier, and was a strict interpreter of the law. In time he was fired by Mayor J. Bracken Lee for raiding a gambling event at which Lee was in attendance. "After Skousen's firing, his model police programs were dismantled, and crime increased, on the average, by 22 percent."[1]

Skousen reports in his book, *The Naked Capitalist,* on a conspiracy among a "mysterious super leadership" intent on ruling the world. I know what you might be thinking at this point, "Oh no—another one-world government piece of nonsense!" Perhaps it is just that, but let me flesh out the dots for you, and then you decide if they connect or not. Skousen bases much of his foundational work on the findings of Dr. Carrol Quigley. Quigley was a professor of history at the Foreign Services School of Georgetown University and the author of numerous textbooks, including the *Evolution of Civilization.* His book, *Tragedy and Hope,* detailed the big bankers' role in world affairs, manipulating the people and managing their governments.

What does money have to do with world affairs? Everything! We don't need a conspiracy theory to enable our search of history and discover that big banks have financed wars throughout modern history. Quigley disclosed the full nature of this in *Tragedy and Hope,* and as an insider to the political events in the world, he essentially tells us that the reason he is now disclosing the information is, and I'll quote Skousen's take on this: "It is now too late for little people to turn back the tide. In the spirit of kindness he is therefore urging them not to fight the noose that is already around their necks. He feels certain that those who do will only choke themselves to death. On the other hand, those who go along with the immense pressure which is beginning to be felt by all of humanity will eventually find themselves in a man-made millennium of peace and prosperity."[2]

"Wow, such audacity," I thought when I first encountered this idea. Sure, we the people are going to be herded like cattle or sheep, and we'll just accept it because, after all, we are being led to greener pastures. Unfortunately, I was much younger then, and I simply dismissed this rhetoric as somewhere between strange and absurd. Maybe I had a strain of self-righteousness running through me, as do many young people who truly believe the myth of self-governance. Thoughts such as, "Now that we're adults, we can choose what we want to do, what we want to become, and how we will do that. This is the land of opportunity, isn't it?"

Today I have a much more sober view of all of this. Living tends to educate those who are aware. So just how does this elite few manage to coerce, intimidate, manipulate, and corrupt millions of people in order to pull off this subversion?

Money Lenders

As Quigley points out, all governments are dependent upon sources of revenue to establish and maintain control, especially in time of emergency. In other words, who doesn't need to borrow money? Quoting Quigley:

> In time they brought into their financial network the provincial banking centers, organized as commercial banks and saving banks, as well as insurance companies, to form all of these into a single financial system on an international scale which manipulated the quantity and flow of money so that they were able to influence, if not control, governments on one side and industries on the other. The men who did this . . . aspired to establish dynasties of international bankers and were at least as successful at this as were many of the dynastic political rulers."[3]

351

Please allow me to fast forward for a minute. I enjoyed many hours-long conversations with a man who himself was cast in the mold of Quigley. Not only was he an insider who had a healthy view of himself as a member of the intellectual elite, but he was also a bit of a renegade in the sense that he would openly discuss matters of this nature with anyone he trusted. His interests owned or controlled gold mines, gold coining facilities, retail establishments, public corporations, real estate companies, and much more.

One evening as I challenged some of his ideas, he shared this scenario with me. Suppose some strangers come to your door and tell you they are taking your house and possessions—get out! What would you do? Of course, you would defend your home and property! However, if the strangers at the door were bankers, informing you that they were repossessing your property due to your failure to keep your word and repay your loans, what would you do? Lower your head in shame and walk away.

Debt—that is just one control mechanism, as we will see. I remember when people could not freely finance such small purchases as appliances. Then the law was changed, and you could buy on time with 10 percent down. Not long afterward, 10 percent down became no money down. It's not at all uncommon nowadays to find that even automobiles can be purchased this way. During the housing boom and subsequent scandal, in the days of subprime loans, many practices employed by mortgage companies led people into home loans they simply never stood a chance to repay. What resulted was a massive redistribution of wealth that caused even nations to go belly up.

Protecting Freddie and Fannie

It is also worth noting at this juncture that Freddie Mac and Fannie Mae made large investments of taxpayer money (government backed) in subprime mortgages. Quoting from the *National Review*:

> The House Ethics Committee quietly joined its Senate counterpart in finding that no members or staffers—or at

least any it claimed jurisdiction over—broke congressional rules while obtaining "VIP" mortgages from Countrywide. This failed lender at one time provided a huge share of the questionable subprime mortgages issued by Fannie Mae and Freddie Mac, the government-backed mortgage lenders that were some of the first players to fall in the 2008 financial collapse . . .

. . . The taxpayer guarantee allowed—indeed, encouraged—the lenders to be reckless, creating a moral hazard. In 2008, this set-up helped bring down the whole house of cards built by subprime mortgages.

But far from being dismantled, Fannie and Freddie have avoided insolvency, thanks to massive taxpayer bailouts. Talk of winding them down has faded on Capitol Hill and is being discouraged by the Obama administration. The two entities, along with the Federal Housing Administration, currently back some 90 percent of new mortgages. Talk about there being no consequences for failure.

Countrywide's most famous client was Democratic senator Chris Dodd, chair of the Financial Services Committee from 2006 to 2010. Although he and Conrad were cleared of ethics violations by the Senate Ethics Committee in 2009, Dodd retired the next year after it became clear that revelations about his involvement with Countrywide had destroyed his political standing in his home state of Connecticut. He was nonetheless able to shepherd the now-infamous Dodd-Frank bill into law before he stepped down. Dodd-Frank is a rat's nest of new regulations on financial firms, but it goes notably light on regulating the housing industry and its cozy relationship with the federal government.

Despite its explosive findings, Representative Issa's committee lacked any jurisdiction to suggest punishment for any individuals. The matter was handed off to the secretive House Ethics Committee, which quietly issued a report just two days after Christmas. This report concluded:

While these allegations concern serious matters, almost all of the allegations concerned actions taken outside, or well outside, the jurisdiction of this committee . . . because they occurred before the third Congress prior to the current Congress. In addition, several of the members and employees mentioned in the allegations are no longer serving in or employed by the House, and therefore are outside the committee's jurisdiction.[4]

Back to the development of the money influence. Returning to Quigley's remarks:

> The greatest of these (banking) dynasties were the descendants of Mayer Amschel Rothschild of Frankfurt, whose male descendants, for at least two generations, generally married first cousins or even nieces. Rothschild's five sons established at branches in Vienna, London, Naples, and Paris, as well as Frankfurt, cooperated together in ways which other international banking dynasties copied but rarely excelled . . .
>
> The names of these other banking families are familiar to all of us and should be more so. They include Baring, Lazard, Erlanger, Warburg, Schroder, Selingman, the Speyers, Mirabaud, Mallet, Fould, and above all, Rothschild and Morgan."[5]

International Bankers

And then there is the differentiation between ordinary and international bankers:

> They remained different from ordinary bankers in distinctive way: (1) they were cosmopolitan and international; (2) they were close to governments and were particularly concerned with questions of government debt; (3) their interests were exclusively in bonds and very rarely in goods; (4) they were accordingly, fanatical devotees of deflation; (5) they were almost equally devoted to secrecy and the secret use of financial influence in political life. These bankers came to be known as international bankers and, more particularly, were known as merchant bankers in England, private bankers in France, and investment bankers in the Unites States. In all countries they carried on various kinds of banking and exchange activities, but everywhere they were sharply distinguishable from other, more obvious, kinds of banks, such as savings banks or commercial banks.[6]

With this brief introduction—and that's all this is, for the purview of this work is not about banking or debt except as it pertains to another gotcha, another means by which we may be controlled as a people, an element in the plan, so to speak—let's take a look at the money game called the Federal Reserve.

The Federal Reserve

It has surprised me just how many people are ignorant of the role the Federal Reserve plays in our lives. Most ordinary people that I have asked know that they regulate interest to some extent and that's pretty much it. The Federal Reserve System (FRS) is the central banking system of the United States. It was created in 1913. Its scope of power reaches much farther than regulating the interest rate banks charge other banks, or the prime rate, as it is called. President Woodrow Wilson signed the law into effect on the December 23, 1913. It was also known at the time as the Currency Bill, or the Owen-Glass Act. It is a privately owned banking system supposedly operating in the public interest.

> The U.S. Congress established three key objectives for monetary policy in the Federal Reserve Act: Maximum employment, stable prices, and moderate long-term interest rates. The first two objectives are sometimes referred to as the Federal Reserve's dual mandate. Its duties have expanded over the years, and today, according to official Federal Reserve documentation, include conducting the nation's monetary policy, supervising and regulating banking institutions, maintaining the stability of the financial system, and providing financial services to depository institutions, the U.S. government, and foreign official institutions. The Fed also conducts research into the economy and releases numerous publications, such as the Beige Book.[7]

There have been a few changes to the FRS since its original design by Nelson Aldridge. Because of Aldridge's influence at the time, he was generally considered to be the "general manager" of the country. He was the Republican leader in the Senate who held a pivotal position on the Senate Finance Committee. He became wealthy as a result of insider investments in rubber, sugar, railroads, and banking. As an interesting aside, your federal income tax liability may well rest squarely on his shoulders as well.

In 1909, Aldrich introduced a constitutional amendment to establish an income tax, although he had declared a similar measure "communistic" a decade earlier. Aldrich was quite candid about his scheme to block the House bill that had been passed, declaring to the Senate, "I shall vote for the corporation tax as a means to defeat the income tax."

The compromise passed unanimously in the Senate and by a vote of 318 to 14 in the House. The corporate excise tax would be levied, and the income tax constitutional amendment would be sent out to the states for ratification—which Taft and Aldrich thought was impossible.

The plan went awry. After 1909, the U.S. underwent a major political transformation. Democrats and progressive Teddy Roosevelt Republicans swept many state elections. Woodrow Wilson won the 1912 presidential election. Democrats controlled both houses of Congress. On February 3, 1913, the legislatures in Delaware, New Mexico, and Wyoming voted for the amendment, pushing the total to the required 36 states. The 16th Amendment was officially adopted on February 25, three and a half years after the Taft-Aldrich compromise had supposedly relegated the income tax to the dust bin.[8]

It should be clear that money held a high position in Aldrich's priorities, and banking interests were married to his wealth. So what is the problem with the FRS, you might ask at this point. Why is it included as a part of the plan, or is it another gotcha?

The FRS controls the quantity of money and thereby has some control over inflation and deflation cycles. Its chief aim is argued to be that of promoting a vibrant economy, but the fact is, what it always does is promote and create more debt.

We have already seen why debt can be a problem, a real gotcha. That said, there is another reason, other than the spiraling size of the debt and concerns about America becoming insolvent, such as the situation in Greece where even the Red Cross is cutting back on the "supply of donor blood to Greece because the country has failed to pay its bills on time."[9]

The relevant reason that I have in mind is the cycle of consumerism that is implicit in this ever-expanding debt model. This is a subject that we will take up in some depth in the chapter on consumerism. For now, the important message exists in that simple story shared with me many years ago: "What would you do if a stranger came to your home to take what you owned?"

Before continuing, I urge you to read Skousen's little book *The Naked Capitalist* and follow up by checking into the works of Quigley. I am not arguing that there is a one-world conspiracy beyond the scope of greed, as suggested in what I have chosen to cover. However, I would be remiss if I didn't inform you that, in my opinion, there is something to the notion that a few elite not only control the wealth of the world but have made puppets of many of the governments in at least indirect ways as well.

Back to the Plan: Debt and Taxes

If you made a long-term plan and developed a strategy and the tactics to carry it out—with the idea that the subordination of the public was the goal, that they should be seen as workers in a beehive, dispensable as individuals but essential collectively, necessary to accumulate more and more treasure—what would you do?

First, provide an economic architecture, a means of trade for their labors, and second, a way to recover at least most of the gains they have made at the end of their usefulness. The answer is two-fold: debt and taxes. We have already given time to a cursory examination of these two techniques, so what's next?

Self-Reliance

America was built on a strong sense of self-reliance. This self-reliance arguably fostered the spread of individualism. It is worth thinking a moment about exactly what *Individualism* means.

> Individualism is the moral stance, political philosophy, ideology, or social outlook that emphasizes "the moral worth

of the individual." Individualists promote the exercise of one's goals and desires and so value independence and self-reliance and advocate that interests of the individual should achieve precedence over the state or a social group, while opposing external interference upon one's own interests by society or institutions such as the government.

Individualism makes the individual its focus and so starts "with the fundamental premise that the human individual is of primary importance in the struggle for liberation." Liberalism, existentialism, and anarchism are examples of movements that take the human individual as a central unit of analysis. Individualism thus involves "the right of the individual to freedom and self-realization." [10]

Now impinging on this idealistic definition is reality. Today the tax load on many is a form of indentured servitude. Each year the length of this servitude extends itself. In 2013, tax freedom for most came on April 18, for example, and that is five days later than in 2012. In other words, for the first four and a half months of the year, everything you earn goes to taxes. That's over one-third of your labors that belong to someone else.

In today's culture there is a sense of "need" that in years past might have been categorized as "want." There exists as well the notion of entitlement—I am entitled to this, the government should do this for us, education should be free, health care should be free, and so forth. Now for my liberal friends, if you're still reading this, I don't mean to imply a preference here but rather describe a situation.

We have people on record stating that they voted one way or another because of the freebies they got. We have a larger and larger proportion of our population taking some form of support from the government. According to the online magazine *Slate*, "Considering only 'means-tested' programs, such as food stamps, Medicaid, and housing assistance, around 35 percent of Americans live in households that benefit from government assistance." [11]

That means that more than a third of our population is dependent upon the tax dollars taken from their fellow hardworking citizens. Now if you add in the Social Security obligation owed by government, you discover that about 49 percent of Americans live in households receiving some form of support from the government. What's the point? Public assistance programs devalue the sense of self-reliance and self-responsibility. Obviously we need and want to support the needy, but the catch-22 may be in how we define *needy*. Do we really have more than one-third of Americans in truly needy roles? If so, then we definitely need to redefine what we mean by a prosperous nation!

Now, as people become more and more dependent upon government, they give up much of their sense of self-reliance or trade it in for a new view.

The New View

One of the psychological mechanisms we discussed earlier is justification. It is human nature to rationalize in ways that justify actions including those that happen to us. The new view gaining traction today is "I deserve it." Governments exist to take care of people; that is, after all, the reason for government in the first place, isn't it? Government is to provide a safe environment, public education, protection from criminals, means of transportation, jobs or income sources, etc. In other words, many have transferred the hard work ethic, that sense of self-reliance and self-responsibility, to the collective. It is the burden of the hive to care for the members. What's more, it's time for those fat bees, the ones with all of the wealth, to take care of the worker bees. It's time to tax them more to pay for all the benefits we deserve.

Now, I do not wish to argue in favor of the multinational corporations or big bankers and so forth, but we should keep in mind two things about this emerging, ever more popular attitude. The first is a lesson that history repeatedly teaches us, and forgive my colloquialism, "But it flat ain't going to happen!" The real money pulls the strings, and whether through a dictator or the pressure on elected representatives by special interest groups, the big money will not pay the bills! What typically takes place is a redistribution of wealth. The middle class is wiped out, and the rich simply get richer as a result.

GOTCHA!

The second concern is as abiding. Giving up our sense of self-reliance has far-reaching consequences. Not only does it pre-dispose us to become genuine dependents in much the same way that children are dependents, but it also robs us of our dignity. In order to mask this nasty fact, it could be argued that the cult of self-esteem was contrived.

The Cult of Self-Esteem

If I can convince you that you are perfect just as you are, that you deserve the cornucopia of all the good things that life has to offer, that additionally, the only reason you have not been able to enjoy the finer things in life is due to the fundamental unfairness brought about by those who already have the finer things, then I have positioned you to expect that you do indeed deserve all of those finer things, this better way of life. What's more, you don't really have to do anything because you should have been given them before now. Like a restitution payment that is due, say, to Native Americans for the acts of our distant relatives, all the goodness life has to offer is due to you. So the first thing that must be done to bring this picture into focus is to sell you on the idea that you deserve self-esteem, you deserve respect, you deserve the best, and what's more—it's yours just for claiming it!

Now if you have ever read any of the many self-help books out there, this theme should be quite familiar to you. Indeed, if you're one of the millions who have read *The Secret,* then you know that all you need to do is focus your attention on what you want, visualize it, declare it to be yours, know that it is coming, let it go, and voilà, it is yours! And of course, that's why there are so many new billionaires—they read *The Secret.*[12]

Forgive my facetiousness, but sometimes the tripe and drivel I see selling millions and millions of copies disturbs me. For when I see this sort of thing I know that whatever the material, it is not necessarily telling you anything other than what you wish were true and want to hear. What's worse, this sort of teaching tends to create narcissists, and that can be quite disturbing, especially given the context of this writing, for as Alice Miller wrote in *Drama of the Gifted Child,* Germany's fall into fascism was only possible because as individuals, each person had become a narcissist.[13]

The idea of hard work and self-denial is unpopular today, largely because the general consensus seems to be that it is not necessary to work in order to have everything that we are entitled to. Bottom line: Not all sides of the self-esteem construct are healthy.

Self-esteem should be built, not passed out. Giving everyone a ribbon for just competing, refraining from identifying winners and losers, fails to build anything real other than the sense that I already deserve it without having to prove, demonstrate, earn, or otherwise pay any dues to gain it. Honestly, I can't think of anything much further from the truth.

Confession

Now as one who has a New Age publisher, I must confess to having partially supported the idea that we are perfect as we are. However, I see it this way. I happen to believe that life has a purpose and that we are more than just a terminal species dwelling for a short time in the evolution of all matter, ultimately destined as individuals to become only atoms of matter again. In my view, we have a Creator; I do believe in some form of Grand Organizing Designer (GOD). To be clear, I believe not in some anthropomorphic deity but in that Unmoved Mover of Aristotle's that I think of as Universal Intelligence, Universal Consciousness, and so forth. For me, this mystery is beyond the capability of our language or intelligence to truly comprehend or communicate. It's like asking the finite to describe the infinite or explaining to someone why division by zero can be shown to lead to all possibilities, or infinity.

My take, then, is that you are created with an awesome potential to manifest your innate talents, to face and overcome all challenges, to rise to a level of human existence that honors you and your creator, and to do so by doing your best with integrity in all matters with service to your fellow human beings as the defining factor in your life. This sort of self-help, self-esteem building, I encourage. This is what I write about and endorse. This is not free self-esteem, no price to pay—you just deserve it—and that's the kind I am criticizing.

Personal Pride

Everyone has probably heard that adage, "You value what you have to earn much more than you value what is free." I am sure every parent has seen this with their children at some point in their maturation. The fact is, the more we get free, the more we expect. If you give someone a phone for free and it breaks, they expect you to replace it for free as well. Why would they expect otherwise?

So the next thing to be taken into consideration in the plan of subjugation is how to encourage people to expect things for free and still maintain a sense of pride about it. This way they can be our assistants in taking more wealth and power from those beneath the elite. Some very interesting facts were recently published by *Zero Hedge:*

> Back in 2010 we started an annual series looking at the (re)distribution in the wealth of nations and social classes. What we found then (and what the media keeps rediscovering year after year to its great surprise) is that as a result of global central bank policy, the rich got richer, and the poor kept on getting poorer, even though as we predicted the global political powers would, at least superficially, seek to enforce policies that aimed to reverse this wealth redistribution from the poor to the rich (a doomed policy as the world's legislative powers are largely in the lobby pocket of the world's wealthiest who needless to say are less than willing to enact laws that reduce their wealth and leverage). Now that the topic of wealth distribution (or rather concentration) is once again in vogue, below we present the latest such update looking at a global portrait of household wealth. The bottom line: 29 million, or 0.6% of those with any actual assets under their name, own $87.4 trillion, or 39.3% of all global assets... What CS does not say is that the bulk of this increase is courtesy of Federal Reserve-facilitated wealth redistribution from the lower and middle classes to the upper class."[14]

In my view, there is no such thing as a free lunch! Getting it free often means, *"Gotcha!"* The free stay in a lovely Florida condo is about selling you that condo; the free trip to the Bahamas, that's about selling you . . . you get the idea.

New Age Religion to New World Government

There are many nonsense ideas in the world. The idea that you are here to manifest material wealth is one such notion. No seriously spiritual, religious, or nonreligious, person believes that to be our prime purpose in life. Indeed, one of the most outspoken and best-known skeptics in America, Michael Shermer, shared with me that it is our highest nature to aid our fellowman.

There is a New Age idea that asserts the need for cooperation. Many proponents of this notion instruct their readers about the natural order and how cooperation is the bond within and between species. I spoke with one such popular author on my radio show, *Provocative Enlightenment.* She shared a story of how her dog and a neighbor's dog learned to share a bone. To her, this was evidence for the "bond."

I challenged that assertion at the time. A stallion will kill a seven-day-old foal just to get to the mare in foal heat. The fact is, anyone who has spent any time in nature and around animals knows how predacious nature is. The idea that nature cooperates is more than a little wacky, unless by *cooperate* we mean "balances life by preying on each other."

Still, the notion of the bond has gained great traction among many New Agers. It seems, after all, very Christian, for it includes the idea of sharing—particularly where the redistribution of wealth is concerned. In repeated interviews with many guests, I have attempted to flesh out this notion. Assume that as a society we were to take all the wealth in the country and divide it evenly among the population. This idea is pleasing to most. Next, assume we took the wealth you just added to your holdings and divided it among all the starving and poor peoples of the world. This is the same idea—share and share alike, regardless of anything other than the fact that you are alive. (I mean, the fact that you are here is your franchise and you need do nothing to reap

363

fabulous benefits; remember the original idea.) Now you have less than you had to begin with!

Charity is wonderful, but few give up everything to take care of those starving in Africa, and that includes the proponents of "share and cooperate." If, however, you were to design a religious/spiritual belief that would nurture the idea of a one-world government, then the idea behind bonding to all in shared wealth is one way to move society in that direction.

America has long been a country that prized individuality and cherished individual freedoms. Immigrants from all over the world come to America to better their station in life. America is a country of entrepreneurs the likes of Steve Jobs. The legend of what Jobs did with Apple and the contribution this one man made to the world in technology and economic impact is formidable. That said, although Jobs was widely considered to be a genius, many have also called him "a bad, mean manager."[15]

Steve Jobs was focused and knew what he wanted. He began with nothing and built an empire, helping the world along with technology that we find everywhere today from the hospital to the parking lot of the local grocery. He was an entrepreneur— a strong individualist and intent on achieving his goals. This is what made Steve Jobs the success that he was, and who he was is anything but a poster boy for *The Bond*.

So the New Age religion focuses on the concept of oneness and equality, but the real world shows that those who have made the biggest contributions to society rarely ever fit this model. So now, let's take it further and see how New Age beliefs can be used to subvert the system that has traditionally desired freedom and independence.

There is a conspiracy theory about a project known as NASA's Project Blue Beam. Blue Beam is allegedly all about misinformation and disinformation. It is rumored to be behind engineered earthquakes, hoaxed discoveries, and such other matters as the "laser projection of multiple holographic images to different parts of the world."[16]

For what it's worth, I tend to believe this belief has little truth in it and is instead packed with fluff and conjecture, but that is only my opinion. Still, there is a statement common to those who insist Blue Beam and other like programs are all about preparing the world for takeover, and it makes a little sense. The argument goes like this:

> We must remember that the New Age religion is the very foundation for the new world government, without which religion the dictatorship of the new world order is completely impossible. I'll repeat that: Without a universal belief in the New Age religion, the success of the new world order will be impossible![17]

Cooperation is important, but so is self-reliance. Freedom and competition form the arena in which entrepreneurship prospers. There is little reason, given an understanding of human nature or the history of civilization, to believe that being given everything while lacking any reward for working hard would result in the world producing another Steve Jobs or Bill Gates or Sam Goldman and so forth.

Protection

To subvert a group, you obviously have to get them to do your bidding, and one of the easiest ways to do this it to give them free stuff. But what else can you do? The answer is to provide them with services. Help them depend upon you for safety. Guarantee the safety of their food and medicine. The fact is, protections have led to numerous gotchas, some of which we have already covered, including the recent extension of "law enforcement," the government's spying abilities, the increase in no-knock searches, the legalized indefinite detention of U.S. citizens under the Patriot Act, and so forth; others, such as food and medicine, we will cover later. For now, it is obvious that the more we depend upon an entity for all things, the less individual sovereignty remains and the easier it is to be controlled by outside forces.

Definitions—Newspeak

As we discussed earlier, in the classic work *1984* by the seer George Orwell, a new language was created. This new language was called "newspeak." It largely redefined the meaning of words.

Newspeak is the fictional language in the novel *1984* written by George Orwell. It is a reduced language created by the totalitarian state as a tool to limit free thought, and concepts that pose a threat to the regime such as freedom, self-expression, individuality, peace, etc. Any form of thought alternative to the party's construct is classified as "thought crime."[18]

Domestic Extremism

Isn't that exactly what Janet Napolitano, former U.S. Secretary of Homeland Security, attempted (and failed at) when she tried to introduce her Domestic Extremism Lexicon in 2009? Just as a reminder, Napolitano ended up rescinding the Lexicon, released as an internal document for the Obama administration in 2009, due to public outrage. This dictionary labeled such groups as returning veterans as potential extremists and thereby inclined to terrorist acts. It was the veterans' inclusion that no doubt tipped the scale of embarrassment leading to the withdrawal—whatever that means. However, there were some obvious political positions in this document—positions that ran contrary to the administration's policies at the time. For example, pro-gun advocates and pro-lifers were included as potential extremists. Indeed, the language of the document is a tutorial for understanding how definitions can be used to marginalize groups:

> The definition reads: "A movement of groups or individuals who are virulently antiabortion and advocate violence against providers of abortion-related services, their employees, and their facilities. Some cite various racist and anti-Semitic beliefs to justify their criminal activities."[19]

This is really interesting. We cannot use the terms "Muslim terrorist" or "black criminal" because these terms engender hate, but we can categorize a "right to life" person as an extremist!

Are you a potential terrorist under such guidelines? Let's see how you answer these questions. Do you pay with cash? Do you complain about your tap water? Are you concerned about your privacy? Do you desire GMO labeling? I could add, are you reading this book?

All but the last activity were formerly classified as terrorist characteristics, but if I am successful at building concern in you for any of these matters, then I suppose that reading this book could be considered as constituting a potential threat.

A piece by Anthony Gucciardi shows us that every American is potentially a terrorist and therefore could be held indefinitely without trial:

> I can show you how literally 100 percent of the population can be classified as a terrorist under the truly outrageous Department of Homeland Security (DHS) and FBI characteristics that define a terrorist or terrorist activity. These broad qualifications of "terrorism" that have spawned a new wave of absolute paranoia within the population regarding their fellow citizens, who the nightly news says may be sleeper cell terrorists.
>
> Paranoia has led to one woman facing an armed 'terrorism taskforce' who demanded a home search without a warrant after she ran a Google search for pressure cookers online—a search that, as it turns out, qualifies for terrorist activity within the United States of America. It has now come out that it was her employer who went and called in the police and subsequent 'terrorism taskforce' after it was discovered that this law-abiding woman and her family had searched for backpacks along with 'pressure cookers' on Google.[20]

Are the actions reported in this article over the top? Many would say so. What have you Googled lately?

Framing and Reframing

I have always argued that if you control the definition, you control the argument. The fact is, all sorts of redefinitions are taking place right in front of us on a daily basis, and most of them go unnoticed.

Think about the many changes made by recent administrations designed to reframe the argument. For example, under President Obama, there is no war on terror. The shooting at Fort Hood was classified as workplace violence, despite the fact that former Major Nidal Hasan states openly that he felt he was on the wrong side of the war, and when he realized that, he changed sides, taking up arms with his Muslim brothers by fatally shooting 13 and injuring 30 others. What advantage is gained by calling this an act of workplace violence?

If we look at the context in which the shooting at Fort Hood happened, it's plain to see that the argument of the day was Al Qaeda was decimated and on the run. Later the slogan became, "We got Bin Laden." All of this was pivotal in a reelection campaign.

Now this is not to point fingers at one side or another. The fact is: it is those seeking to gain an advantage in their argument that are doing the reframing or creating the newspeak. It has become an important part of propaganda and public relations. "Words That Work"[21] is more than the title to a book; it is an expression that goes to the very heart of the matter!

As definitions change, people fall into lockstep, like marchers in a band. Often this is due to pressure placed on them by a small minority championing the changes. Now, before going on to the next example, it is also important we understand that some language changes are good—good in every sense. They raise the level of discourse and provide a much more civilized manner in which we refer to and communicate with each other.

With that bit of introduction, let's do another thought experiment. Imagine that you grow up in an era where referring to a person in a certain way is normal and ordinary. Let's just say you live on the wealthy side of the tracks, and those on the other side are commonly thought of as poor white trash. Let's assume you become friends with a young lady from the wrong side of the tracks. She knows how people talk about her from where you come, so she calls herself white trash from time to time when you're out together doing your thing. Now, let's assume the expression becomes, in time, "hate speech." Then one day you are asked if you ever called someone "white trash." You admit that yes, indeed, you did many, many years ago when it was common. Let's assume that this admission causes you to lose your job and marks you as a bigot. How do you feel?

What to Do if You Want to Subvert the System

Let's continue our thought experiment some. Imagine that one evening you have crossed the tracks to visit your friend. Along the way you were accosted and robbed. You returned home immediately, frightened and mad. The thief had threatened you with a gun. When asked what happened by your family, you shouted something like this, "Some white trash asshole stuck a gun in my face and stole everything I had on me!"

Now assume that you have been asked under oath whether or not you ever called someone "white trash." You answer yes and even explain the situation, but the explanation doesn't matter. What does matter is that you said such a thing in the first place. You are fired and publicly branded a bigot. How do you feel?

Let's further assume that you have not used the words "white trash" for more than twenty years. Times have changed and slurs of that kind are now unacceptable generally and truly unacceptable to you. Knowing that, do you tell the truth or lie when asked have you ever called someone "white trash?"

Let's play with this experiment just a minute or two more. Assume that it's a close friend of yours who is in trouble for calling a thief white trash many years ago. What do you do? Assume for the moment that there is a strong backlash because your friend is a public figure and the folks who used to call each other white trash insist that your friend is a bigot who should be ashamed of himself and does not deserve to be a public figure. These folks are very vocal and attack anyone who tends to suggest that your friend may have done something that at the time was acceptable given the circumstances. Do you stand up to them or do you remain quiet in the background?

Paula Deen

Enter Paula Deen. Here's the story as it appeared in the *Business Insider*:

> Southern-cooking Food Network star Paula Deen is currently being sued by the former general manager of her restaurant, Uncle Bubba's Seafood and Oyster House in Savannah, Georgia.

The manager, Lisa T. Jackson, has accused Deen of racial discrimination and her brother Earl W. "Bubba" Hiers of sexual harassment, according to the *Savannah Morning News*. Jackson also accused Deen's husband of being physically abusive.

The National Enquirer says it obtained a recorded copy of a May 17 deposition related to the lawsuit, and quotes from the alleged recording certainly don't seem to help Deen's case.

In response to a question about whether Deen had ever used the N-word, she said, "Yes, of course," and also admitted to telling racist jokes, according to the *Enquirer*.

She reportedly said, "It's just what they are—they're jokes . . . most jokes are about Jewish people, rednecks, black folks . . . I can't determine what offends another person."[22]

Deen insisted she was not racist. The police report of a black man robbing her at gunpoint when she worked in a bank supported her story. She was nevertheless dropped by the Food Network, where her long-standing show had been a favorite, as well as by Walmart, Caesars, JCPenney, Sears, Kmart, and more. In an appearance on the *Today Show*, "Deen told Lauer she could recall using the "N-word" only once. She had earlier said that she remembered using it when retelling a story about when she was held at gunpoint by a robber who was black; she was then working as a bank teller in the 1980s in Georgia. In a deposition for the lawsuit involving an employee in a restaurant owned by Deen and her brother, she had said she may also have used the slur when recalling conversations between black employees at her restaurants."[21-23]

Herd Pressure

Now the real point here is not whether Paula Deen was racist or not. No, the real issue is, how did you react? Did you condemn her immediately without knowing all of the facts? Did you cast an eye in her direction and think something like, "this Southern woman is a part of the problem, still hanging on to the white supremacy crap?" In the alternative, did you think the entire thing was overblown and much ado about nothing? Or, were you somewhere in between? If you were inclined to think what Deen admitted to did not deserve the treatment she received, my bet is you were relatively quiet about that. Why? Because of the herd pressure!

After Deen had lost many sponsors and her business was ruined, the news turned to some of the merits of her case. Despite the fact that the case against Deen was tossed out of court, reverse racism won the day.

> In a 20-page opinion released Monday, U.S. District Court Judge William T. Moore Jr. tossed out race discrimination claims made by former Savannah restaurant manager Lisa Jackson against celebrity chef Paula Deen and her brother, Bubba Hiers. According to Moore, Jackson, who is white, was at best, "an accidental victim of the alleged racial discrimination." This inconvenient reality will matter little to the civil rights lynch mob and their media enablers who have dedicated themselves to destroying Deen's career. A *USA Today* story announcing Deen's victory exemplifies the success of that effort. It was entitled, "Experts: Paula Deen is done despite legal win."[24]

Reverse Racism

What is reverse racism? Though that is an aside at this point, it's worth pursuing the idea. The dictionary defines the term this way: "Discrimination against members of a dominant or majority group, especially when resulting from policies established to correct discrimination against members of a minority or disadvantaged group." According to this definition, reverse racism can be about a race, a nationality, even a pursuit. What typically happens in such instances is that the majority fails to speak up for fear that they will be identified as the racist, or the bigot, or the homophobe, and so on. We have seen a lot of this sort of labeling in the recent past. Labels of this nature are designed to elevate or denigrate; it's that simple. Sometimes they are there to position an argument favorably. For example, in the right-to-choose and the right-to-life arguments both use titles designed to win support. We don't have a pro-abortion title; rather, we have a right to choose.

When a minority feels wounded or, seemingly of late, sees an opportunity to gain national attention for their cause, they rush to the microphones. We saw this with the Trayvon Martin case. When George Zimmerman was acquitted, many responded to the news as though it was another O.J. Simpson miscarriage of justice announcement. Anyone who dared to defend Zimmerman was attacked immediately. Indeed, one whistleblower may have paid a heavy price.

> A former employee of Florida State Attorney Angela Corey's office is suing the prosecutor, claiming he was illegally fired after he testified on behalf of George Zimmerman, who was acquitted in the death of black teenager Trayvon Martin.
>
> Ben Kruidbos, the former director of information technology for Corey's office, is seeking more than $5 million in damages in the lawsuit filed in Jacksonville, according to legal documents.
>
> Kruidbos was fired after testifying at a pre-trial hearing on June 6 that he believed prosecutors had failed to turn over to the defense, as required by evidence-sharing laws, potentially embarrassing evidence extracted from Martin's cell phone.
>
> His lawyer, Wesley White, said last month that he would file a whistleblower action. This week he filed a separate complaint to the Florida Commission on Human Relations seeking whistleblower status, which could result in the second lawsuit, White said.[25]

Not long after the Trayvon Martin story, another situation occurred which highlighted the contrast to the publicity and interest the nation had in the Martin case.

> Police said the three teens attacked the unidentified 13-year-old victim after he told officials at their dropout prevention school that one of them had tried to sell him marijuana. The victim, who was struck with a flurry of punches and kicks, suffered a broken arm and two black

eyes. He may have an opportunity to testify in two weeks. . . . The three teens arrested in the attack—Lloyd Khemradj, Julian McKnight, and Joshua Reddin—arrived at the Pinellas County courthouse early Tuesday. All three 15-year-olds declined to comment when approached by Fox News. All three were charged with aggravated battery. Reddin is also charged with unarmed robbery . . .

The brutal incident made national headlines, in part because video of the attack captured on the bus's surveillance camera went viral online. It also prompted critics to question why civil rights leaders did not speak up about the assault. The attackers were all African-American and the victim was white, although Gulfport Police Chief Robert Vincent told Fox News the attack did not appear to be racially motivated.

Former Florida Representative Allen West, who is African-American, chided Al Sharpton and Jesse Jackson, noting they condemned Florida in the wake of the Trayvon Martin shooting yet remained silent on the bus attack.

"Three 15-year-old black teens beat up a 13-year-old white kid because he told school officials they tried to sell him drugs," the former Army colonel wrote on his Facebook page. "Do you hear anything from Sharpton, Jackson, NAACP, Stevie Wonder, Jay-Z, liberal media, or Hollywood? Cat got your tongues or is it that pathetic hypocrisy revealing itself once again? Y'all just make me sick."[26]

False Reporting

Regardless of the opinion one might have about the Zimmerman case, understanding how those opinions were formed is critical to becoming awake. Mindful persons search themselves thoroughly enough to understand at least where and why they harbor biases. Even if you're unable to set them aside, knowing that you have them provides insight into why you might think as you do, and sometimes that is in spite of the evidence to the contrary.

Given the human proclivity to hold biases, it should come as no surprise that during the Zimmerman public trial, many reports exaggerated or colored the events. There were also outright lies told by the media.

Reporting in the *Philly Post*, the lead line read, "Three major news organizations, NBC, ABC, and CNN, were forced to 'walk back,' as they like to say."[27] All three networks doctored (edited) a 911 recording in such a way as to make it appear that Zimmerman "volunteered the information that Martin was black."[28] In doing so, race became a pivotal issue in the case and the assault on Zimmerman's character.

CNN went so far as to claim that Zimmerman used the word "coon."[29] Interpretations of this nature obviously gave rise to racial profiling allegations and a rush to judgment by many members of the press. The controversial radio talk show host Rush Limbaugh had this to say about the press's distortions:

> This was a purposeful, racist, hate-oriented decision by a major American network to lie to the American people about a person involved in the Trayvon Martin case, George Zimmerman. Then ABC puts out police video where they claim there's no sign of injury here to Zimmerman. There's no sign of anything he says. He says his head was beaten against the ground, got a bloody nose, there's no sign of that. Then all of a sudden ABC decides that they're gonna enhance the video, and they say that they strip a layer away—this is police video, by the way, now—and that all of a sudden, lo and behold, there is evidence of injury on the back of George Zimmerman's head.[30]

The stories are reported, the networks apologize, the news agencies run retractions, but as we saw earlier, research shows clearly that folks at home do not disregard the information even when they know of the corrections.

Boycotts

Sometimes the efforts to control and intimidate a group include things like boycotts. Personally, I vote my dollar all the time and have no problem whatsoever in refusing to spend money in establishments or on goods where I have an objection to that business. Unfortunately, however, we may be blinded to the real impact of our actions. If I boycott a business, I may well be assisting in the loss of employment for someone. Is that what I want? Is my cause worth it? All things must be considered, and I think integrity means walking the talk. I have seen and heard many object to Walmart for a variety of reasons, and yet most of those folks go right back there to buy their HD-TVs and more. That said, what about boycotting a movie because the author of the book from which the movie was made opposes gay marriage? Is that a valid reason to boycott the movie, which is something that has nothing to do with the author's position on gay marriage? Who really pays the price? Why aren't the sellers of the book, such as Amazon or Barnes and Noble, also boycotted? Why not boycott all of the author's books?

Sometimes activities like boycotts are all about publicity. How much publicity would be gained as a result of a few folks deciding not to buy an author's books? Oh, but protest the movie, especially one with a lot of hype and prerelease publicity, and what would you expect? Why would you want the publicity from boycotting Orson Scott Card's *Enders Game?* Simply put: your action warns others of potential intimidation should you decide to publicly voice your opinion in opposition to the group. Think about that the next time you come face to face with a boycott. Are you giving up your voice or making your voice heard?

> The film *Ender's Game* tells the story of a gifted child sent to a military academy in space to prepare for an alien invasion. It's catnip for the Comic-Con crowd, and Lionsgate Entertainment wants to position it as November's big-budget blockbuster. But the studio is encountering an unexpected publicity nightmare: an activist group called Geeks Out is pushing a boycott of the film, claiming that anyone who pays to see it will effectively be subsidizing antigay "fearmongering."
>
> Geeks Out wants to sink the film to punish Orson Scott Card, who wrote the 1985 novel *Ender's Game* and was one of several producers for the screen adaptation. In 1990, Mr. Card argued in the magazine *Sunstone* that, "Laws against

homosexual behavior should remain on the books" and "be used when necessary to send a clear message that those who flagrantly violate society's regulation of sexual behavior cannot be permitted to remain as acceptable, equal citizens within that society." He was on the board of the National Organization for Marriage, which opposes same-sex unions, from 2009 until this year.[31]

Now, just for the record, I personally believe that gay marriage should be legal because the only honest reasons that can be marshaled to oppose it are religious. The separation of religion and state therefore urge this equalitarian approach. However, if we legalize gay marriage, we should also be prepared to allow other forms of marriage as well, such as polygamy and polyandry.

So we see that definitions do much more than simply reshape a language. They assert tremendous force and effect on behavior, and our behavior in turn gives power to our definitions. Is this another gotcha?

Conspiracy or Master Plan?

Now that you have seen how pervasive the interest and intent on engineering consent has become, it's time to share a technical document with you. The document is referred to as Operations Research Technical Manual TW-SW7905.1 titled "Silent Weapons for Quiet Wars." The document begins with this:

Disclaimer

I want to advise you in advance that this document has supposedly been confirmed as the adopted policy of certain "international elites," as agreed upon at the first Bilderberg Meeting in 1954. Delamer Duverus of Lawfulpath assures us that the document is authentic and has been authenticated by four different technical writers for military intelligence. The entire document is published free on the Internet and readers are encouraged to share it with the world, "The consensus opinion was to distribute this to as many people as who wanted it, to the end that they would not only understand that 'War' had been declared against them, but would be able to properly identify the true enemy to Humanity." To read the document in its entirety, please go to: **www.law fulpath.com/ref/sw4qw/**

The document includes drawings and diagrams illustrating many of the technical points, and I encourage you to read the entire manual. That said, I wish only to bring certain issues to your attention that are so well knitted into our discussion as to make themselves potential linchpins.

The manual opens with this statement:

Security

It is patently impossible to discuss social engineering or the automation of a society, i.e., the engineering of social automation systems (silent weapons) on a national or world-wide scale without implying extensive objectives of social control and destruction of human life, i.e., slavery and genocide. This manual is in itself an analog declaration of intent. Such a writing must be secured from public scrutiny. Otherwise, it might be recognized as a technically formal declaration of domestic war. Furthermore, whenever any person or group of persons in a position of great power and without full knowledge and consent of the public, uses such knowledge and methodologies for economic conquest—it must be understood that a state of domestic warfare exists between said person or group of persons and the public.[32]

Selected highlights from the document continue below:

Social engineering (the analysis and automation of a society) requires the correlation of great amounts of con-stantly changing economic information (data), so a high-speed computerized data-processing system was necessary which could race ahead of the society and predict when society would arrive for capitulation.

Energy is recognized as the key to all activity on earth. Natural science is the study of the sources and control of natural energy, and social science, theoretically expressed as economics, is the study of the sources and control of social energy. Both are bookkeeping systems: mathematics. There-fore, mathematics is the primary energy science. And the bookkeeper can be king if the public can be kept ignorant of the methodology of the bookkeeping.

In conclusion, the objective of economic research, as conducted by the magnates of capital (banking) and the industries of commodities (goods) and services, is the establishment of an economy which is totally predictable and manipulatable.

In order to achieve a totally predictable economy, the low-class elements of society must be brought under total control, i.e., must be housebroken, trained, and assigned a yoke and long-term social duties from a very early age, before they have an opportunity to question the propriety of the matter. In order to achieve such conformity, the lower-class family unit must be disintegrated by a process of increasing preoccupation of the parents and the establishment of government-operated day-care centers for the occupationally orphaned children.

The quality of education given to the lower class must be of the poorest sort, so that the moat of ignorance isolating the inferior class from the superior class is and remains incomprehensible to the inferior class. With such an initial handicap, even bright lower class individuals have little, if any, hope of extricating themselves from their assigned lot in life. This form of slavery is essential to maintain some measure of social order, peace, and tranquility for the ruling upper class.

When a silent weapon is applied gradually, the public adjusts/adapts to its presence and learns to tolerate its encroachment on their lives until the pressure (psychological via economic) becomes too great and they crack up.

Therefore, the silent weapon is a type of biological warfare. It attacks the vitality, options, and mobility of the individuals of a society by knowing, understanding, manipulating, and attacking their sources of natural and social energy, and their physical, mental, and emotional strengths and weaknesses.[33]

The manual continues:

Theoretical Introduction

Give me control over a nation's currency, and I care not who makes its laws.—Mayer Amschel Rothschild (1743–1812).

Today's silent weapons technology is an outgrowth of a simple idea discovered, succinctly expressed, and effectively applied by the quoted Mr. Mayer Amschel Rothschild. Mr. Rothschild discovered the missing passive component of economic theory known as economic inductance . . . Mr. Rothschild had discovered that currency or deposit loan accounts had the required appearance of power that could be used to induce people . . . into surrendering their real wealth in exchange for a promise of greater wealth (instead of real compensation). They would put up real collateral in exchange for a loan of promissory notes. Mr. Rothschild found that he could issue more notes than he had backing for, so long as he had someone's stock of gold as a persuader to show his customers.

Mr. Rothschild loaned his promissory notes to individuals and to governments. These would create overconfidence. Then he would make money scarce, tighten control of the system, and collect the collateral through the obligation of contracts. The cycle was then repeated. These pressures could be used to ignite a war. Then he would control the availability of currency to determine who would win the war. That government which agreed to give him control of its economic system got his support.

Collection of debts was guaranteed by economic aid to the enemy of the debtor. The profit derived from this economic methodology made Mr. Rothschild all the more able to expand his wealth. He found that the public greed would allow currency to be printed by government order beyond the limits (inflation) of backing in precious metal or the production of goods and services.

. . . shock testing in economic engineering, the prices of commodities are shocked, and the public consumer reaction is monitored. The resulting echoes of the economic shock are interpreted theoretically by computers and the psychoeconomic structure of the economy is thus discovered. It is by this process that partial differential and difference matrices are discovered that define the family household and make possible its evaluation as an economic industry . . .

Then the response of the household to future shocks can be predicted and manipulated, and society becomes a well-regulated animal with its reins under the control of a sophisticated computer-regulated social energy bookkeeping system.

Eventually every individual element of the structure comes under computer control through a knowledge of personal preferences, such knowledge guaranteed by computer association of consumer preferences (universal product code, UPC; zebra-striped pricing codes on packages) with identified consumers (identified via association with the use of a credit card and later a permanent "tattooed" body number invisible under normal ambient illumination).

The problem with stabilizing the economic system is that there is too much demand on account of (1) too much greed and (2) too much population.

This creates excessive economic inductance which can only be balanced with economic capacitance (true resources or value—e.g., in goods or services).

The social welfare program is nothing more than an open-ended credit balance system which creates a false capital industry to give nonproductive people a roof over their heads and food in their stomachs. This can be useful, however, because the recipients become state property in return for the "gift," a standing army for the elite. For he who pays the piper picks the tune.

Those who get hooked on the economic drug must go to the elite for a fix. In this, the method of introducing large amounts of stabilizing capacitance is by borrowing on the future "credit" of the world. This is a fourth law of motion, onset, and consists of performing an action and leaving the system before the reflected reaction returns to the point of action—a delayed reaction.

The means of surviving the reaction is by changing the system before the reaction can return. By these means, politicians become more popular in their own time and the public pays later. In fact, the measure of such a politician is the delay of time.

The same thing is achieved by a government by printing money beyond the limit of the gross national product, an economic process called inflation. This puts a large quantity of money into the hands of the public and maintains a balance against their greed, creates a false self-confidence in them and, for a while, stays the wolf from the door.

They must eventually resort to war to balance the account because war ultimately is merely the act of destroying the creditor, and the politicians are the publicly hired hit men that justify the act to keep the responsibility and blood off the public conscience.

If the people really cared about their fellow man, they would control their appetites (greed, procreation, etc.) so that they would not have to operate on a credit or welfare social system which steals from the worker to satisfy the bum.

Since most of the general public will not exercise restraint, there are only two alternatives to reduce the economic inductance of the system.

Let the populace bludgeon each other to death in war, which will only result in a total destruction of the living Earth. Take control of the world by the use of economic 'silent weapons' in a form of 'quiet warfare' and reduce the economic inductance of the world to a safe level by a process of benevolent slavery and genocide. The latter option has been taken as the obviously better option. At this point it should be crystal clear to the reader why absolute secrecy about the silent weapons is necessary. The general public refuses to improve its own mentality and its faith in its fellow man. It has become a herd of proliferating barbarians, and, so to speak, a blight upon the face of the Earth. They do not care enough about economic science to learn why they have not been able to avoid war despite religious morality, and their religious or self-gratifying refusal to deal with earthly problems renders the solution of the earthly problem unreachable to them.

It is left to those few who are truly willing to think and survive as the fittest to survive, to solve the problem for themselves as the few who really care. Otherwise, exposure of the silent weapon would destroy our only hope of preserving the seed of the future true humanity.[34]

Whether or not this manual is, in fact, an authentic document employed by the so-called elite or not becomes somewhat academic in light of all that we have shared thus far. Obviously, the provisos in this manual could be de facto forces behind the direction of governments, even if their actions were taken in ignorance of this plan.

I find this all very disturbing. Do you?

Fear

Perhaps the greatest of all control devices is fear. As we saw in the chapter on how we humans are wired, fear is used to sell us everything. Our fears propel much of our ignorance. We ignorantly allow fear to push us into doing and allowing things that we would never ordinarily even give a second thought to. We give up our constitutional rights because of our fear of terrorism. We hurry to buy products when told there are limited quantities. We elect politicians because the other side scares us (and of course, the other side scares us because their efforts to make us fear the opponent have been weaker than the fear-inducing efforts of those we are voting for). In other words, both sides try to convince us that the other guy should be feared. We give in to spending huge amounts of money on war machines because we are fearful. We are afraid to speak out on some matters for fear that the herd will reject us, or worse yet, brand us in ways that humiliate us. Oh, and yes, a big yes as a matter of fact, we are absolutely afraid of rejection. We are herd animals, and we need the herd, we need love, we need to be touched, we need to be accepted.

The English philosopher Thomas Hobbes insisted that governments exist only as a result of fear. We need them to protect us from the bully. According to Hobbes, we are born into fear, and it is fear that propels self-interested cooperation.

So is it also fear that leads to cooperation? Some would argue effectively—yes! That is a philosophical question beyond the scope of this work, so suffice it to say, fear possibly underlies most of our human motives. Understanding this makes it easy to recognize why fear would be a force used to manipulate and manage the masses.

Now let's assume that we live under the illusion of freedom. We are free to a certain extent, and the very ethnocentrism that we were enculturated by has convinced us that we truly are free people. There are stories of those who have risen from the ashes, so to speak, gone from poor immigrant to successful politician or business owner and so on. We can choose our vocation, where to bank, what car to buy, how to invest our money; we can even vote for our elected representatives. All of this is clearly convincing—we are a free people.

Now if you desired to curtail this freedom a little, but not enough to alarm the people, what would you do? Well, of course, you would slowly remove the freedoms in the name of protection, and the mechanism that would sell this benefit is the fear that would be brought to boil by propaganda designed to convince the public of an imminent danger. We have all seen this work with the Patriot Act in recent years. Building upon fear—fear of economic collapse, fear of terrorist attacks on home and country, fear of noncompliance and so forth, we allow government to quietly nationalize major sectors of our economy, redistribute wealth, censor information and, arguably, even punish whistleblowers, control gun ownership, manage our food and drugs, control our money supply, and more. Is this really all in our best interest? And when looked at this way, what is it about our system of government that makes it superior to the systems of our neighbors and allies?

CONCLUSION

In the end, are we as a country on a path destined to eliminate self-reliance, replace creativity and productivity with ideas of fear and scarcity, and thereby fuel a welfare state while imposing the will of the collective? Is Georg Hegel correct, "Human history could be made to tell a story of contrived outcomes"?

Are we on a path determined to spread the virtue of cultural relativism and consequently break down ideas of right and wrong, leading us further and further away from any possibility of an absolute value, including that of life itself?

Have we become convinced that media can teach us all we need to know without confirming the information for ourselves? Is H.G. Wells correct that we are living under an "Open Conspiracy"?[35] Will the findings of Prussian psychologist Wilhelm Wundt prevail as religion is attacked and ridiculed? (Wundt determined that the individual had no soul.) If the individual is only a cog in the wheel, a disposable asset employed to turn the wheel, and if social Darwinism is combined with this view, then the fittest (our so-called elite) are justified in treating the masses as a herd of animals to be controlled.

Is fear the means of operant conditioning that keeps the masses following the promptings of the herders?

I don't think so. The very fact that you have read this book has already neutralized many of these control mechanisms. Knowledge is power, and now we are putting the knowledge into the hands of the people. It is time to take back your hearts and minds, to be someone you can truly be proud of, and to work to make sure everyone enjoys a life of freedom and independence!

Chapter Twenty-Eight

"Now What?"

Not everything that counts can be counted, and not everything that can be counted counts.

~William Bruce Cameron

From beginning to end, throughout this journey, we have seen the influence of the perceived need to manage the masses through means of engineered consent. Whether in the arena of government or merchandising, the fact is, owning your opinion is their objective. There are many means by which this can be accomplished, and we have not exhausted them in this brief overview. Indeed, it should be patently obvious that the themes I have chosen as examples are but a handful of the current issues before the world today. In that sense, this work is only a primer designed to rough out an idea.

I have tried to be thorough in presenting sufficient dots so that, even if you discard several, the conclusion remains the same: the territory of the mind is the target of opportunity for those seeking power and fortune!

A few today believe we are on the cusp of a consciousness evolution, advancing to stages of shared consciousness and even, some say, telepathy. Frankly, I would like to believe that, but what I see is quite different. However, I do believe that we are at a threshold with respect to the direction that we as individuals and, on a larger scale, the global world itself may go. That threshold is not so much due to an evolution as it is to a conscious revolution.

A conscious revolution is not about violence. It is not about the next thing we can chase down and consume either. It is about critical thinking and mindfulness.

Solutions

It could be very easy to be intimidated by the plethora of information that I have provided and therefore very tempting to throw your hands up in despair, preferring to close your eyes and ears to the problems in favor of the carefree oblivion you lived in before. In that sense, you have the same choice Neo faced in the movie *The Matrix*—the choice between the red or blue pill is very real.

Your mind is a precious treasure. It can be your best friend or your worst enemy. The mind can operate as healer or slayer. The full power of the mind is still not known, but what we do know is amazing. I have discussed much of this in my book *I Believe: When What You Believe Matters,* but the takeaway is that you absolutely can bring about anatomical changes in your brain while rewriting your mind.

For those of you who choose to face reality head-on, who wish to be masters of their fate, you need to cultivate critical thinking, become an activist, practice mindfulness, take personal responsibility, and take some time to explore what life means to you. Let me break these actions down for you.

1. Cultivate Critical Thinking

I have invested most of my life in teaching the notions of critical thinking and mindfulness. Both of these disciplines, and they are indeed disciplines, require fully engaging that eight-pound universe between your ears. I must admit that at times I have felt like throwing my hands in the air in exasperated exhaustion. I have watched videos of petitions being signed by folks eligible to vote—petitions requiring mandatory euthanasia of senior citizens, the addition of carcinogens to drinking water, the legalization of infanticide for children up to three years of age, and I have been both shocked and appalled by the ignorance of so many! (See for yourself here: **youtube.com/watch?v=XoHFWx5JWEk**.)

Now What?

It is often at times like that when I remember the words of Robert Laing from his book *The Politics of Experience:*

> "If I could turn you on, if I could drive you out of your wretched mind, if I could tell you, I would let you know."[1]

Laing continues encouraging us to set aside the normal, which is the absurd, to think critically and evaluate honestly, to take the journey others may ridicule and fail to understand, to search within and take stock of ourselves:

> In this particular type of journey, the direction we have to take is back and in, because it was the way back that we started to go down and out. They will say we are regressed and withdrawn and out of contact with them. True enough, we have a long, long way to go back to contact the reality we have all long lost contact with. And because they are humane, and concerned, and even love us, and are frightened, they will try to cure us. They may succeed. But there is still hope that they may fail.[2]

The drone obeys. The mass of people may well be unplugged from reality. They may indeed be so undereducated that a magic word here or there is all they hear, and when you add words like carcinogen, they have no clue what that means, but in the context they assume it is good. This is exactly the sort of word games and context framing that the social psychologists who specialize in managing perception, are very good at doing. Being alert to this sort of thing requires a special vigilance. One must actually set an intention to be attentive and aware in order to become a critical thinker.

I hope by now that you have realized that we are often our own worst enemy and that to get past our own blocks, attachments, dissonance, and other interfering thought patterns that perhaps have conditioned us to accept propaganda as fact, we must be willing to challenge even our dearest, most sacred beliefs. Otherwise, we remain the blind following the blind. To do this we need to:

i. Be Open-Minded

You can never learn anything new if you think you already have the answers. There may actually be some merit to the words and beliefs of those who are on the so-called opposite side of the fence to you!

ii. Look for Motives

When you understand the motive behind someone's attempt at persuasion, you will have a better chance of making a decision that is actually your own. And this holds regardless of whether you are talking to a salesman or are in the voting booth!

iii. Be Skeptical About Popular Beliefs

If everyone is keen on a new idea, stop and ask yourself *why*. What tactics have been used to gain such widespread support? In the real world, there will always be a diversity of opinions. When an election is won with a 60/40 margin, it is considered a landslide win. When 90 percent of a particular electorate votes one particular way, you can count that many of the tactics discussed in this book have been used! Have you been targeted in this way, too?

iv. Examine Both Sides of the Issue

Go out of your way to examine both sides of an issue. When it comes to politics, I would highly recommend that you vary your news sources. When you watch the same news story being told on different stations, such as Fox News and MSNBC, the biases of both should become apparent. A change in a word here, a different inflexion there, and the entire question can elicit very different emotions. In today's world, all of your news sources will have their own biases. If you think your trusted news source is not biased, then that is just evidence of the efficacy of the programming you have already succumbed to. The key is to understand the bias and then to adjust for it—look for the answers that lie in between, for that is where you have a chance of finding the truth.

v. Choose Your Entertainment Carefully

Pay attention to what you watch, even if you think of it as just another silly movie or another computer game. For decades, the power elite have used your entertainment as a means to win your hearts and minds—there is a constant push to mold your thoughts. How is your current entertainment manipulating your judgment and beliefs? When you see it for what it is, it will lose much of its power.

vi. Ask Yourself 'Why?'

Get into the practice of asking yourself 'why' questions. Why is that politician harping on that subject? Why is the stage arranged that way? Why was that music chosen? Why those color schemes? Why those primes? And so forth. Thinking critically about all aspects of a presentation will assist you in assessing the information based on its merits and not based on techniques that have been demonstrated effective at influencing your choices! It is for sure that you want to avoid being swayed by the handsome/ beautiful person offering up the message in a sincere sounding way. Remember, it is the facts that are important – not the romanticized stories!

vii. Stop Playing the Game and Picking Sides

Real answers lie in the middle. Look for the common ground and don't buy into the sound bite reasoning. The art of compromise is in the ability of both sides to feel the needs of the other. Empathy will inevitably lead to solutions that propaganda will fail to achieve.

viii. Don't Assume 'They' Will Protect You!

As a society, we have developed many safeguards for our protection, and as a result, we have turned off our own sense of judgment. There is much truth in the saying, "Power corrupts and absolute power absolutely corrupts." For our system to work, we must all hold those in power accountable. Fear is one of the most obvious techniques being used to take away our personal liberties. The area of whistleblowers is of particular importance here. Don't automatically assume that whistleblowers against the government are traitors, endangering national security. Listen to the information and then make up your own mind. Remember, national security is not only about keeping you safe; there has been much done in the name of national security that is an invasion of your privacy with the aim of finding more ways to exert control over you and your thoughts.

2. Become an Activist

For me, I have become convinced that we must all be activists. I like this definition of an activist: "advocating or opposing a cause or issue vigorously, especially a political cause."

In the alternative to waking up, engaging our brains, taking the time away from our pitiful entertainment and paltry searches for something more to consume in order to turn our attention to the matters that really count, we deserve to be herded just like cattle. We have repeatedly seen throughout this work that a minority of people, who consider themselves to be the elite, are pulling the strings behind the puppet show while we gaze uncaringly on. It is way past time for a revolution of ideas.

i. Develop New Ideas

We need new ideas. The fact is, when most people encounter a stressful event and attempt to deal with difficult issues, they find themselves falling back on what I think of as the "maze bright hungry rat syndrome." Research that I originally read by Richard Alpert, today known as RamDas, clearly shows what happens when you overstimulate the maze bright rat. Withhold food from the rat, and when you set him down in a maze that he easily handles under ordinary circumstances, the rat is unable to complete the maze or it takes the rat much longer than typical—thus, the dull rat.

People are like the maze bright rats. Provide too much stimuli, create anxiety, fear, and the like, and they also become dull. Our decisions can be clouded and our inspiration lacking. As opposed to reaching toward the highest human potential, unfortunately in this condition we resort to the more primal animal instincts, and those usually lead to more fear and eventually violence!

ii. Understand the Importance of Freedoms

When it comes to personal freedoms, avoid becoming overly comfortable. One of the most common issues in play here are the ideas that go along the lines of, "That doesn't affect me and I am on their side anyway so I don't care if someone else's freedoms are trampled on. They're too stupid to deserve the freedom anyway!" Not long ago, I heard of a Facebook discussion regarding the IRS's targeting of Republicans. A Democrat actually thought (until it was pointed out to her) that it was okay for the IRS to target Republicans because they were continuing to go after the Benghazi story. In her opinion, the Benghazi issue was just political posturing and she had no time for that! She had not stopped to think that tomorrow the IRS could be targeting supporters of something she is passionate about, like GMO labeling.

iii. Develop Self-Reliance

Get into the habit of verifying information and stop expecting someone else to take care of you. Time and time again, the so-called experts have made huge mistakes. Understand that it is perfectly okay for you to get a second opinion (and a third) and then to go check the information for yourself. You are responsible for yourself and your family. Don't expect government regulations to protect you. The more regulations there are in place, the more marketers find a way around them. Eat as naturally as possible, buy organic where possible, and know that convenience foods are only convenient in the short-term. You will also find that eating more healthfully will help you greatly in being healthier, stronger, and happier for as Socrates pointed out, "A healthy body leads to a healthy mind."

iv. Speak Up!

Listen to your inner guidance. Just because everyone else is doing something does not make it right. Do not blindly follow the pack—stop and think for yourself. And when you see that something is wrong, speak up!

v. Take An Active Role in Government.

By this I do not mean that everyone should run for office, but I do mean that you should be taking your voting responsibilities seriously. Do your homework before voting and stop voting based on the most appealing sound bites. Remember too, that very often, the powers that be will use fear to control you.

3. Practice Mindfulness

If we are to avoid becoming willing followers of the elite Procrustes, we need some tools to disarm their methods. There is probably no more powerful tool—when it comes to really getting a grip on who we really are, from where our thoughts and ideas originate, how our thinking proceeds, and therefore, how we can make genuine changes—than the tool known as mindfulness. Mindfulness training is something truly coming of age. Indeed, in a conversation on my *Provocative Enlightenment* radio show with Congressman Tim Ryan, Ryan emphasized the interest members of Congress now have in mindfulness training.

What is mindfulness? In straightforward, uncomplicated rhetoric, it is paying attention to your thoughts and experience in a nonjudgmental way. It is a matter of attending to the moment with your mental resources, ever mindful, if you will, of your present experience, and again without judgment.

In recent years, research has proliferated, repeatedly demonstrating many positive outcomes as a result of mindfulness. One such study demonstrated that mindfulness can indeed increase your self-knowledge. If this book has resonated at all with you, then you realize just how important it is to truly come to "know thyself!"

> Mindfulness—a technique often recognized for its positive effects on mental health—involves paying attention to your current experience (e.g., thoughts, feelings) and observing it in a nonjudgmental manner.
>
> These two components of mindfulness, attention and nonjudgmental observation, can overcome the major barriers to knowing ourselves. Psychological scientist Erika Carlson of Washington University in St. Louis argues that the motivation to see ourselves in a desirable way is one of the main obstacles to self-knowledge. For instance, people may overestimate their virtuous qualities to ward off negative feelings or boost self-esteem. However, non-judgmental observation of one's thoughts, feelings, and behavior might

reduce emotional reactivity—such as feelings of inadequacy or low self-esteem—that typically interferes with people seeing the truth about themselves.

Lack of information is another barrier to self-knowledge—in some situations people might not have the information they would need to accurately assess themselves. For instance, we have a hard time observing much of our non-verbal behavior, so we may not know that we're grimacing or fidgeting during a serious conversation. Mindfulness could also help in this domain, as research has shown that mindfulness training is associated with greater bodily awareness.[3]

A favorite quote brought to my attention by my son Roy aptly places us in a world worthy of contemplation.

> And it seemed to him as he drove on day after day that history was like some vast thing that was always over the tight horizon, invisible except in its effects. It was what happened when you weren't looking—an unknowable infinity of events, which although out of control, controlled everything.[4]

To be aware, I must attend to the moment while viewing it through the lens of the past and future, ever aware of the behind-the-scenes forces that impact my perception.

So we see that mindfulness is more than just another idea. It is much more than simply meditating for a few minutes each day, although that's a great start. Genuine mindfulness is being aware of every thought, sensation, and so forth, moment by moment in the eternal now. And now is more than only now, as some might claim. As Dogen, the founder of Zen Buddhism, might express it, "We may experience only the present right now, but the present exists and is significant only in its relationship to the past and future. To ignore the moment that we live in is to lose reality, because all that is real is that moment, but to ignore the past and the future is to lose the meaning of reality."

Dogen wrote a beautiful poem that I think is apt here:

> Being in the world:
> To what might it be compared?

> Dwelling in a dewdrop fallen from a waterfowl's beak,
> The image of the moon.[5]

Professor Jay Garfield interprets Dogen as saying that our experience of being in the world compares to a dewdrop from a bird's beak—something delicate, impermanent, and unbelievably beautiful. Further, the moon is contained in this tiny dewdrop, just as being in the world entails containing the vastness of reality within us—but only momentarily. The deepest kind of beauty is that which reveals impermanence because in doing so, it reveals the nature of our minds and reality. We can experience reality only if we grasp and celebrate impermanence![6]

Mindfulness can assist us in lightening up as well. It can be all too easy to become somewhat depressed, or worse yet, overwhelmed to the point that you give up in frustration, when you balance the gotchas against your power to bring about change. For even in the midst of our most urgent concerns, mindfulness can change the moment from despair to analysis, from fear to freedom, from confusion to a learning experience, and so on.

Each of us can take some really important steps to minimize the mindless meld into hive consciousness. Six of perhaps the most important steps are the following.

i. Awareness Training

First and most important, you must become mindful! You must actively engage yourself in daily awareness training. We have already discussed the importance of mindfulness, so let me add a couple of easy steps that can help you achieve this important form of awareness. Begin by becoming alert to your every thought. Ask yourself, where does that come from? Why do I think that? What alternatives exist? And so on. The idea is simple: Question everything you think and follow it back to the origin of that belief. As I have shown in my book *I Believe*, there is no such thing as a stand-alone belief! Our beliefs exist in a giant web, and when you tweak one strand of the web, the entire construct vibrates. So, sorting through our beliefs means that one will lead to another, and in exactly that way, we stand a chance to uncover all of the ill-conceived and unproductive foundations behind behaviors that may not be in our best interest.

Remember to carry out this evaluation judgment-free. You are not looking to blame anyone or anything; rather, you are an inquisitor of truth—your very own truth. Thus you move beyond the condition of self-alienation, the condition Robert Laing so eloquently described as the condition of the normal man.

> What we call "normal" is a product of repression, denial, splitting, projection, introjection and other forms of destructive action on experience. It is radically estranged from the structure of being. The more one sees this, the more senseless it is to continue with generalized descriptions of supposedly specifically schizoid, schizophrenic, hysterical "mechanisms." There are forms of alienation that are relatively strange to statistically "normal" forms of alienation. The "normally" alienated person, by reason of the fact that he acts more or less like everyone else, is taken to be sane. Other forms of alienation that are out of step with the prevailing state of alienation are those that are labeled by the "formal" majority as bad or mad.
>
> The condition of alienation, of being asleep, of being unconscious, of being out of one's mind, is the condition of the normal man. Society highly values its normal man. It educates children to lose themselves and to become absurd, and thus to be normal. Normal men have killed perhaps 100 million of their fellow normal men in the last fifty years.[7]

ii. Positioning, Framing, and Agendas

It is imperative that you recognize the sales pitch for what it is: a form of communication with an agenda. What is the agenda? What is the overall message in the movie, in the TV series, in the advertisement? How does the message impact our society, our way of life, our values, and so forth? Is this an agenda you can consciously get behind?

Some of today's entertainment is way over the top in more ways than one, but still its message can be completely lost unless you overtly ask the question. For example, there is an amusing TV comedy series called *How I Met Your Mother*. The sitcom features three main characters who are single and two who are married to each other. Every week the show indulges in the sexual fantasies and achievements of Barney, the oversexed single male who does not want a long-term relationship, only one-night stands, and who has succeeded at this over 200 times. While Barney is using his many "charms" to seduce, the two other single characters are practicing a form of serial relationships, also bouncing from one bed to another with different partners.

The show is funny, and I enjoy it, but what is its message? There is no way you can view this series and not take away the idea that it's okay to have sex with multiple partners. Is that the message you want your children to accept?

Questioning, always alert to uncovering the agendas or the abiding message, is one of your best defenses against many forms of covert mind control.

iii. Suggestion

We have discussed a number of ways in which your mind can be entrained, resulting in a sort of mechanical participation. From conversation hypnosis to the contextual framing of labels, we have seen how easy it is to find ourselves receiving multiple messages that directly bypass critical awareness.

The power of suggestion cannot be overstated. From the placebo effect to outright altered states of consciousness capable of producing a wide range of effects, including blind obedience, it is suggestion that leads the way. Hypnosis is technically nothing more than a hyper state of suggestibility.

There is no such thing as a statement that doesn't contain a question or a question that doesn't contain a statement! Think about that.

I spent many years successfully positioning people in both therapeutic settings and interrogations as a result of simply understanding how powerful suggestion can be and how important the small, simple suggestions are in leading persons down the path you want them to follow. "You're not really a bad person; you're not some scumbag, are you, John?" contains both a suggestion of honesty and a positioning platform. John is likely to answer, "No—I'm a good person."

The next time you are in a conversation or listening to some orator, ask yourself, "How is the power of suggestion being used here?" What techniques are being employed by the speaker, knowingly or not, that fit the models of NLP and conversational hypnosis? How am I being positioned if I reject the arguments of the speaker? Am I accepting the arguments because I don't want to be positioned in the alternative suggested? For example, one may be thinking in the scenario above something like this, "I'm a good person—because if I'm not, then I guess I'm a scumbag, and I don't want to be a scumbag!"

Consciously attending to the nature of the communication, the explicit as well as the implicit meaning, will definitely provide you a special lens of clarity that sparks the ability to reject suggestion and thus come to your own independent conclusions.

iv. Positive Programming

With all of the work being carried out by so many to own your thoughts, is there a way to counteract this—an antidote, so to speak? Is there a way to replace the programming in our subconscious mind with positive programming of our own choice?

As I told you earlier, my work in this field began when, as a lie detection examiner, I wanted to find a way to reduce the number of inconclusive results obtained from the test. I wanted a way to assist innocent people in staying relaxed throughout the test so they did not give a 'false positive' result, and to add more stress to the guilty so that, despite any countermeasures they attempted to employ, they were still unable to beat the test. It was in this scenario that I first utilized an InnerTalk subliminal audio program and the results I obtained were phenomenal! My research then moved to the Utah State Prison where I found a way to reduce hostility and aggression and to increase feelings of self-responsibility in inmates.[8]

Continuing my research and development, in time I developed (and patented) a technology that everyone can use to replace the negative programming with positive programming that would actually enhance their life experience and assist them in becoming the best they could be in whatever area they chose. This technology is called InnerTalk, and you can learn more about it by visiting **www.innertalk.com** and by reading my earlier book, *Choices and Illusions*. I cannot deny that I am very proud of the InnerTalk technology, as it is the only such technology on the market today that has been researched by numerous independent universities and institutions (including Stanford University), and demonstrated effective at priming self-talk. Your self-talk is a mirror on your inner beliefs, and when it changes, so does your life experience.

The simple fact is this: We do not live in a glass bubble. Regardless of our best efforts, we are constantly bombarded with negative programming, from friends and peers who tell us we cannot do something, to the advertisers constantly telling us we are deficient because we don't look or act a certain way, to the power elite who use fear in order to take away more of our personal liberties. Keeping ourselves balanced and on track to achieving our dreams and goals is very difficult to well-nigh impossible in this day and age without some positive effort, and that is why I developed InnerTalk.

v. Choose the Person You Want to Be

Choose the kind of person you want to be and then ask yourself if a course of action will support your desires. What if things were turned around? Practice being compassionate and give the benefit of the doubt.

vi. Understand Your Own Limitations

It is easy for most of us to think that we would never betray ourselves and act in a way that we would be ashamed of. However, it is important to remember the work of Philip Zimbardo, who showed that, in the right circumstances, we can all exhibit an 'evil' side. If you remember, in his study students took on the role of the ruthless guards who found it perfectly okay to intimidate the students who were acting as the prisoners. The biggest mistake you can make is to say that you would never act in such a way. In fact, the only way to prevent this is to guard against it, and you cannot do this by denying it could ever happen. Remember, we all have an obligation to fight for life, liberty, and the pursuit of happiness for everyone, as tomorrow it may be ourselves who need this support.

4. Personal Responsibility

As discussed earlier, I believe we all have a role to play in our democracy. We have seen that some studies suggest that democracy is wasted on Americans because the population is simply not smart enough to take advantage of this marvelous form of government. We have also seen that those who would engineer consent believe, as Bernays did, that the population must be rendered into hive consciousness by way of propaganda in order for a smooth form of government to exist. I think that both of these propositions are fundamentally flawed.

There is no doubt in my mind that the average American possesses the intellectual faculties to be a good citizen. What is missing is the desire to participate. There is an apathy that leads many into allowing whatever because, after all, there's nothing they can do about it anyway. "Why fight city hall?"

It is time for every American to begin to urge their fellow Americans to get involved. When there are important causes, we have seen men and women rise up and lead the way to change. Martin Luther King put it this way:

> Change does not roll in on the wheels of inevitability, but comes through continuous struggle. And so we must straighten our backs and work for our freedom. A man can't ride you unless your back is bent.[9]

Maybe it's time to go back to school, night school, or take online courses, and learn more about our government and how it works. It is definitely time to become involved in grassroots efforts to guide this country in the direction we want for ourselves and for our future generations.

Sitting idly by while the gotchas add up is a certain way to disenfranchise everyone, including yourself!

A brilliant architect friend, Richard Kielbon, recently made a comment relevant to what can happen if we do nothing:

> I'm hearing of people affected by privacy issues. We once had a man from the old Iron Curtain Hungary come to a church. He was a rock star there, nothing here. He talked about what it was like to fear even your brother or mother because of the potential of the state finding out you were not a Communist. That's a stretch from where we are now—but I just realized that that isn't the point: The fact that we *ever* have to pause and wonder who's listening creates the same sick environment of not knowing—of always and at all times wondering.
>
> I study the human mind. Humans suck at understanding 'facts' as opposed to feelings. The *facts?* 'Terrorism' is an extremely insignificant cause of death. It is used totally and absolutely to hold an entire nation of 'free' people hostage in their own land. The frustrating thing to me? *We* the people, by and large, are victims of our own ignorance of our own perceptual failings. The scientifically derived information is massive now about our perceptual failings—*all* of which lead us to blindly walk into propaganda traps, one after another. We really shouldn't blame 'them.' 'They' will always be present, like a virus in the background. *'We'* let it happen by eating intellectual Twinkies all the time and thus becoming intellectually flaccid. All I can do is lob an occasional post. That's a pretty tiny thing to do.

5. Life's Meaning

What is the meaning of life? Why are we here? Why does any of this really matter in the great, grand scheme of time and space? Where will everything be or go if I do nothing and no longer exist? When does the action of one individual really make a difference? Who are we to care? These are all relevant questions, some of which call upon possibilities that we think of as being spiritual in nature.

When is it appropriate to pull out the spiritual card, and does an atheist or agnostic need spirituality to share in the concerns relevant to the meaning of life?

The answer is no. We can all share a common concern—the welfare of our generation and future generations. We all have a built-in preference for freedom. The smallest of children wish to make their own decisions. Without ever articulating the assumption that freedom is a privilege, we all demand it as a right. Even as tiny children, we simply throw tantrums.

When you discover that your acceptance of things as they are has been engineered, when you learn that your every belief has been arranged in a preferred order of perception management, like being given a multiple choice question with alternatives A, B, and C and thereby ignoring the entire rest of the alphabet, when you realize that the very real possibility exists that an elite few use human beings like each of us might use our technology, and when you awaken your own inner resources to properly discriminate, becoming ever more mindful at every level of your being—what then do you do?

From my perspective, I think that each of us has a duty, an obligation, to protect the freedoms we so highly cherish. I think of this as a spiritual duty–spiritual in the sense of enlightenment. Immanuel Kant discussed enlightenment in his essay, "What Is Enlightenment?" He concluded that most live a life of self-imposed juvenility. To live a meaningful life, Kant asserted, we must be grounded in discourse in the public sphere.[10]

I believe that a goal of a meaningful life is to foster the freedom of all, and that is a truly spiritual aspiration. For whatever you subtract from one, you have subtracted from yourself, if by no other means than precedent. I have repeatedly stated my belief, and that, quite simply, is this:

> "Many believe that self-help and self-improvement is about rags to riches, failure to success, and so forth, when indeed it's the beginning of a journey into self-discovery. Inside every human being is an eternal truth and life purpose. Using our mind power is simply starting the engine on that path towards highest self-actualization." [11]

Kant was convinced that knowledge and inquiry required not only intelligence but courage. For him, becoming enlightened marked the difference between childhood and adulthood. As a child we simply let others care for us; we trust that they will do so wisely. As adults we begin to care for ourselves, and not too uncommonly, we discover that the adults who used to care for us were more about taking care of themselves than taking care of us. Becoming the adult signaled enlightenment, and for Kant, that's why Sapere Aude (daring to know) was so important.

Kant thought of a meaningless life this way: "If I have a book to have understanding in place of me, a spiritual advisor to have a conscience for me, a doctor to judge my diet for me, and so on, I need not make any efforts at all. I need not think, so long as I can pay; others will soon enough take over the tiresome job for me."

Professor Jay Garfield of Smith College writes this: "Kant argues that authority, whether political or ecclesiastical, uses the excuse of paternalism and our own terror of disorder in society, as well as our own laziness, to keep us immature and obedient."[12]

Does any of this describe anyone you know today? This description of authority seems strikingly timely, but it was written at the beginning of the Age of Enlightenment when Prussia, Kant's homeland, was going through a period of liberalization. It was published in 1781.

Nevertheless, Kant's message is as true today as ever! If we are to awaken, we must become informed. If we become informed, we are called upon by duty owed to our very life purpose to act in ways that promote freedom and hope for all. This does require courage and intelligence, but then, it might be easier to let someone else do it for you. What are your thoughts?

ENDNOTES

Preface

1. Johnson, M.A. 2015. "Aunt Denies Usaamah Rahim, Killed by Boston Cops, Had Terrorist Links." *NBC News.* June 4, 2015. **www.nbcnews.com/news/us-news/aunt-denies-usaamah-rahim-killed-boston-cops-had-terrorist-links-n370091**

2. Lippman, W. 2010. *Public Opinion.* Wilder Publications Inc.: Blacksburg, VA

And

Clabough, R. 2011. "Bernays' Ideas on Propaganda Continue to Haunt Americans." *Free Republic.* January 21, 2011. **www.freerepublic.com/focus/news/2662605/posts**

3. Emerson, R. W. 1841. "Self-Reliance." Essays: First Series. **www.emersoncentral.com/selfreliance.htm**

Chapter One – Hypothesis: Smiling Masks

1. Laing, R. 1976. *Politics of Experience.* New York: Ballentine Books.

2. Schjoedt, U., et al. 2010. "The Power of Charisma—Perceived Charisma Inhibits the Frontal Executive Network of Believers in Intercessory Prayer." *Social Cognitive and Affective Neuroscience.* Doi:10.1093/scan/nsq023.

3. Saunders, F. S. 1995. "Modern Art Was CIA 'Weapon.'" *The Independent.* November 18, 2013. **www.independent.co.uk/news/world/modern-art-was-cia-weapon-1578808.html**

4. Ibid.

Chapter Two – Basic Protections

1. University of Oxford. 2013. "97 Percent of UK Doctors Have Given Placebos to Patients at Least Once." *ScienceDaily.* March 20, 2013. **www.sciencedaily.com/releases/2013/03/130320212816.htm**

2. Ibid.

3. Associated Press. 2008. "Half of U.S. Doctors Often Prescribe Placebos." *NBC News.* October 23, 2008. **www.nbcnews.com/id/27342269/ns/health-health_care/t/half-us-doctors-often-prescribe-placebos/**

4. Harvard Medical School. 2010. "Placebos Work—Even Without Deception." *ScienceDaily.* December 23, 2010. **www.sciencedaily. com/releases/2010/12/101222173033.htm**

5. Ibid.

6. Staff Writer. 2012. "Pills Filled with Powdered Human Baby Flesh Found by Customs Officials." *The Telegraph.* May 7, 2012. **www. telegraph.co.uk/news/worldnews/asia/southkorea/9250438/ Pills-filled-with-powdered-human-baby-flesh-found-by-customs-officials.html**

7. Ibid.

8. Choi, C. 2012. "Coke, Pepsi Racing for a Better No-Calorie Soda." *Huffington Post.* July 26, 2012. **www.huffingtonpost. com/2012/07/26/coke-pepsi-no-calories-soda_n_1705083.html**

9. Senomyx. *Corporate Profile.* **phx.corporate-ir.net/phoenix. zhtml?c=127189&p=irol-homeProfile&t=&id=&**

10. Warner, M. 2011. "Pepsi's Bizarro World: Boycotted over Embryonic Cells Linked to Lo-Cal Soda." *CBS News.* June 3, 2011. **www.cbsnews.com/8301–505123_162–44043220/pepsis-bizarro-world-boycotted-over-embryonic-cells-linked-to-lo-cal-soda/**

11. Dr. Mercola. 2013. "How Cells from an Aborted Fetus Are Used to Create Novel Flavor Enhancers." Mercola. March 17, 2013. **articles.mercola.com/sites/articles/archive/2013/03/17/ senomyx-flavor-enhancers.aspx**

12. Senomyx. "Regulatory Process." **www.senomyx.com/flavor_ programs/regProcess.htm**

13. Dr. Mercola. 2013. "How Cells from an Aborted Fetus are Used to Create Novel Flavor Enhancers." Mercola. March 17, 2013. **articles.mercola.com/sites/articles/archive/2013/03/17/ senomyx-flavor-enhancers.aspx**

And

Warner, M. 2011. "The Story Behind Pepsi's Upcoming, 'Scientifically Advantaged,' Low-Calorie Soda." *CBS News.* May 13, 2011. **www. cbsnews.com/8301–505123_162–44043121/the-story-behind-pepsis-upcoming-scientifically-advantaged-low-calorie-soda/**

14. Associated Press. 2013. "Farmers Tied to Listeria Outbreak Plead Guilty." *ABC News.* October 22, 2013. **abcnews.go.com/m/ story?id=20643874&sid=81**

15. Health Ranger. 2011. "Blueberries Faked in Cereals, Muffins, Bagels and Other Food Products—Food Investigations." TV Natural News. January 18, 2011. **tv.naturalnews.com/v.asp?v=7ec 06d27b1a945be85e7da8483025962**

16. Avila, J. 2013. "Exclusive: Group Finds More Fake Ingredients in Popular Foods." *ABC News.* January 22, 2013. **abcnews.go.com/ US/exclusive-group-finds-fake-ingredients-popular-foods/ story?id=18281941**

17. Moisse, K. 2012. "Mislabeled Fish Raise Food Allergy Risk." *ABC News.* December 11, 2012. **abcnews.go.com/blogs/ health/2012/12/11/mislabeled-fish-raise-food-allergy-risk/**

18. Staff Writer. 2012. "Top 3 Health Tips: Fraudulent Food Claims." *The Morning Call.* June 9, 2012. **articles.mcall.com/2012–06–09/ health/mc-top-3-health-tips-allentown-0609–20120609_1_fruit-intake-celiac-awareness-gluten-free-certification-organization**

19. Ibid.

20. Singer, N. 2011. "Foods with Benefits, or So They Say." *The New York Times.* May 14, 2011. **www.nytimes.com/2011/05/15/ business/15food.html**

21. Kaye, L. 2013. "Misleading 'Natural' Food Labels May Soon Be History." *Triple Pundit.* September 20th, 2013. **www.triplepundit. com/2013/09/misleading-natural-food-labels-be-history/**

22. Jalonick, M. K. 2011. "FDA: Some Chicken May Have Small Amount of Arsenic." *USA Today.* June 9, 2011. **usatoday30. usatoday.com/money/industries/food/2011–06–08-fda-chicken-arsenic_n.htm**

23. Adams, M. 2011. "FDA Finally Admits Chicken Meat Contains Cancer-Causing Arsenic (But Keep Eating It, Yo!)." Natural News. June 09, 2011. **www.naturalnews.com/032659_arsenic_ chicken.html**

24. Ibid.

25. Hunt, C. 2013. "The Arsenic in Your Chicken." *Huffington Post.* May 13, 2013. **www.huffingtonpost.com/chris-hunt/arsenic-in-chicken_b_3267334.html**

26. Godoy, M. 2013. "What's in That Chicken Nugget? Maybe You Don't Want to Know." *NPR.* October 11, 2013. **www.npr.org/ blogs/thesalt/2013/10/11/232106472/what-s-in-that-chicken-nugget-you-really-don-t-want-to-know**

27. Adams, M. 2013. "TEPCO Admits Deliberately Using Radiation Detectors That Give Deceptively Low Readings; Radiation Leaks Far Worse than Reported." *Natural News.* September 1, 2013. **www.naturalnews.com/041881_Fukushima_radiation_leaks_ deception.html**

28. Ibid.

29. Zero Hedge. 2013. "Tepco Lies Again, Admits Radioactive Leak 'May' Have Started A Month Earlier." *InfoWars.* August 28, 2013.

www.infowars.com/tepco-lies-again-admits-radioactive-leak-may-have-started-a-month-earlier/

30. Ibid.

31. Jeong, E. 2013. "SKorea Bans Fish from NE Japan on Radiation Fears." *The Denver Post.* September 6, 2013. www.denverpost.com/breakingnews/ci_24030301/skorea-bans-fish-from-ne-japan-radiation-fears

32. Kubota, Y. and Obayashi, Y. 2013. "Wrecked Fukushima Storage Tank Leaking Highly Radioactive Water." *Reuters.* August 20, 2013. www.reuters.com/article/2013/08/20/us-japan-fukushima-leak-idUSBRE97J02920130820

33. Staff Writer. *Radiation Impacts.* www.foodandwaterwatch.org/food/foodsafety/the-nuclear-accident-in-japan/

34. Ibid.

35. Willacy, M. 2013. "Fukushima Plant Spilling Contaminated Water into the Sea 'For Years.'" *ABC News.* August 12, 2013. www.abc.net.au/news/2013–08–12/fukushima-plant-workers-raise-safety-concerns/4879960

36. Adams, M. 2013. "The Dentistry Holocaust: How America Has Been Mercury Poisoned by an Industry in Denial." *Natural News.* September 24, 2013. www.naturalnews.com/042193_dentistry_holocaust_mercury_fillings_poisoners.html

37. Ibid.

38. Dykes, A. and Melton, M. 2013. "Did Vaccine Industry-Backed Researchers Hide SV40 Tainted Vaccine Links to Cancer?" *Truth Stream Media.* July 19, 2013. truthstreammedia.com/did-vaccine-industry-backed-researchers-hide-sv40-tainted-vaccine-links-to-cancer/

39. Ibid.

40. Adams, M. 2013. "Merck Vaccine Developer Admits Vaccines Routinely Contain Hidden CancerfViruses Derived from Diseased Monkeys." *Natural News.* September 8, 2013. www.naturalnews.com/041963_vaccines_cancer_viruses_Dr_Maurice_Hilleman.html

41. Ibid.

42. Humphries, S. 2013. *Dissolving Illusions: Disease, Vaccines, and The Forgotten History.* Amazon: Create Space Independent Publishing.

43. Adams, M. 2012. "Vaccination Rights Attorney Patricia Finn Threatened with Criminal Charges; New York State Demands She Surrender Names of All Clients." *Natural News.* February

28, 2012. www.naturalnews.com/035094_Patricia_Finn_
vaccinations_health_freedom.html

44. Berman, B. 2013. "Hospital Holds West Hartford Girl for 9 Months
After Parents Argue Diagnosis." *Fox CT.* November 19, 2013.
foxct.com/2013/11/19/hospital-holds-west-hartford-girl-for-9-
months-after-parents-argue-diagnosis/

45. Wilson, J. 2013. "Virginia Department of Health Acquires
Children's Medical Records Without Parental Consent." July
9, 2013. *InfoWars.* www.infowars.com/virginia-department-of-
health-acquires-childrens-medical-records-without-parental-
consent/

46. Staff Writer. "Stop the Real Stigma." *The Citizens Commission on
Human Rights (CCHR) International.* www.cchrint.org/psychiatric-
disorders/stop-the-real-stigma/

47. Ibid.

48. Miller, G.— "Judge Rotenberg Educational Center: Please Stop
Painful Electric Shocks on Your Students." *Change.Org.* www.
change.org/petitions/judge-rotenberg-educational-center-please-
stop-painful-electric-shocks-on-your-students

49. Benson, J. 2012. "History Shows Polio Caused by Pesticide
Exposure, Then Was Eradicated by Decline in DDT Use."
Natural News. June 25, 2012. www.naturalnews.com/036290_
polio_DDT_pesticide_exposure.html

50. Biotechnology and Biological Sciences Research Council.
2013. "Pesticide Combination Affects Bees' Ability to
Learn." *ScienceDaily.* March 27, 2013. www.sciencedaily.com/
releases/2013/03/130327133347.htm

51. Ibid.

52. Adams, S. 2012. "Killing Babies No Different from Abortion,
Experts Say." *The Telegraph.* February 29, 2012. www.telegraph.
co.uk/health/healthnews/9113394/Killing-babies-no-different-
from-abortion-experts-say.html

53. Ibid.

54. Ibid.

55. Ibid.

56. Sacks, O. 1999. *Awakenings.* New York: Vintage Press.

57. Adams, S. 2012. "Killing Babies No Different from Abortion,
Experts Say." *The Telegraph.* February 29, 2012. www.telegraph.
co.uk/health/healthnews/9113394/Killing-babies-no-different-
from-abortion-experts-say.html

58. Lynne, D. 2005. "Life and Death Tug of War: The Whole Terri Schiavo Story." *World Net Daily.* www.wnd.com/news/article. asp?ARTICLE_ID=43463

59. Walsh, F. 2012. "Vegetative Patient Scott Routley Says 'I'm Not in Pain.'" *BBC News.* November 12, 2012. www.bbc.co.uk/news/health-20268044

60. Burrell, L. 2013. "EMF Exposures Destroy Health and Well-Being, Claims Panel of Top International Scientists." *Natural News.* August 10, 2013. www.naturalnews.com/041575_electromagnetic_fields_cell_phones_public_health.html

61. Barrett, M. 2012. "Cell Phones, EMF Negatively Altering Important Regions of the Brain." *Natural Society.* January 27, 2012. naturalsociety.com/cell-phones-emf-negatively-altering-important-regions-of-the-brain/

62. Ibid.

63. Ibid.

64. Merola, E. 2010. *Burzynski, the Movie.* Merola Films. burzynskimovie.com/

65. Peterson, B. 2013. "GMO Contaminated Alfalfa from Washington Rejected for Export." *Farm Wars.* September 11, 2013. farmwars. info/?p=11459

66. Blomberg, L. 2012. "Eating Our Weight in GMOs." *The Environmental Magazine.* October 22, 2012. www.emagazine.com/daily-news/eating-our-weight-in-gmos

67 Ibid.

68. Staff Writer. 2013. "List of Countries That Ban GMO Crops and Require GE Food Labels." *Natural Revolution.* June 19, 2013. naturalrevolution.org/list-of-countries-that-ban-gmo-crops-and-require-ge-food-labels/

69. Huff, E. A. 2012. "Human Genes Engineered into Experimental GMO Rice Being Grown in Kansas." *Natural News.* May 2, 2012. www.naturalnews.com/035745_GMO_rice_human_genes_Kansas.html

70. Ibid.

71. Peterson, B. 2012. "Syngenta Charged for Covering up Livestock Deaths from GM Corn." *Farm Wars.* June 13, 2012. farmwars. info/?p=8630

72. Staff Writer. 2013. "Stealth GMOs Are Coming: Approved & Unlabeled Everywhere." *Gaia Health.* September 6, 2013. gaia-health.com/gaia-blog/2013–09–06/stealth-gmos-are-coming-approved-unlabeled-everywhere/

73. Ibid.
74. Adams, M. 2013. "Monsanto Leading Super-Secret 'Above Congress' Obama Trade Scheme to Outlaw GMO Labeling Worldwide." *Natural News.* September 09, 2013. **www. naturalnews.com/041965_TPP_GMO_labeling_Monsanto.html**
75. Ibid.
76. Peterson, B. 2012. "Aluminum + Fluoride = Alzheimer's and Dementia." *Farm Wars.* January 22, 2012. **farmwars.info/?p=7791**
77. Thomas, W. 2001. "Chemtrails—U.S. Military Continues to Spray Chemical-Laden Skytrails." *Rense.* **rense.com/general15/ chemusmilitarycontinues.htm**
78. Peterson, B. 2012. "Aluminum + Fluoride = Alzheimer's and Dementia." *Farm Wars.* January 22, 2012. **farmwars.info/?p=7791**
79. Peterson, B. 2012. "Chemtrails and Horizontal Gene Transfer— The GMO Connection." *Farm Wars.* December 4, 2012. **farmwars.info/?p=9583**
80. Ibid.
81. Gucciardi, A. 2013. "Thousands of Genetically Modified Insects Set for Release." *InfoWars.* September 6, 2013. **www.infowars.com/ thousands-of-genetically-modified-insects-set-for-released/**
82. Dr. Mercola. 2013. "Documentary: The Disappearing Male." *Mercola.* August 31, 2013. **articles.mercola.com/sites/articles/ archive/2013/08/31/disappearing-male-documentary.aspx**
83. Staff Writer. 2008. "The Disappearing Male." *Information Liberation.* November 14, 2008. **www.informationliberation.com/?id=26130**
84. Macrae, F. 2013. "Poisoned by Every Day Life: Landmark Study Warns Gender-Bending Chemicals in Your Home, Food, and Car ARE Linked to a Huge Range of Diseases." *Mail OnLine.* February 19, 2013. **www.dailymail.co.uk/news/article-2281394/ Poisoned-day-life-Landmark-study-warns-gender-bending- chemicals-home-food-car-ARE-linked-huge-range-diseases.html**
85. Adams, M. 2012. "Obama Seizes Control over All Food, Farms, Livestock, Farm Equipment, Fertilizer and Food Production Across America." *Natural News.* March 20, 2012. **www. naturalnews.com/035301_Obama_executive_orders_food_ supply.html**
86. Humphrey, T. 2012. "House Bill Bans State Enforcement of Farm Child Labor Law." *Knox News.* March 26, 2012. **blogs.knoxnews. com/humphrey/2012/03/house-bill-bans-state-enforcem.html**

87. Bechman, T. 2011. "How Would New Child Labor Laws on Farms Be Enforced?" *Farm Progress.* November 30, 2011. **farmprogress. com/story-how-new-child-labor-laws-farms-enforced-9–55039**

88. Adams, S. 2012. "Unborn Babies Could Be Tested For 3,500 Genetic Faults." *The Telegraph.* June 6, 2012. **www.telegraph.co.uk/health/healthnews/9315265/Unborn-babies-could-be-tested-for-3500-genetic-faults.html**

89. Staff Writer. 2010. "Everything Is a Lie: The Deliberate Intent to Deceive People Is at an All Time High." *Prevent Disease.* August 10, 2010 **preventdisease.com/news/10//081010_everything_is_a_lie. shtml**

Chapter Three – They Start with Our Children

1. Staff Writer. 2012. "The Ivy-in-Chief: Is the Political Establishment Too Elitist?" *The Urban Politico.* July 8, 2012 **www.theurbanpolitico.com/2012/07/ivy-in-chief-is-political-establishment.html**

2. Keith, J. 1997. *Mind Control, World Control.* Kempton, Ill.: Adventures Unlimited Press.

3. Ibid.

4. Ibid.

5. Ibid.

6. Taylor, E. 2009. *Mind Programming: From Persuasion and Brainwashing to Self-Help and Practical Metaphysics.* Carlsbad, Calif.: Hay House.

7. Salazar, A. 2013. "School Apologizes for Propagandizing Students to Love Obama." *InfoWars.* September 30, 2013. **www.infowars. com/school-apologizes-for-propagandizing-students-to-love-obama/**

8. Morgenstern, M. 2012. "'He's Our Man, Yes We Can!': Pro-Obama Song Taught to Kindergarteners at TX School." *The Blaze.* February 10, 2012. **www.theblaze.com/stories/2012/02/10/ hes-our-man-yes-we-can-shocking-obama-song-taught-to-kindergarteners-at-tx-school/**

9. Ibid.

10. Staff Writer. "Hitler Youth Movement." *History Learning Site.* **www. historylearningsite.co.uk/hitler_youth.htm**

11. Napier, A. 2014. "School Plans Microchip Bracelets." *Stuff.* July 31, 2014. **www.stuff.co.nz/national/60406398/School-plans-microchip-bracelets**

12. Nimmo, K. 2013. "MSNBC Host: Your Kids Belong to the Collective." *InfoWars*. April 6, 2013. **www.infowars.com/your-kids-belong-to-the-collective/**
13. Kimbol, S. "Corporate Ownership of Children." *AntiShyster*, Vol. 1, No. 8. **famguardian.org/PublishedAuthors/Media/Antishyster/V08N1-CorpOwnershipOfChildren.pdf**
14. Orwell, G. 1956. *Animal Farm*. New York: Signet Classics.
15. Lincoln, A. 1859. *Letter To Henry L. Pierce And Others.* **www.abrahamlincolnonline.org/lincoln/speeches/pierce.htm**
16. Pilger, J. 1992. "TV Interview of Noam Chomsky by John Pilger." Transcribed by Rae West. *BBC2*. November 25, 1992. **www.recrea.org/rrf/johnp/jp_noamc.htm**
17. Chomsky, N. 1979. *Language and responsibility: Based on conversations with Mitsou Ronat.* New York: Pantheon.
18. Chomsky, N. 1992. "On Propaganda." *WBAI*. **www.chomsky.info/interviews/199201—.htm**

Chapter Four – Behaviorism

1. Watson, J. B. 1930. *Behaviorism* (Revised edition). Chicago: University of Chicago Press.
2. Wikipedia. "John B. Watson." **en.wikipedia.org/wiki/John_B._Watson**
And
Watson, John B., and Watson, R. R. 1921. "Studies in Infant Psychology." *The Scientific Monthly* 13.6 (1921): 493–515.
And
Watson, J. B., & Rayner, R. 1920. "Conditioned Emotional Reactions." *Journal of Experimental Psychology, 3*, 1–14.
3. Northern Illinois University. "BF Skinner, Behavioralism, & Language Behavior." **www3.niu.edu/acad/psych/Millis/History/2003/cogrev_skinner.htm**
4. Rosen, C. "The New Behaviorist." *New Threats to Freedom.* **newthreatstofreedom.com/news/free-preview/**
5. Ibid.

Chapter Five – Curtailing Freedom

1. Wikipedia. "U.S. Intelligence Involvement with German and Japanese War Criminals After World War II." **en.wikipedia.org/wiki/U.S._intelligence_involvement_with_German_and_Japanese_war_criminals_after_World_War_II**

2. Wikipedia. "Operation Midnight Climax." **en.wikipedia.org/wiki/ Operation_Midnight_Climax**

And

Time Magazine. 1977. "The CIA: Mind-Bending Disclosures." *Time Magazine.* August 15, 1977. **content.time.com/time/magazine/ article/0,9171,915244,00.html.**

And

Hooper, T. 2012. "Operation Midnight Climax: How the CIA Dosed S.F. Citizens with LSD." *San Francisco Weekly.* March 14, 2012. **www.sfweekly.com/2012–03–14/news/cia-lsd-wayne-ritchie- george-h-white-mk-ultra/**

3. Keith, J. 1997. *Mind Control, World Control.* Kempton, Ill.: Adventures Unlimited Press.

4. Ibid.

5. Ibid.

6. The Examiner. 2009. "CIA Behavior Modification: Project Bluebird." *The Examiner.* July 4, 2009. **www.examiner.com/ article/cia-behavior-modification-project-bluebird**

and

Want To Know. "CIA Declassified Mind Control Document." *Want To Know.* **www.wanttoknow.info/mind_control/foia_mind_ control/19520101_140401**

7. Want To Know. "CIA Mind Control Experiments: Declassified Documents Reveal Sex Abuse, More" *Want To Know.* **www.wanttoknow.info/mind_control/cia_mind_control_ experiments_sex_abuse**

8. Richelson, J. T. 2013. "Science, Technology and the CIA." *The National Security Archive.* August 5, 2013. **www2.gwu. edu/~nsarchiv/NSAEBB/NSAEBB54/**

And

www2.gwu.edu/~nsarchiv/NSAEBB/NSAEBB54/st02.pdf

9. Ibid.

10. Ibid.

11. Staff. 1977. "Joint Hearing Before the Select Committee on Intelligence and the Subcommittee on Health and Scientific Research of the Committee on Human Resources" *United States Senate Ninety-Fifth Congress.* August 3, 1977. **www.nytimes.com/ packages/pdf/national/13inmate_ProjectMKULTRA.pdf**

12. Ibid.

13. Supreme Court of United States. 1984. "Central Intelligence Agency, et al.V. Sims, et al." 471 U.S. 159 (1985). No. 83-1075.

scholar.google.com/scholar_case?q=471+U.S.+159&hl=en&as_
sdt=2,33&case=16297847318525168348&scilh=0

14. Wikipedia. "High-Frequency Active Auroral Research Program."
    **en.wikipedia.org/wiki/High_Frequency_Active_Auroral_
    Research_Program**

15. Begich, N. and Manning, J. 2002. *Angels Don't Play This HAARP.*
    Anchorage, Alaska: Earthpulse Press.

16. Anderson, B. 2013. "Alaska's Controversial HAARP Facility Closed
    – Will It Come Back Online?" *Alaska Dispatch.* July 17, 2013. **www.
    alaskadispatch.com/article/20130717/alaska-s-controversial-
    haarp-facility-closed-will-it-come-back-online**

17. Rappoport, J. 1995. "U.S. Government Mind Control Experiments
    on Children." *Perceptions*, March/April 1995, p.58.

And

Rappoport, J. 2002. "Where Are All the Missing Children? CIA
    Experiments with Mind Control on Children." *2ⁿᵈ Sight Research.*
    April 15, 2002. **groups.yahoo.com/neo/groups/2nd_Sight/
    conversations/messages/457**

18. Rappoport, J. 1996. "Mind Control Experiments on Children."
    New Dawn Magazine. No. 34. January/February 1996. **www.
    newdawnmagazine.com/Articles/Mind%20Control%20
    Experiments%20on%20Children.htm**

19. Dulles, A.W. 1956. "Brainwashing From a Psychological
    Viewpoint." *Central Intelligence Agency.* April 25, 1956.
    **www.foia.cia.gov/sites/default/files/document_
    conversions/89801/DOC_0000886487.pdf**

And

Romains, J. 1939. *Verdon: The Prelude.* p. 156.

Chapter Six – Giving Our Rights Away

1. Seligman, M. E. P. 1972. "Learned Helplessness." *Annual Review
    of Medicine,* 23(1), 407–412. **www.annualreviews.org/doi/
    abs/10.1146/annurev.me.23.020172.002203**

2. Nolen, J. 2014. "Learned Helplessness." *Encyclopedia Britannica.*
    January 3, 2014. **www.britannica.com/EBchecked/
    topic/1380861/learned-helplessness**

3. Wikipedia. "Just World Hypothesis." **en.wikipedia.org/wiki/Just-
    world_hypothesis**

4. Milgram, S. 1963. "Behavioral Study of Obedience." *Journal of
    Abnormal and Social Psychology,* 67, 371–378.

5. Lerner, M. J., & Simmons, C. H. 1966. "Observer's Reaction to the 'Innocent Victim': Compassion or Rejection?" *Journal of Personality and Social Psychology*, 4(2), 203–210.
6. Wikipedia. "Just World Hypothesis." **en.wikipedia.org/wiki/Just-world_hypothesis**

Chapter Seven – Propaganda: From the Beginning

1. Cialdini, R. B. 1992. *Influence: Science and Practice.* New York: Harper Collins.
2. Bernays, E. 1928. *Propaganda.* 2005 ed. New York: Ig Publishing.
3. Clabough, R. 2011. "Bernays' Ideas on Propaganda Continue to Haunt Americans." *Free Republic.* January 21, 2011. **www.freerepublic.com/focus/news/2662605/posts**
4. Bernays, E. 1928. *Propaganda.* 2005 ed. New York: Ig Publishing.
5. Bernays, E.L., Cutler, H.W. 1955. *The Engineering of Consent.* University of Oklahoma Press.: Oklahoma.
6. Wikipedia. "Edward Bernays." **en.wikipedia.org/wiki/Edward_Bernays**
And
Tye, L. 1998. *The Father of Spin: Edward L. Bernays and the Birth of Public Relations.* Henry Holt and Co.: New York.
7. Jacoby, J. 1992. "The Public Be Swayed." *The Jerusalem Report.* February 13, 1992. **www.jeffjacoby.com/5708/the-public-be-swayed**
8. Feminism 3.0. *Torches of Freedom.* **www.feminismthreepointzero.com/?page_id=41**
9. MacDonald, K. 2012. "Public Relations." *Cambridge Historical Society.* **www.cambridgehistory.org/discover/innovation/Edward%20Bernays.html**
10. Morris, A. 2013. "What If a Search Engine Could Determine an Election?" *PBS Newshour.* April 2, 2013. **www.pbs.org/newshour/rundown/2013/04/what-if-a-search-engine-could-determine-an-election.html**
11. Cohen, M. 2002. "How the War Party Sold the 1991 Bombing of Iraq to U.S." *Antiwar.* **www.antiwar.com/orig/cohen1.html**
12. Watson. P.J. 2013. "BBC Caught Staging Syria Chemical Weapons Propaganda?" *Infowars.* October 7, 2013. **www.infowars.com/bbc-caught-staging-syria-chemical-weapons-propaganda/**
13. Fisher, M. 2013. "Oops: Azerbaijan Released Election Results Before Voting Had Even Started." *The Washington Post: WordViews.* October 9, 2013. **www.washingtonpost.com/blogs/**

worldviews/wp/2013/10/09/oops-azerbaijan-released-election-results-before-voting-had-even-started/

14. True The Vote. "How Widespread Is Voter Fraud? | 2012 Facts & Figures." *Truth The Vote.* www.truethevote.org/news/how-widespread-is-voter-fraud-2012-facts-figures

15. Bullock, A. 2004. *The Secret Sales Pitch.* San Jose, Calif.: Norwich Publishers.

16. Ibid.

17. Ibid.

18. Tye, L. 1998. *The Father of Spin: Edward L. Bernays and the Birth of Public Relations.* Henry Holt and Co.: New York.

19. Lippman, W. 2010. *Public Opinion.* Wilder Publications Inc.: Blacksburg, VA.

Chapter Eight – Indoctrination via the Media

1. Taylor, E. 2009. *Mind Programming: From Persuasion and Brainwashing to Self-Help and Practical Metaphysics.* Carlsbad, Calif.: Hay House.

2. Taylor, E. 2012. *Self-Hypnosis and Subliminal Technology.* Carlsbad, Calif.: Hay House.

3. Sorrow, A. R. 2012. "Magazine Trends Study Finds Increase in Advertisements Using Sex." *UGA Today.* June 5, 2012. news.uga.edu/releases/article/magazine-trends-study-finds-increase-in-advertisements-using-sex/

4. Association for Psychological Science. 2012. "Exposure to Sexual Content in Popular Movies Predicts Sexual Behavior in Adolescence." *ScienceDaily.* July 17, 2012. www.sciencedaily.com/releases/2012/07/120717162743.htm
And
www.psychologicalscience.org/index.php/news/releases/exposure-to-sexual-content-in-popular-movies-predicts-sexual-behavior-in-adolescence.html

5. Ohio State University. 2012. "Violent Video Games: More Playing Time Equals More Aggression." *ScienceDaily.* December 10, 2012. www.sciencedaily.com/releases/2012/12/121210101344.htm
And
Hasan, Y., Bègue, L., Scharkow, M., and Bushman, B. J. "The More You Play, the More Aggressive You Become: A Long-Term Experimental Study of Cumulative Violent Video Game Effects on Hostile Expectations and Aggressive Behavior." *Journal of Experimental Social Psychology,* 2013; 49 (2): 224 DOI: 10.1016/j.jesp.2012.10.016.

6. Iowa State University. 2013. "Violent Video Games Are a Risk Factor for Criminal Behavior and Aggression, New Evidence Shows." *ScienceDaily*. March 26, 2013. **www.sciencedaily.com/releases/2013/03/130326121605.htm**
And
DeLisi, M., Vaughn, M.G., Gentile, D. A., Anderson, C. A., Shook. J. J. 2012. "Violent Video Games, Delinquency, and Youth Violence: New Evidence." *Youth Violence and Juvenile Justice*, 2012; 11 (2): 132 DOI: 10.1177/1541204012460874.

7. Breen, T. 2013. "Human-like Opponents Lead to More Aggression in Video Game Players, UConn Study Finds." *UConn Today*. May 20, 2013. **today.uconn.edu/blog/2013/05/human-like-opponents-lead-to-more-aggression-in-video-game-players-uconn-study-finds/**

8. Munsey, C. 2006. "Frisky, but More Risky." *Monitor*. American Psychological Society. **www.apa.org/monitor/julaug06/frisky.aspx**

9. University of Bristol. 2013. "Fear Factor Increases, Emotions Decrease in Books Written in Last 50 Years." *ScienceDaily*. March 20, 2013. **www.sciencedaily.com/releases/2013/03/130320212822.htm**

10. McKernan, L. 2002. "Film History." *War and Militarism*. Vol. 14, No. 3/4, pp. 369–389. Indiana University Press: Indiana **www.jstor.org/stable/3815438**

11. Wikipedia. 2013. "List of Allied Propaganda Films of World War II: United States." **en.wikipedia.org/wiki/List_of_Allied_propaganda_films_of_World_War_II#United_States**

12. Waring, R. 2000. "Will the West Wing Cause the Left Swing?" *Picturing Justice*. November 4, 2000. **usf.usfca.edu/pj/westwing-waring.htm**

13. Mataconis, D. 2012. "The West Wing and American Politics." *Outside the Beltway*. October 1, 2012. **www.outsidethebeltway.com/the-west-wing-and-american-politics/**

14. McMillan, G. 2013. "Revisiting The West Wing: A Stirring, Comforting Fantasy." *Time Entertainment*. April 19, 2013. **entertainment.time.com/2013/04/19/revisiting-the-west-wing-a-stirring-comforting-fantasy/**

15. Perkins, S. 2003. "Dirty Rats: Campaign Ad May Have Swayed Voters Subliminally." *Science News*. 163/8, p. 116–117.

www.sciencenews.org/article/dirty-rats-campaign-ad-may-have-swayed-voters-subliminally

16. Ledgerwood, A. & Callahan, S. 2012. The Social Side of Abstraction: Psychological Distance Enhances Conformity to Group Norms." *Psychological Science*, 23, 907–913. And

UC Davis. 2012. "Voters Are Influenced by Friends, Neighbors and Groups, UC Davis Study Says." *UC Davis News and Information.* July 21, 2012. **news.ucdavis.edu/search/news_detail.lasso?id=10295**

17. Logiurato, B. 2012. "Obama Made Everyone Cringe with His Gushing Praise of Aaron Sorkin." *Business Insider.* August 7, 2012. **www.businessinsider.com/obama-aaron-sorkin-writes-the-way-every-democrat-wishes-they-spoke-2012-8**

18. Ponte, L. "HBO's 'The Newsroom' a Liberal Mess." *Newsmax.* June 25, 2012. **www.newsmax.com/LowellPonte/HBO-Newsroom-Sorkin-Daniels/2012/06/25/id/443387** And

Nussbaum, E. 2012. "Broken News: The Artificial Intelligence of 'The Newsroom.'" *The New Yorker.* June 25, 2012. **www.newyorker.com/arts/critics/television/2012/06/25/12062 5crte_television_nussbaum**

19. Indiana University. 2013. "We Live Our Lives Within Our Media, Rather than Simply with It, Expert Says." ScienceDaily. October 29, 2012. **www.sciencedaily.com/ releases/2012/10/121029131825.htm**

20. Indiana University. 2013. "We Live Our Lives Within Our Media, Rather than Simply with It." *IU Newsroom.* October 29, 2012. **newsinfo.iu.edu/news/page/normal/23365.html**

21. Durden, T. 2013. "An Orwellian America." *Zero Hedge.* March 15, 2013. **www.zerohedge.com/news/2013–03–15/orwellian-america**

22. Ibid.

23. Curtis, A. 2012. *Mass Media Influence on Society. University of North Carolina at Pembroke.* **www.uncp.edu/home/ acurtis/Courses/ResourcesForCourses/Media&Society/ MassMediaInfluenceOnSociety.html**

Chapter Nine – Physiology/Psychology

1. Du Sautoy, M. 2009. "Neuroscience and Free Will." **www.youtube.com/watch?v=N6S9OidmNZM&feature=share**

2. Copernicus. 2013. "Free Will an Illusion? Very Likely!" *Brane Space.* August 24, 2013. **brane-space.blogspot.com/2013/08/free-will-illusion-very-likely.html**

3. Ibid.

4. Penfield, W. 1955. "The Role of the Temporal Cortex in Certain Psychical Phenomena." Journal of Mental Science, 1955 101:451–65.

5. Nelson, M. 2012. "Science Explains Why Our Brains May Be 'Hardwired' for God." *Patheos.* **www.patheos.com/blogs/friendlyatheist/2012/06/05/science-explains-why-our-brains-may-be-hardwired-for-god/**

6. Anik, L., Aknin, L. B., Norton, M. I., & Dunn, E. W. "Feeling Good about Giving: The Benefits (and Costs) of Self-Interested Charitable Behavior." *Harvard Business School.* **www.hbs.edu/faculty/Publication%20Files/10–012.pdf**

7. Marsh, J. & Suttie, J. 2010. "5 Ways Giving Is Good for You." *Greater Good.* **greatergood.berkeley.edu/article/item/5_ways_giving_is_good_for_you**

8. St. Joseph's Hospital and Medical Center. 2012. "Discoveries into Perception via Popular Magic Tricks." *ScienceDaily.* May 22, 2012. **www.sciencedaily.com/releases/2012/05/120522180700.htm**

9. LiveScience Staff. 2012. "Like Pinocchio, Your Nose Shows When You Lie." *LiveScience.* **www.livescience.com/25191-nose-reveals-lies-pinocchio-effect.html**

10. Association for Psychological Science. 2013. "In the Land of the Free, Interdependence Undermines Americans' Motivation to Act." *ScienceDaily.* January 22, 2013. **www.sciencedaily.com/releases/2013/01/130122143220.htm**

11. University of Nebraska-Lincoln. 2012. "How Our Brains See Men as People and Women as Body Parts: Both Genders Process Images of Men, Women Differently." *ScienceDaily.* July 25, 2012. **www.sciencedaily.com/releases/2012/07/120725150215.htm**

12. Economic and Social Research Council. (ESRC). 2012. "Our Brains Often Fail to Notice Key Words That Can Change the Whole Meaning of a Sentence." *ScienceDaily.* July 16, 2012. **www.sciencedaily.com/releases/2012/07/120716091921.htm**

13. University of Missouri-Columbia. 2012. "Advertisers Could Target Online Audiences More Efficiently with Personality Scale." *ScienceDaily.* July 12, 2012. **www.sciencedaily.com/releases/2012/07/120712224816.htm**

14. Atalay, A. S., Bodur, H. O. and Rasolofoarison. D. 2012. "Shining in the Center: Central Gaze Cascade Effect on Product Choice."

Journal of Consumer Research. December, 2012. **press.uchicago. edu/pressReleases/2012/July/JCR_1207_Center.html**

15. Madison, L. 2011. "'Birther' Claims Debunked in New Report." *CBSNews.* April 26, 2011. **www.cbsnews.com/news/birther-claims-debunked-in-new-report/**

16. Grabmeier, J. 2013. "False Beliefs Persist, Even After Instant Online Corrections." *The Ohio State University.* January 24, 2013. **researchnews.osu.edu/archive/realtimecorr.htm**

17. Brown, T. 2013. "Bombshell: Document Examiner Tied to Obama Defense Attorney Says Birth Certificate is 100% Fraud." *Freedom Outpost.* Jun 8, 2013. **freedomoutpost.com/2013/06/bombshell-document-examiner-tied-to-obama-defense-attorney-says-birth-certificate-is-100-fraud/**

18. Miller, G. 2013. "Expert Witness from Obama's Law Firm Says 'Obama Birth Certificate' a Fraud." *Ventura County Tea Party.* August 13, 2013. **venturacountyteaparty.ning.com/profiles/blogs/expert-witness-from-obama-s-law-firm-says-obama-birth-certificate**

And

Zane, K. 2013. "Document Expert Could Topple the Obama Administration." *The Western Center for Journalism.* July 20, 2013. **www.westernjournalism.com/document-expert-could-topple-the-obama-administration/**

19. University of Toronto. 2013. "Moments of Spirituality Can Induce Liberal Attitudes, Researchers Find." *ScienceDaily.* February 25, 2013. **www.sciencedaily.com/releases/2013/02/130225131532.htm**

20. Ibid.

21. Press Release. 2013. "Name-Brand or Generic? Your Political Ideology Might Influence Your Choice." *Association for Psychological Science.* February 12, 2013. **www.psychologicalscience.org/index.php/news/releases/name-brand-or-generic-your-political-ideology-might-influence-your-choice.html**

22. Kiger, P. J. 2013. "Are We Hard-Wired to Enjoy Cheating?" *DNews.* September 12, 2013. **news.discovery.com/human/evolution/is-dishonesty-the-best-policy-for-happiness-130912.htm**

23. Ibid.

24. Ariely, D. 2012. *The Honest Truth about Dishonesty.* New York: Harper.

25. Dice. M. 2013. *The Petition for "Mandatory Euthanasia" for Senior Citizens Under Obama Care.* **www.youtube.com/watch?v=t4BEY1lZDyg**

26. Wolchover, N. 2012. "People Aren't Smart Enough for Democracy to Flourish, Scientists Say." *Livescience.* February 28, 2012.

27. Rael. 2008. *Geniocracy: Government of the People, for the People, by the Geniuses.* UK: Nova Distribution.

Chapter Ten – Pushing the Boundaries

1. Wikipedia. "Murder of Kitty Genovese." *Wikipedia.* en.wikipedia.org/wiki/Kitty_Genovese

2. Cherry, K. "The Bystander Effect: Why Bystanders Sometimes Faily to Help." *About.com Psychology.* **psychology.about.com/od/socialpsychology/a/bystandereffect.htm**
And
Latane, B., & Darley, J. 1969. "Bystander 'Apathy.'" American Scientist, 57, 244–268.

3. Bournemouth University 2013. "Investigating the Bystander Effect Using Virtual Reality." *ScienceDaily.* January 11, 2013. www.sciencedaily.com/releases/2013/01/130111092451.htm

4. Milgram, S. 1963. "Behavioral Study of Obedience." *Journal of Abnormal and Social Psychology,* 67, 371–378.

5. Association for Psychological Science. 2012. "Social Identification, Not Obedience, Might Motivate Unspeakable Acts." *ScienceDaily.* July 18, 2012. **www.sciencedaily.com/releases/2012/07/120718164947.htm**

6. Alexander, M. 2001. "Thirty Years Later, Stanford Prison Experiment Lives On." *Stanford Report,* August 22, 2001.

7. Zimbardo, P. 2008. *The Lucifer Effect: Understanding How Good People Turn Evil.* New York: Random House.

8. Dyer, J. 2001. "Ethics and Orphans: The 'Monster Study.'" *Mercury News.* June 10, 2001. **www-psych.stanford.edu/~bigopp/stutter2.html**

9. Listverse. "Top 10 Unethical Psychological Experiments." **listverse.com/2008/09/07/top-10-unethical-psychological-experiments/**

10. Oregon State University. 2012. "Wearing Two Different Hats: Moral Decisions May Depend on the Situation." *Oregon State University.* June 23, 2012. **oregonstate.edu/ua/ncs/archives/2012/may/wearing-two-different-hats-moral-decisions-may-depend-situation**

Chapter Eleven – Information Processing

1. Vague, R. 2012. "The Two Systems of Cognitive Processes." *Big Think.* January 16. 2012. **bigthink.com/delancey-place/the-two-systems-of-cognitive-processes**

2. Kahneman, D. 2013. *Thinking, Fast and Slow.* New York: Farrar, Straus and Giroux.

3. Ferriss, T. and Ariely, D. "Understanding the Dangers of 'Ego-Depletion.'" *Experiments in Lifestyle Design.* **www.fourhourworkweek.com/blog/2012/08/12/understanding-the-dangers-of-ego-depletion/**

4. . University of Iowa 2012. "This Is Your Brain on No Self-Control." *ScienceDaily.* June 6, 2012. **www.sciencedaily.com/releases/2012/06/120606142704.htm**

5. Koch, C. 2011. "Probing the Unconscious Mind." *Scientific American.* October 20, 2011. **www.scientificamerican.com/article.cfm?id=probing-the-unconscious-mind**

6. Taylor, E. 2009. *Mind Programming: From Persuasion and Brainwashing to Self-Help and Practical Metaphysics.* Carlsbad, Calif.: Hay House, Inc.

7. Bornstein, R. F. and Pittman, T. S., Eds. 1992. *Perception Without Awareness: Cognitive, Clinical, and Social Perspectives.* New York: Guilford Press.

8. Taylor, E. 2009. *Mind Programming: From Persuasion and Brainwashing to Self-Help and Practical Metaphysics.* Carlsbad, Calif.: Hay House, Inc.

9. Dulles, A.W. 1956. "Brainwashing from a Psychological Viewpoint." *Central Intelligence Agency.* April 25, 1956. **www.foia.cia.gov/sites/default/files/document_conversions/89801/DOC_0000886487.pdf**
And
Romains, J. 1939. *Verdon: The Prelude.* p. 156.

10. Perkins, S. 2003. "Dirty Rats: Campaign Ad May Have Swayed Voters Subliminally." *Science News.* 163/8, p. 116–117.
And
Perkins, S. 2003. "Dirty Rats: Campaign Ad May Have Swayed Voters Subliminally." *Science News.* **www.freerepublic.com/focus/f-news/853824/posts**

11. Sloan, J. 2013. "Did a British Television Viewer Capture a Subliminal, Encoded Message?" *Disinformation.* January 24, 2013.

disinfo.com/2013/01/did-a-british-television-viewer-capture-a-
subliminal-encoded-message/

Chapter Twelve – Some of What "They" Have Learned

1. SAGE Publications. 2012. "Note to Waitresses: Wearing Red Can Be Profitable." *ScienceDaily*. August 2, 2012.
www.sciencedaily.com/releases/2012/08/120802111454.htm
2. Wiley. 2012. "Strangers on a Bus: Study Reveals Lengths Commuters Go to avoid Each Other." *ScienceDaily*. August 1, 2012.
www.sciencedaily.com/releases/2012/08/120801093615.htm
And
Esther, C. K. 2012. "Nonsocial Transient Behavior: Social Disengagement on the Greyhound Bus." *Symbolic Interaction*.
3. University of Southern California. 2013. "Empathy? Surprising Study Shows That Brains Process the Pain of Villains More than the Pain of People We Like." *ScienceDaily*. October 16, 2013.
www.sciencedaily.com//releases/2013/10/131016132256.htm
4. International Communication Association. 2013. "Humans Feel Empathy for Robots: fMRI Scans Show Similar Brain Function When Robots Are Treated the Same as Humans." *ScienceDaily*. April 23, 2013.
www.sciencedaily.com//releases/2013/04/130423091111.htm
5. University of Texas at Austin. 2012. "Repetitious, Time-Intensive Magical Rituals Considered More Effective, Study Shows." *ScienceDaily*. July 26, 2012. **www.sciencedaily.com/releases/2012/07/120726135234.htm**
6. Ibid.
7. Newberg, A. and Waldman, M. R. 2010. *How God Changes Your Brain: Breakthrough Findings from a Leading Neuroscientist*. New York: Ballentine Books.
8. University of California—Berkeley Haas School of Business. 2012. "The Advantages of Being First." *ScienceDaily*. July 2, 2012.
www.sciencedaily.com/releases/2012/07/120702210301.htm
9. Association for Psychological Science. 2012. "Thinking About Giving, Not Receiving, Motivates People to Help Others." *ScienceDaily*. August 10, 2012.
www.sciencedaily.com/releases/2012/08/120810112812.htm
10. Association for Psychological Science. 2012. "Our Preferences Change to Reflect the Choices We Make, Even Three Years Later." *ScienceDaily*. October 3, 2012.
www.sciencedaily.com/releases/2012/10/121003132416.htm

11. Thadeusz, F. 2013. "Is Your Coffee Too Cheap? Using Brain Waves to Test Prices." *Speigel Online.* October 12, 2013. **abcnews.go.com/Technology/coffee-cheap-brain-waves-test-prices/story?id=20541594**

12. Association for Psychological Science. 2013. "Warning of Potential Side Effects of a Product Can Increase Its Sales." *Press Release.* September 24, 2013. **www.psychologicalscience.org/index.php/news/releases/warning-of-potential-side-effects-of-a-product-can-increase-its-sales.html**

13. Ibid.

14. University of Southern California. 2012. "Whether We Like Someone Affects How Our Brain Processes Movement." *ScienceDaily.* October 6, 2012. **www.sciencedaily.com/releases/2012/10/121006170905.htm**

15. Ohio State University. 2013. "Mitt Romney's Face Looks Different to Republicans and Democrats." *ScienceDaily.* December 12, 2013. **www.sciencedaily.com//releases/2013/12/131212113042.htm**

16. Ibid.

17. Georgetown University Medical Center. 2012. "What You Hear Could Depend on What Your Hands Are Doing." *ScienceDaily.* October 14, 2012. **www.sciencedaily.com/releases/2012/10/121014162904.htm**

18. University of Warwick. 2013. "Too Much Choice Leads to Riskier Decisions, New Study Finds." *ScienceDaily.* March 25, 2013. **www.sciencedaily.com/releases/2013/03/130325093709.htm**

19. Ibid.

Chapter Thirteen – Pulling on Our Emotions

1. Association for Psychological Science. 2012. "How Do We Make Moral Judgments?—Insights from Psychological Science." *Press Release.* September 12, 2012. **www.psychologicalscience.org/index.php/news/releases/how-do-we-make-moral-judgments-insights-from-psychological-science.html**

2. Case Western Reserve University. 2013. "Babies Seeing Violence Show Aggression Later." *ScienceDaily.* June 17, 2013. **www.sciencedaily.com/releases/2013/06/130617110707.htm**

3. Case Western Reserve University. 2012. "Empathy Represses Analytic Thought, and Vice Versa: Brain Physiology Limits Simultaneous Use of Both Networks." *ScienceDaily.* October 30, 2012. **www.sciencedaily.com/releases/2012/10/121030161416.htm**

4. Basque Research. 2012. "Emotion Detector Enables Design of Tailor-Made Election Campaigns." *ScienceDaily*. September 25, 2012. **www.sciencedaily.com/releases/2012/09/120925091605.htm**

5. Ibid.

6. Ibid.

7. Association for Psychological Science. 2012. "The Good, the Bad, and the Guilty: Anticipating Feelings of Guilt Predicts Ethical Behavior." *ScienceDaily*. October 10, 2012. **www.sciencedaily.com/releases/2012/10/121010141452.htm**

Chapter Fourteen – The Power of Suggestion

1. Association for Psychological Science. 2012. "The Power of Suggestion: What We Expect Influences Our Behavior, for Better or Worse." *Press Release*. June 6, 2012. **www.psychologicalscience.org/index.php/news/releases/the-power-of-suggestion-what-we-expect-influences-our-behavior-for-better-or-worse.html**

2. Ibid.

3. University of Chicago Press Journals. 2012. "Does Changing the Price of Medicine Influence Consumers' Perceived Health Risk?" *ScienceDaily*. December 11, 2012. **www.sciencedaily.com/releases/2012/12/121211130323.htm**

4. Lund University. 2013. "Magical Survey Shows Voters Are Less Partisan than Indicated by Polls." *Press Release*. April 11, 2013. **www.lunduniversity.lu.se/o.o.i.s?id=24890&news_item=6037**

5. Association for Psychological Science. 2013. "Extreme Political Attitudes May Stem From an Illusion of Understanding." *Press Release*. April 29, 2013. **www.psychologicalscience.org/index.php/news/releases/extreme-political-attitudes-may-stem-from-an-illusion-of-understanding.html**

6. Ibid.

7. Ibid.

8. Woods, J. 2013. "Aggressive Advertising May Make for Aggressive Men." *PsychCentral*. March 2, 2013. **psychcentral.com/news/2013/03/03/aggressive-advertising-may-make-for-aggressive-men/52140.html**

9. Herbert, W. 2011. "Thinking About Mortality Changes How We Act." *Scientific American*. December 23, 2011. **www.scientificamerican.com/article.cfm?id=two-faces-of-death**

10. Ibid.

11. Jenkins, D. 2006. "Study Suggests Game Link to Marijuana and Alcohol Abuse." *Gamasutra*. April 11, 2006.
www.gamasutra.com/php-bin/news_index.php?story=8866
And
Brady, S. B. and Matthews, K. A. 2006. "Effects of Media Violence on Health-Related Outcomes Among Young Men." *JAMA Pediatrics*. April, 2006. archpedi.jamanetwork.com/article.aspx?articleid=204843

12. Université du Luxembourg. 2012. "Inexperienced Video Gamers Show Macbeth Effect." *ScienceDaily*. July 12, 2012. www.sciencedaily.com/releases/2012/07/120712092441.htm

13. Michigan State University. 2013. "Some Video Games Promote Unhealthy Foods for Kids." *ScienceDaily*. October 7, 2013. www.sciencedaily.com/releases/2013/10/131007151742.htm

Chapter Fifteen – Attention

1. Wolpert, S. 2013. "How the Brain Creates the 'Buzz' That Helps Ideas Spread." *UCLA Newsroom*. July 5, 2013. newsroom.ucla.edu/portal/ucla/how-the-brain-creates-buzz-247204.aspx

2. Brigham and Women's Hospital. 2013. "If You're Not Looking for It, You Probably Won't See It." *ScienceDaily*. July 19, 2013. www.sciencedaily.com/releases/2013/07/130719112134.htm

3. Springer Science+Business Media. 2013. "Gamblers Like Noisy Slot Machines—It Reinforces the Rewarding Feeling After a Win." *ScienceDaily*. July 2, 2013. www.sciencedaily.com/releases/2013/07/130702100348.htm

4. Sullivan, M. 2012. "Dissonant Music Brings Out the Animal in Listeners, Say UCLA Researchers." *UCLA Newsroom*. June 12, 2012. newsroom.ucla.edu/portal/ucla/dissonant-music-brings-out-the-234656.aspx

5. The University of Chicago Press. 2012. "Does Background Noise Make Consumers Buy More Innovative Products?" *Press Release*. June, 2012. press.uchicago.edu/pressReleases/2012/June/JCR_1206_Noise.html

6. Williams, L. E. and Bargh, J. A. 2008. "Experiencing Physical Warmth Promotes Interpersonal Warmth." *Science*. October 24, 2008. Vol. 322 no. 5901 pp. 606-607.

Chapter Sixteen – Conditioning

1. KU Leuven. 2013. "Pavlov Inverted: Reward Linked to Image Is Enough to Activate Brain's Visual Cortex." *ScienceDaily*. March

21, 2013. sciencedaily.com/releases/2013/03/130321092948.
htm

2. University of Missouri. 2013. "Individual Donation Amounts Drop
When Givers Are in Groups, Says MU Researcher." *Press Release.*
April 11, 2013. **munews.missouri.edu/news-releases/2013/0411-
individual-donation-amounts-drop-when-givers-are-in-groups-says-
mu-researcher/**

3. University of Copenhagen. 2013. "Information Technology
Amplifies Irrational Group Behavior." *ScienceDaily.* April 11,
2013. **www.sciencedaily.com/releases/2013/04/130411124005.
htm**

4. San Diego State University. 2013. "Today's Teens: More
Materialistic, Less Willing to Work." *NewsCenter.* May 1, 2013.
newscenter.sdsu.edu/sdsu_newscenter/news.aspx?s=74179

5. Universität Bonn. 2013. "Do Markets Erode Moral Values? People
Ignore Their Own Moral Standards When Acting as Market
Participants, Researchers Say." *ScienceDaily.* May 10, 2013. **www.
sciencedaily.com/releases/2013/05/130510124501.htm**

Chapter Seventeen – Perception

1. Karolinska Institutet. 2013. "Imagination Can Change What We
Hear and See." *ScienceDaily.* June 27, 2013.
www.sciencedaily.com/releases/2013/06/130627125156.htm

2. Max-Planck-Gesellschaft. 2013. "Hunger Affects Decision-Making
and Perception of Risk." *ScienceDaily.* June 25, 2013.
www.sciencedaily.com/releases/2013/06/130625073802.htm

3. Columbia Business School. 2013. "An Expansive Physical Setting
Increases a Person's Likelihood of Dishonest Behavior."
ScienceDaily. June 24, 2013.
www.sciencedaily.com/releases/2013/06/130624133145.htm

4. Journal of Consumer Research, Inc. 2013. "The Geometry of
Persuasion: How Do Seating Layouts Influence Consumers?"
ScienceDaily. June 18, 2013.
www.sciencedaily.com/releases/2013/06/130618101649.htm

5. Ibid.

6. Doucot, A. 2013. "Who Knew? Round Tables Increase Collaboration
and Sense of Belonging." *GovDelivery.* August 14, 2013.
www.govdelivery.com/blog/tag/geometry-of-persuasion/

7. Morris, A. 2013. "What if a Search Engine Could Determine an
Election?" *PBS Newshour.* April 2, 2013.
**www.pbs.org/newshour/rundown/2013/04/what-if-a-search-
engine-could-determine-an-election.html**

8. Barry, M. 2013. *Lexicon: A Novel.* New York: Penguin Group.

Chapter Eighteen – Political Strategies

1. Lepore, J. 2012. "The Lie Factory." *The New Yorker.* September 24, 2012. p. 53. www.newyorker.com/ reporting/2012/09/24/120924fa_fact_lepore?currentPage=all
2. Skousen, W. C. 1998. *The Naked Capitalist.* Cutchogue, NY: Buccaneer Books.
3. Carter, I. 2012. "Positive and Negative Liberty." *The Stanford Encyclopedia of Philosophy.* (Spring 2012 Edition). Edward N. Zalta (ed.). plato.stanford.edu/archives/spr2012/entries/ liberty-positive-negative/
4. Staff. 2013. "Shocking: Fox News Reporting Interview with Unabashed Surfer Receiving Food Stamps." *Fox News Insider.* August 10, 2013. foxnewsinsider.com/2013/08/10/shocking-fox-news-reporting-interview-unabashed-surfer-receiving-food-stamps
5. Staff. 2013. "'Obama Phone' Fraud Exposed: Reporter Gets 3 Free Phones!" *On The Record With Greta Van Susteren.* August 2, 2013. foxnewsinsider.com/2013/08/02/reporter-jillian-kay-melchior-i-got-three-obama-phones-rampant-fraud-lifeline-program
6. Pulaski, R.. 2012. "United Welfare State of America: U.S. Now Spends Over $1 Trillion on Welfare." *Gateway Pundit.* October 19, 2012. www.thegatewaypundit.com/2012/10/united-welfare-state-of-america-us-now-spends-over-1-trillion-on-welfare/
7. Barron, R. 2012. "How much is Welfare Fraud Costing Us? (Welfare Reform Part 12)." *It's Our America.* April 8, 2012. www.roanen. com/1/post/2012/04/how-much-is-welfare-fraud-costing-us.html
8. Adams, M. 2013. "Global Warming Computer Models Collapse; Arctic Ice Sheets Rapidly Expand as Planet Plunges into Global Cooling." *Natural News.* Sept. 10, 2013. www.naturalnews. com/041981_global_warming_computer_models_cooling.html
9. Ibid.
10. Lofgren, K. 2013. "Study Shows Why Global Warming is Adding Ice to the Antarctic." *Inhabit.* April 5, 2013. inhabitat.com/study-shows-why-global-warming-is-adding-ice-to-the-antarctic/
11. Lindzen, R. 2006. "Climate of Fear." *Wall Street Journal.* April 12, 2006. heartland.org/sites/all/modules/custom/heartland_ migration/files/pdfs/20143.pdf

12. Dingfelder, S. 2012. "The Science of Political Advertising." *American Psychological Association.* April, 2012, Vol 43, No. 4, p. 46. **www.apa.org/monitor/2012/04/advertising.aspx**

13. Perkins, S. 2003. "Dirty Rats: Campaign Ad May Have Swayed Voters Subliminally." *Science News.* February 19, 2003. 163/8, p. 116–117. **www.sciencenews.org/article/dirty-rats-campaign-ad-may-have-swayed-voters-subliminally**

14. Dingfelder, S. 2012. "The Science of Political Advertising." *American Psychological Association.* April, 2012, Vol 43, No. 4, p. 46. **www.apa.org/monitor/2012/04/advertising.aspx**

15. Ibid.

16. Lakeoff, G. 2006. *Thinking Points: Communicating Our American Values and Vision.* NY: Farrar, Straus and Giroux.

17. Ibid.

18. Ibid.

19. Ibid.

20. Wikipedia. "Biology and Political Orientation." **en.wikipedia.org/wiki/Biology_and_political_orientation**
And
Kanai, R., Feilden, T., Firth, C. and ReesSee, G. 2011. "Political Orientations Are Correlated with Brain Structure in Young Adults." *Current Biology.* April 7, 2011. Vol. 21, Issue 8, p. 677–680.

21. Wikipedia. "Biology and Political Orientation." **en.wikipedia.org/wiki/Biology_and_political_orientation**
And
Psych Central. 2007. "Brains of Liberals, Conservatives May Work Differently." **psychcentral.com/news/2007/09/10/brains-of-liberals-conservatives-may-work-differently/1691.html**
And
Gellene, D. 2007. "Study Finds Left-Wing Brain, Right-Wing Brain." *Los Angeles Times.* September 10, 2007. **www.latimes.com/news/obituaries/la-sci-politics10sep10,0,2687256.story**

22. Tencer, D. 2010. "Study: Conservatives Have Larger 'Fear Center' in Brain." *The Raw Story.* December 28, 2010. **www.rawstory.com/rs/2010/12/28/conservatives-fear-center-brain/**

23. Laber-Warren, E. 2012. "Calling a Truce in the Political Wars." *Scientific America Mind.* September/October, 2012. p. 23-23
And

Laber-Warren, E. 2012. "Unconscious Reactions Separate Liberals and Conservatives." *Scientific American*. August 2, 2012. **www.scientificamerican.com/article/calling-truce-political-wars/**

24. Association for Psychological Science. 2013. "Name-Brand or Generic? Your Political Ideology Might Influence Your Choice." *Press Release*. February 12, 2013. **www.psychologicalscience.org/index.php/news/releases/name-brand-or-generic-your-political-ideology-might-influence-your-choice.html**

25. Association for Psychological Science. 2012. "Want to Influence Support for Redistributive Tax Policies? Choose Your Words Carefully." *Press Release*. November 2, 2012. **www.psychologicalscience.org/index.php/news/releases/want-to-influence-support-for-redistributive-tax-policies-choose-your-words-carefully.html**

26. Taylor & Francis. 2012. "Comedian's Political Humor Affects Potential Voter's Attitudes About Candidates." *ScienceDaily*. November 5, 2012. **www.sciencedaily.com/releases/2012/11/121105195950.htm**

27. University of Illinois at Urbana-Champaign. 2012. "Answer Three 'Why' Questions: Abstract Thinking Can Make You More Politically Moderate." *ScienceDaily*. November 2, 2012. **www.sciencedaily.com/releases/2012/11/121102151948.htm**

28. University of South Carolina. 2012. "This Is Your Brain on Politics: Neuroscience Reveals Brain Differences Between Republicans and Democrats." *ScienceDaily*. November 1, 2012. **www.sciencedaily.com/releases/2012/11/121101105003.htm**

29. University of Illinois. 2012. "Abstract Thinking Can Make You More Politically Moderate." *Psypost*. November 2, 2012. **www.psypost.org/2012/11/abstract-thinking-can-make-you-more-politically-moderate-14734**

Chapter Nineteen – Physical Control

1. Daniels, K. 2013. "U.S. Army Conducts Military Occupation Drill in Small Town Wisconsin." *Infowars*. August 13, 2013. **www.infowars.com/u-s-army-conducts-military-occupation-drill-in-small-town-wisconsin/**

2. Smolinski, A. 2013. "Small Town Provides Big Training Value." *DVIDS*. August 9, 2013. **www.dvidshub.net/news/111804/small-town-provides-big-training-value**

3. Daniels, K. 2013. "U.S. Army Conducts Military Occupation Drill in Small Town Wisconsin." *Infowars*. August 13, 2013.

www.infowars.com/u-s-army-conducts-military-occupation-drill-in-small-town-wisconsin/

4. Watson, P. J. 2013. "TSA to Purchase 3.5 Million Rounds of Ammunition." *Infowars.* August 19, 2013. www.infowars.com/tsa-to-purchase-3–5-million-rounds-of-ammunition/

5. RT Question More. 2013. "Bush Advisor: Hastings Crash 'Consistent with a Car Cyberattack.'" June 25, 2013. rt.com/usa/michael-hastings-cyber-car-218/

6. Watson, P. J. 2013. "Michael Hastings Feared His Mercedes Had Been Tampered With." *Infowars.* August 22, 2013. www.infowars.com/michael-hastings-feared-his-mercedes-had-been-tampered-with/

7. Gibson, C. 2013. "Exclusive: Who Killed Michael Hastings?" *Occupy.* October 24, 2013. www.occupy.com/article/exclusive-who-killed-michael-hastings

And

Zane, K. 2014. "This Journalist Died After Exposing Bowe Bergdahl's Anti-Americanism." *Western Journalism.* June 9, 2014. www.westernjournalism.com/traitor-bowe-bergdahl-linked-michael-hastings-murder/

8. Watson, P. J. 2013. "Police, Firefighters Ordered Not to Speak About Michael Hastings Crash." *Infowars.* July 9, 2013. www.infowars.com/police-firefighters-ordered-not-to-speak-about-michael-hastings-crash/

And

Global Research News. 2013. "Was Journalist Michael Hastings Murdered? Police and Firefighters on the Scene Told Not to Comment." July 17, 2013. www.globalresearch.ca/video-was-journalist-michael-hastings-murdered-police-and-firefighters-on-the-scene-told-not-to-comment/5343076

9. Lee, O.B. 2013. "The Michael Hastings Police Report - A Critical Examination." *Old Bull Lee.* November 10, 2013. oldbulllee.com/hastings-police-report.htm

And

oldbulllee.com/HASTINGS,%20Michael%20Mahon%20LA%20County%20Coroner%20Report_%20COMPLETE.pdf

10. The University of Texas at Austin. 2013. "UT Austin Researchers Successfully Spoof an $80 million Yacht at Sea." July 29, 2013. www.utexas.edu/news/2013/07/29/ut-austin-researchers-successfully-spoof-an-80-million-yacht-at-sea/

11. Hoopes, H. 2013. "False Sense of Security: Your TV, Car, Neighborhood May Be Hackable." *Gizmag*. August 6, 2013. www.gizmag.com/cyber-security-hacks-defcon-black-hat/28599/

12. Ibid.

13. Dodson, B. 2013. "Creepydol System Can Destroy Your Privacy for About US$500." *Gizmag*. August 6, 2013. www.gizmag.com/wi-fi-track-smartphone-creepydol/28585/

14. Ibid.

15. Electronic Frontier Foundation. 2013. "Mandatory Black Boxes in Cars Raise Privacy Questions." *Electronic Frontier Foundation*. February 11, 2013. www.eff.org/press/releases/mandatory-black-boxes-cars-raise-privacy-questions

16. Marsh, R. 2013. "Wi-Vi System Uses Wi-Fi to See Through Walls." *Gizmag*. July 1, 2013. www.gizmag.com/wi-vi-see-through-walls/28120/

17. Dodson, B. 2013. "DARPA's New 1.8-Gigapixel Camera Is a Super High-Resolution Eye in the Sky." *Gizmag*. February 11, 2013. www.gizmag.com/argus-is-darpa-gigapixel-camers/26078/

18. RT Question More. 2011. "City Lights Spy on Farmington Hills, Michigan." *RT Question More*. November 1, 2011. rt.com/usa/harwood-intellistreets-hills-farmington-321/

19. Scheuermann, C. 2013. "Black Helicopters: Britain's Blind Faith in Intelligence Agencies." *Spiegel Online*. August 21, 2013. www.spiegel.de/international/world/the-cozy-relationship-between-britain-and-its-intelligence-apparatus-a-917689.html

20. Ibid.

21. European Gazette. 2013. "Brain Implants to 'Reboot' Depressed People." *European Gazette*. October 11, 2013. egazette.eu/uncategorized/brain-implants-to-reboot-depressed-people/

22. Nimmo, K. 2012. "Breitbart and the CIA's Heart Attack Gun." *Infowars*. March 7, 2012. www.infowars.com/breitbart-and-the-cias-heart-attack-gun/

23. Whiteout Press. 2012. "Eric Holder, Andrew Breitbart and the CIA Heart Attack Gun." March 8, 2012. www.whiteoutpress.com/articles/q12012/eric-holder-andrew-breitbart-and-the-cia-heart-attack-gun613/

24. Investment Watch. 2013. "FBI Under Pressure to Explain Drone Use, as Obama Names New Director." June 21, 2013. investmentwatchblog.com/breaking-fbi-under-pressure-to-explain-drone-use-as-obama-names-new-director/

25. Golgowski, N. 2013. "Slain Woman in Capitol Police Chase Was Fleeing police for Her Life and Not 'Delusional': sisters." *NY Daily News.* October 7, 2013. **www.nydailynews.com/news/national/slain-woman-capitol-police-chase-delusional-sisters-article-1.1478448**

26 Staff. 2009. "Nancy Pelosi Accuses CIA Of Lying." *The Telegraph.* 15 May, 2009. **www.telegraph.co.uk/news/worldnews/northamerica/usa/5327101/Nancy-Pelosi-accuses-CIA-of-lying.html**

Chapter Twenty – Mind Control

1. Sohn, E. 2012. "Mind-Reading May Be Reality Soon." *News Discovery.* February 1, 2012. **news.discovery.com/human/psychology/mind-reading-120131.htm**

2. Ibid.

3. Radboud University Nijmegen. 2013. "Computer Can Read Letters Directly from the Brain." *ScienceDaily.* August 19, 2013. **www.sciencedaily.com/releases/2013/08/130819141641.htm**

4. Krawczyk, G. 1993. "Mind Control and the New World Order." *Nexus Magazine.* February/March, 1993.

5. Keith, J. 1997. *Mind Control, World Control.* Kempton, Ill.: Adventures Unlimited Press.

6. Weinberger, S. 2008. "Army Yanks 'Voice-To-Skull Devices' Site." *Wired Blog Network.* **blog.wired.com/defense/2008/05/army-removes-pa.html**

7. Weinberger, S. 2007. "The Other MEDUSA: A Microwave Sound Weapon." *Wired Blog Network.* **www.wired.com/2007/08/the-other-medus/**

8. Hambling, D. 2008. "Microwave Ray Gun Controls Crowds With noise." *New-Scientist.com news service.* **www.newscientist.com/article/dn14250-microwave-ray-gun-controls-crowds-with-noise.html**

9. Lutz, D. 2012. "Scientists Read Monkeys' Inner Thoughts." *Washington University in St. Louis.* July 19, 2012. **news.wustl.edu/news/Pages/24043.aspx**

10. Harvard University. 2012. "Using Precisely-Targeted Lasers, Researchers Manipulate Neurons in Worms' Brains and Take Control of Their Behavior." *ScienceDaily.* September 24, 2012. **www.sciencedaily.com/releases/2012/09/120924102658.htm**

11. Cornell University. 2013. "Mental Picture of Others Can Be Seen Using fMRI, Finds New Study." *ScienceDaily*. March 5, 2013. **www.sciencedaily.com/releases/2013/03/130305091000.htm**

12. Coxworth, B. 2013. "Scientists Remotely Control Live Turtles." *Gizmag*. April 24, 2013. **www.gizmag.com/remote-control-turtles/27253/**

13. Hopperton, L. 2013. "Tiny LEDs Can Be Injected into the Brain." *Newselectronics*. April 17, 2013. **www.newelectronics.co.uk/electronics-news/tiny-leds-can-be-injected-into-the-brain/49276/**

14. Anthony, S. 2013. "Harvard Creates Brain-To-Brain Interface, Allows Humans to Control Other Animals with Thoughts Alone." *ExtremeTech*. July 31, 2013. **www.extremetech.com/extreme/162678-harvard-creates-brain-to-brain-interface-allows-humans-to-control-other-animals-with-thoughts-alone**

15. Halverson, N. 2013. "First Human Brain-to-Brain Mind Meld Achieved." *News Discovery*. August 28, 2013. **news.discovery.com/tech/biotechnology/first-human-brain-to-brain-mind-meld-achieved-130828.htm**

16. Langleben DD, Loughead JW, Bilker WB, Ruparel K, Childress AR, Busch SI, Gur RC. 2005. "Telling Truth from Lie in Individual Subjects with Fast Event-Related fMRI." *Hum Brain Mapp*. 2005 Dec;26(4):262–72.

And

Davatzikos C, Ruparel K, Fan Y, Shen DG, Acharyya M, Loughead JW, Gur RC, Langleben DD. 2005. "Classifying Spatial Patterns of Brain Activity with Machine Learning Methods: Application to Lie Detection." *Neuroimage*. November 2005;28(3):663–8.

And

Wolpe PR, Foster KR, Langleben DD. 2005. "Emerging Neurotechnologies for Lie-Detection: Promises and Perils." *Am J Bioeth*. Spring 2005;5(2):39–49.

And

Langleben D, Schroeder L, Maldjian J, Gur R, McDonald S, Ragland, JD, OBrien CP, Childress AR. 2002. "Brain Activity During Simulated Deception: An Event-Related Functional Magnetic Resonance Study." *Neuroimage*. March 2002; 15(3):727–732.

And

www.noliemri.com/

17. Carnegie Mellon University. 2013. "Scientists Identify Emotions Based on Brain Activity." *ScienceDaily*. June 19, 2013. **www.sciencedaily.com/releases/2013/06/130619195137.htm**

18. Ibid.
19. University of California—Irvine. 2013. "Scientists Create New Memories by Directly Changing the Brain." *ScienceDaily.* September 10, 2013. **www.sciencedaily.com/releases/2013/09/130910142334.htm**
20. Scripps Research Institute. 2013. "Possibility of Selectively Erasing Unwanted Memories." *ScienceDaily.* September 10, 2013. **www.sciencedaily.com/releases/2013/09/130910140941.htm**
21. Godlike Productions. 2006. "How to Successfully NEUTRALIZE Mind Control of Ultrasonic and Electromagnetic Wave Lengths." **www.godlikeproductions.com/forum1/message304599/pg1**
22. Ibid.
23. Alexander, J. B. 1980. "The New Mental Battlefield." *Military Review.* December, 1980. **www.icomw.org/documents/alexander.pdf**
24. Wolfe, L. "Americans Target of Largest Media Brainwashing Campaign in History." **rense.com/general15/tr.htm**
25. Ibid.
26. Weeks, B. T. 2001. "Tavistock: The Best Kept Secret in America." *Educate-Yourself.* July 31, 2001. **educate-yourself.org/nwo/nwotavistockbestkeptsecret.shtml**
27. Staff writer. 2007. "Playing Video Games May Sap Emotional Control." *Taiwan News.* December 26, 2007. **www.taiwannews.com.tw/etn/news_content.php?id=578012&lang=eng_news&cate**

Chapter Twenty-One – Data Mining

1. Rosenbach, M., Poitras, L. and Stark, H. 2013. "iSpy: How the NSA Accesses Smartphone Data." *Spiegel Online.* September 9, 2013. **www.spiegel.de/international/world/how-the-nsa-spies-on-smartphones-including-the-blackberry-a-921161.html**
2. KU Leuven. "Top Websites Secretly Track Your Device Fingerprint." **www.kuleuven.be/english/news/several-top-websites-use-device-fingerprinting-to-secretly-track-users**
3. RT Question More. 2012. "NSA Utah 'Data Center': Biggest-Ever Domestic Spying Lab?" March 17, 2012. **rt.com/news/utah-data-center-spy-789/**
4. Ibid.
5. ACLU. 2011. "FOIA Documents Show FBI Illegally Collecting Intelligence Under Guise of 'Community Outreach'." *Press Release.* December 1, 2011. **www.aclu.org/national-security/foia-**

documents-show-fbi-illegally-collecting-intelligence-under-guise-community

6. Greenwald, G. 2013. "NSA Collecting Phone Records of Millions of Verizon Customers Daily." *The Guardian.* June 5, 2013. **www.theguardian.com/world/2013/jun/06/nsa-phone-records-verizon-court-order**

7. Democracy Now. 2013. "NSA Confirms Dragnet Phone Records Collection, but Admits It Was Key in Stopping Just 1 Terror Plot." August 1, 2013. **www.democracynow.org/2013/8/1/nsa_confirms_dragnet_phone_records_collection**

8. Gellman, B. 2013. "NSA Broke Privacy Rules Thousands of Times Per Year, Audit Finds." *The Washington Post.* August 15, 2013. **articles.washingtonpost.com/2013–08–15/world/41431831_1_washington-post-national-security-agency-documents**

9. Ibid.

10. Poitras, L., Rosenbach, M. and Stark, H. 2013. "'Follow the Money': NSA Monitors Financial World." *Spiegel Online.* September 16, 2013. **www.spiegel.de/international/world/how-the-nsa-spies-on-international-bank-transactions-a-922430.html**

11. Ibid.

12 Bamford, J. 2002. *Body of Secrets: Anatomy of the Ultra-Secret National Security Agency.* New York: Anchor Books.

13. Ibid.

14. Kennedy, M. 2013. "Intelink-U Advances Gov Interoperability & Saves Resources with HSPD-12." *Information Sharing Environment.* July 16, 2013. **www.ise.gov/blog/michael-e-kennedy/intelink-u-advances-gov-interoperability-saves-resources-hspd-12**

15. Bamford, J. 2002. *Body of Secrets: Anatomy of the Ultra-Secret National Security Agency.* New York: Anchor Books.

16. Adams, M. 2013. "Warning: Enrolling in Obamacare Allows Government to Link Your IP Address with Your Name." *Infowars.* October 10, 2013. **www.infowars.com/warning-enrolling-in-obamacare-allows-government-to-link-your-ip-address-with-your-name-social-security-number-bank-accounts-and-web-surfing-habits/**

Chapter Twenty-Two – Who Are They Protecting?

1. Gucciardi, A. 2013. "Pentagon Prepping for 'Large Scale Economic Breakdown'." *Infowars.* August 26, 2013.

2. Hsu, S. S. and Tyson, A. S. 2008. "Pentagon to Detail Troops to Bolster Domestic Security." *The Washington Post.* December

1, 2008. www.washingtonpost.com/wpdyn/content/
   article/2008/11/30/AR2008113002217.html
3. FoxNews. 2014. "Where Was Obama? Question Resurfaces of
   President's Whereabouts During Benghazi Attack." *FoxNews*. May
   2, 2014.
   www.foxnews.com/politics/2014/05/02/where-was-obama-
   question-resurfaces-presidents-whereabouts-during-benghazi/
4. Lucas, F. 2013. "WH: Obama Called Hillary on Night of Benghazi
   Attack–More than Six Hours After It Started." *CNS News*.
   February 20, 2013. cnsnews.com/news/article/wh-obama-called-
   hillary-night-benghazi-attack-more-six-hours-after-it-started
5. Kieley, E. 2013. "Benghazi Timeline: The Long Road From
   "Spontaneous Protest" to Premeditated Terrorist Attack."
   FactCheck. May 9, 2013.
   www.factcheck.org/2012/10/benghazi-timeline/
6. Jones, S. 2013. "Benghazi Was About 400 Surface-to-Air-Missiles
   Stolen by 'Some Very Ugly People,' DiGenova Says." *CNSNews*.
   August 13, 2013.
   www.cnsnews.com/news/article/benghazi-was-about-400-
   surface-air-missiles-stolen-some-very-ugly-people-digenova-says
7. Ibid.
8. The Free Dictionary. *Treason*.
   legal-dictionary.thefreedictionary.com/treason
9. Hoyng, H. 2013. "The Manning Verdict: Obama's Defining
   Injustice." *Spiegel Online*. August 5, 2013.
   www.spiegel.de/international/zeitgeist/bradley-manning-verdict-
   use-of-espionage-act-shows-us-hypocrisy-a-914834.html
10. Wikipedia. "Julian Assange." en.wikipedia.org/wiki/Julian_
    Assange
And
Smith, C. 2010. "Police Complaint Filed After Tom Flanagan Calls
    for Assassination of Wikileaks' Julian Assange." *Straight.com*
    (Vancouver). December 4, 2010.
    www.straight.com/article-362941/vancouver/lawyer-files-
    criminal-flanagan-assassination-wikileaks-julian-assan
11. Wikipedia. "Julian Assange."
    en.wikipedia.org/wiki/Julian_Assange
And
CBCNews. 2010. "Flanagan Regrets WikiLeaks Assassination Remark".
    CBC News (Toronto). December 1, 2010.
    www.cbc.ca/news/politics/flanagan-regrets-wikileaks-
    assassination-remark-1.877548

12. Wikipedia. "Julian Assange." **en.wikipedia.org/wiki/Julian_ Assange**
And
Sidiqqui, H. 2010. "U.S. Embassy Cables Culprit Should Be Executed, Says Mike Huckabee." *The Guardian* (London). December 1, 2010. **www.theguardian.com/world/2010/dec/01/us-embassy-cables-executed-mike-huckabee**

13. Wikipedia. "Julian Assange." **en.wikipedia.org/wiki/Julian_Assange**
And
McFarland, K.T. 2010."Yes, WikiLeaks Is a Terrorist Organization and the Time to Act Is NOW." *Fox News.* November 30, 2010. **www. foxnews.com/opinion/2010/11/30/yes-wikileaks-terrorist-organization-time-act/**

14. Wikipedia. "Julian Assange." **en.wikipedia.org/wiki/Julian_Assange**
And
HuffPost Media. "Fox News' Bob Beckel Calls for 'Ilegally' Killing Assange: 'A Dead Man Can't Leak Stuff.'" *Huffington Post.* December 7, 2012. **www.huffingtonpost.com/2010/12/07/fox-news-bob-beckel-calls_n_793467.html**

15. Wikipedia. "Julian Assange." **en.wikipedia.org/wiki/Julian_ Assange**
And
The Guardian. 2010. "Julian Assange Answers Your Questions." *The Guardian.* December 3, 2010. **www.theguardian.com/world/ blog/2010/dec/03/julian-assange-wikileaks**

16. Assange, J. 2013. "Statement by Julian Assange on Today's Sentencing of Bradley Manning." *WikiLeaks.* August 21, 2013. **wikileaks.org/Statement-by-Julian-Assange-on,267.html**

17. La Jeunesse, W. 2013. "ATF Tries to Block Fast and Furious Whistleblower from Publishing Book." *FoxNews.* October 8, 2013. **www.foxnews.com/politics/2013/10/08/atf-tries-to-block-fast-and-furious-whistle-blower-from-publishing-book/**

18. Ibid.

19. Morales, F. 2012. "'The American Military Coup of 2012': Encroachment upon Basic Freedoms, Militarized Police State in America." *Global Research.* June 14, 2012. **www.globalresearch.ca/the-coup-of-2012-encroachment-upon-basic-freedoms-militarized-police-state-in-america/31428**

20. Ibid.

21. Ibid.
22. Smolinski, A. 2013. "Small Town Provides Big Training Value." *DVIDS*. August 9, 2013. **www.dvidshub.net/news/111804/small-town-provides-big-training-value**
23. Knight, D. 2013. "FISA Court: The 21st Century Star Chamber of the Secret U.S. Government." *InfoWars*. October 16, 2013. **www.infowars.com/fisa-court-the-21st-century-star-chamber-of-the-secret-us-government/**
24. Nimmo, K. 2012. "H.R. 347: Another Step in the Elimination of the First Amendment." *InfoWars*. March 5, 2012. **www.infowars.com/h-r-347-another-step-in-the-elimination-of-the-first-amendment/**
25. Rottman, G. 2012. "How Big a Deal is H.R. 347, That 'Criminalizing Protest' Bill?" *ACLU*. March 8, 2012. **www.aclu.org/blog/free-speech/how-big-deal-hr-347-criminalizing-protest-bill**
26. Gucciardi, A. 2013. "Woops! Obama Ordered Gun Report Reveals Guns Actually Save Lives." *Storyleak*. June 27, 2013. **www.storyleak.com/woops-obama-ordered-gun-report-guns-save-lives/**
27. Leghorn, N. 2013. "Chicago Firearms Confiscation Begins." *The Truth About Guns*. July 28, 2013. **www.thetruthaboutguns.com/2013/07/foghorn/chicago-firearms-confiscation-begins/**
28. Alex. 2013. "FBI Planned to Kill Occupy Leaders." *Economic Crisis*. July 3, 2013. **economicrisis.com/fbi-planned-to-kill-occupy-leaders/10769**
29. Chumley, C. 2013. "Big Brother Alert: Cameras in the Cable Box to Monitor TV Viewers." *The Washington Times*. June 17, 2013.

Chapter Twenty-Three – What's a Gotcha?

1. Carey, B. 2012. "Academic 'Dream Team' Helped Obama's Effort." *The New York Times*. November 12, 2012. **www.nytimes.com/2012/11/13/health/dream-team-of-behavioral-scientists-advised-obama-campaign.html?pagewanted=all&_r=0**
2. Penny Press. 2008. "An Examination of Obama's Use of Hidden Hypnosis Techniques in His Speeches." *Penny Press*. September 24, 2008. **www.pennypresslv.com/Obama's_Use_of_Hidden_Hypnosis_techniques_in_His_Speeches.pdf**
3. Breitbart News. 2013. "Obama Admin to Create 'Nudge' Squad to Shape Americans' Behavior." *Breitbart*. July 30, 2013.

www.breitbart.com/Big-Government/2013/07/30/Obama-nudge-squad

4. Heyes, J. D. 2013. "Science Journal Hires Former Monsanto Scientist to Decide Which Papers Should Be Accepted or Rejected." *Natural News.* June 3, 2013. www.naturalnews.com/040607_Monsanto_scientific_studies_Food_and_Chemical_Toxicology.html

5. DProgram. 2013. "Monsanto Protection Act Resurrected to Grant Biotech Giant Legal Immunity." *DProgram.* September 12, 2013. dprogram.net/2013/09/12/monsanto-protection-act-resurrected-to-grant-biotech-giant-legal-immunity/

6. TBL Staff. 2013. "Media Silent on Fukushima Radiation Impact in U.S." *The Liberty Beacon.* June 4, 2013. thelibertybeacon.com/2013/06/04/media-silent-on-fukushima-radiation-impact-in-us/

7. Morris, A. 2013. "What If a Search Engine Could Determine an Election?" *PBS Newshour.* April 2, 2013. www.pbs.org/newshour/rundown/2013/04/what-if-a-search-engine-could-determine-an-election.html

8. Yadron, D. 2013. "Report: NSA Pays Tech Companies for Data." *The Wall Street Journal.* August 23, 2013. blogs.wsj.com/digits/2013/08/23/report-nsa-pays-tech-companies-for-data/

9. Ibid.

10. McCullagh, D. 2013. "Feds Put Heat on Web Firms for Master Encryption Keys." *CNet.* July 24, 2013. news.cnet.com/8301-13578_3-57595202-38/feds-put-heat-on-web-firms-for-master-encryption-keys/

11. Poitras, L. 2013. "Miranda Detention: 'Blatant Attack on Press Freedom.'" *Spiegel Online.* August 26, 2013. www.spiegel.de/international/world/laura-poitras-on-british-attacks-on-press-freedom-and-the-nsa-affair-a-918592.html

12. Ibid.

13. Peterson, J. 2013. "Holder Needs to Explain DOJ's Spying on Journalists, Says Civil Liberties Groups." *The Daily Caller.* May 14, 2013. dailycaller.com/2013/05/14/holder-needs-to-explain-dojs-spying-on-journalists-says-civil-liberties-groups/

14. Ibid.

15. Bloom, J. 2013. "AP, Then James Rosen—How Widespread Is DOJ Surveillance of Journalists?" *The American Conservative.* May 20, 2013. www.theamericanconservative.com/ap-then-james-rosen-how-widespread-is-doj-surveillance-of-journalists/

16. ACLU. 2011. "FOIA Documents Show FBI Illegally Collecting Intelligence Under Guise of 'Community Outreach.'" *Press Release*. December 1, 2011. www.aclu.org/national-security/foia-documents-show-fbi-illegally-collecting-intelligence-under-guise-community

Chapter Twenty-Four – A Little History Continued: Public Relations

1. Turney, M. 2000. "Ivy Lee Was Decades Ahead of His Colleagues." www.nku.edu/~turney/prclass/readings/3eras2x.html
2. Ibid.
3. Ibid.
4. Lee, I. 1934. *The Problem of International Propaganda*. Michigan: The University of Michigan.
5. Glaser, J. 2013. "Media Still Hype Staged Toppling of Saddam Statue as Genuine." *Anti War*. April 9, 2013. news.antiwar.com/2013/04/09/media-still-hype-staged-toppling-of-saddam-statue-as-genuine/
6. Bamford, J. 2005. "The Man Who Sold the War." *Rolling Stone*. November 18, 2005. www.commondreams.org/headlines05/1118–10.htm
7. Miller, L. and Rampton, S. 2001. "The Pentagon's Information Warrior: Rendon to the Rescue." *PR Watch*. Volume 8, Number 4, Fourth Quarter, 2001. www.prwatch.org/files/pdfs/prwatch/prwv8n4.pdf
8. Bamford, J. 2005. "The Man Who Sold the War." *Rolling Stone*. November 18, 2005. www.commondreams.org/headlines05/1118–10.htm
9. Phillips, P. 2010. "U.S. Military Continues to Embeds Active-Duty PSYOPS Soldiers at Local TV Stations." *The Daily Censored*. October 11, 2010. www.dailycensored.com/us-military-continues-to-embeds-active-duty-psyops-soldiers-at-local-tv-stations/
10. Peters, J. W. 2012. "Latest Word on the Trail? I Take It Back." *The New York Times*. July 15, 2012. www.nytimes.com/2012/07/16/us/politics/latest-word-on-the-campaign-trail-i-take-it-back.html?_r=3&pagewanted=all&
11. Bidder, B. 2013. "Russia Today: Putin's Weapon in the War of Images." *Spiegel Online*. August 13, 2013. www.spiegel.de/international/business/putin-fights-war-of-images-and-propaganda-with-russia-today-channel-a-916162.html

12. PRweek. 2004. "Study Slams Philip Morris, Burson for Undue Influence." *PRweek.* August 23, 2004. **archive.tobacco.org/news/176036.html**

13. The Sydney Morning Herald. 2011. "Facebook Admits to Anti-Google Smear Campaign." *The Sydney Morning Herald.* May 13, 2011. **www.smh.com.au/technology/technology-news/facebook-admits-to-antigoogle-smear-campaign-20110513–1el5t.html**

14. Wikipedia. "Burson-Marsteller." **en.wikipedia.org/wiki/Burson-Marsteller**

15. Global Research News. 2013. "Monsanto Protection Act Signed by Obama, GMO Bill 'Written By Monsanto' Signed into Law." *Global Research.* May 25, 2013. **www.globalresearch.ca/monsanto-protection-act-signed-by-obama-gmo-bill-written-by-monsanto-signed-into-law/5329388**

16. Boerma, L. 2013. "Critics Slam Obama for 'Protecting' Monsanto." *CBSNews.* March 28, 2013. **www.cbsnews.com/8301–250_162–57576835/**

17. Packard, V. 1959. *The Status Seekers.* Philadelphia, PA: David McKay.

18. McFadden, R. D. 2008. "Wal-Mart Employee Trampled to Death." *The New York Times.* November 28, 2008. **www.nytimes.com/2008/11/29/business/29walmart.html**

19. Dictionary. "Propaganda." **dictionary.reference.com/browse/propaganda**

20. Wikipedia. "Ludlow Massacre." *Wikipedia.* **en.wikipedia.org/wiki/Ludlow_Massacre**

21. Ibid.

22. Wikipedia. "United States House Select Committee to Investigate Tax-Exempt Foundations and Comparable Organizations." **en.wikipedia.org/wiki/United_States_House_Select_Committee_to_Investigate_Tax-Exempt_Foundations_and_Comparable_Organizations**

23. University of Arkansas, Fayetteville. 2012. "Consumers Develop Complex Relationships with Celebrities to Construct Identity: Identity Formed by Relationships Influences Purchasing Decisions." *ScienceDaily.* November 29, 2012. **www.sciencedaily.com/releases/2012/11/121129093000.htm**

24. Tippett, A. B. 2012. "Getting Your Attention." *University of Delaware.* December 4, 2012. **www.udel.edu/udaily/2013/dec/memorable-ads-120412.html**

25. Dr. Mercola. 2013. "'Consuming Kids' Reveals Shocking Tactics Used to Manipulate Your Children's Preferences and Habits."

Mercola. June 8, 2013. **articles.mercola.com/sites/articles/ archive/2013/06/08/children-marketing.aspx**

26 Ibid.

27. University of California—Los Angeles. 2012. "Which Ads Are Winners? Your Brain Knows Better than You Do." *ScienceNewsline.* April 25, 2012. **www.sciencenewsline.com/ articles/2012042519180033.html**

28. Ibid.

29. American Sociological Association (ASA). 2013. "More Tweets Mean More Votes for Political Candidates, Study Finds." *ScienceDaily.* August 11, 2013. **www.sciencedaily.com/ releases/2013/08/130811005333.htm**

30. Chomsky, N. 2002. *Media Control.* NY: Seven Stories Press.

Chapter Twenty-Five – The Human Vehicle: What "They" Know and Why Propaganda Works

1. Cialdini, R. B. 1992. *Influence: Science and Practice.* New York: Harper Collins.

2. Ibid.

3. Ibid.

4. Feinberg, R. A. 1990. "The Social Nature of the Classical Conditioning Phenomena People." *Psychological Reports,* 67, 331–334.

5. Bornstein, R. F., Leone, D. R. and Galley, D. J. 1987. "The Generalizability of Subliminal Mere Exposure Effects." *Journal of Personality and Social Psychology,* 53, 1070–1079.

6. Milgram, S. 1963. "Behavioral Study of Obedience." *Journal of Abnormal and Social Psychology,* 67, 371–378.

7. Barker, E. 2012. "When an Expert Speaks Does Your Ability to Think for Yourself Literally Shut Down?" *Barking Up The Wrong Tree.* **www.bakadesuyo.com/2012/06/when-an-expert-speaks-does-your-ability-to-th/**

8. Cialdini, R. B. 1992. *Influence: Science and Practice.* New York: Harper Collins.

9. Frankl, V. 1963. *Man's Search for Meaning.* New York: Pocket Books.

10. Cialdini, R. B. 1992. *Influence: Science and Practice.* New York: Harper Collins.

Chapter Twenty-Six – Scandals

1. Heal, L. 2013. "California Schools to Train Kids to Sell ObamaCare." *Heartland.* June 20, 2013. **news.heartland.org/**

newspaper-article/2013/06/20/california-schools-train-kids-sell-obamacare

2. Ibid.

3. Bedard, P. 2013. "Treasury: IRS Targeted 292 Tea Party Groups, Just 6 Progressive Groups." *Washington Examiner.* June 27, 2013. **washingtonexaminer.com/treasury-irs-targeted-292-tea-party-groups-just-6-progressive-groups/article/2532456**

4. Ibid.

5. Sink. J. 2013. "Obama Dismisses Scandals as 'Phony.'" *The Hill.* July 25, 2013. **thehill.com/blogs/on-the-money/economy/313191-obama-talks-up-economy-hits-gop-focus-on-phoney-scandals**

6. Editorial. 2013. "Scandals Hard to Dismiss." *WCF Courier.* July 30, 2013. **wcfcourier.com/news/opinion/editorial/scandals-hard-to-dismiss/article_6d428672-f861–11e2-b6d9–0019bb2963f4.html**

7. Griffin, J. 2013. "Benghazi Witnesses Forced into Silence? New Concerns over Terror Attack Aftermath." *Fox News.* August 2, 2013. **www.foxnews.com/politics/2013/08/02/benghazi-witnesses-forced-into-silence-new-concerns-over-terror-attack/**

Chapter Twenty-Seven – What to Do If You Want to Subvert the System

1. Wikipedia. "Cleon Skousen." **en.wikipedia.org/wiki/Cleon_Skousen**

2. Skousen, W. C. 1998. *The Naked Capitalist.* p. 4–5. Cutchogue, NY: Buccaneer Books.

3. Ibid.

4. Fund, J. 2012. "The Mega Scandal Everyone Has Forgotten." *National Review Online.* December 31, 2012. **www.nationalreview.com/articles/336632/mega-scandal-everyone-has-forgotten-john-fund**

5. Skousen, W. C. 1998. *The Naked Capitalist..* Cutchogue, NY: Buccaneer Books.

6. Ibid.

7. Wikipedia. "Federal Reserve System." *Wikipedia.* **en.wikipedia.org/wiki/Federal_Reserve_System**

8. Wikipedia. "Nelson W. Aldrich." **en.wikipedia.org/wiki/Nelson_Aldrich**

9. Seidl, J. M. 2013. "How Broke is Greece? This Broke." *The Blaze.* February 26, 2013. **www.theblaze.com/stories/2013/02/26/how-broke-is-greece-this-broke/**

10. Wikipedia. "Individualism." **en.wikipedia.org/wiki/Individualism**

11. Palmer, B. 2012. "Exactly How Many Americans Are Dependent on the Government?" *Slate*. September 18, 2012. **www.slate. com/articles/news_and_politics/explainer/2012/09/romney_ says_47_percent_of_americans_receive_direct_government_ assistance_is_that_true_.html**

12. Byrne, R. 2006. *The Secret*. New York: Atria Books.

13. Miller, A. 1996. *The Drama of the Gifted Child*. New York: Basic Books.

14. Durden, T. 2013. "It's a '0.6%' World: Who Owns What of the $223 Trillion in Global Wealth." *ZeroHedge*. June 2, 2013. **www. zerohedge.com/news/2013–06–02/its-1-world-who-owns-what-223-trillion-global-wealth**

15. Reuters. 2011. "Steve Jobs: A Genius but a Bad, Mean Manager." *Technology Inquirer*. October 25, 2011. **technology.inquirer. net/5713/steve-jobs-a-genius-but-a-bad-mean-manager**

16. Monast. S. 1994. "Project Blue Beam." *Educate Yourself*. **educate-yourself.org/cn/projectbluebeam25jul05.shtml**

17. Ibid.

18. Orwell, G. 1950. *1984*. New York: Signet Classics.
And
Wikipedia. "Newspeak." **en.wikipedia.org/wiki/Newspeak**

19. Ertelt, S. 2009. "Obama Admin Terrorism Dictionary Calls Pro-Life Advocates Violent, Racist." *LifeNews*. May 5, 2009. **www.lifenews. com/2009/05/05/nat-5019/**

20. Gucciardi, A. 2013. "It's Official, Everyone Is Now a Terrorist According to the U.S. Government." *StoryLeak*. August 3, 2013. **www.storyleak.com/everyone-now-terrorist-us-government/**

21. Luntz, F. I. 2008. *Words That Work: It's Not What You Say, It's What People Hear*. New York: Hyperion.

22. Engel, P. 2013. "Southern Cooking Star Paula Deen Caught in Racism Scandal." *Business Insider*. June 19, 2013. **www. businessinsider.com/paula-deen-allegedly-admits-to-being-racist-2013–6**

23. Associated Press. 2013. "Paula Deen On 'Today': The Only Person I've Ever Called The N-Word Robbed Me." *NewsOne*. June 26, 2013. **newsone.com/2616195/paula-deen-today/**

24. Ahlert, A. 2013. "Judge Throws out Discrimination Charges Against Paula Deen." *FrontPage Mag*. August 14, 2013. **frontpagemag.com/2013/arnold-ahlert/the-bogus-discrimination-charges-against-paula-deen/**

25. Reuters. 2013. "Trayvon Martin Case: Ben Kruidbos, Fired Employee, Sues Florida Prosecutor." *Huffington Post*. August 2, 2013. **www.huffingtonpost.com/2013/08/03/trayvon-martin-case-ben-kruidbos-sues-florida-prosecutor_n_3698129.html**

26. Bossip Staff. 2013. "No Wonder They're Thugging!: Dad Of 3 Teens Who Beat White Boy up on Bus Speaks Out 'My Son Ain't No Bad Boy' [Video]." *Bossip*. August 13, 2013. **bossip. com/818795/no-wonder-theyre-thugging-dad-of-3-teens-that-beat-white-boy-up-on-bus-speaks-out-my-son-aint-no-bad-boy-and-boys-appear-in-court-video/**

27. Spikol, L. 2012. "Mistakes by NBC, CNN Make George Zimmerman a Hero." *Philly Mag*. April 10, 2012. **blogs.phillymag. com/the_philly_post/2012/04/10/george-zimmerman-cnn-nbc/**

28. Ibid.

29. Ibid.

30. Limbaugh, R. 2012. "Third News Network Admits to False Reporting on George Zimmerman." *Rush Limbaugh*. April 5, 2012. **www.freerepublic.com/focus/news/2868699/posts**

31. Lapidos, J. 2013. "The 'Ender's Game' Boycott." *The New York Times*. July 20, 2013. **www.nytimes.com/2013/07/21/opinion/ sunday/the-enders-game-boycott.html**

32. Hard Truth. 1979. "Silent Weapons for a Quiet War." *Hard Truth*. **www.theforbiddenknowledge.com/hardtruth/ silentweaponsforquietwars.htm**

33. Ibid.

34. Ibid.

35. Wells, H. G. 2006. *The Open Conspiracy: What Are We To Do With Our Lives?* San Diego, Calif.: Book Tree.

Chapter Twenty-Eight – "Now What?"

1. Laing, R. 1976. *Politics of Experience*. New York: Ballentine Books.

2. Ibid.

3. Association for Psychological Science. 2013. "Know Thyself: How Mindfulness Can Improve Self-Knowledge." *ScienceDaily*. March 14, 2013. **www.sciencedaily.com/ releases/2013/03/130314180259.htm**

4. Robinson, K. S. 1993. *Red Mars*. New York: Spectra

5. Garfield, J. L. 2011. *Meaning of Life*. Chantilly, VA: Great Courses.

6. Ibid.

7. Laing, R. 1976. *Politics of Experience*. New York: Ballentine Books.

8. Taylor, E. 2007. *Choices and Illusions*. Carlsbad, Calif.: Hay House.

9. Varghese, J. 2014. "Martin Luther King Day: 50 Influential Quotes by American Civil Rights Leader." *International Business Times.* **www.ibtimes.co.in/articles/535341/20140121/martin-luther-king-50-quotes-inspire-educate.htm**

10. Kant, I. *What is Enlightenment?* **www.columbia.edu/acis/ets/ CCREAD/etscc/kant.html**

11. Taylor, E. 2007. *Choices and Illusions.* Carlsbad, Calif.: Hay House.

12. Garfield, J. L. 2011. *Meaning of Life.* Chantilly, VA: Great Courses.

About Eldon Taylor

Eldon Taylor has made a lifelong study of the human mind and has earned doctoral degrees in clinical psychology and pastoral psychology. He is a Fellow with the American Psychotherapy Association (APA) and an interdenominational minister.

Eldon was a practicing criminalist for over ten years while completing his education. He supervised and conducted investigations and testing to detect deception. His earliest work with changing inner beliefs was conducted from this setting, including a double-blind study conducted at the Utah State Prison from 1986 to 1987. Eldon is president and director of Progressive Awareness Research, Inc. For more than 30 years, his books, audio and video programs, lectures, and radio and television appearances have approached personal empowerment from the cornerstone perspective of self-responsibility, forgiveness, gratitude, and service. Eldon now lives in the countryside of Washington State with his wife and their two sons. Apart from his family and work, his true passion is horses.

To Learn More About Eldon

If you enjoyed this book and would like to learn more about the tools suggested to help you become the person you were meant to be, visit Eldon's websites at **www.eldontaylor.com** and **www.innertalk.com**. You may also tune in to his *Provocative Enlightenment* radio show, where he interviews a fascinating array of guests in his search for answers to the questions that really matter.

InnerTalk Distribution

Global

Progressive Awareness Research, Inc.
PO Box 1139
Medical Lake, WA 99022
1 800 964 3551
1 509 299 3377
www.innertalk.com (English)
www.dialogointerno.com (Spanish)

U.K.

Kiki Ltd.
Unit 4, Aylsham Business Estate
Shepheards Close
Aylsham
Norwich
NR11 6SZ
Tel: 01263 738 663
www.kiki-health.co.uk/products_innertalk.asp

Germany

Axent Verlag
Steinerne Furt 78
86167 Augsburg

Germany
011 49 821 70 5011
www.axent-verlag.de

Malaysia/Singapore/Brunei/Viet Nam

Progressive Awareness Sdn Bhd
2–2 Jalan Pju 8/5E, Perdana Bus. Cntr.
Bandar Damansara Perdana,
47820 Petaling Jaya
Selangor, Malaysia
011 60 37 729 4745
www.innertalk-au.com

Taiwan and China

Easy MindOpen
3F, No. 257, Ho-Ping East Rd. Sec. 2
Taipei, Taiwan, R.O.C
011 886 (227) 010–468(1)
www.iamone.com.tw

Spanish

InnerTalk programs in Spanish can be obtained from:
www.dialogointerno.com

Distribution Inquiries

For information regarding distributing InnerTalk programs,
please contact:
Progressive Awareness Research, Inc.
PO Box 1139
Medical Lake, WA 99022
1 800 964 3551
1 509 299 3377
www.innertalk.com

CPSIA information can be obtained
at www.ICGtesting.com
Printed in the USA
BVOW08s1857071116
467158BV00001B/84/P